Islam, Law and Identity

The essays brought together in *Islam, Law and Identity* are the product of a series of interdisciplinary workshops that brought together scholars from a plethora of countries. Funded by the British Academy the workshops convened over a period of two years in London, Cairo and Izmir. The workshops and the ensuing papers focus on recent debates about the nature of sacred and secular law and most engage case studies from specific countries including Egypt, Israel, Kazakhstan, Mauritania, Pakistan and the UK. *Islam, Law and Identity* also addresses broader and over-arching concerns about relationships between religion, human rights, law and modernity. Drawing on a variety of theoretical and empirical approaches, the collection presents law as central to the complex ways in which different Muslim communities and institutions create and re-create their identities around inherently ambiguous symbols of faith. From their different perspectives, the essays argue that there is no essential conflict between secular law and Shari'a, but various different articulations of the sacred and the secular. *Islam, Law and Identity* explores a more nuanced and sophisticated understanding of the tensions that animate such terms as Shari'a law, modernity and secularization.

Marinos Diamantides is Reader in Law at Birkbeck College, University of London where he teaches constitutional law and theory. He has published extensively on the philosophy of Emmanuel Levinas.

Adam Gearey is a Reader in Law at Birkbeck College. His publications include *Critical Jurisprudence*, authored with Costas Douzinas. He is presently working on a text tentatively entitled *Welfare as Justice*.

Islam, Law and Identity

Edited by

Marinos Diamantides
and Adam Gearey

Routledge
Taylor & Francis Group
a GlassHouse book

First published 2012
by Routledge
2 Park Square, Milton Park, Abingdon, Oxon OX14 4RN

Simultaneously published in the USA and Canada
by Routledge
711 Third Avenue, New York, NY 10017

A GlassHouse book

Routledge is an imprint of the Taylor & Francis Group, an informa business

British Library Cataloguing in Publication Data
A catalogue record for this book is available from the British Library

Library of Congress Cataloging in Publication Data
A catalog record has been requested

ISBN 13: 978-0-415-56681-0 (hbk)
ISBN 13: 978-0-203-80948-8 (ebk)

Typeset in Garamond
by Graphicraft Limited, Hong Kong

MIX
Paper from responsible sources
FSC www.fsc.org FSC® C004839

Printed and bound in Great Britain by
CPI Antony Rowe, Chippenham, Wiltshire

Contents

Acknowledgements

The editors wish to thank the British Academy for enabling this project and Valerie Kelley for her editorial work and advice. We are also grateful to the American University in Cairo and the Dokuz Eylül University in Izmir for their hospitality; and Routledge GlassHouse for their support and understanding.

Notes on contributors

Lior Barshack is Professor of Law and Social Theory at the Interdisciplinary Center Herzliya, Israel. After graduating from Oxford University Lior Barshack pursued post-doctoral studies in Paris and New York and was a member of Centre Marc Bloch in Berlin. His research interests include political theology, political theory, theories of kinship, and relations between politics and the arts.

Dr Katherine E. Brown is a lecturer at King's College London. Her work draws on three intellectual heritages: feminism, human rights, and critical war/security studies. She currently researches the roles of Muslim women in security politics, with a focus on the UK. Her work has been generously funded by the ESRC, British Academy, and King's College London, and she has published and presented her findings widely.

Alexandre Caeiro is a Research Fellow at the Erlangen Centre for Islam and Law in Europe (EZIRE) at the Friedrich-Alexander University in Erlangen-Nuernberg, Germany. He works on integration discourses and the dynamics of religious authority amongst Muslim minorities in the West.

Marinos Diamantides is Reader in Law at Birkbeck College, University of London where he teaches constitutional law and theory. He has published extensively on the philosophy of Emmanuel Levinas [his latest publication is *Law, Levinas, Politics* (Routledge-Cavendish, second edition, 2009)]. He is interested in the relationship of modern political philosophy and legalism with monotheist dogmas. In this and other publications he attempts a comparative study of legalism across monotheist cultures.

Baudouin Dupret is educated in Law, Islamic Sciences and Political Sciences. He is Directeur de Recherche at the French National Centre for Scientific Research (CNRS). He was appointed in 2010 as Director of the Centre Jacques-Berque in Rabat, Morocco. He is also guest lecturer in Islamic law and socio-legal sciences at the University of Louvain and the Institute for advanced studies in the social sciences (EHESS), Paris. He has published extensively in the field of the sociology and anthropology of law, legislation and media, especially in the Middle East. His current work involves a praxiological approach to the production of truth in Arab contexts, including courts and parliaments, scientific expertise, the media, and religious education. He also (co-)edited numerous volumes, the last one being *Narratives of Truth in Islamic Law* (Saqi books, 2008), and authored several single-authored books, for example *Practices of Truth* (Benjamins, forthcoming) and *Adjudication in Action: An Ethnomethodology of Law, Moral and Justice* (Ashgate, forthcoming).

Professor Tasneem Kausar is a graduate of Pakistan College of Law, Lahore and Yale Law School, USA. Presently, she is working as Principal and Associate Professor of Law, at Pakistan College of Law, Lahore. Her areas of interest include Constitutional Law and Politics, Islamic Law, and Criminal Law. Professor Kausar has attended several national and international conferences and seminars in the USA, Canada, France, UK, Nepal, Turkey, India and Australia. Her articles and essays have been published in various prestigious national and international journals.

Satyel Larson is a doctoral candidate in the Department of Rhetoric at the University of California, Berkeley. Presently, she is writing a dissertation on the transformations in legal, medical and religious knowledge of the female body and reproductive technologies in modern Morocco.

Hassan El Menyawi is a PhD candidate in the Department of Sociology at New York University. In his previous work in human rights law, he was the Distinguished Kemp Visiting Assistant Professor at Davidson College and the International Law and Human Rights Assistant Professor at the United Nations University for Peace. He has also been a Visiting Scholar at Harvard Law School and the University of Pennsylvania Law School. He has published and lectured worldwide in the areas of human rights, LGBT rights, gender and sexuality, and the Middle East.

Dr Gül Berna Özcan is Reader in International Business and Entrepreneurship at Royal Holloway, University of London. Dr Özcan has been an expert evaluator for the European Commission since 2003 and a research director of the Gurukul Global Leadership Programme at the London School of Economics. She is the author of several books and numerous articles on local economic development, small and medium-sized enterprises, entrepreneurship and economic transition in Turkey and Central Asia.

Introduction

Politics, theology, sovereignty

Marinos Diamantides and Adam Gearey

I. Secularism, religious faith and state law

This collection invites the reader to turn from the current obsession with the role of Islam in the modern world, and rethink the relationship between law, faith and power; one of the most pressing concerns that we presently face. We cannot hope to come to any sensible conclusions if we address this complex issue from the exclusive standpoint of a European notion of history where secularism is at once defined too narrowly and too broadly. Thus, this collection must be seen as intentionally failing to reach general conclusions about 'Islam, identity and law'. It is a contribution to a much broader debate about monotheism, state law and identity formation; and one that is committed to examining the *agon* between the old and the new, between secularising and religious forces. There are no given or necessary outcomes – only the possibilities of transformation, mutation.

The general conclusions that can be drawn would appear to be self-evident to most educated readers; this *agon* has not stopped with the emergence of European secular states; nor is there any such thing as a monolithic Islam with a singular substantive 'Islamic law' that regulates Muslim social life from Dakar to Luton and from Mecca to Utrecht. Rather, there are different versions of 'Islamic laws' built around a small Qura'nic normative core; a core that is given different interpretations in those diverse cultural and historical contexts where people look to texts for guidance. Muslims articulate their belonging to the political communities that they find themselves in many different ways. Hence it is misleading to suggest that there is something essentially incompatible between modernity, human rights and Islamic religion. Accordingly this collection has no reason to be fixated on fundamentalist Islamism and its opponents. Instead, it addresses those areas of hybridity and overlap, where new forms emerge, such as the construction of 'minority *fiqh*' or, indeed, where social forces assert old patterns against the pressures of historical change. Underlying this theme is a concern with the different possible patterns of identity and recognition in which these conflicts and compromises can be theorised.

It is worth thinking about why these concerns are not evident in the wider debate about Islam and the modern world. We are trapped by certain assumptions, and cannot appreciate the development of new patterns of being and thinking. For instance, the history taught to schoolchildren across Europe records the gradual emergence of the secular nation-state as part of the prevailing of peace backed by practical reason in the aftermath of murderous 'wars of religion'. In this last phrase lie concealed two problematic and unexplored ideas that weigh heavily on debates around identity and religion. The preposition 'of' points to irrational, murderous fanaticism as a necessary feature of religious faith *per se*, independently from theological, political and juridical context. This should not be left unchallenged. One must consider the historically more plausible counter-thesis that the international and internecine conflicts of early European modernity

> ought to be remembered as the first wars of the modern nation-state whose principal purpose was to establish the supremacy of secular authority over every rival power, most especially the power of the church . . . Far from the secular nation-state rescuing Western humanity from the chaos and butchery of sectarian strife, those wars were the birth pangs of the modern state and its limitless license to murder. And religious alliances, and hatreds were used by regional princes for conflicts whose causes, effects, and alliances had very little to do with faith or confessional loyalties. . . . Early modernity was the age . . . of the great political struggle of the independent nation-state to emancipate itself from all the religious, legal, moral, and, sacramental bonds that had ever in any way confined or constrained its total sovereignty over its subjects. . . . The first of the early modern "religious" wars in Europe were waged by the Habsburg Holy Roman Emperor Charles V to shore up his power in his various demesnes: wars that ended in 1555 with the Peace of Augsburg, which established in imperial law the principle that the faith of a people would be determined by its prince.
>
> (Bentley-Hart 2009: 88–90)

The phrase 'wars of religion' refers to 'religion' in general as if the history of Western European Christianity synecdochically covers *all* religions and as if the term 'religion' sufficiently encompasses practices as diverse as voodoo, meditation and participation in the Eucharist. Although evidently wrong this rhetoric operates as a licence to participate in debates over the proper role of 'any religion' in organised social life within contemporary modern nation-states. What is thus lost is the particularity of the history of interaction of *specifically* Abrahamic religions that have, since their inception, challenged the power of rulers. Their dogmas alone centred on *covenants*, which, in pre-modern Christian Europe, gave rise to the *ecclesia* of ecclesiastical states. Later, in the early modern period, these ideas were transformed to become the notion of a 'sacred bond' between people of a specific region and their prince/king. Late modernity saw a further re-working of the sacred bond. It became the self-consciously 'secular' idea of the social contract.

It is, therefore, important to remember that it was in Europe and the Near East – not in pre-colonial Papua New Guinea, Sub-Saharan Africa or Central America – that the issue of 'religious faith' became so central to politics. Moreover, as the essay by Diamantides in this collection highlights, even within the three main monotheistic religions the evolution of the initially similar relation between state and religious authorities has been distinctly different in each case. In pre-Ottoman and pre-colonial Islamic modernity, for example, the state never quite managed to marshal the secular ideologies of 'absolute monarchy' and 'divine right' in order to fashion the notion of absolute state sovereignty as was the case in Western Europe. There are further changes that we should take into account. The post-colonial creation of European-style nation-states everywhere and the reactive emergence of Islamist and Jewish ultra-nationalist politics suggest that the rhetorical collapse of 'religion' into the European history of Christian states has become so pervasive that it is all too easy to forget that the manner in which we discuss the relationship between 'religion' and 'secular' power is framed by Abrahamic and specifically Christian–European ideas and history. It is in the context of such oblivion that, when confronted with calls and violent actions aimed at establishing 'Islamic states' or a purely 'Jewish state', Europeans tend to relive *their* history as if it were a universal necessity. The violent, modern Islamist ideological take on 'Islamic jihad' substitutes for the wars of 'Christianity' in the collective imagination. Jews and Muslims, it then follows, must reform their religions as Europeans did. And yet, it is perhaps true that it is not their religions but their *states* that must be reformed.

As with every other traumatic reliving this represents both a danger and an opportunity. The danger is that, in a desperate attempt to preserve what security one has found, one ends up confirming one's preconceptions where the 'other' features only as a figment of one's own imagination. For example, we often come across the condescending and a-historical 'lesson' that Muslims 'need their own reformation'. It is as if Islam (and Judaism, too, but here we concentrate on the former) needs to be 'corrected' by the secularising forces that have expressed themselves in European history. Not only is this a partial reading of the ongoing dynamics of the Reformation, as Gearey's essay suggests, but it would be historically more accurate to understand that post-colonial Muslims are forced to choose between the absolutist and democratic versions of divinised European statehood as the best imported version of political association or try to come up with something in line with their own tradition in which the state never usurped God's authority.

To elaborate our arguments, we have divided the essays that compose this book into two broad, thematic groups. The first group raise a number of general points about the relationship between monotheistic faith and

Christian theology (for there is no such thing as a coherent Jewish or Islamic theology) on the one hand, and politics and law on the other hand. This is followed by a section that contains essays with a more specific focus on contemporary issues. Whilst we did not want to impose any single methodological frame we feel that there are several points of reference that are common to these essays. All of them can be read as pointing to the limits of the conventional multiculturalist paradigm that has been used for thinking these issues through.[1] It is as if the energies of multiculturalism have resulted in a more or less workable compromise. If we are to continue exploring the challenges of religion and faith, we need a much more complex and subtle appreciation of the networks of overlap, agreement and contestation between traditions, concepts and ways of thinking.

II. European theologies and the modern reduction of the rule of law to mere process

Barshack's elegant and complex essay appears at the beginning of the collection to prepare the reader for the task of rethinking the idea of the rule of law beyond the grounds of state sovereignty and its location in 'secular' liberal political thought. Its main anthropological premise is strikingly simple: no political community can exist by virtue merely of common interests without the constant labour of reference and counter-reference to what is past, dead and seemingly inoperative. This is a political task which is performed by those who are often seen as a-political; apart from village elders and modern historians, it is a task that usually falls to men and women of religion and law. We can appreciate that in both pre-modern and modern traditions law, in particular, becomes embedded in the narrative community of the living *and* their ancestors. Myths of origin suggest that the source of law is 'projected' outside of society onto the immemorial of custom, history and tradition. This means that modern 'secular' sovereignty, too, has to be given a constitutional interpretation that continues to communicate with stranger, more antique and more obviously 'mythical' currents of thought even if these are conventionally thought of as 'superseded' and debunked.

The continuing purchase of old myths, however, should not be seen as licence to let one historical paradigm obscure others. It is of course true that the European fabrication of 'absolute' state sovereignty (sovereignty without reference to anything other than itself) has now been globalised. But the modernity it heralded depended on a peculiar turn not shared by other monotheistic cultures and certainly not by non-monotheistic ones. In Europe the *formal* rule of law – law as process rather than content; controlled and guaranteed by centralised state apparatuses – replaced the absent sovereign

1 We discuss multiculturalism in more detail at the end of this introduction.

in democratic states, that is, states in which the pretension of the absolute monarch to rule 'with the grace of God' had become unsustainable. In turn, the advent of the state opened the possibility of imagining a political community of 'autonomous individuals', namely human beings of certain characteristics (age, ethnicity, property, education, etc.) who have since been required to play, collectively, the role of gods/monarchs unto themselves. This new myth of autonomy was a break with the claustrophobia of generally cohesive pre-modern European communities in which individuals could scarcely be conceived apart from the community.

But one should not deceive oneself that this was a radical and 'progressive' break with the past. Hobbes' *Leviathan* – a seminal early work on secular governance – can be read as a mere variation on the ancient Greek ur-myth told in the *Oresteia*: when the sovereign violence that preserves the community is not projected onto a 'transcendental' deity, but associated with a human figure – the sovereign – the immanent power of the latter is one of permanent violence. This is the failure of transcendental reference. Because sovereignty has not been placed 'elsewhere' its violence tends to remain even within the generality of law. The violence of the immanent community – aiming to eliminate all obstacles to the realisation of human will on nature and other humans – could only cease if communities renounce their absolute power over themselves, and invoke a source of law 'outside of' factionalism and the perpetual war that their contract has failed to bring to a decisive end. The sense of this argument is that law can only mediate between social factions if its source is entirely removed from the human arena of conflict. Hence the notion of ancestral law or, indeed, a divinity located outside of nature and time whose will is expressed in a law given to the ancestors.

To what extent, though, does the conventional thinking of law grasp that behind any formal account of rights there has to be some notion of transcendent (i.e. ancestral) authority? Barshack engages in a study that runs from Hobbes, through Austin to Hart. Do these authors provide the resources to think the absent sovereign? If this thinking remains blind to the problem, it is blindness shared by other forms of contemporary jurisprudence – in particular law and economics. Economic reasoning and rational-choice theory simply cannot grasp the 'excess' on which the law depends, namely its ultimate reliance on reference to something 'transcendent'. Nor can this excess be contained within a theory of adjudication and a community of principle. This, then, is a problem shared by liberal accounts of formal equality. In a final re-working of the rule of law Barshack reinvents the Dworkinian account of the point of political philosophy in order to account for and justify the coercive power of the state other than by reference to the social contract.

Since transcendent reference has – in European history – been theologically framed it would appear that 'secular' liberals need to start reading theology to understand the rule of law. In the history of Christian thought there has been a clear, albeit not discussed, schism regarding the fundamental monotheistic principle of faith in a withdrawn God of creation. On the one side Augustine, Thomas Aquinas and Meister Eckhart (amongst others) remained faithful to the 'realist' theological idea that 'every . . . created thing, no matter how real it might be, is utterly contingent, relying upon Him for any substance that it might possess' (Blond 1998: 7). Opposing theological realism is a position that derives from the 'natural theology' of Duns Scotus (1266–1308) which explains the persistent attempts ever since to derive transcendent reference from a community of principles. Scotus posited a third term – 'being' – that he elevated *above* both the idea of God (now understood as 'infinite being') and His creations ('finite beings'). The consequence of this argument was that 'theology itself became idolatrous' (Blond 1998: 6) whereby the *mind is self-divinised* and understands itself as essentially constructive. This eliminates 'any mind-independent account of ontology and ironically, helps to give "secular" modernity its characteristic immanence' (Blond 1998: 9).

To return to this collection's immediate concerns, this triumph of 'natural theology' has been accompanied by the emergence of a specific form of political 'secularism' that considers itself either agnostic (in the case of liberalism) or atheistic (in the case of applied state communism), oblivious to the fact that it is nothing but a form of idolatrous worship of the mind. However, securalism (whatever its versions) is in reality theistic and committed to presence through the 'deification' of an immanent will expressed by either the social contract or the communist party. In consequence, it seems that the so-called securalist has decided that the *only* possible options for subjectivity are either to affirm itself through acting out desire and dominating nature, or to deny itself 'by positing his consciousness as a consequence of other less human structures . . . which it is suggested only the strong can bear to endure' (Blond 1998: 4). Hence, for example, the two most prominent versions of the 'rule of law' either as a mere 'tool' for the realisation of whatever human objectives or as encapsulating 'substantive' principles (i.e. natural law, biological impulses, linguistic or biopolitical structures).

The crypto-theism inherent in European secularism is problematic for past secular and realist theology. Scholars have also argued that it also fails to provide a way of understanding the intelligibility of politics as such. In the words of Anglican Archbishop Rowan Williams, a politics worthy of the name cannot be based on the assumption that action is nothing but the successful assertion of will, something which subverts the very idea of *intelligible* action as 'contributing to a system of communication, to symbolic exchange' by virtue of being a 'representation of something *prior*, in such a way as to introduce that prior and shaping reality into a continuing narrative of uncovering through response and question' (Milbank 2005: 1–3, italics added). As Williams wisely emphasises, this view of intelligible action is common to faithful Augustine, Hegel and atheist Marx. But it seems to have vanished from our discourse. In the case of those liberal polities which emerged 'triumphant' following the collapse of state communism, this has meant that '. . . the lowest has become the highest, and equality names itself as the only value that cannot be devalued' (Blond 1998: 2). In these circumstances 'critique' becomes at best synonymous with scepticism. Before the disasters that both liberal polities and their erstwhile 'communist' enemies have brought about, scepticism re-emerges as a welcome 'alternative' (for example in the case of deconstruction) only to be exposed as 'too weak a force to confront the present with its ownmost possibilities' because it lacks what Merleau-Ponty called perceptual faith (*la foi perceptive*), namely the faith necessary to:

> understand that *there is a world*, and in all its paradoxical certainty it calls forth for description. To lack faith in the external world, or even to doubt that there is any knowable external to the synthetic activities of the human mind, is to be complicit with the modern oscillation between subjectivity and its indifferent denial.
>
> (Blond 1998: 4, italics added)

Whether or not this is an accurate assessment of the political potential of deconstruction, Diamantides relies on it when he insists on reminding us that Islamic history has followed a different path from that sketched out above. Faithful medieval Muslims never invested in the creation of a theology proper and certainly not the 'natural theology' that flourished in England. The theological category of 'being', which comprises both God and His creations, never took off in Muslim-majority societies nor in Jewish communities. Consequently, and in distinction to the situation in medieval and modern Europe as well as post-colonial 'Islamic' republics and Israel, medieval Muslim (and Jewish) jurists did not respond or engage in the various attempts of state authorities to usurp theological authority and occupy the position of the 'sovereign being' that defines political community. Consequently, even if the political institutions of Muslim-majority (and Jewish-majority) societies have by now been shaped by force according to European models, they should not feel obliged to complete their colonisation by adopting Europe's idolatrous immanentism. Muslim thought, in particular, need not commit itself to the idea of absolute sovereignty, a tendency that Diamantides attributes to *both* Islamists and Muslim liberals. Instead he seeks to summon critical energies that run through Christian, Islamic and Judaic notions of faith in an *unknowable* creator God and to turn these notions of faith against traditions of sovereignty, constitutionalism and positivist jurisprudence that have presented themselves as the only resources for thinking the rule of law in modernity.

There are a number of elements to this argument. Elaborating a thesis of Jean-Luc Nancy, Diamantides asserts that there is an intriguing process of 'auto-deconstruction' that runs through all monotheistic thinking: crudely, monotheism replaces pagan belief in the presence of a powerful God with faith in a withdrawn God; a faith which can survive even contemporary atheism. This makes any crude distinction between faith and secularism, religion and politics, theism and atheism, strictly impossible. It also gives rise to the necessary and difficult way in which one might try to reclaim or re-work a critical thinking of faith. Diamantides retraces the theological origins of the Western positivist belief in the power of the formal (procedural) rule of law, supposedly purged of morality, to provide the basic social structure in which a plural society can hold itself together. He stresses an original point where procedural law assumed, in different 'secular' terms, the theological prerogative of stating the social being. Positive law, it is widely assumed, turns the social bond into the expression of individual wills, bringing to an end arguments about morality and antagonisms about faith, and allowing a coherent and pluralistic political community to found itself. Those theories of constitutionalism and sovereign power that took root in modern North-Western Europe, however, reflect the particular history of North-Western European modernity and a Christian version of monotheistic auto-deconstruction that is no better or worse than what has happened in pre-colonial Islamic modernity. No better but victorious. Through imperialism, colonialism and now so called 'globalisation' and the 'creation' of market economy, the way Christianity secularised itself in North-Western Europe has had a strong influence on societies around the world including Muslim-majority states. The centralised sovereign state has been imposed everywhere. Diamantides is concerned with historical and contemporary elaborations of this pattern, focusing on the scholarship of liberal Muslim Abdullahi an-Na'im whose work is read partly as a tactical reaction to Islamist fundamentalists and partly as an attempt to mend the ruptures between constitutionalism and *Shari'a* that perhaps downplays the more radical (but not fundamentalist) challenges posed by faith to the state.

In contradistinction to the history of European faith and law, Islamic jurisprudence shows that religious, legal and state authority *need to be neither coordinated nor antagonistic*; and that sophisticated bodies of law can develop without reference to sovereign power and singular authority. Diamantides refers to 'faithful jurists' in both Islamic and Judaic traditions who developed subtle and nuanced jurisprudences on the basis of the 'withdrawn God' – one who would *not* guarantee the 'truth' or the correctness of their interpretations of 'His' word. In distinction to the Weberian notion of officials and the Hartian notion of legal personnel as a *sine qua non* of the modern rule of law, this jurisprudence points at a peculiar idea: that complex law can exist despite or, even on the basis of, a certain *disinvestment* from the idea that state action is the ultimate guarantor of meaning. Within contemporary Islam, and in spite of both Islamist and liberal ideologies, one can still find the refusal to merge faith and state power, a fact that accounts for the 'still born' nature of sovereignty within Islamic political history but also the possibility of a different way of thinking universally about law and the state. The latter part of the essay reads this thesis into contemporary arguments about legal theory and reflexive politics and seeks a genealogy for itself in Christian political theology.

Gearey's essay also takes the position of the long *durée*. Although focused on a reading of the British case law concerning the Islamic veil, it seeks to put this case in a much broader historical and intellectual context. The *Begum* case is read as a modern manifestation of the old dispute over the faith that attaches itself to instruments. In modern terms this is an argument over human rights, but human rights must themselves be seen as the way in which a certain logic of the reformation plays itself out. This argument returns us to our thesis that supposedly 'secular' terms contain within themselves theological residues. The essay concludes with an examination of Rowan Williams' position on *Shari'a*. His proposal for the formal recognition of *Shari'a* within the UK correctly identifies the need to bring Islamic law within a human rights framework. This is not the 'triumph' of supposedly secular human rights against benighted faith; nor is it an argument that the state can define the terms of political community. The following passage, from Dr Rowan Williams' consideration of faith and plurality, gives some sense of the consequences of the argument:

> Societies that are in fact ethnically, culturally and religiously diverse are societies in which identity is formed . . . by different modes and contexts of belonging, 'multiple affiliations'. The danger is in acting as if the authority that managed the abstract level of equal citizenship represented a sovereign order which then *allowed* other levels to exist. But if the reality of society is plural – as many political theorists have pointed out – this is a damagingly inadequate account of common life, in which certain kinds of affiliation are marginalised or privatised to the extent that what is produced is a ghettoised pattern of social life, in which particular sorts of interest and of reasoning are tolerated as private matters but never granted legitimacy in public as part of a continuing debate about shared goods and priorities.
>
> (Williams 2008)

Whilst, in the light of Barshack and Diamantides' arguments, this position might not be entirely acceptable, the shared point of reference is that the state is a latecomer. Whilst it must in the last instance arrange the terms of common being, it has absolutely no claim to its definition, either through rights or constitutionalism, which remain 'derived' forms and entirely secondary. This rests on an argument about the nature of 'common life' that cannot be defined by the state, determining by fiat, as it were, what groups could participate in the life of the community. Such versions of the state have proved weak. The distinction between private matters of faith and public expressions of secular belonging do not allow strong communities to be created, where the legitimacy of political institutions is provided by the fact that they give form to an inclusive common culture.

Thinking these issues through requires a redefinition of one of the key terms that has justified the sovereignty of the state: the rule of law. The dominant version of this political philosophy would hold that it is necessary for the state to guarantee the equality of its citizens. The fundamental way in which this is achieved through access to the courts, and the discourse of equal rights. In recent years, the rule of law (as we have seen) has become linked to the idea of human rights. This perhaps strengthens the rights of the citizen against executive authority, but the argument still works with fundamentally the same terms of the doctrine of the rule of law. Dr Williams offers a partial critique of this idea. The rise of human rights has brought with it a privileging of the idea that all citizens are essentially individuals, with rights claims that can be pressed against other citizens and the state. It becomes difficult to think of political community as something that is shared between people and requires a public culture. Values such as 'civility' and conventional communally orientated ethical codes are replaced by 'individual rights'. However, this is not to condemn the state. It is to seek a new balance between state and community:

> The role of 'secular' law is . . . the monitoring of [social] affiliations to prevent the creation of mutually isolated communities in which human liberties are seen in incompatible ways and individual persons are subjected to restraints or injustices for which there is no public redress.
>
> (Williams 2008)

III. The essays: friction, resistance, hybridity

In order to step outside of Western Europe, but to retain our concern with the malleability of concepts like secular state and identity, we turn to El Menyawi's attempt to read the *aporias* of Egyptian family law. These have developed around conflicts between the secularists and the conservative champions over the precise form that both law – and the state – should take. The terms of the conflict were laid down in the last century. Modernising secularists were forced to compromise on their drive to re-make Egyptian law on a European model. Religious elites and their supporters were placated by maintaining family law as an Islamic core – around which the programme of modernisation could then be completed. The cost of this compromise was the sacrifice of women's rights, such as the provision of no fault divorces; a pattern that has repeated itself in more recent years. How can this peculiar tension be described? At one level, it is a successful political strategy that allows a secularising project to continue. From a different perspective, though, it is a strategy that is only possible because Egyptian women are kept in a perpetual limbo or an indeterminate zone, where secular reforms and, hence, more complete and better protection of rights are always promised and forever delayed. It would appear that the preservation of an Islamic legal core has become the very condition of secularising reform; secular norms are only possible if, at the heart of the Egyptian legal system, there are deep-seated principles that contradict them, but, at the same time, allow them to exist. Further reforms continue to be threatened by this peculiar situation and its affects. Recent feminist attempts to work in Islamic terms, and to improve women's rights by presenting their arguments as essentially Islamic, have not been productive and, furthermore, run the risk of strengthening resistance to future reforms. It may be that this system can be perpetually 'managed' as a constituent tension of the Egyptian state. Alternatively, it may be the case that it can be pushed in a progressive direction.

El Menyawi's concerns are perhaps a variation on themes that we can also find in Barshack's essay. Barshack draws attention to the inherent violence of secular legal systems that lack transcendental reference. El Menyawi, too, is concerned with the violence 'walled up' within law. For him, however, Egyptian law can be neither properly secular nor religious for there can be no 'transcendental reference' as there is no general agreement over the symbols that can be shared. Therefore, there is ongoing conflict over the terms of the law and irresolvable violence, which in the Egyptian case plays itself out over the perennial question of the status of women's rights. This is why El Menyawi is so concerned to find the appropriate theoretical path that navigates between the Derridean logic of sacrifice and Agamben's concern with abandonment.

El Menyawi draws on Baudrillard's account of the simulacra to push the logic of Egyptian law to its limit. Crudely, the simulacra presents a copy of reality as if it was real or, more precisely, creates a zone of ambiguity where what is real, inauthentic and copied is impossible to distinguish from the real and authentic: the 'gift' of ambiguity. The focus for this strategy is on the reforms contained in Article 20 of Law No 1 of 2000, which draws on the Islamic concept of the *khul'*. The *khul'* allows a wife to divorce on the condition that she surrenders any financial rights against her husband. When the *khul'* was enacted as law, the condition that a wife receives her husband's permission was absent. Could this be seen as a 'hyper real *khul'*', a law which appears to be consistent with the norms of Islam whilst containing within it a radical secularist 'virus'? The *khul'* law split the conservative religious elite. Whilst the *Sheikh* of Al-Azhar University – an influential religious scholar – supported Article 20, others argued that there were no textual sources to justify divorce initiated by the female spouse. Despite these differences, there seemed to be a popular understanding that the law was indeed coherent with Islam. Liberal modernisers and feminists appeared to have created a zone of indeterminacy, a site where it might be possible to develop further secular principles as if they were religious (or indeed, to seize the secularising potential of religious principles).

Dupret's essay seeks to demolish the idea that Islamic family law represents the last stand of something 'authentically religious' within the jurisdiction of the 'secular' Egyptian state. Read more broadly, however, his argument also suggests that those states that label themselves 'Islamic' actually do not make consistent use of 'religious law'. The hard and fast distinction between secular and religious state is thus rendered yet more oblique. Dupret's approach is based on praxiology, an attempt to get closer to the ways in which law is practised and interpreted, and to leave on one side over-arching, general concepts that appear to have little to do with daily life. Thus, claims to the 'intrinsic authority' of Islamic family law have to be assessed against the background of how lawyers, judges and litigants actually compose and contest their understandings of particular claims. Rules appear to have no authority beyond the way in which claims are made within any given context. It would be easy to get this argument wrong. It does not seek to replace 'law in books' or classifications, secular or otherwise, with law 'in action'. Nor does Dupret's argument reject analyses of rules in terms of power relationships or the implicit or explicit cultural assumptions that animate and underlie religious or secular rules. Praxiology requires that the analytical focus is firmly on those instances where (to repeat a jurisprudential catchphrase) people do things with rules.

So what does Dupret's study of a series of Egyptian decisions about personal status tell us? If we suspend the assumption that these cases are a privileged site for the application of the norms of religious law, we can begin to see the actual practices which articulate the norms themselves. At this level we have to observe that in the place of learned deliberations on fine jurisprudential points there is in fact very little 'religious law' in judicial practices. Rather, these cases suggest much more narrow concerns with procedure, the construction of fact and court routine. We are a long way from some 'orientalist' fantasy of learned religious disputation and, instead, are in the routine, bureaucratised world of a working court.

With Larson's essay we move from Egypt to the Islamic Republic of Mauritania. The concept of *Kafā'a* in Sunni jurisprudence determines the legal idea of a 'suitable marriage' and thus constructs the sense in which the parties can be seen as equivalent in terms of their genealogy, social standing, piety and wealth. Focusing on the development of the concept in the Islamic Republic of Mauritania, Larson argues that *Kafā'a* relates to a complex of interpretations and practices that show tensions between notions of equality before the law as a Mauritanian citizen, and ethnic/cultural articulations of legal identity. Larson traces the development of the term in Maliki jurisprudence and the way in which understandings of equalities between partners have been transformed. Her history of the term is then linked to two contemporary cases on personal status discussed by the Mauritanian scholar, Zekeria Ould Ahmed Salem, in which rival ideas of clan and ethnicity play themselves out. Lying behind these conflicts are different ideas of belonging.

It is significant that the cases were heard in the 1990s, after the promulgation of the democratic 1991 Constitution but prior to the publication of the 2001 Code of Personal Status. This time-frame raises the question of how the state deals with notions of personal status in Islamic law, and its rival interpretations. Is there an interpretation of *Kafā'a* that stresses the equality of Muslim citizens? These issues are analysed in the third section of the essay.

The Mauritanian cases can be read as pointing to some general themes about the problems of post-colonial law. In conventional theory the law of a nation coordinates with the customs of a people who are themselves coordinated with a territory that will be a nation-state. At the same time, though, these principles must be rooted in specific local 'conditions', and the law of the nation-state must be able to mediate these foundational conditions. The jurisprudence of *Kafā'a* suggests the possible resolution of a fundamental problem of foundation. Nationality and religious or ethnic belonging can be combined. Recognising *Kafā'a* jurisprudence allows the state to present itself as 'multi-ethnic' – respecting different interpretations of the term; at the same time the potential ambiguities inherent in *Kafā'a* can be resolved by a court speaking for the coherence of Mauritanian citizenship. But is such a use of these terms possible, particularly after the traumatic ethnic cleansing of 1989? The fundamental problem is a tension between two 'measures' of equality: that of the citizens of a democratic European-style nation-state who are formally equal before the law, and that of notions of status defined by ethnic and religious norms which, in this case, ultimately further the power of elite groups. If these concepts can be brought together by the court speaking for the nation, it needs to deal with the problem of foundations. After independence, pre-national forms of life must express themselves in the terms of an Islamic nation-state defined by sovereign law. The problem is that these forms carry forward into the democratic nation-state inequalities that characterised its multi-ethnic history. The past casts a long shadow.

What do we make of these arguments? Larson's argument points away from conventional liberal thinking. Take, for example, Kymlicka's notion that societal culture defines social being and allows people to achieve their identity through a complex of meanings; the network of shared significations that make life in its totality understandable. This definition is meant to stress the importance of 'common institutions and practices' (Kymlicka 1991: 165), and ultimately to underlie Kymlicka's account of minority rights and the multicultural state that defends the diverse 'cultural heritage[s]', a culture that is somehow recognisably 'ours' (Kymlicka 1991: 165). Although Kymlicka has worked to refine this model to make it applicable to other cultures, Larson's work suggests that the construction of common 'narratives' is far more complex than liberal thinking might suggest. Moreover, it points towards the notion that minority rights may not be as stable a concept as Kymlicka allows; indeed, minority rights may be subject to the tensions of definition of the concept of *Kafā'a* and equally as unstable.

Özcan's essay examines the moral world of Muslim entrepreneurs in Kazakhstan, Kyrgyzstan and Uzbekistan. Born and educated in the atheist Soviet Union these individuals discovered as adults two previously unavailable 'gods': the free market and Islam. Özcan is concerned with this peculiar conjunction; how are Islamic norms used to delineate and justify business practices? Her thesis is that the sudden withdrawal of Soviet power opened up a complex conjuncture where different moral codes, including still influential communist ideas, were pragmatically combined. In particular, there was a growing public appreciation that markets required public morality. What norms could be invoked? The picture that emerges is another exercise in understanding hybridity and complexity; the way in which different individuals bring together the different norms and ideologies that have influenced them, and attempt to use them to make sense of their worlds. The implicit suggestion is that ideologies operate not because they are somehow doctrinally pure but precisely because their ideas and beliefs are malleable. This research warns us against positing a 'pure' idea of Islam that forms a substratum of core principles articulating a post-communist moral world. Kazakh and Kyrgyz interpretations of Islam had already been nuanced by their own pragmatism and animistic folk cultures; and are further combined with secular influences acquired through Soviet education.

Working out and acting on hybrid moralities is a difficult process. The paper focuses on elaborating three 'ideal types' of business morality: a type that draws on communist ideology, a second that is articulated through Sufi ethics and a third that is animated by utopian Islam. These moral codes are exemplified through a close study of the moral worlds of three businessmen based on field research and interviews. These studies show how the combination of different ideas, lead to the privileging or downplaying of certain concerns relating to the structure and objectives of business activities. In general, the tensions between different norms can lead to a sense of moral dissonance but equally those who attempt to think of business in moral terms derive comfort from their beliefs in times of frustration and failure. Whether or not individual commitment to codes of behaviour in itself is sufficient for a functioning market, however, remains an open question. Özcan's conclusion, echoing Durkheim, suggests that unless there is some consistent effort to provide over-arching moral norms, a crippling sense of anomie will paralyse public life.

Kausar's essay addresses the role that religion played – and continues to play – in the foundation and coherence of The Islamic Republic of Pakistan. Her essay draws attention to the difficulties that arise when modern law and constitutionalism speak for the divine in a modern Muslim majority setting. As Kausar notes, Pakistan, like Israel, is a modern European-style nation-state explicitly founded on a notion of religious faith. The problem is that the intense moment of identification of people, faith and nation in 1947 has not been sustained in the decades of the country's history and the various problems that the new territorial nation-state both brought about and had to contain or solve. Dividing the history of Pakistan into four representative periods, Kausar argues that the notion of 'Islamic unity' has failed to mediate the ethnic, territorial and ideological tensions that characterise the nation-state. The foundational moment requires the creation of a unique Islamic identity, distinct from and incompatible with the dominant Hinduism of India. In this sense, the coordination of faith and nation remains 'reactive' and, once the forces that oppose its objectives are overpowered or removed, the notion of a nation synonymous with a religion collapses under its own weight. Indeed, the separation of Bangladesh from Pakistan evidences the failure of a common Muslim identity. These themes are traced into the politics of constitution-making, and the attempts to give the foundational idea of religion a viable legal form. This results in an uneasy tension between ethnicity and nationalism. These themes communicate with other pieces in the collection, notably those of El Menyawi and Larson.

Kausar suggests that the dynamic of Pakistani politics might have produced different ways of articulating common belonging, had it not been for various factors that revivified *religious forms of expressing national cohesion*. External support for the Islamist pretensions of President Zia's military dictatorship – a product of cold war alliances – enabled an unprecedented 'Islamisation' of national life. In Zia's wake, though, it became increasingly clear that this process had not furthered national coherence, as struggles broke out between Shi'a and Sunni factions over the form that an Islamic state should take; problems exacerbated by the Iranian revolution. Democracy proved unstable, and General Musharraf's coup returned the country to military dictatorship in 1999. Musharraf had a more moderate approach to Islam and in his desire to modernise Pakistan sought to distance himself from Zia. The events of 9/11, and Musharraf's decision to ally himself with the US, have opened a new phase in the history of Pakistan. If Jinnah's vision remains a lodestar for this essay, it is only right that he is left the final word: what is the form of the relationship between state and religion?

For the final two essays we move back to the West. Caeiro's essay examines the life of Muslims who live in Christian-majority secular states. He focuses on the attempts by Muslim scholars and public intellectuals to create a 'European' or 'Western Islam' through a Muslim jurisprudence for minorities (*fiqh al-aqalliyyat* or minority *fiqh*). This kind of thinking comes out of *fiqh* councils such as the European Council for Fatwa and Research and the *Fiqh* Council of North America. Indeed, it is precisely the mobility of minority *fiqh*, the fact that it is constituted by so many different writers, working in different traditions and raising diverse concerns, that makes it such a vital phenomenon. Although it appears to be innovative in terms of its practitioners and modes of dissemination – in particular through the internet – it also has a presence within traditional Islamic thought and scholarship, and receives notices and support from powerful establishment figures. Minority *fiqh* is thus a mixture of tradition and innovation. It seeks to reconfigure Islamic scholarship and define how the faith is to be lived within a globalised world characterised by migration.

'Minority *fiqh*' raises issues around the creation of a discourse specific to the realities of Muslim communities living in Christian/secular states and, although it covers a variety of issues from critical engagement with human rights to the status of Islam in public discourse, it seems to be focused upon the peculiar difficulties faced by Muslim minorities. How is this status to be understood? How are the challenges to a life lived in faith to be navigated within secular democracies? In particular, how can faith be practised publicly, in those nations where it is seen as primarily a private matter? Yusuf al-Qaradawi, one of the most influential scholars of minority *fiqh*, has argued, for instance, that Muslim minorities are necessary for the spread of the religion and that there is no compulsion to move to an Islamic state. This thesis requires a particular articulation of the relationship between the community and the state. Al-Qaradawi roots authority in the community and its authorised scholars but also asserts that Muslims must politically engage in order to achieve legal recognition and equal rights. This development of minority *fiqh* often echoes critical approaches to liberal equality – and suggests the need to develop those resources of social capital that work outside formal arguments about equality.

However, the problems experienced in France by the Imam of Bordeaux, Tareq Oubrou, suggest the limitations of this way of thinking. Oubrou sought unsuccessfully to reposition Islam culturally and re-negotiate the relationship between religious and republican norms. In the hands of men like Tariq Ramadan, minority *fiqh* has taken on a different and more radical form that moves away from the notion of an Islamic minority, and shows how it is possible to conceive more broadly of Islamic citizenship. Ajil al-Nashmi has also been critical of how the very notion of minority rights has limited the spaces in which Islamic 'agency' can be understood and practised; others have been concerned as to how international law and minority rights can be brought together. Indeed, they might point towards a much more expansive concept of a 'public Islam', as suggested by Salah Sultan's argument. Sultan has asserted that American Muslims have a duty to ensure the general spread of literacy as a public good, and also as a chance to encourage the reading of the Qur'an and engagement with the Islamic community.

However, as Caeiro stresses, it would be wrong to impose a false consensus on minority *fiqh*. He thus focuses on a debate between Taha Jabir al-Alwani and 'Ajil al-Nashmi to suggest how even those committed to the promulgation of the discourse radically disagree about its terms and content; the two scholars have very different ideas about the status of the Sunna and interpretation of key passages from the Qur'an. It is not Caeiro's intention to mediate in this debate but to see the positions that the two scholars take as representative of the wider tensions that characterise the field.

Brown's essay takes us to the complex structuring of Muslim identity in the United Kingdom. The fundamental question she poses is: how can a hybrid British Muslim identity be created? This must be based on a notion of citizenship and thus the exercise of the rights and duties that define the citizen. However, a British Muslim identity as a citizen must take into account those religious and ethnic differences that are as important to self-definition as belonging to a national community. Her essay takes entrance to higher education as its focus. This is a particularly interesting site for studying the emergence of new identities. For instance, civil society and campus-based groups are active in encouraging young Muslim women to take up university places. This has created tensions with traditional ideas that are resistant or hostile to women's education. Those promoting education for women have stressed that education does not necessarily mean turning away from faith. The tensions between these positions inform debates around appropriate clothing and facilities. Rather than reading such tensions as the assertion of 'fundamentalist' doctrines, it is necessary to be sensitive to the fact that they are about the terms in which a notion of Muslim citizenship could be composed.[2]

The 'politics of fear' that have resulted from the 'war on terror' make it more difficult to navigate the intricacies of such problems. Despite the best efforts of the British government to separate notions of moderate and fundamentalist or radical Islam, adoption of or requests for Islamic forms of dress are now seen as the mark of 'suspect populations' – ready to assert a radical identity against the tolerance of their host community. Brown warns that 'security policy' threatens to homogenise a complex set of positions, and to limit the very tendencies that would be helpful in the fabrication of a cultural position that could negotiate the old and the new, the secular and the sacred.

Brown's essay fits into the broader pattern of concern over fundamentalism and the perceived failure of multiculturalism. Primitivist or fundamentalist assertions of Islamic identity are seen to be linked to a rejection of modernisation, secularism and liberalism. The problem that Brown stresses is that

2 Kathleen Moore's *The Unfamiliar Abode* (2010) offers a striking analysis of how Muslim communities in the United States and Great Britain articulate their identities around strategies of 'diasporic legality' (6) which combine both Islamic and secular legal resources to negotiate the diverse tensions that are attendant on assuming a public position as a Muslim. The resonant concept of the 'unfamiliar abode' describes the difficulties of stating an identity when the terms that the law offers are characterised by both indeterminacy, and a 'universal' that only pretends to be 'open, rational and pluralistic' (10). Is it possible for Muslims to make a claim to a public 'faith' identity without being considered either as a fundamentalist threat to national values, or un-Islamic? The unfamiliar abode is a product of contradictory tensions playing themselves out in the migrations caused in part by globalisation: the need to assert an identity, when 'solid' reference points appear not to be available.

fundamentalism cannot be read as the failure of multiculturalism. To do so would be to throw out doctrines that have proved themselves resilient and adaptable. Multiculturalism remains a useful paradigm. However, we need to stress the way in which identity can be fabricated. This fabrication goes beyond the old sense in which ethnicity or religious identity is somehow taken for granted and opposed to other cultural terms which are equally as rigid. One broad conclusion from the essays above is that conventional multicultural analysis has not developed the necessary analytic tools to perform this kind of analysis.

IV. Conclusions

In their different ways these essays suggest that it is necessary to move beyond conventional multiculturalist positions which mirror the individualist versus communitarian divide.[3] Liberals like John Rawls or Ronald Dworkin aspire to an ethically neutral legal order where every individual is assured the opportunity to pursue his or her conception of the good. Implicit in these views is the standard Lockean understanding of the primacy of the individual as the fundamental component of political association. In this approach, we also come across the idea of a separation between the 'public' and 'private' spheres where, predictably, religion is allocated in the latter. For many this way of thinking is deeply embedded in specifically modern European cultural and intellectual contexts. By contrast, communitarians, such as Charles Taylor, disputing the ethical neutrality of the law, expect the liberal state to open up to diverse specific conceptions of the good life, including, if need be, those that prize collective over individual rights. However, in recent years, the debate has become less polarised; a softening of positions due, in

3 The fundamental claim of multiculturalism is that 'minority cultures or ways of life are not sufficiently protected by ensuring the individual rights of their members and as a consequence should also be protected with special *group* rights or privileges' (Moller Okin 1997). We need to distinguish our understanding of multiculturalism from that of the 'secularists' or champions of 'enlightenment values'. To give an example: Cohen argues that the state must 'commit itself to secularism; to offer full religious freedom, while striving to keep religion out of the public sphere. Leaving all considerations of principle aside, secularism is the only ideology that can make a multi-faith society work. The alternative is a future of competitive grievance and unremitting vexatious litigation' (Cohen 2008). These secularist arguments are similar to those put forward by critics like Barry (2002) who asserts that multiculturalism leads to the fragmentation of the nation-state and the collapse of national cultures. Whilst such arguments are difficult to disprove, it would seem that the state has proved itself able to accommodate a wide range of multiculturalist demands (Joppke and Lukes 1999). Indeed, multiculturalism can itself become part of official legitimising discourses. Grillo draws attention to a tendency in recent American political and social thinking that has articulated versions of 'strong pluralism'. He cites K.H. Claghorn's arguments that judges should be able to speak minority languages (Grillo 1998: 189).

part, to a re-examination of the precise terms of law's ethical neutrality.[4] For us, the specific challenges for the law that are raised by Muslim cultural and religious identities – both in the form of minorities within non-Muslim majority states but also within Muslim-majority European-style nation-states – represent an opportunity to go even further.

We need to redefine the debate by reflecting on the mutual transformations that come from the encounter between monotheistic faith and state sovereignty. Multiculturalism has been successful in re-articulating the terms in which one belongs to a nation-state only up to a point.[5] From this perspective, multiculturalism is less of a threat to the norms of liberal democracies than was perhaps first imagined.[6] But can we really stretch its premises so as to defend liberal democracies from more radical implications of the cultural traditions of minorities?

If we consider the United Kingdom, the accommodation of cultural and religious difference has been achieved incrementally. As Parekh[7] (2006: 243) stresses, the law took into account the importance of certain cultural practices that are discriminated against by an insensitive enforcement of common rules. For instance, the amendment of the law in 1976 that required Sikhs to wear crash helmets whilst riding motor cycles went some way to realising this principle. Similar reforms were made in the construction industry where health and safety legislation made wearing hard hats obligatory. Another example would be the resolution of the dispute over appropriate uniforms brokered by the General Nursing Council. The Council was able to compromise over the demands of Asian women who sought to wear *shalwar kameez* whilst

4 See, for example, Brian Barry (1995) and Will Kymlicka (2001).

5 This idea of the centrality of the state to any realisation of community runs through the different understandings of how potentially threatening and disruptive differences can be legitimately managed. Following Parekh's (2006: 199–206) instructive typology, these can be broadly defined as: proceduralist, civic assimilationist and the Ottoman *millet* model. Proceduralism tends to stress the intractable nature of cultural difference and accepts it as an inconvenient fact of political community. The task of the state is to remain largely 'formal and neutral': as it would be illegitimate to impose its own understanding of the good life it must instead articulate minimum rules that relate to behaviour and keep social conflict to the minimum. Civic assimilationists favour the creation of a strong public culture that allows different communities to agree upon common institutions and goals. The state, as the pre-eminent part of public culture, articulates what is held in common. Civil society and the family are accorded a greater expression of diversity. The legitimacy of the state rests on its ability to police the boundary between the public and the private. The millet system acknowledges more than the other two models the primary importance of culture, and sees the state as merely providing the over-arching administrative and legal framework in which different minorities can be left to their own devices.

6 See Gutmann (1994).

7 Given limitations of space, we are using Parekh as a representative figure. There is clearly more to theorising multiculturalism but Parekh's work has the virtue of providing a well-articulated general account of how liberal democracies can accommodate multicultural demands.

performing official duties. However, it is not the case that the courts have always made decisions protecting cultural differences. The so-called 'objective necessity' test was successfully used to prevent Muslim men with beards from working in food preparation. This 'instrumental' approach to the law appears insensitive and inflexible (Parekh 2006: 246).

So, we are not trying to suggest that there is always a possibility of compromise. Tensions, even profound tensions, can and do emerge.[8] Parekh (2006) recognises that the 'British' model has hit boundaries. Perhaps one of the most contentious matters in recent years has been the insistence of Muslim women on their right to wear the *hijab*. To an extent the problem is one of perception. To return to Brown's point, the right is not exclusively claimed by fundamentalist Islamists. The ongoing '*affaire du foulard*' in France in the late 1980s is symptomatic. It was prompted by the assertion of three French girls of North African descent that they should be allowed to wear the *hijab* in the *lycée*. The French establishment was not sympathetic and argued that any visible display of a religious symbol threatened the *laicité* of the French state. This was particularly worth upholding in schools to encourage the formation of universal secular cultural values. Counter-arguments stressed that Christians or Jews were not prohibited from wearing religious symbols and that the French state should be open to plurality. The attempts of the Ministry of Education to distinguish between the 'discrete' wearing of religious symbols, and those that tended to 'proselytise' or were inherently discriminatory, did not resolve matters. One of the features of the whole episode was the sense in which the state and the media, on the whole, sided with the principle of *laicité*. However, the '*affaire du foulard*' shows just how high levels of anxiety and misunderstanding about Islamic cultural 'otherness' have become.

This volume aspires to contribute to the undoing of this 'othering'. From the first group of essays, we can extract the following theme: rather than reading history as a singular process of secularisation with the emergence of positive law as a necessary part of it, we want to see it as a study of the malleability of concepts that can be used to fabricate a notion of the social bond. This allows us to see the Western liberal order as based on specifically

8 The recent decision of the the French Senate (September 2010) to prohibit the wearing of face-covering veils in public would be a good example of a profound tension between the state (speaking for a national community) and a religious minority. The ban should become law in spring 2011. The Justice Minister, Michèle Alliot-Marie, was quoted as saying 'The full veil dissolves a person's identity in that of a community. It calls into question the French model of integration, founded on the acceptance of our society's values. Living with one's face uncovered. . . . was a question of dignity and equality'. It is interesting that the face, and the figure of the veiled face, becomes an image of equality and individuality. The obscuring of the face is the sign that the individual has not transcended the 'community' – whilst the visible face is the symbol of the citizen who belongs to the public space of the nation. See www.guardian.co.uk/world/2010/sep/14/france-senate-muslim-veil-ban. On the veil and 'Islam in Europe', see Motha (2007).

Western European theological concepts that have been adapted to political exigencies and secularising arguments. These have been used to suggest that the terminal point of a tradition is an absolutely sovereign state – even a human rights state – that grants and sustains the terms of social being. We want to elaborate a counter-argument to this assertion of the European nation-state as a source of singular codified state law. Religious faith (and critical thinking) can harbour infinitely more complex understandings of social being when disjointed from the demands of sovereignty. These articulations of being together are to be found in those nodes where people share the truths that circulate amongst them; or even, in Diamantides' terms, in the productive yet unresolved anxiety and the non-paralysing 'moral trembling' of the type shown by medieval Jewish and Muslim jurists.

These jurists were concerned with the rule of law and its logical coherence but were equally able to reach a number of varying, and equally valid, solutions to the problems they posited. They were not concerned with the state's need to turn law into a means for the efficient implementation of centrally made decisions throughout huge territories. Such faith-induced indifference to general legislation certainly is antithetical to today's states – including many of the post-colonial, 'Islamic republics', which emulate the medieval European reduction of faith into state idolatry in all but name. But it is worth bearing in mind at the same time that religious humility before an unknowable God (or a thinking that works with doubt and irresolution) also prevents the abuses that contemporary human rights ideology struggles to contain. To refuse to legislate for others for reasons of religious humility or from doubts as to the possibility of generalising one's own position is as far away from the situation of 'dictatorship of majorities' that embarrasses modern democracies as we can ever wish to arrive. Faith-based humility prevents what human 'rights' defend against.

This conclusion, however, does not mean that Islam, Judaism or other forms of faith offer ready-made alternatives to liberal democracy. This is because organised religion is now largely in the service of statist ideals throughout the world. It would, therefore, be grossly misleading to suggest that faithful Muslims (or Jews or Christians) would necessarily be disloyal to nation-states. What conclusions can we draw? We can take Larson and Dupret's work as pointing in the following general direction. Despite the arguments of some, there is authority to maintain that Islamic thought has never held that the simultaneous belonging to the community of believers, the *umma*, and a state is impossible. Likewise, it would be unrealistic to think that Islamic faith can operate in isolation from its political and legal context. Dupret, El Menyawi and Larson offer examples of this hybridity at a micro level in Egypt and Mauritania, while Kausar takes a macro perspective in the context of Pakistan. So, we would not disagree with Dr Rowan Williams' conclusion that 'even in a predominantly Muslim state', a Muslim has 'something of a dual identity' as s/he is both a 'citizen and a believer' (Williams

2008). However, a caveat may be necessary: the historical process which accounted for hybrid identities in pre-colonial Muslim contexts differed significantly from that in Europe, as well as from post-colonial Muslim-majority states. Specifically, government in the Christian West has operated as part of a particular economy of coordinated division between secular and religious institutions from very early on.[9] In this regard the relevant thesis recently articulated by Giorgio Agamben (2007) is likely to lead to further research in this direction. How can the agonistic duality between the secular and the sacred be understood in the Muslim context, rather than from that articulated by liberal constitutional arrangements?

References

Agamben, G. (2007) *Il Regno e la Gloria: per una genealogia teologica dell'economia e del governo*, Vicenza: Neri Pozza.

Barry, B. (1995) *Justice as Impartiality*, Oxford: Oxford University Press.

Barry, B. (2002) *Culture and Equality*, Cambridge: Polity Press.

Bentley-Hart, D. (2009) *Atheist Delusions: the Christian revolution and its fashionable enemies*, New Haven, CT: Yale University Press.

Blond, P. (ed.) (1998) *Post-Secular Philosophy – between philosophy and theology*, London: Routledge.

Cohen, N. (2008) 'A cast iron case for a secular society', *The Guardian*, Sunday, 3 August 2008, available at www.guardian.co.uk/commentisfree/2008/aug/03/race.equality

Grillo, R.D. (1998) *Pluralism and the Politics of Difference*, Oxford: Oxford University Press.

Gutmann, A. (ed.) (1994) *Multiculturalism*, Princeton: Princeton University Press.

Joppke, C. and S. Lukes (1999) *Multicultural Questions*, Oxford: Oxford University Press.

Kymlicka, W. (1991) *Liberalism, Community, and Culture*, Oxford: Oxford University Press.

Kymlicka, W. (2001) *An Introduction to Political Philosophy*, Oxford: Oxford University Press.

Milbank, J., Creston Davies and Slavoj Zizek (eds) (2005) *Theology and the Political – the new debate*, Durham, NC: Duke University Press.

Moller Okin, S. (1997) 'Is Multiculturalism Bad for Women', *Boston Review*, available at www.bostonreview.net/BR22.5/okin.html

Moore, K. (2010) *The Unfamiliar Abode*, Oxford: Oxford University Press.

Motha, S. (2007) 'Veiled Women and the Affect of Religion in Democracy', *Journal of Law and Society*, 34 (1), 139–62.

Parekh, B. (2006) *Rethinking Multiculturalism*, Basingstoke: Palgrave Macmillan.

Williams, R. (2008) 'Address to Royal Courts of Justice', available at www.archbishopofcanterbury.org/1575

9 This could be dated to the theological consensus on the triadic nature of God.

Chapter 1

Transcendence and interpretation

Introductory notes on the theology of the rule of law

Lior Barshack[1]

While the core idea underlying the rule of law is debated among lawyers, there is general agreement on the operative implications of that contested idea. The rule of law is taken to constrain law-making and law-enforcing branches of government. The main imperatives addressed to the legislator are those of drafting general, prospective, consistent and clear laws. The law-enforcing branches are expected to act in conformity with pre-established law and to be able to adduce before the public evidence for their conformity with the law. The rule of law has been generally associated with liberal values such as negative liberty and fair notice. In his seminal treatise on the rule of law, written in the mid-thirties, Franz Neumann described the rule of law as historically anchored in the liberal ideas and economic interests of the bourgeoisie. While many of Neumann's observations remain definitive, the rule of law cannot be situated exclusively within the history of liberal ideas and reforms and seen as a response to distinctly liberal concerns. Rather, the various injunctions that are cited in the name of the rule of law are based on the proposition that the law originates outside the society in which it is in force. The rule of law is premised on the notion that ultimate law-making power does not vest among the living. This idea is neither distinctly liberal nor alien to the liberal tradition. Indeed, it is a fairly widespread if not universal idea which establishes continuity between liberalism and older worldviews, such as the monotheistic religions. I will argue that the relegation of ultimate law-making power outside society and the observance of the prescriptions that make up the formal aspect of the rule of law are inseparable institutional achievements. The absence of sovereignty depends on society's deference to the formal principles of the rule of law, which in turn depend on the projection of sovereignty outside society.

1 The Radzyner School of Law, The Interdisciplinary Center Herzliya. Earlier versions of this essay were presented at the British Academy conference in Izmir, the faculty seminar of the Radzyner School of Law at the Interdisciplinary Center Herzliya, and a workshop on interdisciplinary approaches to the law organised by Michael Anderheiden and Stephan Kirste at the ZIF in Bielefeld. I am grateful to participants in the different discussions for their comments.

I. Ancestral authority and the reconciliation of unity and plurality

The most immediate objection to the assertion I just made would be that the rule of law does not depend on the transcendence of sovereignty because immanent sovereignty can constrain itself and abide by self-imposed rules and principles. An alternative response would be to deny that the fiction of a sovereign subject, immanent or transcendent, has a role to play in an account of the rule of law. The 'abolition of sovereignty within the body politic of the republic' was praised by Arendt as 'perhaps the greatest American innovation in politics' (Arendt 1963: 153). In the following paragraphs, I will outline one view of the contribution of theological notions of sovereignty to our understanding of the rule of law. According to the proposed view, the relegation of ultimate law-making power to an external realm conditions the transformation of lawless founding violence into principled violence.

I will suggest that the problem of violence to which the projection of sovereignty is the response does not consist in the war of all against all described by Hobbes but rather in total social cohesion. It consists in excess of unity rather than diversity. In the apolitical state to which philosophers refer as the state of nature, individuals are not set against each other but disappear into a single collective body, which devours its individual organs and in which sovereignty is vested. The passage from state of nature to rule of law proceeds through the dispersion of social unity. The rule of law presumes the reconciliation of unity and diversity among individuals. Employing the metaphor of projection, it can be said that founding violence is overcome through the expulsion of the sovereign collective body outside the social. The idea that the sovereign unity of society lies outside society is one that can be intuitively grasped. The projection of unity makes room for individuality and diversity within the social. It also implies that the contours of the social body are superimposed upon society by a transcendent principle. In other words, it is not up to society itself to draw its own boundaries in the normal course of affairs. Thus, the absence of sovereignty prevents society from excluding parts of itself from the protection of the law.

The dependence of the rule of law on the projection of sovereignty is illustrated in Aeschylus' play *Eumenides*, one of the most illuminating literary investigations of the rule of law. The play charts the passage from archaic justice to legal disputation. Haunted by the furies (the *Erinyes*) for having murdered his mother Clytemnestra in order to avenge the blood of his father Agamemnon, the fate of Orestes is to be finally decided in court. Orestes is spared the torments inflicted by the *Erinyes*, the earthbound furies in charge of vengeance and retaliation. The passage from retaliation to legal resolution of disputes is accompanied by the transformation of the furies into *benevolent beings* (*Eumenides*) that guard the order laid down by the Olympian gods. The metamorphosis of the furies into benevolent beings can be read as an allegory for the process of projection of sovereignty and the sacred (in particular, of the sovereign power over life and death) from the terrestrial sphere onto a superior realm with the foundation of a legal order.

In Greek mythology and in Aeschylus' play, pre-political deities such as the *Erinyes* pervade the realm inhabited by humanity and perpetuate a cycle of violence. These deities were contrasted by the Greeks with the Olympian gods and goddesses of the polis.[2] The terrestrial presence of the pre-Olympian deities leaves no space for rational human self-government and does not allow for legal regulation of social conflicts. The emergence of an independent temporal realm is signalled in the play by the transformation of the furies into protectors of the Olympian order and, before that happens, by Athena's refusal to settle the conflict between Orestes and the *Erinyes*, by her decision to found instead a human court for homicide, and by the status that she and Apollo receive in court. Athena and Apollo behave in court like ordinary mortals. Their sanctity is not allowed to interfere with the logic of the legal proceeding. In the conclusion of the trial Athena insists that her vote for the acquittal of Orestes should count like any mortal vote. Apollo plays an unspectacular role in court as a witness and advocate of Orestes. The story of the furies, the savage, relentless agents of archaic justice, records the projection of sovereignty outside the space inhabited by humanity. The furies cease to wander freely across the earth; they are renamed *benevolent beings* and integrated into the *polis* as guardians of the order presided over by the Olympian gods. The setting apart of the human realm from the superior realm of the gods, notwithstanding the gods' frequent intervention in human affairs, conditions the establishment of the rule of law.

Hobbes offers a different account of the process of projection through which peace and order are established. According to Hobbes, the pacification of the war of all against all is accomplished through the monopolisation of violence by an immanent sovereign, that is, by a living human being. Hobbes acknowledged the contribution of the rule of law to efficient government but stressed that

2 While classical scholars have often warned against simplifications and overstatements of the opposition between the two families of gods, the distinction between gods of the polis and pre-political gods has parallels in many religious systems. For example, in his account of Tallensi religion Fortes records a distinction between ancestors and the wild 'bush sprites'. The latter, in contrast to the ancestors, 'are not mystical agencies ritually incorporated in the total system of human social life and therefore having mystical rights to intervene in human affairs. There are no shrines or altars at which they can be approached. In short, they do not complement or even contrast with humanity; they simply negate all that is human, being totally lawless and without any moral capacity, such as is vested in the socially incorporated mystical agencies' (Fortes 1987: 260). On the primordial and implacable nature of the *Erinyes* in comparison to the Olympian gods, see Sewell-Rutter (2007) at 88. Sewell-Rutter lists a number of interpretations of the pacification of the *Erinyes* in Aeschylus' play which differ from the proposed interpretation associating pacification with the projection of sovereignty.

the sovereign is unbound by it. The Hobbesian sovereign exercises founding violence permanently. While Hobbes did not expect the sovereign to show respect for the rule of law in the first place, the reasons for which Hobbes' social design fails to tame the violence of the state of nature entail that immanent conceptions of sovereignty will fail to secure the rule of law even when they purport to do so.

Contrary to Hobbes' prediction, the war of all against all and the uncertainty of the state of nature are bound to persist as long as ultimate law-making power remains immanent and self-grounded. As long as power lacks an extra-social sanction it remains factional and retaliatory, even where man-made law wears the guise of generality and neutrality. Without a superimposed normative framework that dictates the scope of jurisdiction, and in which any claim to power must be grounded, officials and ordinary citizens alike will have no certainty as to who enjoys the protection of the law. Citizens will be as uncertain as they were in the state of nature, and civil war will be perpetuated. Only once a superimposed principle delineates jurisdiction and constrains the pleasure of the king can the law serve as a neutral mediator of disputes between factions.

Hobbes would concede the allegation that law and power remain in his account factional. His response to the intransigent partiality of power consists in urging citizens to erase any trace of individuality and difference and to form a single faction headed by the sovereign. By sacrificing their individuality citizens are likely to evade the wrath of the sovereign and somewhat improve their condition in comparison to the state of nature. Hobbes does not in fact ask citizens to renounce their innermost beliefs, only to pretend in public that they endorse the sovereign's.

Contrary to the Hobbesian scenario, the display of absolute unanimity would only heighten distrust among citizens and between subject and sovereign. It will fail to produce civic peace. This is illustrated in Hegel's reflections on Terror in his account of the French Revolution. Once the Revolution dissolved the objective social differences that made up the old regime, order could only be conceived in terms of absolute oneness. The demand of universal and absolute loyalty to a common cause, Hegel's account shows, escalates violence since every individual seems to constitute a separate faction. Every individual, as an individual, is suspected of conspiracy and deviance: '. . . subjective virtue, whose sway is based on disposition only, brings . . . the most fearful tyranny' (Hegel 1944: 450).[3] While Hobbes, unlike the Jacobins, does not expect the sovereign truth to penetrate the minds and hearts of individual citizens, the imperative of complete outward accord would trigger suspicion and terror even without an expectation of 'subjective

3 On Terror as the realization of abstract reason's tendency to eradicate any instance of particularity, see Hegel (1977) at 359–60.

virtue'. When the protection of the law depends on loyalty, overt or covert, and not on status bestowed by a superimposed principle, it is bound to be uncertain and to inspire both conspiracy and suspicions of conspiracy. Indeed, totalitarian regimes which followed several of Hobbes' recipes offered a spectre of uncertainty that approximated the Hobbesian state of nature more closely than any other regime.

It is thus questionable whether rational considerations of self-preservation will lead individuals to resign their natural freedom to an immanent sovereign as Hobbes asks them to do. In exchange for a complete waiver of autonomy, the members of Leviathan are subjected to a constant threat of denunciation and persecution. Immanent sovereignty entails terror. Furthermore, the dangers of immanent sovereignty are greater than what can be gathered on the basis of the Hobbesian assumption of man's self-preserving rationality. Historical evidence of senseless bloodshed in episodes such as civil wars, revolutions, interregna and carnivals suggests that the presence of sovereignty sets self-preserving rationality in abeyance.[4] Once sovereign, arbitrary power over life pervades society, ruthless violence is unleashed. The affirmation of life, on which the Hobbesian social contract is premised, can no longer be taken for granted. Violence is asserted for its own sake by a society which, as medieval and early modern society perceived itself during carnival, sheds its humanity and is temporarily given over to sinister powers.

Monopolisation of violence by an immanent sovereign can pacify the war of all against all only as a transitional measure. Violence will have to undergo two further, *interdependent* transformations which were rejected by Hobbes: it will have to become principled and impersonal, and to be grounded in a principle that is superimposed upon the living. The renunciation of sovereignty on the part of the living creates the social conditions which give rise to self-preserving rationality. It endows the subject's status as a subject of the law with determinacy. It allows for the accommodation, and legal regulation, of social divides within a single political body whose boundaries are superimposed upon the polity.

The Hobbesian account of the war of all against all in the state of nature is one among several possible points of departure for an account of the origins of sovereignty. According to an alternative line of thought, the political institution of sovereignty is meant to alleviate a condition of interpersonal communion rather than interpersonal strife. The state of nature can be conceived in terms of excessive unity rather than excessive division. Contrary to Hobbes' position, the role of the political is to overcome, not to generate, conformity. In the state of nature, with the absolute conformity which

4 See, for example, Paravicini-Bagliani's account of ritual plundering in Rome prior to the election of a new pope; Paravicini-Bagliani (2000) at 99–107, 150–155.

characterises it, the group enacts its collective body. Since sovereignty vests in the collective body, the state of nature is one of immanent sovereignty. The presence of the collective body collapses boundaries between individuals as well as between the living and the dead, since the collective body is the common body of all generations.[5] I use the terms communal body and corporate body to designate the collective body in two different positions that it can occupy in relation to the social: the 'communal body' designates the collective body of all generations when it is enacted by the group while the 'corporate body' refers to the collective body once projected outside the social. When the group contains its sovereign unity, no room is left for the law as a mediator between alienated and antagonistic groups and individuals and between generations. Individuation and the rule of law depend on the projection of the sovereign collective body outside the social.

The two accounts of the social predicament to which the projection of sovereignty can be the response – oneness and fragmentation – are not as inconsistent as they appear. Excessive unity and excessive fragmentation are two sides of the same coin. Hobbes' depiction of atomisation and dispersal in the state of nature turns into a spectre of total social conformity. As Hegel's discussion of Terror shows, atomisation and uprootedness lead to absolute social uniformity which leads back to fragmentation and civil war. Arendt's comments on the loneliness of the individual in the midst of the totalitarian crowd expand upon Hegel's observations (Arendt 1973: 476). 'Groundless' individuals, namely, individuals whose identity is not solidly grounded in objective social and legal categories that are in turn anchored in transcendent authority, disappear into a collective body which then disbands and sets them against each other. The enactment of the collective body in transitional 'constitutional moments' makes society appear at the same time totally fragmented and totally unified. The presence of the sovereign collective body unleashes destructiveness and self-destructiveness which compel its projection. The projection of the collective body outside the social anchors the social order in an external foundation, a mythical reference which endows society with unity while allowing it to accommodate and adjudicate factional divides.

When projected outside the social, the collective body of all generations is personified by ancestral authority since ancestors are taken to extend through the bodies of their descendants across the generations.[6] The projection of the oneness of the group onto the realm of the ancestors means that communal bonds are loosened in favour of an overarching legal unity. Ancestral law comes to embody the unity of society in a way that allows for the reconciliation of unity and division within the social. By dispelling communal unity and ordaining

5 On sovereignty, intergenerational communion and the body corporate, see Barshack (2006b) at 185 and Barshack (2009).

6 On ancestors and the social body, see Fortes (1969) at 304.

interpersonal separation and a separation of powers, ancestral law establishes itself as the repository of any unity that can still be attributed to society.[7]

Traditional representations of the law in different media – learned, figurative, ritual, or oral-popular – point to law's origin in ancestral authority. Moreover, cultural representations of ancestors rarely omit references to their juridical capacities. Ancestors are depicted as sovereign in the lands inhabited by their descendants and as members of an ultimate tribunal whose infallible decisions are appropriately never fully predictable.[8] Mythical law-givers, founders of dynasties, and the founding fathers and mothers of modern nation states count among the more familiar instances of law-giving ancestral authority. While many of these figures are historical, their authority is embedded in narratives which display repetitive mythical patterns.[9]

The origin of the law in ancestral authority entails that behind the changing positive articulations of the law lies an ancestral law which binds all generations. I will refer to ancestral law interchangeably as eternal law, higher law or fundamental law, notwithstanding historical variations between these terms and possible analytical distinctions between categories of norms that claim an ancestral origin.[10] The eternity in question derives from the idea of corporate perpetuity, the potentially or fictively perpetual succession of generations, not from the metaphysical notions of eternity that informed Aquinas's philosophy of law. Eternal law is explicitly or implicitly recognised by legal systems in the official narratives of their origins. Such accounts legal systems have of their historical and normative foundations blend ancestral law and ancestral myth. Legal systems come into being through the postulation of an ancestral authority which vindicates the claims of a political centre for universal jurisdiction. The unity of law in a legal system is produced through

7 On law as a national symbol, see Beaune (1991) at 245–65.

8 In an essay on ancestral authority, Meyer Fortes gathered observations on the jural aspects of ancestral authority scattered throughout his extensive work. Fortes writes: 'The ancestors are the ultimate source of life both for the individual and, much more obviously of course, for the descent group which would not exist if there had been no ancestors. But this implies the converse: that ancestors have the sole right and power to terminate the life of an individual or of a corporate group, phrased often in terms of summoning the deceased as if before a judicial tribunal'. [. . .] 'Ancestors are projected as figures of authority to whom powers of life and death are attributed – judicial figures – rather than bountiful deities' (Fortes 1976: 1, at 12, 14). While the model of descent groups that is associated with the British school of structural anthropology does not apply to all societies, the general category of ancestral authority is much more broadly applicable. For an argument to that effect see, for example, Scheffler (1966) at 541–51. Fortes' remarks on ancestors as ultimate rulers exercising power over life and death derive from Freud and reflect Freud's considerable influence on his work.

9 On analogies between legends that relate the achievements of different lawgivers, see Szegedy-Maszak (1978) at 199–209.

10 On the history of the term 'fundamental law' and of other terms denoting types of higher law, see Thompson (1986) at 1103.

the imposition of a standard ancestral reference, the establishment of an official pantheon. Jurisdiction is a relationship between the subject and ancestral authority, a relationship in which the humanity of the subject is anchored since it is ancestral law which disperses the communal body and clears the temporal realm for habitation by the living.

Finley has observed that the idea of ancestral law recurs across civilisations and historical periods because it is rooted in the temporal structure of human existence. In an essay entitled 'The ancestral constitution' Finley remarked that the grounds of the ancestral constitution lie 'in the very nature of man, who alone possesses both memory and the prescience of inevitable death, leading unconsciously to a desire, a need, for something that will create a feeling of continuity and permanence' (Finley 1975: 34, at 47). While Finley's view of the ancestral constitution as a response to the temporal predicament of humanity is illuminating, it seems to me that he misconceived the nature of that predicament. According to Finley, the authority of the ancestral constitution stems from the continuity it forges between the generations and which alleviates the sense of transience and futility that besets human existence. Contrary to Finley's suggestion, I have argued that the primary role of ancestral law is to separate rather than connect the generations: ancestral law disbands the communion of the generations that takes place when society enacts its sovereign collective body (Barshack 2009). The temporal predicament of humanity consists in the arrest of time that results from the simultaneous presence of all generations in the 'state of nature' and in constitutional moments. Once the collective body is projected outside the social, the generations succeed each other in time instead of being simultaneously present. By transforming the communal into a corporate body ancestral law launches the flow of time.

A general point which can be raised in relation to the subject's fidelity to ancestral authority is that social aversion toward the law is as crucial to the rule of law as the love of law. The externality of law to the social can be preserved only if a tension between the law and social practices, modes of enjoyment and aspirations, is maintained. The rule of law is consistent with large-scale deviance and is conditioned by a fair amount thereof. One of the most reliable indications for the vigour of the rule of law in a society is the cultivation of certain forms of transgression accompanied by a measure of laxity in law enforcement. The rule of law is animated and sustained by regular instances of transgression on the part of citizens and, as we shall see, even branches of government. The following sections sketch an understanding of the rule of law that is centred on the idea of ancestral law, through a cursory overview of central questions in the theories of legislative, judicial and executive powers. I cannot even begin to do justice to the complexity of these questions in the present discussion. My aim is only to suggest how they can be approached from a perspective in political theology which, unlike Schmitt's, takes the rule of law seriously.

II. Lawmaking

A. Myths of immanent sovereignty (divine kingship and parliamentary sovereignty)

One of the guises in which ancestral law appears in different cultures is that of immemorial custom. The prominence of custom accounts for the arduous crystallisation of the modern concept of legislation. While modern notions of the rule of law regard custom with distrust and champion legislation as a source of law which can provide individuals with accurate information about their rights and duties in changing social conditions, the idea of custom captures the core of the rule of law, the view of the past as a legitimate source of constraints upon the living.

Historians of the common law debated the approximate point in history in which legislation had been distinguished from the articulation and application of existing custom. McIlwain famously argued that the concept of legislation was not clearly distinguished from application before the seventeenth century, and that until then parliament was regarded primarily as a court of justice (see, in particular, McIlwain 1910). Acts of parliament were perceived as articulations and restatements of existing custom devised for the instruction of lower courts. The debates to which McIlwain's claims gave rise reveal an underlying agreement over the prominence of ancestral, immemorial law. Some of his critics have argued that a concept of legislation as strictly distinct from mere application of custom emerged earlier than he thought. This critique does not challenge the idea of ancestral law because it is not contested that statutes, however sharply distinguished from judicial decisions, were still conceived as bound by higher law (see, for example, Plucknett 1962). Furthermore, the difficulties that beset the crystallisation of the modern idea of legislation attest to the tenacity of the idea of ancestral custom irrespectively of the precise or approximate date in which this conceptual crystallisation took place.

Another response to McIlwain's argument consisted in challenging the very notion of permanent custom which his account allegedly presupposed. Various critics have claimed that custom itself was ever-changing rather than stagnant, and that legislation, before being clearly distinguished as a separate source of law, formed part of the ongoing and varied activities through which custom recast itself.[11] This line of thought, too, only demonstrates the persistence

11 Plucknett writes: '. . . our common law is custom, and . . . the various modes of legal change in the reign of Edward I were conceived (if this interpretation can be sustained) as being changes within that mass of fluctuating customary law . . .' (Plucknett 1962: 10–20). See also Cheyette (1963) at 362. For Plucknett's initial critique of McIlwain, see Plucknett (1922) at 26–30. As McIlwain explained, he had never contested the fact that parliament made and changed law, only that it *conceived* of its role in terms of law-making.

of the idea of ancestral law. The all-inclusiveness and liberality of custom reveal the robust sense of continuity which was attributed to the law, and which was undisturbed by constant innovations and adaptations. In fact, the idea of ancestral law as a mediator between the generations implies legal *continuity through change*, a formula which captures each generation's simultaneous *identity with* and *difference from* all other generations.

In *The Concept of Law* Hart famously argued against theories of immanent sovereignty, such as Hobbes' and Austin's, that 'The statement that a new legislator has a right to legislate presupposes the existence, in the social group, of the rule under which he has this right' (Hart 1961: 58). The fallacy of Hobbes' theory consists in its attempt to perpetuate a state of divine kingship. A political authority that emanates entirely from personal charisma or naked power can only be short lived. It can exist in periods of foundation, transition or abrupt decline (De Heusch 1962: 215–63). While the divine king embodies the charisma of the founding moment, his successors derive their authority from an established principle. Authority comes to be vested in kingship as an office and loses its personal, private character.[12] Prototypically, the office of *pater familias* subjects its changing occupants to a law personified by the lineage founder and renders them mere guardians of the family's property and long-term interests. Similarly, the king is obliged to exercise his power as guardian of the interests of the realm as a cross-generational entity.[13] He is constrained by fundamental laws that safeguard the interests of future generations in the name of an ancestral authority that decreed the perpetuity of descent and of the realm.

See McIlwain's brief review of Gough's *Fundamental Law in English Constitutional History* in McIlwain (1955) at 109–10.

12 Historians have often traced the emergence of a system of offices – and, by implication, of the rule of law – to the Gregorian Reform. The separation between the temporal and spiritual realms in the Gregorian Reform secularised the royal body and turned kingship into an office. On the impersonalisation of authority, see Strayer (1970) at 6, Wolter (1997) at 17–36, and Hollister and Baldwin (1978) at 867–905. According to Cheyette, the distinctions between office/person, rule of law/rule of man, public/private crystallised in the second half of the eleventh century; see Cheyette (1978) at 143–78. For a wealth of illustrations of the secularisation and professionalisation of kingship in the course of the twelfth century, see Leyser (1982) at 241–67. See also Mayali (1992) at 129–49.

13 It has often been remarked that the theory that the divine right of kings exempted the monarch, in his various capacities, from subjection to higher law is not in tune with dominant views in the history of Western constitutional thought. The very idea of divine right implies that royal power is circumscribed by higher law. On medieval constitutionalism generally, see McIlwain (1947), chapters 4, 5. On the history of fundamental law in England, see Gough (1961) at 45, especially the claim that the medieval belief in the supremacy of natural law was shared by early modern lawyers. On inalienability, see Kantorowicz (1954) at 488–502. On fundamental law in France, see Lemaire (1907) and Giesey (1961). For a recent discussion, see Taylor (2001) at 358.

Hart's critique of Austin demonstrates that the rule that confers law-making powers upon a king establishes an intergenerational continuity that is characteristic of legal systems. Hart did not make the further step of recognising that in order to establish intergenerational continuity social rules have to be perceived as issuing from an ancestral, fictive authority which endows successive generations with a common identity. Hart also did not recognise that the rules that confer law-making power impose enforceable substantial constraints on that power. He admitted, however, that '. . . it is difficult to give general criteria which satisfactorily distinguish mere provisions as to "manner and form" of legislation or definitions of the legislative body from "substantial limitations"' (Hart 1961: 70, 75).

This is a statement which Hart makes in relation to parliaments and which equally undermines the theories of absolute monarchy and parliamentary sovereignty. Hart seems to concede here the familiar argument that any answer to questions such as '*What is the parliament?*' and '*Who are its members?*' will imply substantial limitations on legislative power in addition to limitations of manner and form. These substantial limitations stem from the cross-generational nature of the common good. Parliaments, like kings, derive their law-making power from rules and principles that establish intergenerational continuity and impose substantial constraints on the law-making powers of the living in the interest of other generations and of corporate perpetuity. The parliament, like other instances of temporal power, makes decisions about the common good for the foreseeable future and these must comply with ancestral law since the foreseeable future partakes of eternity.

Advocates of parliamentary sovereignty would respond that even if the existence of substantial constraints on law-making power is granted, the courts are not necessarily the best guardians of the ancestral constitution. The parliament's take on the demands of ancestral law and the interests of other generations, they would argue, should prevail. Contrary to such a position, I believe that the well-nigh universal idea of an ancestral constitution is inseparable from that of enforceable substantial constraints upon the law-making power of the living. In the first place, the very idea of ancestral law depends on, and in turn decrees, the waiver of institutional omnipotence, that is, a genuine division of powers between branches of government that secures the projection of sovereignty outside the social. The second reason is that a doctrine of parliamentary (or royal) sovereignty is interwoven into an entire network of principles, doctrines and conventions that forms the core of a legal tradition, of custom, or of an ancestral constitution. As such, it is interpreted and qualified in the light of other doctrines and principles. As I have briefly hinted above, due to the dynamic nature of intergenerational relations the ancestral constitution is not a stagnant law; its implementation involves an ever-innovative negotiation between legal principles, doctrines and conventions. Once a concrete doctrine of immanent sovereignty such as parliamentary sovereignty is subjected to continuous re-interpretation, it is likely to become qualified due to the gradual crystallisation of its own underlying reasons and of competing principles, the incessant transformation of institutional configurations and the recurrence of hard cases. This argument was mounted in the debate on parliamentary sovereignty in Britain by Paul Craig and other public lawyers identified in recent years as the school of common law constitutionalism (CLC). T.R.S. Allan, Paul Craig and others have convincingly insisted on the seemingly innocuous proposition that the doctrine of parliamentary sovereignty is itself a doctrine of common law. Whether or not the rule of recognition differs from other legal rules in the ways indicated by Hart, it is interwoven into the fabric of the common law body of doctrine. As such, it might be challenged in certain circumstances, it can be asked to justify itself and it is exposed to limitations and qualifications.[14]

B. *Generality*

According to Neumann, the generality of laws is the kernel of the rule of law and the source of the other dictates associated with it. Neumann regarded the prohibition on retroactivity and the separation between law-making and law-applying powers as institutional guarantees of the generality of law. He traced the advent of generality to the rise of competitive bourgeois society. Generality, he argued, expressed the bourgeoisie's interest and belief in open economic competition and enabled the spread of capitalism (Neumann 1986: 213). The roots of generality and of the maxims that derive from it can be seen as theological rather than economic. If constituent power dwells outside society, higher law and the ordinary laws that are deduced from higher law have to be general. A transcendent law-giver is blind to the personal circumstances of individual subjects and has no partisan stake in the feuds and rivalries that divide the group of his or her descendants. Higher law was fictively laid down by the ancestors at the beginning of time in order to govern the lives of their descendants ever after. It must be abstract and impersonal. Insofar as ordinary legislation is a concretisation of higher law, it should by and large partake of its generality and impersonality.[15]

14 Craig called for a renewed 'awareness of the need for principled justifications for the existence of sovereign power', an awareness revealed by the 'constitutional discourse of previous generations' (Craig 2000: 224). For an attempt to ground parliamentary omnipotence in the theory of the rule of recognition, see Goldsworthy (1999).

15 In tribal societies, ancestral law often comprises non-general norms which prescribe an allocation of territories or constitutional powers among particular, named clans. In such cases, the law records a founding treaty between the different clans which fixed certain allocations for perpetuity. Fortes describes how Tallensi law allocates offices among different groups of clans in a way that made sense of the founding myth of Tallensi. See Fortes (1968) at 53–88, 65, 78. The system of statuses and privileges that made up pre-modern European law can be largely understood in terms of the legal and political device of constituent distribution of resources among descent groups that are united under a single jurisdiction.

Once we shift the focus from the law-givers to the subjects of the law, the externality of sovereignty seems to entail generality because it entails *equality* among the subjects of the law. While criteria for the attribution of humaneness are historically and culturally variable, they typically establish a relation to ancestral law which places humans in a an equal position vis-à-vis the law. Individual bodies are humanised, that is, disentangled from the collective body, through the protection of ancestral law which endows each individual with a package of rights and entitlements that safeguard individuation. To have legal status means to enjoy equal rights by virtue of shared descent and the equal standing vis-à-vis ancestral law which descent implies.[16] The notion that all citizens should be treated with equal concern and respect is rooted in the position of the living before a law of which they are not the principal authors. It is beyond my present purpose to assess how thick this notion of equality is, but contrary to the view of legal philosophers of analytical bent generality is not only a logical feature of the language of the law.[17] It is inseparable from some notion of substantial equality. The Nuremberg laws, for example, while general in their formal structure – they did not refer to individual Jews by proper names – violated the thinnest conceivable notion of equality and hence the externality of sovereignty to the legal system. Leaving aside the question of their legal validity, the Nuremberg laws amounted to a manifestation of immanent sovereignty and were contrary to the rule of law.

According to Neumann, the prohibition on retroactive legislation derives from the idea of generality. Retroactive legislation can be more easily tailored to handle particular persons and events, implicating the law in retaliatory violence. Neumann writes: 'If law provides for an indefinite number of future individual cases, a retroactive law cannot possibly be law; because those facts already realized are computable, and therefore the law is confronted with a definite number of particular cases' (see Neumann 1986: 222). Cicero linked retroactivity to lack of generality in his implacable orations against Verres, a Roman provincial governor who was brought to justice in Rome for grave abuses of power. Cicero accused Verres of applying new rules of inheritance to past testaments in order to divert the course of one particular bequest.[18] Throughout history, retroactive legislation has been deemed abominable because it re-enacts retaliatory violence by collapsing the correlative impersonality of the makers and the subjects of the law. It has been considered tolerable only in certain dramatic constitutional moments, such as revolutions, in which the polity's break with its own past and the redefinition of the body

16 Descent is of course a symbolic rather than biological category. On equality as a fundamental feature of corporate descent groups, see Fortes (1969) at 304.

17 For an example of the analytical approach, see Marmor (2004) at 1, 11. For a critique of the thin, formalistic reading of the idea of equality contained in the rule of law, see Allan (2001). Allan bases his critique on political morality, not constitutional theology.

18 Cicero, *Second Speech against Verres*, Book I, sections 41–4.

politic allow the use of retroactive legislation. Even retroactive dispensations such as amnesties are typically limited to constitutional moments, such as interregna, declarations of independence, states of emergency, changes of regime, and inter- and intra-national reconciliations.[19]

III. The rule of law in court: a note on the anthropology of interpretation

When applied to adjudication, the rule of law requires that courts derive their decisions from pre-existing law. The rule of law is often thought to entail the vague method known as judicial formalism. According to the formalist view of adjudication, crudely characterised, when courts decide cases they use a toolbox of distinctly legal reasons – for example, the obligatory force of precedent – whose operative consequences in each case tend to be straightforward and uncontroversial, and which are placed in relation to each other within the overall structure of a legal argument by a second-order legal rule, such as Hart's rule of recognition. While such a view of adjudication has little to do with reality, it plays a role in the self-understanding of participants in the judicial ritual and in certain justifications of judicial power. Formalism has been regarded as a component of the rule of law because it seems to draw the contrast between lawmaking and application with particular starkness and to guarantee in this way the generality and prospectivity of the law. It seems to provide a solid institutional anchor for the distinction between legislation and application which dispels sovereign presence. However, on closer examination the idea of absent sovereignty turns out to challenge rather than call for formalism. The absence of sovereignty renders every application of the law, in Dworkin's words, thoroughly interpretive.

The association of the rule of law with formalism is related to a view of judicial controversy as a hindrance to the rule of law. Several authors have argued against this assumption that interpretive controversy forms one of the essential manifestations of the rule of law. Dworkin's portrayal of the rule of law as a quest for the realisation of the political rights of parties to legal disputes implies the inevitability of interpretive controversies over the content and scope of rights.[20] Neil MacCormick suggested that argumentation should be viewed as a component of the rule of law since it reduces the arbitrariness of state power. Argumentation, for MacCormick, extends beyond traditional legal arguments to encompass almost any appeal to reason. The rule of law requires that defendants in criminal and civil proceedings be

19 On amnesties, see Gacon (2002).

20 As conceived by Dworkin, interpretation does not detract from the generality and prospectivity of the law because it does not involve judicial creativity of any sort; see Dworkin (1986) at 11–17.

given the opportunity to challenge legal certainties by appeal to a wide range of reasons in a way that detracts from the predictability of judicial decisions (MacCormick 1999: 163).

Martti Koskenniemi has observed that the kernel of the rule of law lies not in adherence to rules but in argumentation over how law's 'functional objectives' are to orient the application of rules: '. . . the rule of law . . . relates to the way the law-applier (administrator, public official, lawyer) approaches the task of judging within the narrow space between fixed textual understandings (positivism) on the one hand, and predetermined functional objectives (naturalism) on the other, without endorsing the proposition that the decisions emerge from a "legal nothing" (decisionism)' (Koskenniemi 2007: 12). The rule of law is realised through the 'constitutional mindset of interpretation'. Adopting a Kantian perspective on law and autonomy, Koskenniemi claims that the underlying values of the Kantian worldview should orient the application of laws because constitutionalism and respect for law are grounded in that worldview. In other words, these values are inherent in the enterprise of law. He writes:

> The Pietist search for self-improvement, *Bildung*, and spiritual perfection prepares a constitutionalist mindset from which to judge the world in a manner that aims for universality, impartiality, and all the virtues of the inner morality of law: honesty, fairness, concern for others, the prohibition of deceit, injury, and coercion. Though this is a vocabulary of moral regeneration, it is also the vocabulary of constitutionalism.
>
> (Koskenniemi 2007: 33)

While I agree with Koskenniemi that certain values are inherent in legal interpretation, I shall argue that these inherent values do not derive from a Pietist understanding of moral regeneration, or from any other moral doctrine, but from the fiction of absent sovereignty on which interpretation in law (and elsewhere) is premised.

The persistence of interpretive controversy is a consequence of absent sovereignty. The externality of sovereignty compels a resort to interpretation and is in turn consolidated by practices of interpretation. Externality implies the existence of a layer of hidden meanings behind that of the legal materials haphazardly accumulated in the course of history. The fiction of a hidden law that infuses the entire legal system with life and meaning ties legal materials to their presumed absent origin, the source of their unity. Moreover, contrary to Hart's account of the standard legal case in *The Concept of Law*, no viable conception of the judicial role can spare judges the obligation to uncover the law that lies behind the surface. Hidden meaning has to be constantly mined in order to regenerate the authenticity of the text and of its message, which cannot rest solely on the circumstances in which the text originated. Interpretive controversy establishes the status of the text as a repository of higher law and reason and makes possible the recovery of its 'proclamation', as Gadamer would describe the process. It endows the text with ever-renewed relevance and authority. In order to animate perpetual controversy, higher law must remain elusive and unfathomable. It can never be fully spelled out by the courts.

As 'priests of the law', judges are obliged to find answers to legal questions within established legal materials. Neumann argues compellingly that this conception of judicial authority is equally fundamental in continental and common law systems. The power of common law judges to set precedents, Neumann argues, is merely that of correctly applying existing precedents to novel situations. Continental and common law systems are equally premised on the fiction, championed by Blackstone and Montesquieu, that judges declare existing law.[21] However, existing law must remain perennially uncodifiable and controversial if it is to retain a link to its absent source of reason, legitimacy and vitality. Every court decision, as Dworkin argues, rests on a complex and contested interpretation of an entire history of a legal system. Viewed in light of the idea of corporate perpetuity, the goal of such synoptic interpretations is the articulation of an ancestral law that binds all generations.

The claim that courts are obliged to engage in a pursuit of higher law lends support to the conception of judicial review known as common law constitutionalism (CLC). According to CLC, modern constitutional judicial review is just a subcategory of a general inherent judicial power to review laws made by the living. Leading exponents of CLC, such as T.R.S. Allan and Paul Craig, find in Coke's judgements in Dr Bonham's case and other cases a prime illustration of their approach. Among the theoretical influences on CLC, Dworkin's has been particularly consistent. Allan and Craig ground CLC in the assertion that the common law is an embodiment of reason. Another possible ground for CLC – one which derives from the present understanding of the rule of law – is the assertion that the common law embodies ancestral law. The two arguments coincide if reason is understood in terms of a circumspect adherence to ancestral law and custom. Coke understood in this way the common law's claim to embody reason. Coke's view of the role of ancestral law and immemorial custom in common law illuminates the workings and claims of interpretation in many other, if not all, legal traditions. Craig seems to endorse today Coke's flexible association of reason

21 Both systems assume 'that the legal system is closed and that every decision is a mere application of a code, a statute, or of customary law' (Neumann 1986: 246). But in neither system, Neumann adds, can decisions be straightforwardly deduced from the law. Neumann challenges the presumed contrast between common and civil law: '. . . the belief that an appropriate clause in a statute or in a code can easily be found and as easily determined, is obviously a myth, as everyone knows who is even slightly conversant with Continental law' (Neumann 1986: 242).

and tradition.[22] Allan advocates a more ambitious account of the common law's intrinsic reason. He views disputation in court as a paradigm of rational public deliberation and implies that the principles that evolve in common law are the most philosophically defensible moral principles.[23]

As an ordinary feature of adjudication, interpretive controversy not only reflects the externality of sovereignty but reproduces and consolidates this externality. It dispels sovereign presence and underscores the boundary between the living and the dead. Interpretation can be viewed as a generative, *liminal* practice which postulates hidden meanings through the fabrication of controversy. Scant familiarity with learned discourses in law, religion or criticism suffices to confirm that interpretation not only responds to problems of meaning but amplifies and multiplies them. In literature and the other arts, as in theology and law, the purpose of interpretation is to set up a superior realm occupied by an absolute other who looms large behind the human author, and with whom readers communicate through the artwork.[24] The more intense the controversies over the meaning of an artwork or of scripture, the more abstract and elusive its divine author. The protestant idea that each believer is an authoritative interpreter of scripture pushes the correlation between the transcendence of the author and the plurality and individuality of interpretations to an extreme. Any centripetal move toward the sealing and reification of scripture, whether in literature, theology or law, leads to a centrifugal pressure toward dispersal of meanings. Any process of codification and canonisation is accompanied by a parallel elaboration and sophistication of interpretive tools.

By cultivating the differentiation between layers of meaning, practices of interpretation reproduce the corporate structure of society as a structure that is premised on the absence of the intergenerational, sovereign unity of the group. Without the critical construal of man-made law in the light of higher law, sovereignty would be re-appropriated by the living. The law would become incapable of safeguarding individual rights vis-à-vis a unified and unfettered community. The formal conditions of the rule of law, such as generality and prospectivity, can be secured for long only where man-made law is subject to interpretation in the light of ancestral law. At the same time, however, the *liminality* of interpretation implies that interpretation

22 Coke famously stated in Dr Bonham's case that 'when an act of Parliament is against common right and reason, or repugnant, or impossible to be performed, the common law will control it, and adjudge such Act to be void'. Craig embraces a traditional common law model in which '[t]he common law was seen as being based on reason and principle, and could be fashioned to meet the challenges of a new age' (Craig 2000: 211, at 234). On the CLC school, see Poole (2003) at 435.

23 On the rationality of deliberation in common law courts, see Allan (2001) at 75–85, 290.

24 On art as a medium through which individuals contemplate the corporate unity of the group, see Barshack (2010).

occasions a moment of sovereign decision that violates the law's generality and prospectivity. The sovereign character of judicial decisions is already implicit in the claim that interpretive practices regenerate order by fabricating interpretive controversies. However solemn and sedentary, interpretation refounds the normative order through its suspension. The authority of the judiciary probably derives from the *liminal*, sovereign character of interpretation much as it does from the contradictory and more explicit fiction that judges apply existing law. The interpreter, like top executive power, occupies a *liminal* position between constituent and constituted powers, a point which has been elaborated in different ways in discussions of the place of paradox in the law.

The *liminality* of interpretation, like that of other activities, can be understood by reference to the idea of the collective body of the group. *Liminal* practices and activities render the sovereign, intergenerational unity of the group immediately present and then re-establish the normative order through repetition of the founding projection of sovereignty outside the social.[25] The enactment of the communal body implies the dissolution of the normative order as a network of boundaries among the living as well as between the living and the dead. The projection of the collective body re-establishes spatial boundaries among the living and temporal boundaries between the generations. Gadamer's notion of *fusion of horizons* captures the *liminal* experience of intergenerational fusion that occurs in interpretation: the distance between the present moment and the founding revelation, between the living and the dead, is suspended.

Needless to say, in interpretation *liminality* is highly domesticated. The interpreter's appropriation of sovereignty is tame because it takes place in the course of an engagement with a text that is accepted as authoritative.[26]

25 For an account of *liminality* in terms of the enactment of the intergenerational unity of the group, see Barshack (2009) at 553. On the *liminal* and hence paradoxical nature of the legal proceeding, see Barshack (2006a) at 145.

26 An account of interpretation as a *liminal* activity is consistent with a non-interpretive account of the preliminary process of identification of the authoritative texts to be interpreted. Contrary to Dworkin's claim that the rule of recognition itself is contested among judges, the demarcation of the site of interpretation has to be governed by formal criteria. The relation between the formal boundaries of legal scripture and the *liminal*, interpretive engagement with meaning can be explicated by analogy to the structure of rites of passage. In Van Gennep's well-known formulation, rites of passage consist of a succession of rites of separation, rites of transition and rites of incorporation. Interpretive controversy stands to the formal delineation of the legal text as rites of transition do to rites of separation. In other words, interpretation is preceded by a phase of 'separation' in which the law-applier enters the realm of law. A boundary is crossed between the secular and the sacred, between the realm of the living and the realm of the dead. Rites of separation in law and elsewhere are typically highly formalised. Legal form demarcates law from non-law, setting up a closed realm in which the interpretive quest for higher law can be launched. On the highly formal character of rites of separation in comparison to the subsequent stages of rites of passage, see, for example, Leach (1961) at 132.

Furthermore, the lawlessness of interpretation is domesticated through the introduction of guiding principles. Manuals of interpretation are devised to contain the interpretative encounter with the dead within a method, in terms of Gadamer's opposition between *truth* and *method*. Alongside methodological guidelines, legal interpretation is oriented by values that are intrinsic to any interpretive practice. Since interpretation is premised on the absence of sovereignty it is inherently loyal to the rule of law and to other institutional manifestations of society's renunciation of sovereignty. Competent interpreters produce interpretations that sustain the rule of law and concomitant principles, such as, the separation of powers, the separation between the sacred and the secular and the affirmation of temporal existence, and equality before the law. Interpretation is naturally oriented toward the introduction of novel distinctions and sub-distinctions and the delimitation of existing powers and ideas since differentiation and division consolidate the projection of the group's sovereign unity.

IV. Aside: the courts under fascism

Neumann concluded his treatise with a brief account of the rule of law under fascism and Nazism. Writing during its inception, Neumann succeeded in capturing the essence of the Nazi legal regime (as well as the uniqueness of Carl Schmitt's approach in 1934–5, unperturbed by the legal innovations even in comparison to the most enthusiastic Nazi jurists). Neumann noted the violation of standards of generality and prospectivity and the complete dissolution of the separation of powers. Nazi law, he observed, found in the will of the leader an immanent foundation.[27] Neumann pointed out a tension in the Nazi conception of the role of the judiciary: judges were expected to obey both the law and the tenets of National Socialism (Neumann 1986: 294–5). According to Neumann, the gap between the two expectations was largely bridged by a new conception of the law which transformed the judiciary into a bureaucracy carrying out written executive decrees, including retroactive and individual ones, and which postulated an ultimate identity between the law and the will of the leader.

The postwar literature on Nazi courts did not pursue Neumann's attempt to overcome the tension between formalism and teleology. Immediately after the war Radbruch famously drew a picture of Nazi courts as slavishly following formal methods of application of the law. In contrast to Radbruch's account, historians in recent years have argued that Nazi courts were not formalist

27 The authority of the law is immanent since 'Law is nothing but the will of the Leader' (Neumann 1986: 293), and since the Leader's own authority is immanent ('The identification of the people with the movement, and of the movement with the Leader is a trick used by every dictator who intends to justify his rule immanently, and not by invoking transcendental justifications' (Neumann 1986: 289).

enough and that they frequently deviated from the letter of the law in order to advance Nazi policies. The courts, it has been argued, were eager to promote the interests and spirit of the people and the homeland, and engaged in full-blooded political, teleological reasoning (Radbruch 1946: 1–11. On teleological reasoning, see Müller 1991).

Contrary to these competing explanations, the distinctive characteristic of courts in totalitarian regimes is neither excess nor shortage of formalism, but the refusal to consider formal and substantive arguments in light of each other. The collapse of the rule of law under totalitarianism cannot be explained in terms of the relative predominance of formal or substantive reasoning. It results from the impoverishment of the interpretive, controversy-generating mediation between different categories of considerations. The will of the people or the leader as the ever-present fount of the law implies an obscenity of meaning which leaves no room for interpretation. In non-fascist legal systems, interpretation ascertains the externality of sovereignty and subordinates both formal and ideological guidelines to higher law by attuning them to each other in a way that induces controversy. Interpretation consolidates the corporate structure of society and the independence of legal vis-à-vis political reasoning which cannot be secured by formalist procedures.

Formalism, no less than undisguised teleological reasoning, attests to the community's appropriation of sovereignty. Formalism can temper the manipulation of the law by the regime only where it serves as a prelude to interpretation. When formal rules are not applied in the light of underlying principles, their political manipulation outside and inside the court becomes all too easy. While blind formalism seems to be grounded in the ideas of absent sovereignty and separation of powers, it severs legal norms from their transcendent source of reason and authority and turns the law into an incarnation of a violent communal body. Moreover, formalism eventually becomes in itself an instance of teleological reasoning: divorced from underlying principles of reason, reified and idolised, the arbitrary legal form becomes an ultimate *political* end, an embodiment of the fall of reason and of holy inevitability.[28] Totalitarianism revels in form and often excels in adherence to formalities. Under fascism, form comes to epitomise the community's immanent sovereignty by expressing the complete sway of arbitrary forces over individual fates.

The rejection of interpretation is a general characteristic of a society that holds fast to its sovereignty. Hitler expected his artists to produce an unambiguous and transparent art which does not call for interpretation and therefore does not

28 Weber was wrong, in my view, to assert that 'formal justice is repugnant to all authoritarian powers, theocratic as well as patriarchic, because it diminishes the dependency of the individual upon the grace and power of the authorities' (Weber 1978: 812). On the worship of arbitrary fate in authoritarian religion, see Fromm (1950) at 35.

presuppose transcendence.[29] In an essay entitled 'What National Socialism has done to the arts', Adorno writes: 'It is just this taboo of expressing the essence, the depth of things, this compulsion of keeping to the visible, that fact, the datum and accepting it unquestionably which has survived as one of the most sinister cultural heritages of the Fascist era . . .' (Adorno 1945: 373, at 381). True art, like real law, invites the subject to contemplate an absent sovereign body through the interpretive engagement with hidden meanings. Nazi art, by contrast, draws no line between the overt and the covert, surface and essence, society and its body, and relieves the subject of the burden of interpretation. It seeks to render the sovereign body, the common body of all generations, immediately present and withhold any reference to an absent ideal or goal. It is perceived uniformly by all members of the political community finding their oneness immediately present in it. A longer discussion may be able to demonstrate the actual contribution of fascist aesthetics to the collapse of the rule of law.[30] Insofar as the rule of law is premised on the absence of sovereignty, it is arguably consolidated by practices of artistic creation and interpretation.

V. Legality and founding violence

In recent years, legal scholars occupying different theoretical standpoints have claimed that also in liberal democracies founding violence is neither renounced nor transformed in the course of normal politics. For some, the blame for the persistence of executive lawlessness is laid at the door of the idea of emergency: once emergency powers are recognised they cannot be effectively demarcated in time and space, and inevitably spill over into everyday government. For others, founding violence inheres in the ordinary operation of the state and cannot be eliminated through the curtailment or abolition of emergency powers. The latter view goes back to Benjamin's 'Critique of violence' [1921] where Benjamin introduced the distinction between founding and conserving violence in order to call it into question (Benjamin 1996: 236). Benjamin's distinction reminds us that the passage from the state of nature to political society is accomplished by means of utter violence. In order to preserve its authority over its citizens, Benjamin's discussion suggests, the state continuously terrorises them by means of unlawful and murderous violence.

Benjamin's 'Critique of violence' can be read as a socio-critical elaboration of the psychoanalytic and anthropological theme of the founding murder. Indeed, the persistence of founding violence is often expressed in terms of a

29 On Hitler's notion of clarity, see Miller Lane (1968) at 189.
30 On aesthetics and the rule of law, see Procaccia (2007) at 140.

permanent sovereign power over life and death.[31] Traditional examples of the power over life include capital punishment and the right to dispatch citizens to the battlefield. Judicial killing has been traced to ludic and sacrificial spectacles of manslaughter, such as the Roman arena games.[32] While such rituals have been suppressed in the civilising process, they arguably reveal the archaic roots of political authority in an arbitrary power over life. The lawlessness of the power over life has also been detected in apparently lawful executions. Benjamin noted that capital punishment cannot be fully understood in terms of conserving violence. Capital punishment allows the violence upon which the law is founded to resurface and re-establish the law (Benjamin 1996: 236, at 242). In the *Soirées de Saint-Pétersbourg* Joseph de Maistre famously described the executioner as a spectre of divine wrath who grounds the social order in terror. Girard claims that the criminal sanction, even in its civilised and attenuated forms and irrespectively of its overt justifications, re-enacts founding sacrificial violence.[33]

Perhaps the most glaring instance of executive lawlessness is the fabulous imagery surrounding intelligence agencies and other secret branches of executive power. The mystique of the secret services, which has not received yet the scholarly attention that it deserves, plays a pivotal role in civil religion. Alongside its references to absent sovereignty and the rule of law, civil religion disseminates the idea of executive powers that lie beyond the reach and knowledge of the law. These powers are intimated in official communication and less subtly in espionage literature, a genre distinguished by its compounding of obscenities, sexual and political. Like the pardoning power, the power to appoint and command intelligence forces retains a distinctly personal character. Bond's license to kill is granted by the queen in person. In most types of regime, secret services are answerable directly to the head of the executive who occupies a *liminal* position between constituted and constituent power. The more power is personal and inscrutable, the more it approximates the sovereign, self-conferred and undivided power of the first, divine king, and the less constrained it is by the rule of law and the separation of powers. However legally regulated the secret services may have become in liberal democracies, they always maintain a direct link to a quasi-sovereign personal will which animates them. While the power to appoint and command special forces, like the pardoning power, may be recognised in the constitution, the personal nature of these powers places them in an intermediate position between constituent and constituted powers.

31 Influenced by Foucault's work on the power over life and death, Agamben (1998) couches the permanence of the exception in terms of a constant and arbitrary power over life. For a recent survey of the historical origins of the power of life and death, see Gaughan (2010).

32 On the political functions of the Roman games see Veyne (1976), Hornum (1993), and Clavel-Lévêque (1986).

33 On punishment as a rationalized form of sacrifice, see Girard (1977).

Advocates of the idea of absent sovereignty can hardly deny that founding violence infiltrates and punctuates ordinary state violence.[34] Sovereignty always retains some of the original unbridled character which preceded its pacification into a system of rules.[35] However, the residue of executive lawlessness does not refute the externality of sovereignty to society and the distinction between founding and conserving violence. Unlike founding violence, the residue of executive lawlessness occupies the margins of an established legal order, the periphery of the rule of law. While the lawlessness of founding violence is often overt, once a constitutional order is established the residue of founding violence is relegated to the crepuscular zones of political representation and civil religion. Under the rule of law only the arbitrariness of sovereign mercy is publicly conceded.

Moreover, the lawlessness of ordinary state violence consolidates in various ways the corporate, legal organisation of social life in the face of communal aspirations for the enactment of the communal body. The head of the executive, with its power of life and death, is placed between constituted and constituent powers in order to anchor the constitutional order in its externality. Furthermore, it is arguable that the imaginary power over life prevents the petrifaction and eventual disintegration of institutional structures by virtue of its lawless and unsettling nature.[36] Finally, the exercise of founding violence allows the state to confirm beyond doubt its exclusive possession of the power

34 The notion of the 'crypt' that Derrida borrows from the work of Abraham and Torok is apt to describe the residual presence of founding violence. An instructive analogy for the lingering of founding violence can be found in Nietzsche's account in *The Birth of Tragedy* of the role of the chorus as a residue of ritual, ecstatic presence and of the real within representation. Nietzsche's is one of many accounts of the disruptive but persistent presence of the negative in art; see Nietzsche (1967), section 8.

35 The limits of the judicial review of the executive sometimes reflect an implicit recognition of a sphere of executive lawlessness. Contrary to the position of certain authors, these limits cannot derive from a superior institutional aptness of the executive to make good decisions in certain areas. Even if such difference in competence is real, it cannot transform the executive into the final interpreter of higher law, a role which belongs to the judiciary. On institutional competence as the justification for judicial underenforcement of the constitution in certain areas, see Sager (2004). The difference between Sager's position and mine stems from a deeper divergence over the nature of the judiciary. While Sager regards the judiciary as 'partners' with other branches of government in the task of constitutional interpretation, many constitutional theorists view the judiciary as privileged 'agents' of higher law.

36 In a famous passage that would elicit perennial controversy Hegel remarked that war rejuvenates the state 'just as the blowing of the winds preserves the sea from foulness' (1821, section 324). Hegel also argued that the legal order *continually* grounds itself in the monarch's personal power, in a pre-legal moment which persists within the established constitutional order but which is largely confined to symbolic gestures. The personal aspect of political power, however inconsistent with the rule of law, is not unique to monarchy. It can also be found in democracies, for example in the pardoning power which often retains a distinctly personal character. The pardoning power should be understood as an extension of constituent power into normal politics.

over life. It demonstrates that the state's authority originates in a prepolitical undomesticated violence, and that its hold over that violence is both ongoing and exclusive. It shows that the constitutional/corporate order is not challenged by persistent unintegrated and undomesticated forces.

These considerations suggest that the somewhat paradoxical idea of permanent special forces reinforces rather than undermines the projection of sovereignty outside society. As long as the lawlessness of these forces is confined to a largely imaginary realm of 'mysteries of state',[37] it does not attest to the permanence of immanent sovereignty and founding violence. Contrary to appearances, the general literary fascination with lawless instances of power betrays the love for the rule of law, since the alternative to the mystique of the secret forces is the communal exercise of terror in full transparency. The rule of law is conditioned much as it is threatened by the lack of complete transparency.

References

Adorno, T. (1945) 'What National Socialism has done to the arts', in R. Leppert (ed) *Essays on Music*, Berkeley: University of California Press, 2002.

Agamben, G. (1998) *Homo Sacer*, Stanford: Stanford University Press.

Allan, T.R.S. (2001) *Constitutional Justice: A liberal theory of the rule of law*, Oxford: Oxford University Press.

Arendt, H. (1963) *On Revolution*, New York: Viking.

Arendt, H. (1973) *The Origins of Totalitarianism*, Orlando: Harcourt.

Barshack, L. (2006a) 'Between ritual and theatre: judicial performance as paradox', in O. Perez and G. Teubner (eds) *Paradoxes and Inconsistencies in the Law*, Oxford: Hart.

Barshack, L. (2006b) 'Constituent power as body: outline of a constitutional theology', *University of Toronto Law Journal* 56(3): 185.

Barshack, L. (2009) 'Time and the constitution', *ICON: The International Journal of Constitutional Law*, 7(4): 553–576.

Barshack, L. (2011) 'The constituent power of architecture', *Law, Culture and the Humanities* 7(2): 217.

Beaune, C. (1991) *The Birth of an Ideology: myths and symbols of nation in late-medieval France*, trans. S. Ross, Berkeley: University of California Press.

Benjamin, W. (1996) 'Critique of violence', in M. Bullock and M.J. Jennings (eds) *Selected Writings Vol 1 1913–1926*, Cambridge, MA: Harvard University Press.

Cheyette, F.L. (1963) 'Custom, case law, and medieval "constitutionalism": a re-examination', *Political Science Quarterly* 78: 362.

Cheyette, F.L. (1978) 'The invention of the state', in B.K. Lackner (ed) *Essays on Medieval Civilization*, Austin: University of Texas Press.

Cicero, *Second Speech against Verres*, Book I, sections 41–4.

Clavel-Lévêque, M. (1986) 'L'espace des jeux dans le monde romain: hégémonie, symbolique et pratique sociale', ANRW II.16.3.

Craig, P. (2000) 'Public law, political theory and legal theory', *Public Law* 211: 224.

De Heusch, L. (1962) 'Pour une dialectique de la sacralité du pouvoir', *Écrits sur la royauté sacrée*, Bruxelles: Editions de l'université de Bruxelles, 1987, 215–63.

37 On the notion of mysteries of state, see Kantorowicz (1955) at 65–91.

Dworkin, R. (1986) *A Matter of Principle*, Oxford: Oxford University Press.
Finley, M.I. (1975) 'The ancestral constitution', in *The Use and Abuse of History*, London: Windus, 34.
Fortes, M. (1968) 'Ritual and office in tribal society', in M. Gluckman (ed) *Essays on the Ritual of Social Relations*, Manchester: Manchester University Press.
Fortes, M. (1969) *Kinship and the Social Order*, Chicago: Aldine.
Fortes, M. (1976) 'An introductory commentary', in W.H. Newell (ed) *Ancestors*, The Hague: Mouton.
Fortes, M. (1987) *Religion, Morality and the Person: essays on Tallensi religion*, Cambridge: Cambridge University Press.
Fromm, E. (1950) *Psychoanalysis and Religion*, New Haven: Yale University Press.
Fuller, L.L. (1969 revd edn) *The Morality of Law*, New Haven: Yale University Press.
Gacon, S. (2002) *L'amnistie. De la commune à la guerre d'Algérie*, Paris: Seuil.
Gaughan, J.E. (2010) *Murder Was Not a Crime: homicide and power in the Roman republic*, Austin: University of Texas Press.
Giesey, R. (1961) *The Juristic Basis of Dynastic Rights to the French Throne*, Philadelphia: The American Philosophical Society.
Girard, R. (1977) 'The unity of all rites', in *Violence and the Sacred*, Baltimore: Johns Hopkins University Press.
Goldsworthy, J. (1999) *The Sovereignty of Parliament: history and philosophy*, Oxford: Oxford University Press.
Gough, J.W. (1961) *Fundamental Law in English Constitutional History*, 2nd edn, Oxford: Oxford University Press.
Hart, H.L.A. (1961) *The Concept of Law*, Oxford: Oxford University Press.
Hegel, G.W.F. (1821) *Philosophy of Right*, trans. T.M. Knox, Oxford: Oxford University Press.
Hegel, G.W.F. (1944) *The Philosophy of History*, trans. J. Sibree, New York: Wiley.
Hegel, G.W.F. (1977) *The Phenomenology of Spirit*, trans. A.V. Miller, Oxford: Oxford University Press.
Hollister, C.W. and Baldwin, J.W. (1978) 'The rise of administrative kingship: Henry I and Philip Augustus', *American Historical Review* 83: 867–905.
Hornum, M.B. (1993) *Nemesis, the Roman State and the Games*, Leiden: Brill.
Kantorowicz, E.H. (1954) 'Inalienability: a note on canonical practice and the English coronation oath in the thirteenth century', *Speculum* XXIX: 488–502.
Kantorowicz, E.H. (1955) 'Mysteries of state. An absolutist concept and its late mediaeval origins', *The Harvard Theological Review* 48(1): 65–91.
Koskenniemi, M. (2007) 'Constitutionalism as mindset: reflections on Kantian themes about international law and globalization', *Theoretical Inquiries in Law* 8(1): 9.
Leach, E.R. (1961) 'Time and false noses', in *Rethinking Anthropology*, London: Athlone.
Lemaire, A. (1907) *Les lois fondamentales de la monarchie française*, Paris: Thorin.
Leyser, K.J. (1982) 'Some reflections on twelfth century kings and kingship', in *Medieval Germany and its Neighbours, 900–1250*, London: Hambeldon Press.
MacCormick, N. (1999) 'Rhetoric and the rule of law', in D. Dyzenhaus (ed) *Recrafting the Rule of Law: the limits of legal order*, Oxford: Hart.
Marmor, A. (2004) 'The rule of law and its limits', *Law and Philosophy* 23: 1, 11.
Mayali, L. (1992) 'De la *juris auctoritas* à la *legis potestas*. Aux origines de l'Etat de droit dans la science juridique médiévale', in J. Krynen and A. Rigaudière (eds) *Droits savants et pratiques françaises du pouvoir*, Bordeaux: Presses Universitaires de Bordeaux.

McIlwain, C.H. (1910) *The High Court of Parliament and Its Supremacy: an historical essay on the boundaries between legislation and adjudication in England*, New Haven: Yale University Press.

McIlwain, C.H. (1947 revd. edn) *Constitutionalism: ancient and modern*, Ithaca: Cornell University Press, chapters 4, 5.

McIlwain, C.H. (1955) 'Review of Gough's *Fundamental Law in English Constitutional History*', *The American Historical Review* 61(1): 109–10.

Miller Lane, B. (1968) *Architecture and Politics in Germany, 1918–1945*, Cambridge, MA: Harvard University Press.

Müller, I. (1991) *Hitler's Justice: the courts of the Third Reich*, Cambridge, MA: Harvard University Press.

Neumann, F. (1986) *The Rule of Law: political theory and the legal system in modern society*, Leamington: Berg.

Nietzsche, F. (1967) *The Birth of Tragedy*, New York: Vintage, section 8.

Paravicini-Bagliani, A. (2000) *The Pope's Body*, Chicago: University of Chicago Press.

Plucknett, T.F.T. (1922) *Statutes and their Interpretation in the First Half of the Fourteenth Century*, Cambridge: Cambridge University Press.

Plucknett, T.F.T. (1926) 'Bonham's case and judicial review', *Harvard Law Review* 40: 30–70.

Plucknett, T.F.T. (1962) *Legislation of Edward I*, Oxford: Oxford University Press.

Poole, T. (2003) 'Back to the future? Unearthing the theory of common law constitutionalism', *Oxford Journal of Legal Studies* 23(3): 435.

Procaccia, U. (2007) *Russian Culture, Property Rights and the Market Economy*, Cambridge: Cambridge University Press.

Radbruch, G. (1946) 'Statutory lawlessness and supra-statutory law', *Oxford Journal of Legal Studies* 26(1): 1–11.

Sager, L. (2004) *Justice in Plainclothes: a theory of American constitutional practice*, New Haven: Yale University Press.

Scheffler, H.W. (1966) 'Ancestor worship in anthropology: observations on descent and descent groups', *Current Anthropology* 7(5): 541–51.

Sewell-Rutter, N.J. (2007) *Guilt by Descent. Moral inheritance and decision making in Greek tragedy*, Oxford: Oxford University Press.

Strayer, J.R. (1970) *On the Medieval Origins of the Modern State*, Princeton: Princeton University Press.

Szegedy-Maszak, A. (1978) 'Legends of the Greek lawgivers', *Greek, Roman and Byzantine Studies* 19: 199–209.

Taylor, C. (2001) 'The Salic law and the Valois succession to the French throne', *French History* 15(4): 358–77.

Thompson, M.P. (1986) 'The history of fundamental law in political thought from the French wars of religion to the American Revolution', *The American Historical Review* 91(5): 1103–28.

Veyne, P. (1976) *Le pain et le cirque*, Paris: Seuil.

Weber, M. (1978) *Economy and Society*, G. Roth and C. Wittich (eds) Berkeley: University of California Press.

Wolter, U. (1997) 'The *Officium* in medieval ecclesiastical law as a prototype of modern administration', in A. Padoa-Schioppa (ed) *Legislation and Justice*, Oxford: Oxford University Press.

Chapter 2

Shari'a, faith and critical legal theory

*Marinos Diamantides**

I. Legal theory and the misleading obsession with *Shari'a*

Public discussion by Muslims and non-Muslims about 'Islam' has, for some time now, been dominated by polemics between Islamists – 'crusaders' with a crescent instead of a cross – and Islamophobes, the new antisemites. Two of the symptoms of this unholy alliance are the increased rhetorical identification of the '*Shari'a*' with Islam; and the tendency to essentialise the 'civilisational' differences between, on the one hand, a 'European' culture that is presented as Greek and Christian (downplaying its Jewish and Islamic influences) and an 'Islamic' one, which is presented as essentially 'Eastern' and which could never have absorbed the influences of Greece and Christianity. In this second regard much too much commentary has been made on S. Huntington's approach to deserve further mentioning here. A more recent, and perhaps more disturbing, example, in France, was Sylvain Gougenheim's deeply flawed but widely publicised *Aristote au Mont-Saint-Michel – Les racines grecques de l'Europe chrétienne* (Gougenheim 2008). Focusing on the figure of James of Venice, the twelfth-century Greek who translated Aristotle's *Posterior Analytics* directly from the Greek (bypassing the Arabic translations), the book suggests that the much studied Arab/Muslim contribution to European enlightenment has been exaggerated and proposes, in its place, a mythical version of a Christianity that managed to become 'purely European' (specifically Greek and Norman with all Semitic elements excised), ecumenical and at peace with itself (forgetting the great schism in 1054 or the sacking of Constantinople). While this mythical Europe is presented as harmoniously incorporating its Greek and Christian heritage – the spirit of scientific curiosity and philosophical reflection embedded in a religious tradition that the Church sought to guarantee – the book presents a picture of the Arab/Muslim world as only superficially Hellenized due to two essential features: a

* School of law, Birkbeck College, University of London. Email: m.diamantides@bbk.ac.uk

Semitic language (Arabic, pejoratively qualified as idiom) that is structurally incapable of expressing scientific and philosophical ideas contrary to Indo-European languages (Gougenheim 2008: 126, 136), and a religion (Islam) that is inherently contrary to reason (for example, Gougenheim 2008: 101). Of course such works do not go unanswered by serious scholarship and Gougenheim's in particular has encountered devastating criticism by a dedicated volume (Büttgen 2009). What is more harrowing is the realisation that this book is only the most recent in a long history of attempts by Europeans to 'salvage' the Greek heritage from its Arabo-Muslim pollutants; something which complements other more crudely formulated anti-Semitic/Islamophobic views. Centuries ago St Thomas Aquinas, while compiling his theology, also sought access to the original Greek texts in order to bypass the neo-platonic Arab translations: chronologically his writings coincide with his vociferous anti-semitism.

In this newly re-focused and re-energised anti-Semitic European environment formerly insular academic experts in Islamic religion, culture and law have increasingly engaged in interdisciplinary discussions concerning the modernisation of '*Shari'a* and Islam'. While initially welcomed, as a means to counterbalance the combined threat of Islamophobia and Islamist extremism, it is time that said contributions be critically re-evaluated in so far as they also display an essentialist approach. As Baudoin Dupret has put it, much of the literature on the norms and law in societies dubbed 'Muslim' follows a culturalist–interpretativist model and has, as a whole, displayed an essentialist attitude with the battle between traditionalists and modernisers raging around the interpretation of this or that source of Islamic law, all the while taking for granted that a coherent body of laws called *shari'a* exists and deserves to be referred to as the primary expression of the religion of Islam (Dupret 2000, 2006, 2007). While I agree entirely with Dupret, I wish to argue that in order to combat the present dangers, one needs to do more than expand on his praxiological alternative. It is certainly indispensable, bearing in mind his faulting the literature that adopts an essentialist approach to cultures in Muslim-majority societies and that portrays 'Islamic law' as characterised by a distinctively 'Islamic' legal sensibility, ethics and politics. Such approaches subscribe to interpretive theory according to which law is a 'cultural code of meanings' for both understanding and creating meaning in Muslim societies and cultures. On the other hand, however, we have to remember that praxiology's exclusive ethno-methodological focus (on micro-processes of construction of local and unfixed meaning on the basis of temporarily stabilised common preferences, choices and means-end schemes) undoes essentialism at the acknowledged cost of *all* cultural specificity, whereas a distinction can be made between 'thick' and 'thin' versions, namely between those that assume the existence of fixed-meaning characteristics and properties and other, more nuanced versions. My concern is that in fixing their view to 'micro' in order to avoid essentialism, praxiologists are unable to partake in the critique of those who insist that the approach of *positivist* jurisprudence to constitutionalism and the rule of law, understood as neutral and universally valid procedural devices, represents the optimal rational framework for thinking rationally and ultimately containing the conflict between Muslim traditionalists and modernisers.

In what follows I will exemplify this position with reference to the work of Abdullahi an-Na'im, a popular representative of liberal faithful Muslims in North American academic circles, whose thesis is at once essentialist and universalist. It is essentialist in so far as it advances the view that 'Islamic law' and state law are entirely different types of normative systems. It is universalist in so far as it believes that Muslims and everyone else *need* the liberal secular constitutional state in order to practise their religion or not, out of conviction alone. It is to achieve this that Muslim-majority societies must be now organised in such a way that people are only legally required to respect those norms that belong to *morally neutral* positive legal systems. What lies beneath this liberal position is a conviction that the way positivists – such as H.L. Hart – understood 'law' has universal purchase. This, of course, is not a controversial view – and *that* should worry us. Similarly, for example, the take of the psychoanalytically inclined (Hegelian/Lacanian) on positive law is that Hart's point of view masterfully exemplified that:

> every society needs a regime of positive law, which officials enforce regardless of whether they agree with its substantive content.
>
> (Schroeder 2008: 42)

The point is that in *every* culture the agent of what Lacanians call 'master discourse' occupies a position or function that must be obeyed unconditionally or just so that humans can cope with life's uncertainties and their mortality (Schroeder 2008: 42). To put it extremely crudely, the idea is that belief in master signifiers mitigates mortals' anxiety. The direct result of this argument is that it turns the positive function of legal form in western history into a synecdoche of humanity's (supposedly) common psychological 'crutch'. As such, I argue, it makes it impossible to think of law otherwise than in Hegelian terms – as property and contract. Hegel thought that the most primitive intersubjective relationship is private law – property and contract – and that state-enforced positive law is the optimal framework for its operations. Is this the ultimate truth? What if such unconditional reliance on contract is not really a universal 'crutch' but, merely, a secularised European *crosier* with the missing cross very much present if only by its absence? In this case we need to expose the theological underpinnings that belie the positivist's claim to moral neutrality. Aware that we are operating under the spectre of our broken cross-turned-liberal contract (which supersedes our belief in the indispensable function of positive law), we realise the need to beware of further slippage into liberal millenarianism, namely the assumption of an inevitable universal process toward Western-type pseudo-secularisation within the context of the constitutional nation state obscuring the theological underpinnings of the modern state (cf Diamantides 2010). If not, far from advancing universal principles of rational co-existence, we risk necessarily importing through the back door – unconsciously and without acknowledgement – specifically European conceptions of law. In fact, when philosophical speculation is coupled with historical and anthropological narrative we are reminded that late-modern contract theories and legal positivism operate as master signifiers not just anywhere and not 'just because', but specifically in the context of the European state and only as always-already justified; that is, as the equivalent of what, in earlier times, was seen as justified with reference to now abandoned, albeit still operative, substantive theological structures and beliefs. We thus recognise that our focus on law's contractual form is the latest expression of a specifically monotheistic dogma centred on *covenants*, which, in Christian Europe, gave rise to the *ecclesia* of ecclesiastical states and, in atheistic Europe, operate as a misnomer of Greek *demos*. In this regard, although all psychoanalytical jurisprudence accepts that the harsh laying down of *a* law is necessary if the human individual, with its myriad and conflicting desires, is to be able to enter the symbolic universe as a civilised ('castrated') subject, not everyone equates this function with legal positivism. Pierre Legendre has dedicated his life to arguing that it is precisely modern legal bureaucracy that is unable to perform this function. More recently, Alain Supiot's legal anthropology relates this function to unconditional, constitutive human submission to *substantive*, collective visions of justice (Supiot 2007). The general idea of law or justice (*la loi*, as opposed to posited rules, *le droit*) refers to the anthropological function of substantial dogmatic beliefs, varying from culture to culture, to institute humans as rational beings by linking together the biological and symbolic dimensions that make up our being and connecting our infinite mental universe with our finite physical existence. While such substantive visions are constantly re-interpreted, the specificity of each normative culture is guaranteed by the techniques of legal interpretation that are particular to its legal system's dogmatic resources. The dogmatic idea of law-as-contract is specific to monotheistic cultures, while the idea of the individual rights-holder (what he calls *Homo Juridicus*) is specifically Christian.

To ignore this is to offer a snapshot of the late-modern subject in liberal regimes as a synecdoche of humanity 'without strangers'. It is also to speak from the 'end of history', free from the spectres of the dogmatic legal past in the context of Christian European states, adopting a 'constitutive' stance. However, tracing positive law to, say, the Theodosian and Justinian legislative acts, we see that these were undertaken *in the guise* of merely codifying Roman law, and followed preambles which stated that the ruler was concerned with nothing but the public good and guided by God. It was through such false modesty, and not unabashed power exhibitionism, that power started to express itself primarily through legislation in Western Europe. Such initial false humility became gradually redundant thanks to legal and theological experts making possible first the idea of absolutist sovereignty in the name of God; then the useful fiction of the social contract in the place of God; and, finally, the idea of individual autonomy as the rightful *self-legislation of the propertied* classes, which now, following the linguistic turn, is reinterpreted as the right to legislate *as a means of self-realisation* of the possessing but no longer *self-possessed* split subject. Currently, complex processes are responsible for violently transposing this idea out of its historical and territorial context and onto a world that is imagined as 'globalised', 'de-territorialised', etc. To consider that contract, property and positive law are elementary forms of law that cut across cultures is, I think, to fall for the myths of Western political theology/theory that turned the historically contingent trajectory of sovereignty in Christian Europe into a necessity.

If social contract theories and their positivistic inception are specific products of European history we can additionally examine them as variations on a common theme aptly called, by Jean Luc Nancy, the 'monotheistic model of social organisation'. Nancy includes in the composition of this model the Greco-Roman legacy, that is to say the philosophical and statist-juridical legacy of Greece and Rome and Semitic faith in a withdrawn creator God. In the case of Judeo-Christianity Nancy speaks of a tight symbiosis between Greco-Roman consciousness and the monotheistic frame of mind developed during the Hellenistic era (Nancy 2003: 39). By symbiosis he means the awareness of a logico-techno-juridical universality and its splitting from the realm of salvation, which was gradually hereafter conceived as an entirely interior or private care. Nancy's clear thesis needs no further elaboration from me apart from adding that, as with any symbiosis, the one that developed between Greek reflexivity and Semitic faith has been anything but a neutral experience. The enquiry over plural *final* causes of all things can neither integrate nor displace the persisting Semitic faith in one creator but withdrawn God as a singular *efficient but useless* cause. This difficult Greek-Semitic symbiosis – Aristotle meets Woody Allen – has been managed in a specific way in the context, and for the benefit, of the European state of law as institutional inheritor of the Roman statist-juridical legacy.

My qualification – that the symbiosis has always been traumatic – complements Nancy's further thesis, namely the existence of what he calls endemic 'auto-deconstructionist' characteristics common to all three monotheistic cultures. Of these, two are of particular importance for my discussion. The first and most evocative characteristic is that, paradoxically, 'monotheism is in truth atheism' since it invokes Abraham's *faith* to a uniquely withdrawn, absent God in contrast to religion proper understood as theism, which invests in *belief* in the presence of power that assembles the world and guarantees its meaning (Nancy 2003: 41–42). Therefore, the Christian West's 'secular' modernity, the meaning of which is but a work in progress (or promised), *continues* the tradition of monotheistic covenants based on a promise that is paradoxically already realised and yet to come, and of meaning that is both taken for granted and absented in its very presence. Nietzsche, in this sense, is not only the last prophet of Christianity but of all monotheism since, in announcing the death of God, he only made explicit the principle of a world without God that monotheism has accommodated within itself since its inception. The second, auto-deconstructionist characteristic of monotheism flows from the first: it is 'demythologisation', or monotheism's auto-interpretative history, in which it understands itself in a less and less 'religious' manner to the extent that a religion implies mythology, and more and more through narratives that relate directly to the human condition among which narratives of and about the law must take a prominent place. In the West, Rousseau's term 'civic religion' captures the web of such interconnected narratives and rightly places, at the very heart of this web, the crypto-theological idea of the social contract.

Elsewhere I worked on this basis to explain the excessive anxiety, or terror, that prevails when Islamic and Christian/secular signifiers are in close proximity with reference to the fact that, *up to a point*, in both cultures law, rather than God, functions as master signifier (Diamantides 2006). In the West we went from Jesus 'rendering unto Caesar . . .', to Popes and Emperors, in the person of whom the temporal and the spiritual merged as expressed by the notion of sovereignty, the juridical and theological basis of which has been explained in the seminal work of Ernst Kantorowicz (1997). In Islam, by contrast, the similar early endemic attempts to invest exclusive interpretative authority in the image of a ruler, as both just and sovereign, was undermined by the same jurists that created the sophisticated body of Islamic laws because that image was reserved exclusively for Mohammed, the prophet and first ruler of the Islamic state. Since then, the function of producing Islamic justice has been performed at local community level by numerous popular Islamic jurists belonging to several Islamic schools of interpretation. Hence, in Muslim states, the legal fiction of 'sovereignty' was stillborn. This situation was only partially and temporarily reversed by the Ottoman state which, much closer to European sovereign states than any other Muslim-majority state, rendered the *Hannafi* as the state's official *madhab*, controlled the administration of Islamic justice through a system of centralised appointments of *qadis* and, in the nineteenth century, invested in the process of codification of law. After the collapse of the Ottoman state the problem of the missing Islamic sovereignty has only been superficially neutralised by the imposition of European-style sovereignty in the colonial and post-colonial Muslim-majority states and by the attempts to appropriate it by Islamists.

But if Europe and its Muslim emulators could not endure the paradoxical symbiosis of Semitic faith and Greek reflexivity within the new 'sovereignty' framework of the old Roman statist legacy (in which the state's power to enforce positive law was both juridically and theologically justified), that was not the case for the faithful jurist. For centuries, Muslim and Jewish jurists have developed a highly rational jurisprudence while rejecting the (Hartian) maxim 'every society needs a regime of positive law, which, in rational legal systems, officials enforce regardless of whether they agree with its substantive content'. (I should add that I reject categorically the Weberian view of 'qadi justice' as primitive.) The jurists did that thanks to their faith in one absolutely withdrawn God – faith, which, as J.L. Nancy has written 'undoes theism' as much as contemporary atheism does. This meant that the jurists exercised practical freedom (interpreting holy texts; devising solutions for moral dilemmas and legal disputes, etc.) while 'trembling', namely without any hope for certainty that they were either 'good' *or* 'right' and, consequently, failing to become officials. Consequently, Muslim *ulema* and Jewish rabbis have played a more radical role politically than the one Hart attributes to legal officials ensuring, on the one hand, that the subject *obeys* the law simply because it is the law and not due to the merits of its contents (as with positivists and psychoanalytic approaches) but, on the other hand, that the subject also *disinvests from the institutionalization/étatisation* of law's function. In short, the message was to obey the law as dictated by your local wise man, not the one appointed by the state. This could be why sovereignty was stillborn in Muslim empires and, also, why the highly complex and elaborate systems of Islamic laws incorporate in legal practice diverse understandings of key concepts to the point that a litigant can rely on different *madhahib* ('schools of interpretation') in relation to different aspects of the same legal case. Similarly it explains why, until the emergence of Zionism, Jews had nothing else to go by when looking for 'authoritative' guidance, but the aporetic and truly liberating double maxim: *make a rabbi for yourself* (*Aseh lecha rav*) (Pirkei Avos 1:6) and *acquire for yourself a friend* (*Kneh lecha chaver*) which, as Maimonides explained, involves the freedom to choose unqualified, unprofessional masters lacking authority and pedigree, and treat them as your 'friend', meaning with fierce loyalty, commitment and love as is the case with one's spouse.[1]

II. The secular legal politics of Abdullah Ahmed An-Na'im

If the Muslim world never truly successfully developed its own version of sovereignty by refusing to merge the theological and the legal as Europe did; and if European 'secularism' is a travesty in so far as it qualifies states which, by virtue of their self-understanding as 'sovereign', are necessarily theistic; then one can speculate about the potential Muslim lessons for a truly *radical* European politics that aims to salvage the 'political' (the use of constitutive power) from the business-as-usual of a small 'p' politics in the context of

1 The Hebrew verb *kneh*/acquire has the same route as marriage.

liberal constitutional states, where all and any political initiative must first and foremost bow to the crypto-theocracy of positive law (with the state as God). But before we get there it is first important to salvage the Muslim difference (the lack of sovereignty) from those who, like the Ottoman *High Porte*, wish to annul it. Confusingly, today these are seeming enemies: liberal Muslim (as well as Zionist) modernisers and their supposed nemesis Islamists (and ultra-orthodox Jews). My example will be Abdullahi Ahmed An-Na'im (2008).

The strength and value of An-Na'im's thesis is his point that Islamic religious, political and juridical cultures (note the plural) suffer when Shari'a law is promulgated via positive law by governments. I can think of nothing that will negate his historically demonstrated argument that:

> whatever the state enforces in the name of shari'a will necessarily be secular and the product of coercive political power and not superior Islamic authority.
>
> (An-Na'im 2008: 7)

He is also descriptively right that:

> [T]he notion of an Islamic state is in fact a postcolonial innovation based on a European model of the state and a totalitarian view of law and public policy as instruments of social engineering by the ruling elites.
>
> (*ibid.*)

And:

> [A]ll Muslims today live under what is commonly referred to as the nation-state, which is based on European models that have been established around the world through colonialism, even in regions that were not formally colonized.
>
> (An-Na'im 2008: 86)

And:

> . . . European colonialism and its aftermath have drastically transformed the basis and the nature of political and social organisation within the territorial states where all Muslims live today . . . [so that] . . . a return to pre-colonial political philosophies and systems is practically impossible.
>
> (An-Na'im 2008: 125)

Less useful are his 'conclusions'. First, he concludes that faithful Muslims *need* the secular liberal constitutional state because it alone can facilitate the possibility of religious piety out of honest conviction; they can, at most, externalise their beliefs by working to 'influence the development and interpretation of state law and contribute to its legitimacy' through substantive 'influences on the formulation of public policy and legislation' (An-Na'im 2008: 89). Second, he concludes that 'Islamic law' and state law are 'different types' of normative systems, each based on its own sources of authority and legitimacy and that the two can be 'complementary' with Islamic law, as a system of jurisprudence that is not state-enforced (An-Na'im 2010).[2]

In response, it seems one has to first reiterate the rather well-known argument that the notion of religion as 'private' matter within a 'morally neutral' constitutional modern state functions ideologically in obscuring the theological structure of the sovereign authority of the state as *persona ficta* and the related (Hobbesian) juristic theory of representation. Moreover, it needs to be pointed out that this structure, whether explicit or concealed, has been indispensable in *containing* the 'paradoxical distinction' between the state/state law and politics which An-Na'im evokes and which, when uncontained could have radical, constitutive, political implications. This distinction – otherwise known as the 'constitutional paradox' regarding the distinction between constituted and constituent power – is a very fragile one and the ability to act on it should not be taken for granted, as An-Na'im does. Historically, the acknowledgment of the paradox emerges with modern constitutionalism after centuries of forced conflation at the hands of non-democratic states. Nowadays, we can all agree that within the confines of liberal constitutional states it is regularly swept aside whenever a state of emergency is declared as well as under so-called acts of state. From a more sceptical/critical point of view, liberal constitutionalism fails to maintain the distinction even in times of normality between what in French is called the political (*le politique*) and politics (*la politique*). In sum, its critics point out that 'constitutionalism must face the fact that constituent power is not free-floating, but appears to come always already implicated with constitutional form, the instituting already coupled with the instituted' (Christodoulidis 2007: 191). Moreover, not only does the constitutional state *not overlap* with the political domain, but its *primary* feature is to *contain* potentially transformative political conflict within the established framework of politics, in a manner that is ultimately depoliticising.

2 His view is premised on a 'difficult distinction between state and politics' (Pirkei Avos, p. 4). 'Since complete autonomy is not possible . . . it is sometimes important to recall the state's political nature. Paradoxically, this reality of connectedness [between the state and politics] makes it necessary to strive to separate the state from politics, so that those excluded by the political processes of the day can still resort to state organs and institutions for protection against excessive use or abuse by state officials' (Pirkei Avos, p. 5). 'This necessary though difficult distinction can be mediated through the principles and institutions of constitutionalism and the protection of the equal human rights of all citizens' (Pirkei Avos, p. 6).

Second, even though Islamic law developed in relative distance from the demands of sovereign rulers (for the reasons mentioned earlier), it is an essentialist fantasy to say that this is because of the specificity of its 'normative nature' as An-Na'im believes. The notion of Islamic law 'naturally' being free from the political exigencies of the various states in which it developed is not helpful as it only begs a hypothetical question that it raises: what would 'Islamic law' mean without these states? It seems clear to me that starting from the creation of a Quranic vulgate under the commission of 'Uthman, the third Caliph (23/644-35/655), which gave the 'legally minded a *textus receptus* on which to draw' (Hallaq 2007: 34), 'Islamic law' has always been actively desired by the various Muslim states in which it was formulated, and its history reflects this even though it never quite became the province of a 'sovereign' ruler as in the West. The story of the creation of the *Sunnah* as the second most important normative source after the Qur'an also attests to the important state-ulamma dialectic as a source of law. While the Prophet's authority during his lifetime was anchored in the Quranic event and, therefore, he was and according to Islamic theology still is nothing more than a human being, this is not the whole story. As Hallaq notes, by the time of the prophet's death his mission had already met with great success and he was the most important living figure the Arabs knew together with the charismatic men who surrounded him. As a result, very soon after his death, history records an intense preoccupation with Prophetic material (reflected in a considerable body of writings found in papyri, inscriptions and numismatics). In order to shore up their authority the successor Caliphs – until at least the middle of the second/eighth century – tended to see themselves as God's direct agents (baring titles such as 'God's Deputy on Earth' and 'The Commander of the Faithful') with the mission to implement His statutes, commands and laws. In fact they 'held their own courts and personally acted as *qadis*' (Hallaq 2007: 44). To be sure, the authority of those early Caliphs did not yet derive from the office itself and they were not 'independent agents of legislation' (Hallaq 2007: 45). However, in accordance with pre-Islamic Arabic tradition, all laws were meant to reflect generally accepted custom and the *sunan* (note the plural), that is, various commendable practices of earlier Caliphs, the Prophet and his companions but also '. . . in fact any good model' (*ibid.*). The development by the *ulama* of stringent techniques for 'authenticating' the sources of the 'true' Prophetic *sunna* (dispensing with apocryphal elements) was precisely a means to control the process of legitimation of state power by association with (invented) good practice. Later the 'Abbasid Caliphs' attempt to create a single coherent and extensive body of Islamic law, with the Caliph as supreme interpreter, expressed more directly their desire to go a step further and *sanctify their office* and, recalling Nancy, to complete the process of demystification/secularisation of Islam. To what extent this succeeded or failed and why it did not lead to a European-style political theology of sovereignty of the type Kantorowitz described with the expression 'the King's two bodies' is a most interesting and complex question that is not answered by saying that inherently 'Islamic law' is normatively alien to state law.

One partly speculative, partly historical, explanation for this contingent (not structural) difference ascribes a crucial role to the faith-induced rebellious actions of those eminent Muslim jurists who resisted the invitation to serve power directly. I call these jurists 'faith-induced', drawing on Nancy's double insight that Abrahamic faith – as opposed to pagan belief – is fundamentally not a power discourse (since it is directed towards not an intervening Master but a withdrawing God). But for them, the auto-deconstructionist path of Islamic faith could have been the same as in the West where it was collapsed into belief in the value of first, absolutist sovereign rulers and later into sovereign state-backed contract law. In this regard the narratives around jurists such as Imam Malik Ibn An-Naas are inspirational. A faithful man as well as brilliant jurist, Imam Malik Ibn An-Naas rejected offers and extreme pressure by the Caliphs of his time to have his jurisprudence 'canonised', on the grounds that he respected other *madh'Ahib* (schools of Islamic law). He was punished for it. This stance has been emulated by most historically prominent Muslim jurists and it *should not be underestimated*. It effectively signals a different (and earlier than the European) modernity in which the classical Muslim-majority societies underwent (what systems theorists call) functional differentiation *instead of* stratification and centralisation. By contrast, European societies *transitioned from* stratification to functional differentiation much later on. As a result, one has always been able to stand in a court of Islamic law and simultaneously use aspects of *different madh'Ahib* in the *same* case and, indeed, do so independently of whether the *madh'Ahib* in question are prevalent or even have any followers in the country where s/he lives or not. 'Disarmed' by the *sunna* of the Prophet who apparently said that 'my [Islamic] community will not err', An-Naas and the other great jurists were simply not able/interested in discrediting opposing interpretations, but were willing to 'let a thousand flowers blossom'. This was all at the expense of the desire of powerful statesmen intent on increasing the overlap between Islamic jurisprudence and the specific *raisons d'etat* they were advocating, and who were spending considerable amounts of money at the time in order to develop coherent legal and political ideologies for all their imperial subjects (Muslim and non-Muslim), including the use of Aristotelian logic, helped by their sponsoring of the great translation movement. It was indeed in their time that 'Islamic law' came to mean not only *Qur'an* and *Sunnah* but also the highly rational and huge body of *fiqh*. Alas, for them, this body of jurisprudence was never streamlined into one state-sanctioned Islamic canon law but remains divided into mutually respecting schools for the reasons mentioned.

An 'evil' consequence of this failure to streamline theology and law was the stifling of the development of an integrated Islamic political tradition wherein the religio-legal and the philosophical strands of Muslim political philosophy could have merged (cf. Brown 2000: 51, 57) and, perhaps, given rise to the fiction of the sovereign state as a sine-qua-non of politics, as it happened in the West. With such and such Imam Malik Ibn an-Naas and others like him, have rendered successive Muslim polities relatively defenceless before the expansionist energies gathered by the sovereign Western states. This, I think, is what both today's Islamists and liberals like An-Na'im are – naively – attempting to 'correct' respectively by striving to establish Islamic sovereign states and putting Islamic theology in the legitimating service of western secular constitutional states (*minority fiqh* would be a good example). Liberal An-Na'im, invites Muslims to substitute their aporetic faith for a pagan belief in the Unity of the Representing Hobbesian State and its power to turn the people from a multitude into a commonwealth. In so doing, *ironically, he is not structurally dissimilar to proponents of so-called 'Islamic states'* where justice follows the implementation of supposedly divine Islamic law albeit in a territorial, nation-state context (e.g. Islamic Republic of Iran). I say 'naively' because this happens at a time when governmentality/securitisation pose an existential threat to state sovereignty and legal positivism, and where, consequently, constitutional theory turns away from both Hobbes's juristic theory of representative sovereignty of the state and Kelsen's hypostatisation of the constitutional legal order into a self-grounding and self-sustaining system of rules, towards the likes of Carl Schmitt.

In this connection what is thought-provoking in the narratives around medieval Muslim jurists is that even as, for reasons of state, the doors of interpretation of Islamic law were declared to be 'closed' and, therefore, the officially recognised *madh'Ahib* today can be counted by the fingers of one hand and are ostensibly the same as hundreds of years ago, their founding jurists' faith-driven rebellion constitutes an exemplary act of powerless resistance as well as an assertion that the *umma* (the Islamic community) may retain its integrity despite – perhaps because of – lacking in representable doctrinal *and* political unity be it of the Kelsenian (normative) or the Schmittian (substantive) sort. This, I must stress, is not a communitarian embrace of pluralism; it is an indifference to the problematic of unity/pluralism. Nor does it require war; it is disinterestedness in power and territory. And it requires patience and endurance two qualities that are very short in the faithless human. It is the sort of subjective stance that both psychoanalysis and deconstruction expect of us.

III. Reflexive jurisprudence and a-theistic faith today

This takes me to the paper's last part. If monotheistic faith can defy power and if, per Nancy, contemporary a-theism paradoxically realises such faith, I speculate on the possibility that monotheistic *and* humanist faith may have potentially equal implications for a truly radical politics, one that disinvests from the power or powerlessness of the contemporary centralising state, to the extent that they remain disinterested in and un-co-opted by its power or lack thereof. Setting our states' pseudo-secular credentials aside, seeing how they are nothing other but successors to, rather than replacements of, their politico-theological predecessors we could seek inspiration in how to gain critical distance from them also from the faithful Muslims, Jews and Christians who defied them.

Critical social-theoretical debates identify ours as the 'late modern age' in the context of the reflexive modernisation thesis (Beck 1992, 1994, 1999; Giddens 1990, 1991). In these, dystopic, visions of modernity, the term 'reflexivity' takes the semantic content of continuous self-confrontation. As Beck argues, reflexive modernisation occurs as a stage of the modernisation process and not via its repudiation. Applying modern principles to modernity itself we find it lacking. In this sense, the reflexive quality of contemporary late modern societies is a deeply *political* quality. It paves the road for a creative self-destruction of an entire epoch: that of industrial society. It is not a big leap on my part to add that this disenchantment may also become directed towards the constitutional state's legal system. The depoliticising management or containment of this self-confrontation is the other side to our late modern age, however. Our societies are 'risk societies' in the sense that we are constantly forced to deal with the unintended consequences of their developmental trajectories; but also in that our biggest problem is not with the production and distribution of 'goods' (hence old-fashioned 'experts' are obsolete) but the prevention and minimisation of 'bads' through expert systems. Consequently, in our times, positive law's function to justify power is performed by lawyers and judges who have adapted to the circumstances. Thus, for example, a judge may or may not declare 'water boarding' to be torture depending on the severity of the perceived threat by terrorism. A lawyer may help her client realise that settling her claim against a powerful corporation is preferable, if money is what she desires, although the claim could succeed, because of the costs/delays involved. The 'legal risk expert' no longer aims to justify centralised power positively (i.e. with reference to some utilitarian, or more traditional, transcendental good); rather, s/he justifies the dispersed, national and transnational, networks of power only indirectly and negatively, by encouraging the calculation of risks that come with dis/obedience among plural, potential masters and letting the individual decide, from the point of view of her desire. In this context the continuing liberal emphasis on individual choice and desire expresses the form in which the subject is addressed by power in late-industrial societies *as* the 'post-modern individual' who is no longer seen as self-possessed (in the sense of the self-coincidence of the individual autonomous subject; but also in the sense of the self-coincidence of the national body) but which possesses means for self-actualisation (individual or sovereign capital and property). Indeed, the care of the self is seen as one arena within which the colonisation of the life-world by 'expert systems' unfolds. The sceptic may question whether legal practice which in reality falls somewhere between litigation and negotiation and judicial review, which in reality falls between constitutional interpretation and accommodation of immediate pragmatic considerations, may not be part of these mechanisms.

Setting aside those members of contemporary monotheistic societies who, despite these significantly new circumstances, still believe and invest in the power of state legal systems to 'contain' the energy released by modernity's self-confrontation, be they 'secular liberals' of 'religious fundamentalists', I want to turn to *immanentist*, materialist, critics of the modern European legal system who wish to unlock the politically constitutive potential of modernity's crisis from the 'shackles' of a jurisprudence still worshiping state-sovereignty and constitutional 'entrenchments', and turn towards 'purely reflexive' accounts of law and politics as separate sub-systems (*cf.* Christodoulidis 2007). The ultimate aim is to enable the thinking of some new kind of political entity as a genuine heterogeneous alternative to the sovereign state, cosmopolis or community all of which presuppose a capitalist economy of representation. For example, Emilios A. Christodoulidis seeks to defend Carl Schmitt's thesis that the origin of political action is already political (without the heteronomy of representation and law) against Kelsen's objection that the members of a polity cannot identify any set of qualities which would univocally and uncontroversially define them as a political unity (thus the 'unity' of a people is possible only in a normative sense: constitution 'of' a people). This criticism is relative, Christodoulidis writes, even as he concedes that political unity requires recognition, because such recognition is itself contingent (Christodoulidis 2007: 192). Having affirmed this contingency Christodoulidis thinks – *or hopes?* – that pure constituent power can give rise to revolutionary changes if only we resist the collapse of the 'constituent' into the pathways of the instituted whereby any attempt to bring about something new is seen as a 'crisis' in need of constitutional containment. This resistance is all the more difficult, he concedes, in the current conditions of globalisation where recognition is available only from within the dialectic of global and communal with anything else rendered invisible and, consequently, political participation only finds outlet in the largely reactionary upsurge of community politics, of state (and sub-state) nationalism that presents itself as the only entry point into the public sphere. How do we resist? The challenge is to theorise the 'constitutional thinking of dissensus', which turns out to mean, again, no more than to reflect on resistance as constituting the very framework of recognition for the kind of political entity that it wants to bring about.

Christodoulidis, for one, is adamant that opportunistic conflict alone is needed, not faith. Semitic traditions' faith in particular is, once more, excised and ridiculed. He derides Lacanians for reducing the political to politics because they emphasise the human fear of the return of the, necessarily lawless, political (Christodoulidis 2007: 193). Alongside he derides Derridians, too, who, in response to this fear, propose not revolutionary struggle, but patient, endless, work of deconstruction and reconstruction (*ibid*.). For them, he decries, the visibility of 'the political' is verified only indirectly, as memory or trace. Instead, Christodoulidis wants to shed ample theoretical light on 'the political' as a pure universal idea, which he seems confident that he *thinks* as human, not as European, Christian, Greek, etc. He also derides Lefort's formulation of democracy's institution of the locus of power as an 'empty place'. Christodoulidis, I gather, wants to fill this empty place with the bio-political bodies of individuals and social groups, which may (indeed) have their own power of resistance against structures.[3] In short he derides all positions that take seriously human weakness and its religious expression, but especially those which, following through monotheism's auto-deconstruction, recall a specifically Jewish and Muslim anti-theological ethos of combining tolerance of juridical uncertainty with persistent faith. The materialist that he is Christodoulidis is explicitly mocking such a-theistic faith. Complaining against a 'proliferation' of theories that draw their inspiration from the impossibility of containment of constituent within the constituted within the institution, he concludes,

> . . . a new faith has emerged at the interstice of the mystical and the political thinking of resistance. Traces, specters, surpluses, and remainders dominate thinking here. I will not pursue this path because resistance to structures of oppression requires political opportunities rather than mystical faith.
>
> (Christodoulidis 2007: 193–194)

This is a perfect example of deriving from Kant not the much advertised freedom of 'daring to know', but to 'know how to dare' (Negri and Hardt 2009: 17). But the question is: is this ambitious project of 'reflective resistance' – which can change the framework of our politics without appeals to heteronomy – a plan or an aspiration? Could it be that this reflexivity can never be 'purified' from Semitic faith and revert to the thinking of the new in the way that Aristotle could (who, after all, was confident that the heavens were solid and harmonious, unlike us)? In reverse, could the politics of resistance not be explained by an economy of rebellious a-theistic *faith*, specifically *Abrahamic* faith, even – especially – at this stage, when both atheists and truly spiritual faithful people must contend with formidable 'believers' and their apologists (be they believers in the market, science, the constitutional state law, global de-territorialised law or one or other caricatural version of

3 Bio-political research agendas share three maxims: 'bodies are constitutive components of the biopolitical fabric of being', bodies 'have to resist in order to exist' and 'corporeal resistance produces subjectivity, not in an isolated or independent way but in the complex dynamic with the resistances of other bodies' (D'Ancona 2005: 31).

the God of Abraham)? Admirable and crucial as their goals may be, I want to point out that the materialist critics' failure to realise that their 'atheism' is nothing but the *realisation* of monotheistic faith (in the paradoxical sense of Nancy mentioned earlier) renders their confidence in the possibility of a 'purely reflexive' politics faulty. Not realising that the spectres of the European past cannot be 'reflected away' but only confronted as *part of* the process of modernity's self-confrontation, they end up driving (again) an artificial and unhelpful wedge between humanist faith and monotheistic faith. As I argued earlier the two kinds of faith are, in fact, *equally* products of monotheism (in other words, being an 'atheist' is not a universal category but specifically situated in late modern monotheistic settings). In this respect they are not reflecting but repeating – as if by 'reflex action' – biases and mistakes by a European humanism that has denied and disavowed its monotheistic provenance. In this regard a lot is to be gained by the study of Jewish and Muslim legal and political histories and in particular the role of *aporetic faith* in preventing the merging of law and politics and the emergence of an integrated political philosophy out of the encounter of philosophy (especially Muslim *falsafa*) with rational dialectical theology (in particular Islamic *kalam*). There was no lack of brilliant, erudite, minds to work for this integration; among the many medieval Muslim philosophers, stand out careful neo-platonists such as Avicenna (with his distinction between essence and existence) (*cf.* Wisnovsky 2005) and Averroes (whose influence extended beyond European scholasticism to Jewish medieval philosophical thought (Taylor 2005: 186) and who taught that the truth of religion and philosophy are one and the same and that the Scriptures contain three kinds of texts that, respectively, must be read literally, interpreted allegorically and contested). Moreover, Muslim rulers strongly supported the philosophers' efforts towards an integrated political philosophy and spared no means to achieve it (e.g. al-Kindi was the tutor of Ahmad, the son of Caliph al-Mu'tasim; he was also the editor of the *Theology of Aristotle* which was nothing but a paraphrase of the *Enneads* with Neo-Platonic emanationist principles such as the existence of the soul prior to birth – which rendered compatible Aristotle's immanent *Metaphysics* with Semitic creationism, most importantly that of God as an agent and efficient cause) (D'Ancona 2005: 24).

There is one last, and more unpleasant, historical reason to warn against the unrestrained turn towards 'reflexivity without faith'. The history of cross-fertilisation and mutual repulsion between Greek reflexivity over final causes and Semitic faith in one efficient but useless cause (i.e. the creator but subsequently withdrawn God), is replete with instances of Europeans eagerly seeking to purify the former from the latter (read: to repress) and the intended and unintended consequences of their efforts must not go amiss. While neo-Platonist philosophers such as Plotinus, and some of the neo-platonic Muslim philosophers, and even early Christian clergy such as St Augustine, had managed to be neither anti-Aristotelian nor anti-Semitic, the same cannot be said of their successors who specifically sought to bypass neo-platonism including by seeking out translations of Aristotle directly from the Greek. Like Aristotle Plotinus had identified the highest level of being – divine Intellect – with reflexive thinking; at the same time he sharply criticised Aristotle's doctrine of substance and denied that such a principle can be the first uncaused cause of things (D'Ancona 2005: 11, 24). For him the One lies 'beyond being', like the Good of the *Republic*. Plotinus consequently identified the 'fall of the soul' with the inevitable *tension* between pure contemplation and divisive action – a tension that for him constitutes the natural mode of existence of the soul (cf. *Ennead* IV.8.6–7). He left it to each person to determine how to seek 'authenticity' within this tension. Berber St Augustine's favourable view of Neo-Platonist thought contributed to the baptism of Greek thought and its entrance into the Christian and subsequently the European intellectual tradition, mostly through translations from the Arabic by scholars and philosophers who were as much Neo-Platonic as Augustine. Augustine had no time for individuated strategies of authenticity and taught that salvation was none other than the love of God pure and simple. The idea of a *decisive self* made its comeback with the shift from the Augustinian Neo-Platonic view of the Good as the 'love of God' to Aquinas's 'purely Aristotelian' rational teleological theology where man is responsible for pursuing his salvation; it underwent a further mutation with the protestant identification of the Good with performance of one's worldly tasks under the doctrine of 'pre-determination'; it got secularised in Machiavellian and consequentialist/utilitarian accounts whereby the 'Good' is disassociated from the divine and its pursuit is entrusted in the hands of a rational, calculating autonomous subject. Finally, in the post-enlightenment atmosphere the idea of self is returned to us, minus its association with the Good, in the various contemporary formulations of subjectivity that centre around the key hermeneutical insight that man makes himself in hermeneutical reflexivity in a plethora of theories. In fact, however, the whole intellectual history of the West since Aquinas and Duns Scotus through to reformation and its secular philosophical aftermath is characterised by intensifying efforts to 'purify' Aristotelian reflexivity with the combined effect of, first, rendering the Good fully rational and, secondly, replacing God with a subject of constant action – becoming – that synthesises the divide between potentiality and actuality. It is perhaps no coincidence that another characteristic of European intellectual tradition since Aquinas and Scotus is its insipient anti-Semitism and Islamophobia.

References

An-Na'im, Abdullahi Ahmed. 2008. *Islam and the Secular State – Negotiating the Future of Shari'a*. Cambridge, MA, Harvard University Press.

An-Na'im, Abdullahi Ahmed. 2010. "The Compatibility Dialectic: Mediating the Legitimate Coexistence of Islamic Law and State Law." *Modern Law Review*, Vol. 73(1): 1–29.

Beck, Ulrich. 1992. *Risk Society: Towards a New Modernity*. London, Sage.

Beck, Ulrich. 1994. The Reinvention of Politics: Towards a Theory of Reflexive Modernization. In Ulrich Beck *et al.* (eds). *Reflexive Modernisation: Politics, Tradition and Aesthetics in the Modern Social Order*. Cambridge, Polity Press.

Beck, Ulrich. 1999. *World Risk Society*. Cambridge, Polity Press.

Beck, Ulrich, Anthony Giddens, and Scott Lash. 1994. *Reflexive Modernisation: Politics, Tradition and Aesthetics in the Modern Social Order*. Cambridge, Polity Press.

Büttgen, Philippe. 2009. In Alain De Libera, Marwan Rashed, and Irène Rosier-Catach (eds). *Les Grecs, les Arabes et nous, Enquête sur l'islamophobie savante*. Paris, Fayard.

Christodoulidis, Emilios A. 2007. "Against Substitution: the Constitutional thinking of Dissensus." In Martin Loughlin and Neil Walker (eds). *The Paradox of Constitutionalism: Constituent Power and Constitutional Form*. Oxford, Oxford University Press.

D'Ancona, Cristina. 2005. "Greek into Arabic: Neoplatonism in Translation." In Peter Adamson and Richard C. Taylor (eds). *The Cambridge Companion to Arabic Philosophy*. Cambridge, Cambridge University Press.

Diamantides, Marinos. 2006. "Towards a Western-Islamic Conception of Legalism." In L. Barshack, P. Goodrich, and A. Schutz (eds). *Law, Text, Terror*. London, Glasshouse Press, pp. 95–118.

Diamantides, Marinos. 2010. Review Essay "No bad conscience please, we're speculating. Lacanian views on the relation of ethics and positive law in Jeanne Lorraine Schroeder's The Four Lacanian Discourses or Turning Law Inside-Out." *International Journal for the Semiotics of Law* Vol. 23(3): 339–354.

Dupret, Baudoin. 2000. *Au nom de quel droit*. Paris, Centre d'Études et de Documentation économique, juridique et sociale.

Dupret, Baudoin. 2006. *Le Jugement en Action – Ethnométhodologie du Droit, de Morale et de la Justice en Egypte*. Geneva and Paris, Librairie Droz.

Dupret, Baudoin. 2007. "What is Islamic Law? A Praxiological Answer and an Egyptian Case Study." *Theory, Culture & Society* Vol. 24(2): 79–100.

Giddens, Anthony. 1990. *The Consequences of Modernity*. Cambridge, Polity Press.

Giddens, Anthony. 1991. *Modernity and Self-identity: Self and Society in the Late Modern Age*. Cambridge: Polity Press.

Gougenheim, Sylvain. 2008. *Aristote au Mont-Saint-Michel, Les racines grecques de l'Europe chrétienne*. Paris, Seuil, "L'Univers historique".

Hallaq, Wael, B. 2007. *The Origins and Evolution of Islamic Law*. Cambridge, Cambridge University Press.

Kantorowicz, Ernst H. 1997. *The King's Two Bodies: A Study in Mediaeval Political Theology*. Princeton, NJ, Princeton University Press.

Nancy, Jean-Luc. 2003. "Deconstruction of Monotheism." *Postcolonial Studies* Vol. 6: 37–46.

Negri, Antonio and Michael Hardt. 2009. *Commonwealth*. Cambridge, MA: The Belknap Press of Harvard UP.

Pirkei Avos. www.torah.org/learning/pirkei-avos/#. Accessed 12 March 2010.

Schroeder, Jeanne Lorraine. 2008. *The Four Lacanian Discourses or Turning Law Inside-Out*. London, Birkbeck Law Press.
Supiot, Alain. 2007. *Homo Juridicus – On the Anthropological Function of the Law*. London and New York: Verso.
Taylor, Richard. 2005. "Averroes." In *The Cambridge Companion to Arabic Philosophy*. Cambridge, Cambridge University Press, chapter 9.
Wisnovsky, Robert. 2005. "Avicenna and the Avicennian Tradition." In Peter Adamson and Richard C. Taylor (eds). *The Cambridge Companion to Arabic Philosophy*. Cambridge, Cambridge University Press, chapter 6.

Chapter 3

One law against another?

Reading the veil cases: the foundational reference, Shari'a and human rights

*Adam Gearey**

I

This paper is an analysis of what remains veiled; a covered face that is the figure of one law coming up against another. How are we to read this peculiar tension? What can the veiled woman tell us about the relationship between secular and divine authority? In broadest terms, the argument can be outlined as follows. This paper reads the case of *Begum*[1] through Legendre's theory of the foundational reference to reveal the dynamics of the strange encounter between Shari'a and common law.

Commentators have suggested that the 'veil cases' in the UK and other jurisdictions reveal a scene of opposition between two legal orders. This approach obscures a deeper problem about the spaces where subjectivity is articulated – the agonistic that exists between the common law's construction of human rights and *Begum*'s arguments about religious law. It would perhaps be more accurate to see *Begum*, and the veil cases in general, as a conflict over the precise relationship of the divine and the secular.

Perhaps we have been distracted, therefore, by the argument that the veiled woman is somehow alien to our secular order. The figure of the veil will take us to a function of the law that in psychoanalytic terms underlies the very possibility of culture. However, this is not to suggest that there are no tensions between common law and Shari'a. We have to plot a complex relationship between the content and form of the foundational reference that underlies both secular and divine law; a function that shows itself only through 'misleading forms' (Goodrich 1997: 137). Might it be that the very possibility of a common law articulation of human rights depends on the veiled woman and what she represents?

One of the key themes of this essay is the argument that both contemporary liberal and multicultural theory has largely failed to appreciate the

* Thanks to Valerie Kelley, Marinos Diamantides and Mary Gearey for their help in writing this paper.

1 *R. (On the Application of SB) v Headteacher and Governors of Denbigh High School* [2006] UKHL 15 (*Begum*).

terms in which these issues are enacted. This is not to delight in obscurity, nor to reject multiculturalism. Rather, it is to argue that certain forms of scholarship remain reluctant to engage with an understanding of symbols and legal communication that draws on psychoanalysis, and thus fail to appreciate the issues at stake.

The argument will develop as follows. It is necessary, first of all, to engage with the history of the common law, and to revise the idea that it is simply a secular body of law. This will provide the re-working of the misleading assertion that the veil cases show secular and divine law in opposition. Admittedly, this introduces a long-term historical perspective into our consideration of the law, but engaging with deep-seated structures will allow an appreciation of the foundational reference and its dogmatic communication through texts, symbols and rituals. We will argue that an account of the foundational reference takes us towards a theory of the contemporary law of human rights; the most recent manifestation of an ancient jurisdiction over the soul. The next sections will show why contemporary liberal and multiculturalist accounts of rights largely fail to understand the structure of the law. Having cleared away these problems, we will engage in a close reading of *Begum* before concluding with a recent speech on Shari'a and human rights by Dr Rowan Williams, the Archbishop of Canterbury. The Archbishop's approach was condemned by many media pundits who, in so doing, displayed a wider cultural failure to locate the resources that would allow informed discussion of religion, rights and law.

II

The starting point is the Legendrian notion of the foundational reference. This takes us to the Reformation. The passage below shows how the triumph of secular power over the church courts was essentially an inclusion of their spiritual jurisdiction into that of the ascendant common law courts:

> The expansion of the monarchical jurisdiction or regia potestas was to transfer the 'government of the soul' to the civil magistrate . . . the civil subject was now properly reflected in the mirror of the constitution. The icon of the Crown and the spiritual unity of secular authority formed a model in which the subject could narcissistically see his own face . . . Its art, the art of the law, held the subject fascinated, magnestised or bound to an already established law . . . The establishment of an identity, the constitution of a community, and the capture of subjectivity are first a matter of establishing a collective or national identity whose virtue will be matched only by the evil of those who do not belong to it.
>
> (Goodrich 1995: 89)

There are a number of important themes. To stress the main point: the creation or production of the secular state is based on its assumption of the power of the civil magistrates for the care of the believer's soul. Spiritual matters are now to be decided in the name of the state; a state that speaks for a national church. Impacted in this comment are complex ideas of the relationship between the prince and the church that provide the foundation of the modern state. However, for the moment we need to leave such concerns to one side.

Why is the constitution described as a mirror? This is more than a metaphor. The civil subject discovers itself in the reflection of its status that it finds in the law of the state. The crown as icon adopts the essential function of the church: the fashioning of subjectivity. This is why law is an art; it brings into being a civil identity that provides the support for what would otherwise be an incoherent being or, perhaps, an entirely private life sunk into the dark world of the family. These ideas may be somewhat strange to us. We tend to think of the law in rather narrow terms. Once we allow that this is only possible on a forgetting of the history of the common law, we can start to recover the sense in which law creates the very possibility of an identity, a function that it effectively took over from the church. The identity offered to the civil subject by the law is over time increasingly coordinated with the nation state and becomes, ultimately, an understanding of a nation defined by the rights and liberties of the common law.

In order to understand the issues raised by *Begum*, we need to realise that this constitution of the subject is no longer necessarily that of the nation, but an international community whose identity is provided by human rights. Human rights thus repeat the process of Reformation. Just as the nation state took over the jurisdiction of the church and granted itself the power to speak for the believer's soul, to articulate the truth, so too, in more recent times, human rights determine the terms of social being. Rights are now the truth of the social bond.

In the same way that the state replaced the mysticism of the church with the transparency of rational organisation (which it could only do through the inclusion into itself of the spiritual jurisdiction), human rights now claims to be the most rational and humane articulation of political organisation (and must, thus, at some level, carry forward yet again the remains of the spiritual jurisdiction). In psychoanalytic terms, human rights are the new icon, replacing the crown as the imago or mirror in which the subject is meant to see himself or herself as a rational being whose inherent dignity is the mark of his or her equality with all other human beings. To return to our previous point, human rights become so by taking on the original religious function: the care for the believer's soul. Human rights might change the terms in which religion operates but, in so doing it effectively claims for itself the power to determine the relationship of religion to the state.

III

At this point in our argument we will elaborate further what we mean by the foundational reference, for this will take us to the heart of dogmatic communication, and hence to the way in which human rights takes over the original power of the church to fashion the identity of the political subject. To clarify our terms further we will now refer to the believer not as the subject of a specifically Christian polity, but as the political subject. This signifies that we are dealing with western modernity and the political community created by the nation state.

What, then, is the foundational reference? Psychoanalysis argues that the human subject has to be brought into being through the imposition of a structure that will mark it off from the dumb chaos of nature. At the most primal level, this is the work of the incest taboo that creates a cultural order by prohibiting certain expressions of sexual desire. In more sophisticated terms, the structuring imposition must stand in for 'something' that is absent but, nevertheless, powerful and capable of providing and guaranteeing the coherence of being.

The great monotheistic religions developed conceptualisations of this guarantor of order in the sublime majesty of the one true God. Religion mediates between the deity and the world, providing the differentiation of two levels – heaven and earth. Religious symbols and rituals speak of the divine order present in its absence. In monotheistic religions, the mediation between the divinity and the world is also linked to the coming of a prophet; a representative of God, in whose name the church or the priesthood will found itself. Thus, the foundational reference and its dogmatic communication through symbols, rituals and sacred practices guarantees a coherence of being, at both a personal and communal level. This organisation of being must always be 'propped up' through the correct interpretation of those rites and devotions that stand in for an impossible and infinite God in the world of time and finite being.

In the history of the west the inheritance of Christian monotheism is communicated through Roman law. This can be demonstrated in myriad ways but one example will have to suffice. Consider the Veronica. The Veronica is a representation of the face of Christ which the believer, in venerating, considers not only an image of divinity but also an image of her own true self. Although the believer recognises the *imago dei* as a reflection of the true self, it is also a representation of 'something incommensurable' (Goodrich 1995: 228): complete alterity or divinity. The *imago dei* counters the threat of emptiness; the loneliness of the created in the absence of the creator.

In Roman law, in the period of the Empire, the Veronica can be linked to the imago. The imago was a wax image of the face and shoulders of the Emperor. Imagos were set up in law courts and in public places; indeed, wherever there were official acts the 'imperial effigy' had to be present. The imago allows law to speak; to declare its verdicts.

Given the European heritage of human rights, a link between rights, Roman law and the Christian tradition is not too farfetched. Let us return to the imago. The imago that now lies behind human rights is not that of the Emperor but a notion of the human being as a subject of rights. This presupposes the logic of Reformation; the movement from the sacred to the secular, and the enshrining of human being as self-founding and self-justifying. From this position, and particularly given the international provenance of human rights, the foundational reference has become the subject of rights. Human rights are where we recognise ourselves. The universal maps onto the particular: 'I am', to the extent that I am a subject of human rights. Through a process of identity formation, too complex to trace here, when we come before the image of what we should be, we see ourselves as we really are: subjects of rights in the international community of human rights.

IV

To advance our argument we need to make a distinction between the content and the form of the foundational reference. It has been implied in the argument so far that there is a difference between the form that the foundational reference takes, and the content of that function. The form of the foundational reference is structural, and underlies the very possibility of an organised society and shared cultural meanings. The content, however, is variable and historically determined. We have suggested that in the West a Christian religious content was taken over or adapted by Roman law. In more recent history the content of the foundational reference has again changed. The processes begun by the Reformation have led to the nation state and then human rights becoming the fundamental terms of the social bond. We will go on to suggest that the veil cases represent a struggle over the precise content that the foundational reference will take. The terms of the foundational reference are always open to dispute. Precisely because symbols and texts have no indisputable meanings, their correct interpretation must always be a matter of conflict. This truth relates to the meaning of the veil and the meaning of human rights. Given the indeterminacies of human rights law (itself related to religious struggles over the correct interpretation of doctrine), we cannot presume that there is no 'room' for a European Islamic identity, nor that Islam is 'other' or 'alien' to Christianity. Extending this principle, we could go on to suggest that the meaning of the veil, or indeed the right to wear or not to wear a veil, may still be to come.

V

How, then, do we understand the veiled woman? As many commentators have already pointed out, the veil is a complex symbol.[2] Whereas in some

2 Supra n. 1, at para.94. Baroness Hale presents a useful summary of this literature as it applied to the issues raised in Begum. She refers to Yasmin Alibhai-Brown (Who do we

cases it is undoubtedly imposed on women by patriarchal religion, in other instances it is adopted as a symbol of religious authenticity or personal autonomy. It is a common place that the veil has no single meaning. This points to the inevitable conflict over the interpretation of symbols. We need to focus our analysis of the foundational reference on the veil. The practice of veiling can be seen as a specific example of the way in which symbols meditate between two levels: the human and the divine. The veil can be understood alongside the Veronica, for example, as a way in which a coherent order of being is maintained. Our first point, then, is that the veil cannot be denounced as other to the order of symbols which we inhabit. It is as central to our inheritance as the crucifix or the civil code.

We can elaborate some of these points by briefly considering the evidence on veiling practices presented to the court in *Begum*:

> The main sources of the Muslim religion are the Holy Quran, which Muslims believe to represent the word of Allah, and Hadiths, or sayings of the Prophet Muhammad, on different topics. A secondary source of authority is a canon of practices and sayings that are ascribed to Muhammad. These are known as the Sunnah, and a combination of the Holy Quran, the Hadiths and the Sunnah provide the basis for the Islamic laws known as the Shari'a. Scholars differ about the authority of the Sunnah, and some of these differences are apparent in the present dispute. In this field familiar problems arise when early traditions pass down the generations by word of mouth, and there is much scholarly dispute about the authority and authenticity of the earliest surviving written texts.[3]

All Muslims endeavour to follow the teachings in the Holy Quran, which include the following:

> And tell the believing women to lower their gaze and guard their sexuality, and to display of their adornment only what is apparent, and to draw their head-coverings over their bosoms. . . . O Prophet, tell your wives

think we Are? (2000), p. 246). Baroness Hale explains: 'What critics of Islam fail to understand is that when they see a young woman in a *hijab* she may have chosen the garment as a mark of her defiant political identity and also as a way of regaining control over her body.' Baroness Hale goes on to refer to Parekh's 'A Varied Moral World, A Response to Susan Okin's "Is Multiculturalism Bad for Women"' (*Boston Review*, October/November 1997): 'In France and the Netherlands several Muslim girls freely wore the *hijab* (headscarf), partly to reassure their conservative parents that they would not be corrupted by the public culture of the school, and partly to reshape the latter by indicating to white boys how they wished to be treated. The *hijab* in their case was a highly complex autonomous act intended to use the resources of the tradition both to change and to preserve it'.

3 *R. (On the Application of SB) v Headteacher and Governors of Denbigh High School* [2005] EWCA Civ 199, at para.32.

> and daughters and the believing women to draw their outer garments around them when they go out or are among the men.
>
> A Hadith of the Prophet states: 'Whenever a woman begins to menstruate, it is not right that anything should be seen except her face and hands'.[4]

This pithy summary of complex theology stresses a couple of central points about scripture and interpretation. Before we engage in more detail, however, it is necessary to anticipate objections to our argument. Switching from a discussion of the Reformation to Islamic theology is a risky move. A proper development of our argument would require more time and space than is available in this collection. However, this compression is justified as we are attempting to present the essential arc of a broad historical thesis, and the need to argue for the connection of themes takes priority at this stage to the presentation of detail. The second point is more problematic.

Our assumption is that if this elaboration of our central argument was attempted, it would have to be clearly shown how Legendre's thesis, developed primarily with relation to Christian and Roman law sources, can be adapted in order to 'read' a different tradition. This could be seen as an example of the most simplistic reductivism. Whilst there is indeed an element of reductivism in our claims, it is worth pointing out that Legendre stresses that the structural function is the most 'empty' of categories. We suggested above that its content is always culturally and historically specific, and so our comments here attempt merely to outline the way in which, as far as the basic summary of Islamic theology above is concerned, the foundational reference is 'apparent'.

After summarising the textual sources, the court stresses that '[a]ll Muslims endeavour to follow the teachings in the Holy Quran'.[5] This is hardly surprising. Islam is one of the great religions of the book. The sacred text records the divine message; the Quran is the word of the prophet, the mediator between God and man. The divine message is, however, destined for interpretation, hence the scholarly disputes over its authority and meaning. The point is, moreover, that the teachings have to be followed. The truth of the text has to be discovered in order that the message of the text is translated into a coherent set of practices that define a culture and a way of being. Interpretation enacts the need to discover the truth of the authoritative speech that will call being into existence and sustain ways of living.

The passage quoted above thus represents a secular court reminding itself of the essential function of the foundational reference. One law coming up against another.

4 Ibid., para.33.
5 Ibid., para.33.

The verses cited from the Quran take us directly to the notion that subjectivity has to be created by the foundational reference. Just as Roman law creates legal categories that are distinct to the sexes, the verses from the Quran lay down rules that define gendered subjectivity. It is worth stressing, however, that the terms of the foundational reference can always be disputed. Indeed, these disputes are often a matter of life and death, because the foundational reference is itself, in the most literal way, a fundamental question of the construction of life.

VI

As the focus of this essay is on Begum's case, we now need to turn our attention to the tension between the understanding of the veil in Islamic law, and its construction in European human rights law. Our first point will be to stress that this is not a jurisprudential clash of civilisations. We need to show how human rights take over the foundational reference from religion and, secondly, how this determines the context of the veil cases.

The sequence of our argument will open with a brief consideration of the response of liberal scholars and multiculturalists.

VII

What resources does liberal theory or multiculturalism have for identifying the problems that we have outlined? Can it comprehend the problematic of the foundational reference? Liberal responses to 'the veil cases' have taken a variety of forms. A brief review of the field suggests that human rights are seen as central to any possible articulation of the problem. Human rights can achieve a 'fair balance between competing interests' as human rights provide the 'language, discourses and, in some cases, institutional structures for mediating and resolving headscarf-hijab debates' (McGoldrick 2006: 308–9). In this section of the chapter, these claims will be examined in more detail. Our argument will be that neither liberal theory nor multiculturalism understands the structural function of human rights.

In turning to Kymlicka's work on minority rights, it is not suggested that this is directly drawn upon by all liberal writers on the headscarf debate. However, it does perhaps display, in one of the more articulate and consistent forms, an extended attempt to engage with the problem of what are framed as minority rights. Rights enable the very possibility of fair solutions. Our criticisms are, in part, a recuperation of Modood's argument that liberal theories of rights cannot provide the 'neutral' grounds for the articulation of plural identities (Kymlicka 1989). However, it is also an attempt to find out why liberal theories of rights lack the analytical focus to articulate the symbolic spaces where law takes hold of the subject.

It might be that Kymlicka appreciates the 'inside', the psychic space of the foundational reference, but his model of a market of equality and cultural equivalence deprives a theory of rights of the appreciation of the necessary agonistics that has to inform a sensible appreciation of the tensions inherent in the communication of rights.

So, Kymlicka's theory of rights and freedom stresses that lives should be lived from 'the inside' (Kymlicka 1989: 12). People need to live from the values that they have 'endorsed' rather than being somehow benignly guided by some higher agencies' understanding of what is good for them. Precisely because we live from our own beliefs and can revise our own understanding of the values to which we have committed ourselves, we need to be able to live as social beings with 'the resources and liberties' to enable this activity. People require 'the cultural conditions' that allow them to 'acqu[ire] an awareness of different views about the good life' and to examine critically the options available (Kymlicka 1989: 13).

How is this worked out? Kymlicka posits a market mechanism that effectively shares social resources out to those choices that are freely made. Minority rights protect those practices that are so embedded in cultures as to be markers of identity, and which thus require special treatment. Rights protect a kind of special status in the cultural market place. Precisely because they are not in the majority, certain cultural practices are fragile and, for this reason, these circumstances have to be taken into account in determining what is fair. The market is a mechanism that measures 'what is in fact equitable' (Kymlicka 1989). Culture takes on an exchange value; it enters a general structure of equivalence which is enabled by the protection of certain interests through minority rights.

This move from culture to the market is far too precipitous and obscures the fundamental logic that we have been arguing is central to the foundational reference. There is an implicit assumption in Kymlicka's argument that the operation of markets, as understood in liberal theory, has the interpretative power to articulate the meaning and possibility of exchange or otherwise of cultural symbols. This is how Kymlicka can move from the 'internal' notion of a life lived from its own centre, to a suggestion of how an 'external' public culture can somehow agree on the terms of acceptable practices. However, a market cannot articulate the terms in which the foundational reference operates as this underlies the very possibility of a culture in the first place. The foundational reference simply cannot be traded. This is not to say, however, that the content of the foundational reference is not open to articulation. Whether or not this can be grasped in Kymlicka's thought is unlikely. Our concern is with scholarly disputes over the meaning of being that are not exchanges or tradeoffs. They are forms of speech: dialogues over the meanings of texts. We cannot hope to engage in meaningful discussion about the meaning of symbols if they are thought of as merely problems about the public distribution of resources.

VIII

Perhaps Parekh's understanding of multiculturalism comes much closer to this sense of the lived meaning of symbols than Kymlicka's liberalism. Indeed, Parekh's thesis is based on a notion of dialogue that is explained by reference to Heidegger and the hermeneutical tradition. The grounding elements of human culture are the 'inclination' of human beings to interpret themselves. This interpretative faculty presupposes the embedding of human beings in cultural communities. However, these communities are not somehow sealed off from each other and self-defining. They may have a hold over individuals to the extent that they provide the means through which the world becomes intelligible, but they are not impregnable. Cultural values are the products of 'dialectical' (Parekh 2006: 127) tensions between the inherent internal and external relationships of different communities. Human values come out of 'cultural dialogue' that realises the 'comparative' nature of '[m]oral discourse' (Parekh 2006: 128).

Thus, culture is a dynamic process that both nurtures individuals in 'local' contexts and brings those contexts together. The human being is a cultural creation, a creation in and of discourses. Ultimately, this is underpinned by 'human worth'. If human beings are language-using, symbol and ritual creating creatures, then one has to assume that the practices that they create are inherently meaningful for them and hence deserve respect. Human beings must be accorded 'dignity' for the expression of 'unique and worthwhile capacities' (Parekh 2006: 139) that define their different cultural worlds.

Rights, as in Kymlicka's account, mediate and balance out the tensions between communities. The constitution must, at its minimum, contain an 'enshrined system of fundamental rights' (Parekh 2006: 208). Fundamental rights have a twofold role to play: they guarantee that minorities are not subject to populist political attack and thus allow minorities to interact on equal terms with the majority. The risk is that a divided society lacks agreement over the terms of a catalogue of fundamental rights. In such a situation, a bare minimum should be agreed by negotiation and act as a way of achieving some kind of consensus.

Whilst this account of culture is certainly useful, it needs to be supplemented with a psychoanalytic approach if we are to understand in greater detail how the agonistics between the various interpretations of symbols by different groups interface with human rights. Without at least some notion of the foundational reference it becomes difficult to think how a community might perpetuate itself. We would, of course, have to make the important distinction between the form of the foundational reference and the inevitable tensions over its content. It is the latter issue that takes us to Parekh's concern with the way in which cultural change redefines a community's mores. To be precise, we would have to see this as enabled by a structural function which is not susceptible to change or cultural negotiation. However, the key point is that Parekh's work neglects the peculiar logic of Reformation. This is the horizon for any discussion of fundamental rights and common values. If any values emerge, they would do so out of an agonistics of interpretation that put in issue the very sense of their commonality. It may be that new values emerge that challenge an old consensus, creating a new community of interpreters. In turning to a specific dispute over headscarves, we need to plot how these warring interpretations can define a new informing social tension.

IX

How, then, does European human rights law take over the foundational reference and re-articulate its content? Answering this question means reading the cases that were central for the arguments in Begum. However, we need to read these texts in a double way: both to the law they reveal, and the arguments about the structural function that they obscure.

The first case is the case of *Otto-Preminger-Institut v Austria*.[6] Our reading of the case will stress that the imago of human rights is not necessarily a secular idea. In the jurisprudence of the court human rights are always already an acknowledgement of a particular religious heritage. *Otto-Preminger-Institut v Austria* can be read as a clash between Article 10 and Article 9 but, more precisely, as an interpretation of the precise terms of Article 9. After all, Article 9 reduces the Reformation to three paragraphs. It is founded on the assumption that a secular court can determine the boundaries of acceptable religion.

The Otto Preminger Institute undertook a screening of a film, *Das Liebeskonzil*, based on a satirical play by Oskar Panizza that was, in part, a reconstruction of the writer's trial and conviction for blasphemy in 1895. The Innsbruck diocese of the Roman Catholic Church requested that criminal proceedings be instigated against the Institute for 'disparaging religious doctrines', an act prohibited by section 188 of the Penal Code. The case was referred to the European Court of Human Rights (ECtHR) by the European Commission of Human Rights (ECHR) in April 1993. The ECHR accepted that the seizure of the film had been necessary to safeguard the rights of others; or, more precisely, the faith of others. This can be elaborated by examining the way in which the court relied on the judgement in the case of *Kokkinakis v Greece* of 1993.[7]

In *Kokkinakis* it was determined that:

> Article 9 . . . is one of the foundations of a democratic society within the meaning of the Convention. It is, in its religious dimension, one of the

6 *Otto-Preminger-Institut v Austria* (13470/87) [1994] ECHR 26 (20 September 1994).
7 *Kokkinakis v Greece* (Application No. 260-A) Ser. A. (1994); 17 EHRR 397.

> most vital elements that go to make up the identity of believers and their conception of life.[8]

Thus, as far as the content of the film was concerned:

> The respect for the religious feelings of believers as guaranteed in Article 9 can legitimately be thought to have been violated by provocative portrayals of objects of religious veneration; and such portrayals can be regarded as malicious violation of the spirit of tolerance, which must also be a feature of democratic society.[9]

The civil magistrates protect the sensibilities of the believer. Within the European polity, and in the name of human rights, the court can affirm that a democratic society can attach protection to objects of religious veneration. The European Court of Human Rights, then, rather like the old ecclesiastical courts, is concerned with the faith that attaches itself to instruments. But how is this faith to be governed? Not by the church or the churches, but by the executive. If there is no consensus over what constitutes the correct balance between the values of freedom of religion and artistic expression, the European Court of Human Rights has to allow the executive of the state a 'certain margin of appreciation' in determining the precise nature of the relationship. The margin of appreciation is the echo of the power of the reformed secular state to determine the precise boundaries of state religion. But, as we are within the empire of human rights, the power of the executive is limited. The powers of the executive have to be interpreted within the context of the European Convention on Human Rights. As a matter of fact, in this case, the European Court of Human Rights determined that the Austrian government were not in breach of Article 10: the correct balance between the right to artistic freedom and the right to respect for religious beliefs as guaranteed by Article 14 of the Basic Law had been struck.

So, *Otto-Preminger-Institut v Austria* shows the extent to which the European Court of Human Rights adopts and elaborates its jurisdiction over the governance of souls. It is willing to see a limitation of Article 10 in protecting Christian religious sensibilities. The jurisprudence of human rights thus includes within itself a jurisdiction that once rested with church courts, was claimed by secular common law courts (at least in England) and now defines and demarcates human rights law.

In turning to *Leyla Şahin v Turkey*[10] we have a further definition of the jurisdiction of human rights over matters of belief. The case raises the question of the extent to which the court is willing to protect the religious sensibility

8 Ibid., para.31.
9 Supra n. 6, at para.47.
10 *Leyla Şahin v Turkey* (Application No. 44774/98), 29 June 2004.

of Moslems rather than Christians. We will see that the court can only assert the universal nature of human rights by deferring to the specific histories of member states.

X

The applicant in this case, Leyla Şahin was a Turkish national who was a medical student at Istanbul University. In 1998, the University prohibited the wearing of Islamic headscarves. Şahin considered it her religious duty to wear a headscarf and refused to comply with the ban.

The ECtHR argued that there had been no breach of Article 9. As the interference in religious freedom was both justified in principle and proportionate to the aims pursued, it was therefore 'necessary in a democratic society'.[11] The European Court of Human Rights relied on a ruling of the Turkish Constitutional Court which had held that freedom of dress was not absolute in higher educational institutions; furthermore, the court determined that authorising students to 'cover the neck and hair with a veil or headscarf for reasons of religious conviction'[12] in the universities was in breach of the Constitution. There were also rulings of the Supreme Administrative Court that had held wearing Islamic headscarves was incompatible with Constitutional principles. The ban on headscarves at the University had been in place long before Şahin had enrolled as a student.

The interference with Şahin's religious freedom was justified from a slightly different perspective. It achieved the legitimate aim of protecting both the rights and freedoms of others, and preserving public order. The values that were protected were those of 'secularism and equality'.[13] The Constitutional court had repeatedly held that secularism underlay such democratic values as freedom and equality; it also prevented the state from promoting any particular set of religious values, thus maintaining its neutrality. A ban on outward manifestations of faith protected individuals from 'pressure from extremist movements'[14] and also helped to further gender equality.

Şahin presents a real insight into the law of human rights. Whilst Turkey as a non-Christian state cannot be thought of in terms of the European Reformation, the case shows how the secularising logic of Attaturk that founded the Turkish Republic over-determines any other meaning to be given to religious freedom. Most specifically, the case shows the court linking this logic to the contemporary value of sexual equality. Whilst this does update the content of the structural function, it does so in a very specific manner.

11 Article 9, cited in *Leyla Şahin v Turkey*, ibid, para.70.

12 Ibid., para.35.

13 Ibid., para.38.

14 Ibid., para.109.

The structural function that founds Turkey and defines the modes of living, the symbols and rituals of secular power, is articulated in such a way as to deny any rival interpretation through Shari'a law. Claims as to justifiable interference in Şahin's right to wear a headscarf thus seem a rather flimsy excuse for a decision that is more properly understood as an uncompromising statement of both the form and content of the structural function.

However, it would be incorrect to conclude that human rights law will always simply acknowledge the power of the state to define the acceptable use of religious symbols. In *Hasan and Chaush v Bulgaria*[15] the European Court of Human Rights stated that:

> [The court] recalls that, but for very exceptional cases, the right to freedom of religion as guaranteed under the Convention excludes any discretion on the part of the State to determine whether religious beliefs or the means used to express such beliefs are legitimate.[16]

This suggests that the state itself cannot interfere with the sensibilities of believers. It would seem to be a contradiction not only of Şahin, but of our argument above that human rights law adopts the power of the magistrate to determine acceptable symbols of faith.[17] This would be to misunderstand another equally important element of Reformation: the understanding that it is necessary to accept deviations in Christian doctrine in the spirit of tolerance. As the Reformation plays itself out, the civil magistrate becomes willing to accept the legitimacy of religious expression. From our perspective, this represents the achievement of political stability of the secular order. Having redefined the terms of the social bond, religious expression is allowed a status within civic life provided that it is a private matter. At the level of structural function this produces two understandings of the state. In the case of France (a similar argument could be made in relation to Turkey) it leads to the uncompromising assertion of the secular appropriation of the dominant content of the structural function. In the United Kingdom it produces the compromise where a national church remains central to the symbology of the state, but is deprived of all forms of 'real' power.[18]

15 *Hasan and Chaush v Bulgaria* (Application No. 30985/96), 26 October 2000.

16 Ibid., para.78.

17 This is a claim about how the spirit of the Reformation influences the thinking of the ECHR not about historical processes of reformation in Bulgaria.

18 As the court comments in *Begum*, supra n. 1, at para.61: 'The United Kingdom is very different from Turkey. It is not a secular state, and although the Human Rights Act is now part of our law we have no written Constitution. In England and Wales express provision is made for religious education and worship in schools in Chapter VI of the 1998 Act. Schools are under a duty to secure that religious education in schools is given to pupils, and that each pupil should take part in an act of collective worship every day, unless withdrawn by their parent.'

The comments above are not meant to suggest that the settlement between secular and religious power is unproblematic. The later history of the Reformation (an epoch that we remain within) is still animated by the policing of the boundaries of symbols. However, as we have seen, the assumption of the dominant form and terms of the structural function by human rights means that in our times the negotiation of this particular legacy is in very particular terms. We will see below that this historical articulation of the content of the foundational reference can help us to understand the decision of the English courts in *Begum*.

XI

To what extent can the norms of Shari'a become a content of human rights law? Is the cost of this an acceptance of a certain idea of Reformation, where human rights speaks for religion?

Could it be said that in *Begum*, the 'state' has missed the opportunity to sanction within human rights law a female, Muslim subjectivity? We must now turn our attention to the case.

XII

Shabina Begum, a devout Muslim, was a pupil at a state-maintained school that required pupils to abide by its uniform policy. This policy had been developed in consultation with a number of local religious groups. It allowed female pupils to wear a variety of forms of dress including the *shalwar kameeze*. The *shalwar kameeze* was a form of dress of Pakistani origin, which included a headscarf. The majority of pupils at the school were Muslim, and the issue of school uniform had not arisen before the litigation occasioned in this case. Indeed, it was noted that the claimant had herself been happy to comply with the uniform rules when she first attended school. However, Begum argued that the *shalwar kameeze* was not an acceptable form of dress and she began to attend school wearing the *jilbab*. The *jilbab* provided covering for the wearer's arms and legs. Begum was suspended from school because she refused to stop wearing the *jilbab*. She applied for judicial review of the decision to exclude her, arguing that the school's policy was in breach of Article 9 and Protocol 1 of the Convention. Her case was dismissed and an appeal to the Court of Appeal ensued.

The court held that Begum's rights under Article 9 had been breached:

> Although her belief that the shalwar kameeze was not a religiously acceptable form of dress was shared by only a minority of Muslims in her community, it was sincerely held. It was not for school authorities to pick and choose between religious beliefs; every shade

> of religious belief, if genuinely held, was entitled to due consideration under Article 9.[19]

How does the court argue this particular articulation of the faith which may attach itself to objects and symbols? To return to Section II above, this reflects the particular articulation of the spirit of Reformation. Refracted through the language of human rights, the court is asserting the possibility of coordinating public and private symbols. This is done by reference to Article 9: the right to 'manifest' one's religion. Arguably, with this concern, we return to the scene of the manifestation of an inner sense of belief: how does one display the truth upon one's heart?[20]

The court returned to *Hasan and Chaush* on this point: '[The court] recalls that, but for very exceptional cases, the right to freedom of religion as guaranteed under the Convention excludes any discretion on the part of the State to determine whether religious beliefs or the means used to express such beliefs are legitimate.'[21] It would thus follow from *Hasan and Chaush* that the school's uniform rules were limiting Begum's right to manifest her faith.

The rhetoric is interesting because it gives us an insight into the dogmatic communication of human rights. This involves a transmission of messages that are predicated upon reference back to the fundamental truth of the foundational reference. The transmission of the text is the dissemination of a discourse that for the society in question has the status of truth. To engage with the text is to accept its hold, to submit to a pre-existent embodiment of the truth. The text itself bestows on the reader the authority to interpret and thus carry forward the function of reference. In other words, the truth

19 Supra n. 3, at para.94.

20 How is this expressed in the language of human rights? The 'correct starting point' was, first of all, to accept that the claimant had a valid right to 'manifest her belief'. The onus was then on the school to show that there was a legitimate aim that justified restricting the claimant's religious freedom. Indeed, it may have been possible to justify the refusal to allow the claimant to wear the *jilbab* with reference to a policy of inclusiveness which could not accommodate some forms of clothing. The Court of Appeal made reference to the European Court of Human Rights in *Kokkinakis v Greece*, which, as we have seen asserts that Article 9 is a foundation of 'democratic society'. The broader idea of religious freedom implies the 'freedom to manifest [one's] religion'. Article 9 also refers to the 'freedom to manifest one's religion or belief'. However, to what extent was it true to assert that the *shalwar kameeze* was not a correct form of Islamic dress for a mature woman? The evidence given suggested two schools of thought: the first, representing mainstream opinion among South Asian Muslims, was that the *shalwar kameeze*, if worn with a headscarf, was sufficient. The other school of thought, and a minority position amongst British Muslims, was that the *shalwar kameeze* was insufficient, and that the *jilbab* must be worn. This would suggest that the *jilbab* is a manifestation of religious faith, albeit a minority position within a faith.

21 Supra n. 3, at para.49.

of the text is largely a notion of the conditions of its own remembrance, perpetuation and continued dissemination.

What truth has the civil magistrate pronounced? It has affirmed and restated its own foundational truth: the human right to manifest one's religion. At the same time it asserts that it is the prince or the state that can limit human rights. Most precisely, the rights to faith can be limited in the name of human rights; in other words, the limits allowed by Article 9.[22]

XIII

The decision of the Court of Appeal was overturned by the House of Lords. This decision is interesting because it turns on a re-inscription of the values of the sacred and the secular. Lord Bingham's argument rests, in part, on ECHR cases[23] that show that Article 9 'does not protect every act motivated or inspired by a religion or belief'.[24] This reasoning re-asserts through the language of human rights, the power of the state to determine what is and is not an acceptable use of a religious symbol. Lord Bingham supports this argument with a reference to *Ahmad v United Kingdom*:[25]

> . . . the freedom of religion, as guaranteed by Article 9, is not absolute, but subject to the limitations set out in Article 9(2). Moreover, it may, as regards the modality of a particular religious manifestation, be influenced by the situation of the person claiming that freedom.[26]

Lord Bingham points out that the ECHR has not looked favourably on breach of Article 9 arguments. The case law suggests that broad limitations on Article 9 are permissible; in particular in instances when an individual has voluntarily accepted contractual terms that might limit their freedom

22 Begum won her appeal on an argument about the correct interpretation of Article 9, and the restrictions that can be placed on Article 9 rights. Can the restrictions be applied to Begum's choice of the *jilbab*? Evidence given to the court suggested that if some students wore *jilbab*, others viewed them as extremists. This would have a negative effect on school discipline, leading to 'divisiveness'. There were also fears expressed on health and safety grounds. However, in order to address these issues, a school would have to address the following questions: has the claimant a valid Article 9 right? Was interference with that right justified under Article 9? (In other words, did the interference have a legitimate aim?) The school did not ask these questions, nor approach the issue in this way: 'Nobody who considered the issues on its behalf started from the premise that the claimant had a right which is recognised by English law, and that the onus lay on the school to justify its interference with that right. Instead, it started from the premise that its uniform policy was there to be obeyed: if the claimant did not like it, she could go to a different school'. Supra n. 6, at para.76.

23 *Leyla Şahin v Turkey*, supra n. 10 and *Kalac v Turkey* (1997) 27 EHRR 552.

24 Supra n. 1, at para.32.

25 *Ahmad v United Kingdom* (1981) 4 EHRR 126.

26 Supra n. 1, at para.32.

to manifest their faith. Lord Bingham resolutely asserts the dominance of secular concerns over the public manifestation of one's inner desires.

XIV

Baroness Hale took a somewhat different approach to the issues of the case. Although she agreed with the majority that the appeal should be overturned, her reasoning is interesting as it directs our attention to the very issue of the articulation of the content of the foundational reference:

> If a woman freely chooses to adopt a way of life for herself, it is not for others, including other women who have chosen differently, to criticise or prevent her. Judge Tulkens, in *Sahin v Turkey* at 46, draws the analogy with freedom of speech. The European Court of Human Rights has never accepted that interference with the right of freedom of expression is justified by the fact that the ideas expressed may offend someone.[27]

To approach the issue of the veil through the figure of the autonomous female choosing the way of life she will lead, invokes the central concern of human rights. The subject is not the obedient believer in thrall to sacred mysteries, or the unquestioning follower of the rules of traditional culture. Rather, it is the reasoning individual who willingly adopts a symbol as a form of self-expression. The analogy with freedom of speech is thus quite apposite. Speech, in this instance, is literally a saying of the self: a figure of the self-creating subject who chooses a mode of dress, a manifestation of faith that appropriates what would otherwise be patriarchal symbols; it is a new coordination of self and symbol.

Note that Baroness Hale approaches the issue from an explicitly feminist perspective. This is a peculiar moment. Might it be the point at which a certain idea of Islam might correspond with the imago of human rights? Might this be a moment that, if sustained, would represent a redefinition of the foundational reference's content? It is hard to say. At the very least, we could suggest that *Begum* cannot be understood as one law coming up against another. Reading Baroness Hale's argument brings us to a realisation that the case opened the possibility that a particular conjunction of sacred law and common law could be worked out.

What sense does this make?

XV

In February 2008, the Archbishop of Canterbury, Dr Rowan Williams, gave the foundation lecture at the Royal Courts of Justice.[28] In his address, Dr

27 Ibid., at para.34.

28 At www.archbishopofcanterbury.org/1575.

Williams engaged with the status of Shari'a law in the United Kingdom. We will read his speech as an attempt to apply the logic of Reformation in a sensitive way to Shari'a law in the United Kingdom.

Shari'a has been subject to a certain degree of misrepresentation at the hands of self-appointed spokesmen for western 'liberal' values. Their proletysing has led to a simplistic idea of a 'clash of civilisations' where the enlightened values of human rights are opposed to a strict pre-medieval social code based on violent punishment and profound social conservatism. Even if our arguments about the structural equivalence of human rights law and Shari'a are ignored, this view of benighted Islamic law and enlightened common law is unsustainable. Whilst Shari'a law has been used by extremist movements as exemplary of their 'primitivist' understanding of Islam, traditions of Islamic jurisprudence are far too complex and sophisticated to be reduced to such caricatures.

In arguing that Shari'a can be understood as a complex practice of interpretation, Dr Williams' ideas come close to our understanding of the articulation of the foundational reference. Rather than a 'monolithic' set of enactments or a 'single code', the Shari'a is a way in which the Koran and other sacred texts have been read so as to 'actualise' the principles of Islam in 'human history'.[29] Indeed, the major traditions of Islam are identified with different ways in which the Shari'a can be interpreted. These traditions are now established, and have such historical authority that there can be no further attempts to open new ways of interpreting the sacred texts. However, there are also a 'good many voices' arguing that new interpretations can be forged by 'reasoning from first principles' rather than entirely remaining within the historical traditions.[30] It is from this position that it might be possible to outline a 'just and constructive relationship between Islamic law and the statutory law of the United Kingdom'.[31] It is possible, in other words, to re-articulate the content of the foundational reference, even though conventional approaches to the sacred texts would hold that there is no need for further interpretation.

Where does this argument lead? Dr Williams refers to the need to think about whether or not there could be 'something like a delegation of certain legal functions to the religious courts of a community'[32] – a question not just of Shari'a, but of other bodies of religious law. The problem with such an enhanced presence for a religious court might be that it strengthens the hand of those who speak for the 'retrograde'[33] aspects of faith traditions. Women in particular tend to be disadvantaged by elements of family law

29 Ibid., no page numbers.
30 Ibid.
31 Ibid.
32 Ibid.
33 Ibid.

concerning divorce settlements and inheritance. The fundamental response to these concerns is simple:

> [i]f any kind of plural jurisdiction is recognised, it would presumably have to be under the rubric that no supplementary' jurisdiction could have the power to deny access to the rights granted to other citizens or to punish its members for claiming those rights.[34]

In building this argument, the Archbishop returns to the logic of Reformation. The law of the secular state serves to licence the acceptable forms of social communication, and sees itself as the dominant way in which public discourse is constituted. However, once it is accepted that religious opinions have to be taken seriously, it raises the question of plural jurisdictions. Is Dr Williams suggesting that, in certain circumstances, the common law might have to give way to a court with jurisdiction over religious matters? This important concern takes us to one of the most interesting parts of the lecture: should we question the fundamental ideas of universal rights, and the principle that all come before the law on equal terms?

To the extent that European cultures can be traced back to the Enlightenment revolt against Church authorities that could not justify their claims to legitimacy through reasoned argument, any return to special privileges for faith is to go against the fundamental movement of western culture. This does not mean, however, that the logic of Reformation is not incompatible with courts that remain bound by human rights having some form of jurisdiction over matters of faith. Picking up on Dr Williams' point about the re-interpretations of the Shari'a, might this not lead to the creation of those institutional sites where the promulgation of a 'reformed' set of religious laws might take place?

XVI

This chapter has argued that the foundational reference brings together both secular human rights law and religious law. This argument requires an immediate distinction between the structural function and the content of this fundamental anthropological operation. The structural function runs through diverse bodies of law. Thus, whether we are concerned with the law of the Christian Church, Shari'a law or human rights law, we have to recognise that these bodies of law serve to determine the symbols and practices that will define forms of being. This does not mean that the content of these bodies of law is the same or even similar. There are many different ways in which life can be given form. The pressing task is to determine the precise content of a Shari'a law that is somehow compatible with human rights. However,

34 Ibid.

this requires us to recognise that human rights are unthinkable outside of the logic of Reformation. This suggests that notions of autonomy and personal authenticity will be the imagos that animate any fusion of rights and Shari'a. Far from a prohibition on the wearing of headscarves, such a hybrid body of law would seek to re-negotiate the tensions between the sacred and the secular.

The terms of this important task have not been understood properly by either the liberal or the multicultural commentators. The media response to Dr Williams' speech also suggests that there has been a wider failure to mobilise the intellectual resources necessary for a proper consideration of the issues raised by re-assertions of religious identity. It is indeed necessary to tread a careful line between criticisms of human rights and a resistance to monolithic ideas of Islam. If the resources for such a thinking can be found, they come from within the depths of our own histories and the ambiguities of the symbols we use to speak of ourselves.

References

Goodrich, P. (1995) *Oedipus Lex*, Berkeley: University of California Press.

Goodrich, P. (ed.) (1997) *Law and the Unconscious: A Legendre Reader*, Basingstoke: Macmillan.

Kymlicka, W. (1989) *Liberalism, Community, and Culture*, Oxford: Oxford University Press.

McGoldrick, D. (2006) *Human Rights and Religion – The Islamic Headscarf Debate in Europe*, Oxford: Hart.

Parekh, B. (2006) *Rethinking Multiculturalism*, Basingstoke: Palgrave Macmillan.

Williams, R. (2008) Address to Royal Courts of Justice. At www.archbishopofcanterbury.org/1575

Cases

Ahmad v United Kingdom (1981) 4 EHRR 126.

Hasan and Chaush v Bulgaria (Application No. 30985/96), 26 October 2000.

Kalac v Turkey (1997) 27 EHRR 552.

Kokkinakis v Greece (Application No. 260-A) Ser. A. (1994); 17 EHRR 397.

Leyla Şahin v Turkey (Application No. 44774/98), 29 June 2004.

Otto-Preminger-Institut v Austria (13470/87) [1994] ECHR 26 (20 September 1994).

R. (On the Application of SB) v Headteacher and Governors of Denbigh High School [2005] EWCA Civ 199, at para.32.

R. (On the Application of SB) v Headteacher and Governors of Denbigh High School [2006] UKHL 15.

Chapter 4

The gift of ambiguity

Strategising beyond the either/or of secularism and religion in Islamic divorce law

*Hassan El Menyawi**

> Truth is such a precious quantity, it should be used sparingly.
>
> Mark Twain

> The simulacrum is never that which conceals the truth – it is the truth which conceals that there is none.
> The simulacrum is true.
>
> *Ecclesiastes* (Baudrillard 1994: 1)

I. Introduction and background

This article attempts to demonstrate that women's rights have been sacrificed throughout the twentieth century in the context of Egyptian family law. In the nineteenth and early twentieth centuries, secular liberal male elites envisioned a secular legal system with European legal transplants and a Civil Code modelled on the French system. Ultimately, to achieve this, the secular, liberal elites had to keep the Islamic character of family law intact in exchange for making the rest of the legal system largely secular. This has had significant costs for women's rights, including women being unable to exercise no-fault divorce.[1] After providing a brief background on Egyptian

* New York University, hem251@nyu.edu. I would like to thank Craig Calhoun (NYU), Judith Stacey (NYU), Juan Amaya Castro, Shannon Gilreath and Ben Francisco for the many conversations, which deepened and enriched my thinking on this topic. Thanks to the editors Adam Geary and Marinos Diamantides for their comments and editorial suggestions on earlier drafts. A version of this paper was presented and discussed at Wake Forest Law School, November 2009 during the Distinguished Lecture Series. My thanks to the participants at Wake Forest Law School for their valuable comments and responses.

1 See El Alami and Hinchcliffe (1996: 3) describing how, in the Muslim world, marriages are most commonly dissolved by the husband exercising his right of *talaq* (divorce). Islamic law grants the husband the power to unilaterally terminate the marriage rendering it analogous to no-fault divorce in contemporary Western family law systems. However, in Islamic law, only the husband is eligible to take this course of action. The husband is not required to demonstrate cause and does not require any recourse before a court of law.

family law, the article examines the idea of sacrifice as contemplated by Jacques Derrida in his *Gift of Death* (Derrida 1995), which explores the biblical story of Abraham's sacrifice of his son, Isaac. Similar to Abraham's sacrifice of Isaac, the liberal elite have sacrificed women's rights as part of a project of largely – not totally – secularising the legal system. This sacrifice is reiterated again and again throughout the late nineteenth and twentieth centuries: legislative reforms and judicial decisions can be characterised as perpetually compromising – 'splitting the difference' – between the demands of feminists and those of the religious intelligentsia. By splitting the difference between feminist and Islamic arguments, the liberal elites have produced an either/or dichotomy that impels a choice between secularism and religion.[2]

Drawing on Giorgio Agamben (1998), the article contemplates women as abandoned by the liberal elites. Women have been in a state of 'exceptional secularism', a limbo in which they have opportunities to establish feminist legal reforms yet never achieve a fully fledged liberal family law. The question is what should be done? The strategy of relying on liberal male elites to liberalise family law has been less than effective, particularly when considering the past century of family law jurisprudence. Making reference to Jean Baudrillard's idea of simulacra (Baudrillard 1994: 3), the article contemplates new strategic possibilities in which normatively powerful religious language is deployed to achieve substantive liberal effects. To demonstrate this, the example of *khul'* reform in Law No. 1 of the year 2000 in Egypt is explored. This statutory reform by the Egyptian state allows a wife to elect to divorce without her husband's permission (and without the mediation of the courts) if she surrenders her financial rights over family property.

The ultimate aim of this article is to determine possible strategies to advance feminist goals in Islamic family legal systems across the Middle East. While the paper takes up the example of Egyptian family law, many family legal systems in the Middle East are similar in that they have adopted a largely secular legal system, but have preserved the religious character of family law. In order to examine new strategies for the secularisation of family law, the article begins with an overview of the legal background. It then turns to explore Derrida's notion of sacrifice and Agamben's idea of abandonment. By means of a conclusion, the article draws on Baudrillard's idea of hyperreal and simulacra to advance a strategic approach that furthers liberal, secular reforms in family law without having to compromise with the religious intelligentsia.

2 This either/or choice is analogical to the manner in which Soren Kierkegaard examines the choices individuals must make between living within an aesthetic sphere or the ethical sphere in his text, *Either/Or*. See Kierkegaard (1971, 1843). See Anderson (1968: 209, 217–24).

II. Background: the example of Egyptian family law

The history of Egypt is marked by a contestation between two emergent identity groups at the turn of the century: the religious intelligentsia and liberal, secular elites. The liberal intelligentsia includes enlightened liberal *ulema* (religious scholars) and liberal *muftis* (who are licensed to deliver *fatwas*), liberal judges and jurists, and the secular nationalist elites who govern through the legislature and judiciary. (While the *ulema* and *muftis* are, of course, religious, the more liberal among them have generally been supportive of the overall secularisation of the legal system, and thus are included in this category.) The religious intelligentsia includes conservative *ulema* (religious scholars) and *muftis*, as well as the religious right more generally, which includes the leadership of political parties such as the Muslim Brotherhood. The secular elites seek to advance progressive reforms that are not necessarily loyal to a textual Islamic conception as approved by the religious intelligentsia, but that are instead liberated from the requirement for family law reforms to be articulated in religious terms (Holyoake 1896: 51).[3]

Egyptian secular liberals have been under attack for the past century by the religious intelligentsia. This antagonism can be traced through the recesses of Egyptian law; it is particularly evident in family law, but also visible in the recent implementation of criminal law. It is primarily in family law where feminists and secular elites battle conservative Islamic scholars – each with a particularised 'imaginary' of the Egyptian nation, each increasingly viewing the other as their polar opposite – the ultimate adversary of their would-be social utopia.[4]

Let us briefly recount the historical narrative of how family law became such a vital battleground. Beginning at the end of the nineteenth century and continuing throughout the early twentieth century, Egypt's Islamic legal rules were dissolved in favour of secular laws transplanted from Europe.[5]

3 The current article defines secularism in a similar manner to the inventor of the term, George Holyoake. Holyoake considered secularism to be a realm of thought or practice separate from that of religion. In other words, secularism (or secularist thought) is not dependent on religious inspiration, thought or practice. While Holyoake seems to suggest that free thought requires the elimination of religious discourses and approaches, in the context of this article, secularism is defined – in slightly different terms – as not *necessitating* religious discourses and approaches (as opposed to entailing the elimination of religious discourses and approaches). The Egyptian secular elites in fact occasionally use religious legal discourses, but begin from the premise that reforms do not necessarily require a religious justification to be legitimate. The secular elites are open to considering legal approaches that are not grounded in *shari'a* (or Islamic law) or that have been adopted in non-Muslim countries. The secular elites' legal approach is in stark contrast to the religious intelligentsia who seek to justify their actions and practices exclusively through Islamic (religious) texts.

4 See Anderson (1983: 6) describing the nation as 'an imagined political community'.

5 See Anderson (1968: 209, 217–24) detailing the legal changes resulting from European legal transplants in the latter half of the nineteenth century.

However, one legal area was kept intact, wholly in its Islamic form: family law.[6] When the first Civil Code was adopted in post-colonial Egypt in 1949, its drafters deliberately excluded family law.

In the late nineteenth and early twentieth centuries, Egyptian elites sought to modernise the nation, with increased secularisation as one of their primary goals. This project of modernisation occurred over an expanded period of time but began to lose momentum (though never came to a complete halt) by the middle of the twentieth century. Determined to change most areas of law, Egyptian liberal elites replaced Islamic laws with imported European legal transplants. However, these same liberal elites kept the 'religious' or 'Islamic' character of family law rules intact, hoping this would appease the religious intelligentsia. While it may have appeased them temporarily, it led to the eventual construction of family law as the last bastion of Islamic law surrounded by a sea of 'impure godless legal secularity'. It served as a reminder that Islamic law was *not* used in the rest of the legal system, tantalising the religious intelligentsia with the possibility of full rule by Islamic law. This led them to a demand for further reforms to 'Islamicise' the law and, most of all, for feminists to 'lay their reformist hands off' family law.[7] In fact, feminists have been viewed by the religious intelligentsia as traitors and have been constructed as allies of the 'colonial West' because of their calls for reform. But, rather than appeasing the religious intelligentsia as was the intention of the secular elites, they have instead sustained a paroxysm of furious debate about the imagining of the status and role of women in Egypt and, correspondingly, a debate about how the Egyptian state can be imagined. This sustained crescendo has brought feminists, secular elites, and the religious intelligentsia, into a single story – with the feminists seeking to wholly liberalise family law, the religious intelligentsia seeking to preserve the Islamic character of family law, and the liberal elites attempting to split the difference between the demands of feminists and those of the religious intelligentsia. Since the middle of the twentieth century, this game of splitting the difference between theories has made family legal reforms slow, difficult and limited.

The secular elites' strategy of splitting the difference is reflected in both legislative reforms by legislators and in judicial decision-making by judges. In the case of legislative reforms, consider Law No. 100 in 1985. Law No. 100 reformed family law by including a bundle of new rights for women. Arguably, the most significant right was that of a woman to divorce

6 See Crecelius (1974: 67) stating that 'the scope of the shari'ah [Islamic law] was reduced to personal status law (marriage, divorce, inheritance, etc. . . .)' (1974: 75, 79). During the process of secularisation, family law 'involved the *ulema* in constant political conflict with their modernizing government' (1974: 83–4).

7 See Najjar (1988: 319, 323–25) providing a description of how religious, conservative opposition of family law reforms in the twentieth century viewed themselves as defending Islam from the onslaught of Western secularism and feminism.

her husband on the grounds of harm. While significant, these new rights do not grant women access to no-fault divorce. Feminists had aggressively agitated for no-fault divorce, but harm-based divorces were seen by secular elites in the nation's legislative body – the Egyptian National Assembly – as the best compromise to appease the religious intelligentsia. The legislators split the difference by allowing women access to harm-based divorces, but without permitting no-fault divorces. The strategy of splitting the difference has also been reflected in judicial decision-making. Consider the 1994 Supreme Constitutional Court family law decision that found that a wife is entitled to divorce if her husband marries another woman. In this case, judges responded to feminists' concerns by providing a woman the right to divorce in the event that her husband marries another. However, the decision fell short of fulfilling the liberal feminists' desire for judges to expunge polygamy from family law. The judges split the difference. They allowed a wife to divorce her husband if he marries another woman, but they did not strike out what members of the religious intelligentsia consider a Muslim male's God-given right to polygamy.

Splitting the difference has resulted in the emergence of a paradox: the secularisation of Egyptian family law preserves Islamic principles. These paradoxes can be approached through Jacques Derrida's aporias; it appears that the very possibility of secularism is the condition of its impossibility.[8] To put this slightly differently, secularism is legitimated through the paradoxical violation of the very ideas and principles of liberty and equality (between spouses) that it allegedly seeks to advance. In other words, to secularise, one must not secularise. Feminist reformist demands and women's rights (applicable within the context of family law) have been 'trumped' in favour of secularising the remainder of the Egyptian legal system (in a way that is historically parallel to many Middle Eastern states). We might want to argue that women have been made the 'object'[9] of sacrifice for secularism's (virtual) adoption. At the same time, they have also become constructed as the site of national imagination – the site of discursive contestation about the state of the nation, its vision, goals and ideals. Both the male liberal, secular elites and the religious intelligentsia, have sought to speak on behalf of the 'subaltern' (Spivak 1994). We could say that women have been abandoned, expelled from secularism, while simultaneously held within it, never able to achieve complete 'emancipation' in the ways contemplated by feminists.

By splitting the difference between feminist and Islamic arguments, the liberal elites have produced a strict either/or dichotomy between secularism

8 See Derrida (1994: 12) saying that 'the impossible that seems to give itself to be thought here: these conditions of possibility of the gift (that some "one" gives some "thing" to some "one other") designates simultaneously the conditions of the impossibility of the gift'.

9 See De Beauvoir (1989: xxxv) stating that women '. . . liv[e] . . . in a world where men compel her to assume the status of the Other. They propose to stabilize her as object . . .'.

and religion, reinforcing the construction of two groups – the liberal feminists advancing women's rights, and the religious intelligentsia advancing Islamic law. Once created, the dichotomy is difficult to escape: every advantage for one group is a loss for the other. The prospect of a so-called win-win scenario is impossible. Instead, an eternal oscillation between feminists and religious elites defines the legal system.[10] For the liberal, secular elite this perpetual back-and-forth, this ongoing oscillation is a stabilising force in Egyptian law. By focusing the attention of the religious intelligentsia on one single area of law, their reformist gaze is not drawn to the rest of the legal system, in turn preserving the overall secularity of the legal system. There are many legal cases in family law that demonstrate how the oscillation between feminist and religious demands produce bounded spaces in which feminists cannot simply liberalise the entirety of family law in a single instance.

In 1980, the Egyptian legislature amended Article 2 of the Egyptian Constitution in response to a vocal call by the religious intelligentsia. The amendment altered the wording from the milder 'the principles of Islamic *shari'a* are a principal source of legislation' (of the 1971 constitution) to the more aggressive and all-encompassing 'the principles of Islamic *shari'a* are *the* principal source of legislation' (emphasis added).[11] This has led to a flurry of legal cases in which the religious intelligentsia challenged what they saw as secular legislation that violated the *shari'a*. To demonstrate how the Supreme Constitutional Court (SCC) navigated their decisions by splitting the difference, three examples are explored.

In a 1997 legal decision, the SCC was asked to determine the constitutionality of Article 11 of the 1929 law of the family that gives the judge the capacity to grant a woman a divorce in the event that it is impossible for the spouses to reconcile their differences. The court concurred with the plaintiff that the Qur'an gives a husband an absolute right to divorce his wife[12] and argued that while the arbitrators should attempt to reconcile the spouses, the law did not specify what subsequent actions should be taken if

10 See Vattimo (1992: 10) describing an oscillation between belonging and disorientation.

11 See Foblets and Dupret (1999: 63). The authors describe the decision of a 1985 constitutional case, explaining that the Supreme Constitutional Court interpreted the applicability of Article 2 to extend to legislation that follows the article's date of coming into force, which is 22 May 1980. Legislation that pre-dates Article 2 is not subject to its requirement, but legislation enacted after the 22 May 1980 date must conform to the principles of Islamic law. See El-Morr (1997: 8); also see Balz (1999: 231, 234–5).

12 Case No. 82, Judicial Year 17, 1997, at 5: 'Divorce (*talaq*) has been permitted by God who gave the power to man because he is wiser and more rational . . .', translation by author. 'When there is discord between husband and wife, arbitrate between them based on the commands of God', 'And when it is feared that discord will erupt between husband and wife, send an arbitrator from his family and also one from hers; if they seek reconciliation, God will ease tensions between them. . . .', citing verse 4:34 of the Qur'an, found in the chapter (*sura*) titled Women (*Al-Nisa*) Case No. 82, Judicial Year 17, 1997, at 6 (translation by author).

they fail to achieve a reconciliation.[13] The court concluded that Article 11 was not unconstitutional, since it merely grants the arbitrators the power to make a recommendation of divorce to the judge.[14] By making this argument, the court forestalled the possibility for no-fault divorce in Egyptian family law. The court seems both to advance women's rights and yet to block retrospectively significant liberal reforms by its interpretation of Islamic law.

In this case, as in most cases, there are two countervailing positions – a religious one and a feminist one. The court appears to take the middle ground between them. The religious position is that polygamy is the absolute right of any man, and the feminist position is that polygamy should be prohibited. The court splits the difference by allowing women a way to leave a marriage through a restricted ground of divorce, but also upholds the right of men to engage in polygamy.

In a 1996 case, the SCC was asked to determine whether the Minister of Education had the right to prohibit the wearing of the veil or headscarf (*niqab* or *hijab*) in primary and secondary schools.[15] The Minister of Education issued an executive order that non-university female students were to remove their headscarves. This provoked such a fury of controversy from religious fundamentalists that liberal elites in government amended the language of its order, requiring instead that schoolgirls who personally elect to wear the headscarf must obtain permission from their parents. Even though the government had compromised by requiring parental permission, the religious intelligentsia were relentless and challenged the executive order in the highest court of the land.[16] In deciding the case, the liberal justices of the SCC directly interpreted verses in the Qur'an that relate to the issue of the headscarf. They ruled that women are required to cover some parts of their bodies but that there was no conclusive evidence to suggest that women were required to cover their hair or face.[17] After rigorous exploration of the verses and *hadith*

13 See Case No. 82, Judicial Year 17, 1997, translation by author. Jurists have struggled to determine who has the power to enforce divorce in the event that the discord between spouses is irreconcilable. Some jurists have argued that in the event of irreconcilable tensions, the arbitrators have the power to divorce the wife from her husband. But other jurists have argued that the jurisdiction of arbitrators remain limited to negotiating and reconciling the interests of the spouses in the pursuit of the goal of terminating the discord between them.

14 The judge grants a divorce to the wife in the place of – on behalf of – the husband.

15 Case No. 8, Judicial Year 17, 1996. For a discussion of this case, see Abu Odeh (2004: 1043, 1140).

16 See Benner Lombardi (1998: 81–108): 'Under the new edict, schoolgirls could wear the *hijab* . . . Plaintiffs, however, continued to fight the decrees in court. . . .'.

17 See Benner Lombardi (1998: 81–108): 'The author reports that "the SCC first identified two passages of the *Quran* which require women to cover up those parts of their body that are sexually appealing to men, but it found none that specifically required women to cover their hair or their faces".'

(sayings and actions of the Prophet), the court explained that the binding principle determining what a woman should wear is 'modesty'. The court ruled that a woman's modesty can be preserved without having to wear a headscarf. The SCC upheld the Minister of Education's executive order, requiring non-university female students wishing to wear the headscarf to obtain permission of their parents. Again, the court predictably split the difference, offering a compromise between religious and feminist positions. The court affirmed that women's dress could be regulated and that it is limited by the principle of 'modesty', but it did not consider the headscarf as a requirement of modesty.

The third case, decided in 1994, concerns a law that entitled a wife to obtain a divorce in the event that her husband marries another woman.[18] The plaintiff argued that allowing a woman the right to obtain a divorce without the consent of her husband violates the explicit language of the Qur'an that a man can marry up to four wives.[19] The argument was that the law violated a man's right to engage in polygamy. In its ruling, the court explained that the law did not violate the explicit dictates of the Qur'an. The Justices concurred with the plaintiff that men have an 'absolute right'[20] to marry up to four wives.[21] However, while insisting that men had a right to marry up to four women, they explained that a woman who obtained a divorce when her husband married another woman is merely a 'restriction of the right and not a cause of it'.[22] Splitting the difference between feminists and the religious intelligentsia, the court crafts a middle-ground position between the argument that divorce is the sole right of the husband and not of the wife, and the feminist position that asserts an equal right to (no fault) divorce: the court allowed a judge to use his authority to end a bad marriage on behalf of the wife, while simultaneously upholding the right of a man to marry up to four wives.

To bring an end to these judicial compromises, feminists have been seeking novel strategies. A new strategy that is gaining ascendancy is premised on the idea that instead of sacrificing liberal feminism to save the preponderance

18 Case No. 35, Year 9, 1994. See El Alami and Hinchcliffe (1996: 58) citing Article 11 of Law No. 25 of 1929, as amended by Law No. 100 of 1985: '[a] wife whose husband takes a second wife may petition for divorce from him if she is affected by some material or moral harm of a kind which would make it impossible for a couple such as them to continue living together, even if she has not stipulated in the contract that he should not take further wives'.

19 See Case No. 35, Year 9, 1994, at 3: 'The plaintiff argues that the provision in contention violates the text of the Qur'an that authorizes polygamy.' (translation by author).

20 Sometimes the Supreme Constitutional Court describes this 'absolute right' as a 'license'.

21 Case No. 35, Year 9, 1994, at 3.

22 Case No. 35, Year 9, 1994, at 8: 'Since polygamy is based in fairness – which is a restriction of the right and not a cause of it – no harm or injustice will inflict the wife when her husband marries another' (translation by author).

of secular law, women's rights may be reconciled with Islamic law.[23] The goal of this strategy is to Islamicise family law, but in a decidedly liberal fashion. This alliance, however, possesses significant potential costs. Fundamentally, the new alliance replaces one sacrifice for another. Before, liberal feminism was sacrificed to preserve legal secularism, and now – according to this new strategic line of thinking – secularism would be sacrificed for liberal feminism. Let us develop these points.

The new feminist strategy of reconciliation certainly has compelling elements. Since there is little Islamic law in contemporary Egyptian law, the Islamic character of family law is constantly being discursively guarded by religious groups. Any time feminists demand reforms, they are criticised and vociferously attacked by the religious intelligentsia in the Egyptian media and in the mosques. To stifle such criticisms, feminists have begun to deploy Islamic texts to demonstrate exegetically that their proposed reforms are reconcilable with Islamic legal tenets. The importance of this strategic shift is that it attempts to evade the limited dichotomous space that is marked by ideational scarcity and a lack of creativity. So, feminists are now attempting to ally themselves with the religious intelligentsia in the hope of persuading them that their liberal reforms are consistent with the tenets of Islamic law (*shari'a*). In other words, this new strategy advocates the establishment of a state based on the *shari'a* in the hope that it will effectively achieve the goals of secular, liberal feminists.

However, there are real dangers inherent in an alliance with the religious intelligentsia. While the normative power of Islamic law is undeniably powerful, it results in a new sacrifice into which liberal, secular discourses – which are increasingly influential among the Egyptian public – cannot be drawn to advance women's rights. Furthermore, such Islamic laws can begin as liberal, and later be transformed into more conservative forms, depending on what is seen as 'Islamic'. Liberal feminists may be promised liberal effects in return for an alliance to Islamicise Egyptian law, but there is no guarantee that the law will not gradually (or even suddenly) be interpreted in conservative ways. There is also the risk that conservative religious forces will become strong enough to go beyond the present compromises of the courts – with detrimental results for the limited gains made so far by feminists and secularising modernists.

III. The sacrifice of women's rights

One way of exploring the sacrifice of women's rights in the context of family law, is to make reference to the story of Abraham – as described by Derrida.

23 See An Na'im (1990) building a liberal (as opposed to conservative) interpretive methodology applicable to Islamic law.

In the *Gift of Death*, Derrida analyses notions of sacrifice and responsibility. In the Genesis story, God demands that Abraham commit 'that most cruel, impossible, and untenable gesture: to offer his son Isaac as a sacrifice' (Derrida 1995: 5–6). God tells Abraham: 'Take your son, your only son Isaac, whom you love, and go the land of Moriah, and offer him there as a burnt offering' (Genesis 22:2 Revised Standard Version).

This sacrifice that God demands is not explained. Instead, the sacrifice is made in silence, in solitude and in total absence of knowledge. Furthermore, this sacrifice is absolute because it entails the loss of someone who is 'unique in terms of its being unique, irreplaceable, and most precious' (Derrida 1995: 58). In the case of Abraham, the sacrifice is of 'what is one's own or proper, of the private, of the love and affection of one's kin' (Derrida 1995: 95). Abraham must sacrifice the person that he is most intimate with – his son – and this is why the sacrifice can be called the 'gift of death'. Ultimately, when Abraham puts the knife to his son's throat, it is 'the moment when Abraham gives the sign of absolute sacrifice, namely, by putting to death or giving death to his own, putting to death his absolute love for what is dearest, the only son' (Derrida 1995: 95).

To carry out this sacrifice, Abraham informs neither his son, Isaac, nor his spouse, Sarah and in so doing, he violates the bond and commitment to them, establishing 'a sort of rupture of marriage, an infidelity to Sarah, to whom Abraham says not a word at the moment of taking the life of his son, their son' (Derrida 2003). Derrida identifies Abraham's singularity and solitude in his decision-making to sacrifice his son as central in his conception of responsibility. Responsibility 'consists in always being alone, entrenched in one's own singularity at the moment of decision' (Derrida 1995: 60).

Finally, the angel of God tells Abraham, 'lay not thine hand upon the lad, neither do thou anything unto him: for now I know that thou fearest God, seeing thou hast not withheld thy son, thine only son, from me' (Genesis 22:12 Revised Standard Version). 'I see that you have understood what absolute duty means, namely, how to respond to the absolute other, to his call, request, or command' (Derrida 1995: 72). Ultimately, the story of Abraham enacts an aporia: to act responsibly one must be irresponsible:

> Absolute duty means that one behaves in an irresponsible manner (by means of treachery and betrayal), while still recognizing, confirming, and reaffirming the very thing one sacrifices, namely, the order of human ethics and responsibility.
>
> (Derrida 1995: 67)

Abraham's decision is absolutely responsible in the sense that it is a decision made 'before the absolute other' (Derrida 1995: 77). It is also simultaneously and paradoxically irresponsible as it is not guided by reason, by ethics, human rights or the rule of law. One cannot do both: be responsible before the absolute other and be responsible 'at the same time before the other and before others, before the others of the other' (Derrida 1995: 77). This paradoxical contradiction occurs in the moment of decision-making 'for every man and every woman' (Derrida 1995: 78).

What can this allegory of responsibility tell us about the problems we have been studying? The condition for the possibility of Abraham's responsibility is also the condition for its impossibility. He cannot be responsible without being irresponsible, and his irresponsibility is itself the basis of his absolute responsibility. This is also true of the male liberal, secular elite that determined that family law must remain Islamic in order to establish a largely secular legal system in Egypt: the condition of the possibility of secularism is also the condition of its impossibility. The liberal, secular elite cannot be true to the secular principles of autonomy, equality and mutual exchange in the context of family law in order to retain the continuity of a secular system.

Of particular relevance to the liberal, secular elites is the assumption that secular liberal principles ought to apply throughout the legal system writ large. However, instead of carrying this out, liberal scholars such as Sanhuri (see Hill 1988: 148–49), who drafted the first Egyptian Civil Code, are known to betray those principles as part of the response to the sacrificial demand of the 'absolute other' – in this case, the absolute other paradoxically being 'Secularism'. Sacrificial responsibility involves a singular relationship with an unknown other. In the Christian tradition this other is named God but, in the case of Egyptian family law, we might name this other 'the Secular'. This responsibility can be acted upon only in silence, in solitude and in the absence of knowledge. This responsibility was indeed acted on without the consent or advice of feminists or women. It was instead determined by male secular elites who felt it best to keep the character of family law Islamic. Their judgement was that it was necessary for the overall advancement of the nation to sacrifice family law, and with it – women – who sought greater autonomy and equality in family law. Just as Abraham violated the bond of commitment and fidelity to Isaac and Sarah, the liberal elite has done the same with their feminist allies. It would not be stretching this point to suggest that – in the terms of our allegory of responsibility – this represents the sacrifice of a feminism that is part of the same political family as liberalism.

There are other ramifications worth pursuing. The secular elites appear 'sad and dangerous' (Koskenniemi 1999: 488, 510), ready to violate – to sacrifice – the very values they espouse publicly and collectively: autonomy, consent, gender equality, liberty and mutual exchange. It is as if they are bound up in an aporia – involving at once a public espousal of obligations to women's rights, and a secret relationship to the singular other of 'Secularism', which legitimates the betrayal of those obligations and underpins the jurisprudence of family law, as conceived and implemented by liberal, secular elites throughout the twentieth century and onwards. For the liberal elite to be responsible, they must be irresponsible towards women and feminist allies, sacrificing women's rights on the altar of secularism.

IV. The abandonment of women

While the Derridean allegory of responsibility might describe the secular elites' strategy to secularise the legal system, it may be seen to pay too much regard to a paradigm where we have to think in terms of the absolute other. As suggested above, whilst we can make these moves, it might be more useful to look to an alternative way of thinking about sacrifice. Consider Giorgio Agamben's idea of *homo sacer* that combines formal law with biopolitics.[24] For Agamben, the interpretation of those destroyed or abandoned by the state within a sacrificial doctrine or through 'the prestige of the mystical' (Agamben 1999: 26–33) originating from the Bible, is unwarranted. Agamben argues that the price individuals pay for inclusion in the state should be understood in a more secular manner – through the concept of abandonment rather than the more religious notion of sacrifice. Roman law contained a figure known as the *homo sacer* who is abandoned by the sovereign power. *Homo sacer* is the sacred man 'who *may be killed and yet not sacrificed*' (Agamben 1998: 8). Agamben describes the *homo sacer* as follows:

> The sacred man is the one whom the people have judged on account of a crime. It is not permitted to sacrifice this man, yet he who kills him will not be condemned for homicide; in the first tribunitian law, in fact, it is noted that 'if someone kills the one who is sacred according to the plebiscite, it will not be considered homicide.' This is why it is customary for a bad or impure man to be called sacred.
>
> (Agamben 1998: 71)

If someone was a *homo sacer*, Roman law did not apply. Although law did not formally apply, the *homo sacer* was defined in a manner that included him in the juridical order solely through his exclusion. The *homo sacer* was both excluded from the law, while also included by the law that excluded him. We could apply this logic to the struggles over Egyptian family law. Women can be seen as *homo sacers* of secularism. By rendering family law external to secularism as a means to retain the largely secular character of the state's laws, women are cast as within (or internal to) secularism to the extent that they are external to it. Their inclusion in secularism is defined by their exclusion.

24 For Agamben's argument that the biopolitical paradigm of the Nazi concentration camp should *not* be interpreted within a biblical doctrine of sacrifice, see Agamben (1999: 26–33).

The *homo sacer* echoes Franz Kafka's short parable, 'Before the Law' (1992: 165–6): this is the story of a man from the country who journeys to the doors of the law and stands before the law – mesmerised by its brilliance. There, he finds the doors open, but guarded by a gatekeeper who refuses to let him in. Although he refuses him entrance, the guard allows him to see through the door. The man from the country waits, waits and waits – wasting away his time – perpetually asking the gatekeeper when he might be able to enter. At the end of the story, when no other person has come to the door, the gatekeeper informs him that the door was meant only for him – and that now he is going to close it. The parable points to how the citizen-subject stands before the law – transfixed by its brilliance – awaiting for the gatekeeper to allow him to enter the kingdom of the law. The citizen-subject 'is delivered over to the potentiality of law because law demands nothing of him and commands nothing other than its own openness' (Agamben 1998: 50). The law holds the man from the country in a holding position by 'includ[ing] him in excluding him' (Agamben 1998: 50).

The gatekeeper, represented in Kafka's story as a guard, is analogous to the liberal elite that guard the law's secularity. Women (and feminists) are patiently waiting at the door of the law, not knowing what an invitation into the law may bring. Feminists wait at the doors of the law hoping for reforms to expand autonomy and equality. But these hopes have been frustrated by the secular elites' imposed compromises. The doors remain closed. But the compromises tantalise feminists into continuing their wait in the hopes that their ideological allies will one day implement the very ideals they purport to support.

By compromising, liberal secular elites have inadvertently reinforced the influence and importance of the religious intelligentsia in the politics of family law, thereby reinforcing their legitimacy and encouraging them to persist in advancing their religious agenda in family law (and other areas of Egyptian law as well). This oscillation between feminists and religious groups produces a legal system that is never fully secular and never fully religious. Both groups develop a sense that the law is on a journey towards completion, in turn waiting for an invitation to enter through the doors of the law.

Women have been abandoned from secularism and its values. This has produced a type of feminism that is never complete, always waiting for expression, for implementation. It is an incomplete feminism of the *homo sacer* – a *homo sacer* feminism in which women are both within secularism, but also external to it. Women's excluded inclusion makes Egyptian secularism – to draw on Agamben's language in his *State of Exception* – a type of 'exceptional secularism' in which the judiciary imposes an imagined compromise in which secularism is suspended only in the case of the exception – in this case, women in the context of family law. Agamben describes the importance of investigating the 'exception in the following way':[25]

25 See Schmitt (1985: 15) saying that '[t]he exception explains the general and itself'.

> The exception is more interesting than the regular case. The latter proves nothing; the exception proves everything. The exception does not only confirm the rule; the rule as such lives off the exception alone . . . The exception explains the general and itself. And when one really wants to study the general, one need only look around for a real exception.
>
> (Agamben 1998: 16)

The exception is more interesting than the regular case because it illuminates how the system operates. In a sense, the 'general' of Egyptian law is that it is secular. However, this is not entirely accurate because its underlying structure is kept intact by keeping family law religious. Secularism justifies the exclusion of women who must endure the very opposite of secularism including unequal treatment in the event of divorce.

V. Strategic ambiguity: simulacra of the religious and the secular in Islamic divorce law

Earlier, we discussed new strategies that feminists are considering. The twentieth-century feminist strategy of accepting imposed compromises of the secular, liberal male elites has not been successful in liberalising family law. The newly conceived strategy to ally feminists with the religious intelligentsia in the hope of creating a state system that is governed through Islamic law – but results in liberal, feminist substantive effects – is also problematic and riddled with risks. The goal is to examine an alternative possibility that explores deploying both religious and secular languages that contain normative power. To explore this further, an examination of *khul'* will be undertaken. *Khul'* is a ground of divorce that came into effect in the year 2000 in Article 20 of Law No. 1 (2000) Egypt.

For years, feminists have sought to achieve no-fault divorce for women. Currently, the law of divorce (*talaq*) in Egypt entitles men to the right to obtain no-fault divorce. Throughout most of the nineteenth and early twentieth centuries (onwards), a woman was entitled to a unilateral right of divorce if her husband delegates his right of divorce to her at the inception of the marriage. A woman could also obtain a divorce if her husband willingly divorces her at her request. Men can divorce their wives with the expectation that their wife must forfeit her financial rights, primarily by requiring the wife to return some or all of her *mahr* (dowry) or the deferred part of the *mahr* back to the husband. This ground of divorce is known as *khul'*. If the wife cannot obtain the permission of her husband for divorce, she can only obtain a divorce under restricted conditions such as the absence of her husband, the imprisonment of her husband, or if her husband engaged in anal sexual intercourse.

It was not until the reforms of 1985 (Egyptian Law No. 100) that a judge was capable of granting a wife the ability to divorce outside the previous grounds, but only in the event of harm caused by the husband to the wife (and proven accordingly) or in the event that the husband continuously fails to provide his maintenance obligations. The previous grounds remain valid grounds for a woman to obtain divorce to this day. In each of these cases, divorce stops short of no-fault divorce. A woman cannot autonomously determine that she needs to divorce her husband. She must either obtain the permission of her husband or obtain a judicial divorce through the courts.

But in the year 2000, statutory reforms (Law No. 1) were introduced that were later ratified. These enabled a woman to autonomously obtain a divorce without the permission of her husband or the mediation of the courts even, in exchange for the forfeiture of her financial rights to her husband. The reforms named this ground of divorce *khul'* after the original version – although *khul'* as originally practised required the permission of the husband.[26]

Law No. 1 of 2000 caused an uproar of opposition with discussions about *khul'* taking place in the media and at Egypt's Al Azhar University – the oldest Islamic university in the world and an influential institution in policy debates. The official position of Al Azhar was supportive. The position of the Grand Mufti of Al Azhar was that *khul'* was in accordance with religious injunctions. But considering the fact that there was no textual evidence supporting *khul'* as being triggered based on the choice of the wife (rather than the husband), many other *ulema* (scholars) disagreed. Despite opposition, the final draft was approved by the National Assembly and became law. In this case, the approach of splitting the difference was less relevant as many religious scholars and conservative Muslims saw *khul'* as a genuine ground of divorce in Islam. The reality is that the application of the term *khul'* to this novel ground of divorce created debate within the religious intelligentsia about its legitimacy and, in fact, was seen by many believing Muslims (who themselves are not trained in the details of Islamic jurisprudence (*usul ul fiqh*)) as legitimately Islamic. Many Muslims did not realise that *khul'* was historically not a ground of divorce that the female spouse was allowed to pursue autonomously.

26 See El Alami and Hinchcliffe (1996: 27–8) providing a general explanation of *khul'* divorce. See El Alami and Hinchcliffe (1996: 174). In a *khul'* divorce, a woman in general agrees to give up some or all of her financial rights in exchange for an exit from the marriage. The woman does not have to base her request on one of the grounds for divorce established by the law. As one author put it, 'apart from the divorce effected by the husband, marriage may be dissolved by mutual consent by the wife giving the husband something for her freedom . . .' (Nasir 2002: 12–3, 115). The new legislation on *khul'* divorce passed in Egypt allows the wife to buy her freedom from the marriage without getting her husband's consent. Esposito (2001: 47, 60): 'Under a new law that came into effect in March 2000, a woman can divorce her husband, with or without his agreement, in exchange for returning to him any money or property he paid to her upon their marriage. This is a variation on *khul'* divorce'. The reason why this is a variation of *khul'* is that in the case of *khul'* divorce the consent of the husband is needed.

To explore this approach further, consider Jean Baudrillard's idea of simulation and simulacra. Using Baudrillard's framework, one can advance a strategy that is not religious in intent or in effect, but is religious only at a superficial level. The newly conceived *khul'* in the proposed statutory reforms of Law No. 1 is crafted as religious, but not merely in name; it also genuinely seems similar to the original institution (as interpreted textually) that was contemplated in the *Qur'an* and by the Prophet as attested in the *hadith* (sayings and actions of the Prophet Muhammad). In the case of *khul'*, it is an institution that has often been differentiated from other grounds of divorce as being based on the willingness of the female spouse to surrender her financial rights. However, Islamic textual laws on *khul'* never contemplated that a female spouse would exercise autonomy in the way envisaged in the reforms of Law No. 1 (2000).

This newly conceived *khul'* seems to be an example of – in Baudrillard's words – a third-order simulation (also referred to as the fourth phase of the sign). In a third-order simulation, the system (e.g. model, machine) does not attempt to imitate the real, but rather to imitate the very difference between the system and the real that allows their equivalence (Baudrillard 1994: 3). For example, the clone, android or replicant is not equivalent to man, but the generation of the real by its model through genetic technologies, or digital, electronic technologies (Baudrillard 1983: 105). There is a collapse of difference between what is true and what is false (Baudrillard 1994: 3). Somehow the real is replaced by the hyper-real, 'something perfectly real, truer than true' (Baudrillard 1999: 275), or 'more real than real' (Baudrillard 1994: 3), in Baudrillard's words. And in the example of the android, the hyper-real is represented as something more human than human. In Baudrillard's words, the hyper-real is '. . . the generation by models of a real without original or reality' (Baudrillard 1983: 1).

The hyper-real is a realm where the distinction between the real and the imaginary is a tautology, in turn making the imaginary impossible, since reality is itself imaginary. In the hyper-real, difference is constantly generated, produced to sustain the illusion of reality. Baudrillard states the following:

> Now the image can no longer imagine the real, because it is the real. It can no longer dream it, since it is its virtual reality. It is as though things had swallowed their own mirrors and had become transparent to themselves, entirely present to themselves in a ruthless transcription, full in light and in real time. Instead of being absent from themselves in illusion, they are forced to register on thousands of screens, off whose horizons not only the real has disappeared, but the image too. The reality has been driven out of reality.
>
> (Baudrillard 1999: 275)

Khul' as envisaged by Law No. 1 can be described as a hyper-real instantiation of the original *khul'* being transformed to something else, but so similar (simulacra) that it conflates the original *khul'* into the new form of *khul'* (as represented in Law No. 1). The new version of *khul'* redefines *khul'*, altering it in ways that make it seem as though it was always historically practised in the way envisaged in Law No. 1. This approach of collapsing a new *khul'* with liberal effects into the old *khul'* – practised for centuries and once seen as antithetical to feminists' goals – is now bringing divorce law closer to no-fault divorce. In a sense, the new *khul'* is a clone of the older version of *khul'* – one that the public (and even Islamic scholars) cannot distinguish and, therefore, one that cannot be overturned by the lobbying efforts of right-wing factions of the religious intelligentsia.

In this case, women – cast as exceptions – speak the language of religion as a means of opening the doors of the law – not through splitting the difference with the religious intelligentsia – but rather, through the de-stabilisation of the boundaries between secularism and religion. This strategy is based on ambiguity. In other words, the state of exception that marked family law remains a state of exception at the perceptual level (of the judiciary, the secular elites and the religious intelligentsia), but is truly a 'hyper-real state of exception'. This hyper-reality of the state of exception that at once marks women as an exception yet simultaneously speaks on behalf of women's rights, is produced through the ambiguous collapse of secularity and religion. In this contemplated strategy religion speaks the hidden goals of secularism while secularism hides itself in the language of religion. This is the Gift of Ambiguity.

VI. The *différance* of *khul'*

The ambiguous collapse of secularism and religion echoes Derrida's ideas on ambiguity. In order to explore how the reformed version of *khul'* harnesses ambiguity, we will make reference to Derrida's notion of *différance*. How is *khul'* made both the same and yet different? The 'same yet different' quality of *khul'* produces ambiguity, again suggesting strategic opportunities in Islamic divorce law.

Derrida's *différance* (see Derrida 1974: 141; Derrida 1978: 278) is developed as part of a critique of the epistemological conceptions of such philosophers as Plato, Aristotle, Immanuel Kant and Jurgen Habermas. He describes how such philosophers prioritise what *is* above what *is not*; this becomes the privileging of the present over the absent that characterises a great deal of philosophical thought. For Derrida, however, signs are used as a way to bring presence to the absence. He explains this in the following way:

> Signs represent the present in its absence; they take the place of the present. When we cannot take hold of or show the thing, let us say the present, the being-present, when the present does not present itself, then we signify, we go through the detour of signs. We take up or give signs; we make signs.
>
> (Derrida 1996: 441, 447)

Drawing on De Saussure's model (see de Saussure 1959: 1907–11) of how signs represent something that while not present, could be potentially present, Derrida's conception of 'arche-writing' (Derrida 1996: 453) differs from De Saussure in that signs perpetually and persistently refer to more signs and these signs again refer to yet other signs *ad infinitum*. Derrida refers to this as *différance*. *Différance* can also be referred to as deferral – described by Derrida as a type of 'interposition of delay, the interval of a spacing and temporalizing that puts off until "later" what is presently denied, the possible that is presently impossible' (Derrida 1996: 441). '"To differ" in this sense is to temporalize, to resort, consciously or unconsciously, to the temporal and temporalizing mediation of a detour . . .' (Derrida 1996: 447). But *différance* is more than the deferral produced by spacing and temporalising. It also includes the type of 'differing' that 'signifies non-identity'. This notion of non-identity is inclusive of the idea of *différance*. It is 'the other sense of "to differ" [*différer*] . . . [I]t is the most common and most identifiable, the sense of not being identical, of being other, of being discernible' (Derrida 1996: 446). But through this deferral (brought on by its spacing and temporalising movement), *différance* also signifies sameness. *Différance* represents the two movements of differing: deferral brought on by spacing and temporalising, but also difference 'as sameness which is not identical' (Derrida 1996: 441).

The newly invented version of *khul'* is marked by the deferral described by Derrida. A type of sameness that is not identical, the newly conceived *khul'* (in Law No. 100) appropriates religious language and legitimacy, while also surreptitiously containing a different (distinctive) signified from the original *khul'* as practised in the past millennium (in *taqlid* law). The fluid boundaries between the original and the newly invented *khul'* led to vigorous debates between Islamic scholars. By debating the legitimacy of *khul'*, Islamic scholars extended the impression that it was potentially a legal ground of divorce. The debate was largely a contestation about whether the new *khul'* was similar enough or too different from the original *khul'*. To scholars, it seemed that the two versions of *khul'* were both similar and different, producing confusion and rampant undecidability. They were, as Derrida puts it, engaged with a sameness that was not identical.

The original *khul'* included the right of a woman to divorce, but only conditional on a husband's consent so long as she forfeits her financial rights. The newly conceived version of *khul'* enabled a female spouse to obtain *khul'* without consent, but still retained the requirement that she unilaterally forfeit her financial rights in exchange for her husband's non-consensual divorce. Does this suggest that *khul'* has three sub-parts: a wife's demand to obtain a divorce, a husband's consent that she can be divorced from him and a wife's willingness to forfeit her financial rights in exchange for the divorce? Or does it merely contain two discrete sub-parts: a wife's demand to obtain a divorce and the forfeiture of a wife's financial rights in exchange for divorce?

Might it be that this version of *khul'* abandons a husband's consent in exchange for the wife's forfeiture of her financial rights? Can forfeiture of a wife's finances be seen as a tacit form of consent in that she is 'paying' for consent? Is this an accurate reading of Islamic law? What makes *khul' khul'*? These issues not only confused the *ulema* and *muftis* at Al Azhar, but questions continued to multiply as they debated. The debate led to the collapse of the signified of *khul'* and the signifier *khul'*, in turn enabling this newly invented ground of divorce to come into existence.

Of course, the term *khul'* played a further role in disorienting those considering the question, and the public did not understand the differences, viewing it as Islamic by virtue of its name, and simultaneously viewing it as a purely academic debate. By producing the question, 'is it Islamic?', feminists won the debate. The question is framed in a manner that presupposes it is within the spectrum of religious legitimacy. By producing ambivalence about the authenticity of the legality of *khul'*, it suggested its own potential legal validity. In turn it also divided the scholarly community and provided an opportunity for feminists to be viewed as using Islamic conceptions to address their concerns rather than secular ones that are often identified with the colonial West.

Khul' became law because it was both the same as the Islamic concept, and different from it. This disorientation has been described by Derrida as the undecidability of words – whose meanings are in constant deferral. In this case, the attempt to uncover a reality in the term *khul'* was separate from the Islamic idea of *khul'* as practised throughout history. This follows Derrida's discussion of the substitution of signs. On this topic, he states the following:

> Following this classical semiology, the substitution of the sign for the thing itself is both secondary and provisional: it is second in order after an original and lost presence, a presence from which the sign would be derived. It is provisional with respect to this final and missing presence, in view of which the sign would serve as a movement of mediation.
>
> (Derrida 1996: 447)

The original way in which *khul'* was historically practised is secondary and provisional. The original is lost at the moment that the term *khul'* emerges. There is no inherent meaning to *khul'*. In a sense the sign is flexibly unmoored to a zero institution, in which meaning is imbibed from without, with the perpetual potential of transforming into something else. Instability.

To examine how religious discourses can provide a road toward secularism's goals, consider Walter Benjamin's *The Work of Art in the Age of its Technological Reproducibility* (Benjamin 1936), and the notion of aura. Benjamin's work on aura sought to capture the groundbreaking cultural shift from authenticity to replication, from uniqueness to seriality, and from the original artwork to its 'soulless' mechanical copy. Benjamin describes aura in the following way:

> One might subsume the eliminated element in the term 'aura' and go on to say: that which withers in the age of mechanical reproduction is the aura of the work of art. This is a symptomatic process whose significance points beyond the realm of art. One might generalize by saying: the technique of reproduction detaches the reproduced object from the domain of tradition. By making many reproductions it substitutes a plurality of copies for a unique existence.
>
> (Benjamin 1936)

Benjamin's conception of aura as applied to works of art – particularly painting and photography – can be analogically extended to such religious institutions as *khul'*. *Khul'* represents a type of traditional institution similar to that of Benjamin's initial work of art (in the domain of tradition) prior to its mechanical reproduction (or copy). Drawing on such religiously coded and traditional institutions as *khul'*, the replication and reproduction of *khul'* (and other religious institutions) leads to a loss of its religious aura. While it seems to be religious, its religious traditional conceptions that were once historically practised for the duration of a millennium are withering every time it is reproduced within a largely secular legal system. Its traditional content is detached from its original object – in this case a sign – as its original unique existence is unmoored from the new discourses that inevitably become attached to its reproduction. While not a 'mechanical' reproduction, it is a 'linguistic' reproduction of the sign itself, *khul'*, containing new signifieds. While Benjamin laments the reproduction of works of art, such reproductions of religious language bring forth the strategic possibility of a move toward secularism. Perhaps this could be more accurately described as a move away from conservative interpretations of religious law that draws on religious signs that contain secular signifieds. These signifieds themselves carry an underlying secular logic or purpose which also strangely shields them from being interpreted as overtly secular. The reproduction of *khul'* enables the loss of its religious aura by detaching itself from its original religious significations.

VII. Conclusion: a single bloc of secular/religion instead of an either/or of secular/religion

The new form of *khul'* does not in itself mean the achievement of no-fault divorce for women, but it does bring us ever closer to the possibility of no-fault divorce. It is the ambiguity – the hidden abstraction – the hyperreal version of *khul'* – that enables it to become the law. That, in effect, assures that the door of law will not be closed on feminists and women's rights advocates. It provides enormous mileage since it is seen by the public – and even by Islamic scholars (*ulema*) – as genuinely and inherently religious. Now, instead of sacrificing women's rights, the sacrifice takes place in the realm of the hyper-real – seemingly remaining religious as an act of appeasement, but never sacrificing. A hyperreal sacrifice.

A passage from Deleuze and Parnet's book, *Dialogues*, originally written in reference to the idea of dialogue, is potentially applicable to the idea of achieving secular effects from religious language and institutions:

> The question 'What are you becoming?' is particularly stupid. For as someone becomes, what he is becoming changes as much as he does himself . . . The wasp and the orchid provide the example. The orchid seems to form a wasp image, but in fact there is a wasp-becoming of the orchid, an orchid becoming of the wasp, a double capture since 'what' each becomes changes no less than 'that which' becomes. The wasp becomes part of the orchid's reproductive apparatus at the same time as the orchid becomes the sexual organ of the wasp. One and the same becoming, a single bloc of becoming . . .
>
> (Deleuze and Parnet 1977)

The dichotomy of secular and religious has led to a socially constructed legal landscape – one created at the hands of the liberal, secular allies of feminists – in which the only possible answers are either liberal/secular or conservative/religious. To move away from this either/or of secular versus religious, we do not assume that it is necessarily possible (although sometimes it is) to achieve feminist goals through the liberal elites splitting the difference between feminists and the religious intelligentsia. We also do not accept that it is altogether easy or possible to accomplish the fully-fledged creation of an Islamic legal system in Egypt that will necessarily be sympathetic to the goals of feminists. Instead, we advance a strategy to deploy religious language that advances a liberal, secular agenda while hiding this agenda from immediate view. By collapsing the hyper-real with the real – by seeing the religious wasp and the liberal, secular flower as one block – ambiguously inter-connected and interwoven with one another – and not separating or dichotomising secular and religious – it is possible to come closer to achieving the liberal goals for which feminists have been waiting for more than a century.

Secular elites contemplated a strategy that figures family law as the exception that must be sacrificed to advance secularism. In other words, secularism's condition is also a condition of its impossibility – to bring it into existence. But while extant, it simultaneously undermines itself by advancing the overall secularity of the law by sacrificing a single person or group. But by drawing on the language of religion, the goals of secularism can be advanced. This contrasts sharply with the sincere, transparent and truthful advancement of secularism through the language of secularity. Such clarity and knowability can produce strategic losses. The goal should be to separate the religious sign from its religious signified, in turn introducing a strategy that results in the loss of traditional, religious auras. This will move the Egyptian legal system away from 'exceptional secularism' to a hyper-real 'exceptional secularism' characterised by contingency and unknowability. Such a political tactic does not guarantee the entrance of feminists through the doors of the law, but rather introduces sufficient contingency, unknowability and uncertainty into the ontology of legal institutions in family law (and more broadly throughout Egyptian law) and, by doing so, in turn advancing possibilities for change in Egyptian family law and the family legal systems throughout the Middle East. As Slavoj Zizek says, 'it changes the very parameters of what is considered "possible" in the existing constellation' (Zizek 1999: 119).

References

Abu Odeh, L. (2004) 'Modernizing Family Law: The Case of Egypt', *Vand. J. Transnat'l Law* 37/4: 1043, 1140.

Agamben, G. (1998) *Homo Sacer: Sovereign Power and Bare Life*, trans. by Daniel Heller-Roazen, Palo Alto, CA: Stanford University Press.

Agamben, G. (1999) *Remnants of Auschwitz: The Witness and the Archive*, trans. by Daniel Heller-Roazen, New York: Zone Books.

Anderson, B. (1983) *Imagined Communities: Reflections on the Origins and Spread of Nationalism*, London: Verso.

Anderson, J.N.D. (1968) 'Law Reform in Egypt: 1850–1950', in *Political and Social Change in Modern Egypt*, P.M. Holt (ed.), London: Oxford University Press.

An Na'im, A. (1990) *Toward an Islamic Reformation: Civil Liberties, Human Rights, and International Law*, Syracuse, NY: Syracuse University Press.

Balz, K. (1999) 'The Secular Reconstruction of Islamic Law: The Egyptian Supreme Constitutional Court and the "Battle over the Veil" in State-Run Schools', in *Legal Pluralism in the Arab World*, Baudouin Dupret et al. (eds), The Hague: Kluwer Law International.

Baudrillard, J. (1983) *Simulations*, trans. by Paul Foss, Paul Patton, and Philip Beitchman, New York: Semiotext(e).

Baudrillard, J. (1994) *Simulacra and Simulation*, trans. by Sheila Faria Glaser, Ann Arbor: University of Michigan Press.

Baudrillard, J. (1999) *The Perfect Crime*, London and New York: Verso Books.

Benjamin, W. (1936) *The Work of Art in the Age of its Technological Reproducibility*, at www.marxists.org/reference/subject/philosophy/works/ge/benjamin.htm (downloaded October 2010).

Benner Lombardi, C. (1998) 'Islamic Law as a Source of Constitutional Law in Egypt: The Constitutionalization of the Sharia in a Modern Arab State', *Colum. J. Transnat'l L.* 37: 81, 108.

Crecelius, D. (1974) 'The Course of Secularization in Modern Egypt', in *Religion and Political Modernization*, Donald Eugene Smith (ed.), New Haven, CT: Yale University Press.

De Beauvoir, S. (1989) *The Second Sex*, trans. by H.M. Parshley, Vintage.

Deleuze, G. and C. Parnet (1977) *Dialogues 1*, Paris: Flammarion.

Derrida, J. (1974) 'That Dangerous Supplement . . .', trans. by Gayatri Chakrovorty Spivak, in *Of Grammatology*, Baltimore: The John Hopkins University Press.

Derrida, J. (1978) 'Structure, Sign, and Play in the Discourses of the Human Sciences', in *Writing and Difference*, trans. by Alan Bass, London and New York: Routledge.

Derrida, J. (1994) *Given Time I: Counterfeit Money* Volume I, trans. by Peggy Kamuf, Chicago and London: Chicago University Press.

Derrida, J. (1995) *The Gift of Death*, trans. by David Wills, Chicago: University of Chicago Press.

Derrida, J. (1996) 'Speech and Phenomena and Other Essays on Husserl's Theory of Signs', in *The Continental Philosophy Reader*, Richard Kearney and Mara Rainwater (eds), London: Routledge. (Originally published as Derrida, J. (1973) *Speech and Phenomena and Other Essays on Husserl's Theory of Signs.*)

Derrida, J. (2003) '"Le Parjure", *Perhaps*: Storytelling and Lying', in *Acts of Narrative*, Carol Jacobs and Henry Sussman (eds), Palo Alto, CA: Stanford University Press.

de Saussure, F. (1959) *Course in General Linguistics*, trans. by Wade Baskin (Charles Bally et al. eds), New York: The Philosophical Library Inc.

El Alami, D.S. and D. Hinchcliffe (1996) *Islamic Marriage and Divorce Laws of the Arab World*, London: Kluwer Law International.

El-Morr, A.M. (1997) 'Judicial Sources for Supporting the Protection of Human Rights', in *The Role of the Judiciary in the Protection of Human Rights*, Eugene Cotran and Adel Omar Sherif (eds), Kluwer Law International.

Esposito, J.L. (2001) *Women in Muslim Family Law* (2nd edn), New York: Syracuse.

Foblets, M.-C. and B. Dupret (1999) 'Contrasted Identity Claims Before Egyptian and Belgian Courts', in *Legal Pluralism in the Arab World*, Baudouin Dupret et al. (eds), The Hague: Kluwer Law International.

Genesis, 22:2 *The Bible* (Revised Standard Version).

Hill, E. (1988) 'Islamic Law as a Source for the Development of a Comparative Jurisprudence, the "Modern Science of Codification" (1): Theory and Practice in the Life and Work of Abd Al-Razzaq Ahmad Al-Sanhuri', in *Islamic Law: Social and Historical Contexts*, Aziz Al-Azmeh (ed.), London: Routledge.

Holyoake, G. (1896) *The Origin and Nature of Secularism*, London: Watts and Co.

Kafka, F. (1992) 'Before the Law', in *Metamorphosis and Other Stories*, trans. by Malcolm Pasley, New York: Penguin.

Kierkegaard, S. (1843) *Either/Or* Volume I, trans. by David F. Swenson and Lillian Marvin Swenson (1971 edn), Princeton, NJ: Princeton University Press.

Koskenniemi, M. (1999) 'The Silence of Law/The Voice of Justice', *International Law, the International Court of Justice and Nuclear Weapons*, Laurance Boisson de Chazournes and Philippe Sands (eds), Cambridge University Press.

Najjar, F.M. (1988) 'Egypt's Laws of Personal Status', *Arab Studies Quarterly*, 10/3: 319–333.

Nasir, J.J. (2002) *The Islamic Law of Personal Status* (3rd edn), London: Graham & Trotman.

Schmitt, C. (1985) *Political Theology: Four chapters on the concept of sovereignty*, trans. by George Schwab, Cambridge, MA: MIT Press.

Spivak, G.C. (1994) 'Can the Subaltern Speak?', in *Colonial Discourse and post-Colonial Theory*, Patrick Williams and Laura Chrisman (eds), New York: Columbia University Press.

Vattimo, G. (1992) *The Transparent Society*, trans. by David Webb, Baltimore: John Hopkins University Press.

Zizek, S. (1999) *The Ticklish Subject: The Absent Centre of Political Ontology*, London: Verso.

Cases

Case No. 8, Judicial Year 17, 1996.
Case No. 35, Year 9, 1994.
Case No. 82, Judicial Year 17, 1997.

Egyptian legislation

Law No. 25 of 1929, as amended by Law No. 100 of 1985.

Chapter 5

What is Islamic law?*

A praxiological answer and an Egyptian case study

Baudouin Dupret

I. The nature of Islamic law

Neither law nor religion is endowed with intrinsic, substantial and natural authority. There are only punctual situations where people orient to something that they identify as being religious law, the authority of which they publicly acknowledge. There is henceforth no way to examine the reference to Islamic law outside its circumstantial and situated uses, that is, outside practices of referring to an object explicitly characterised as Islamically legal in various contexts, each one having its own constraints.

A. Searching for law in Islam

Literature on norms and law in societies dubbed Muslim has, as a whole, an essentialist attitude. According to interpretive theory, law is a cultural code of meanings for interpreting the world. In this hermeneutic project, words are the keys to understanding societies and cultures, and to giving them a meaning. Geertz (1983: 185) gives the example of the Arabic word '*haqq*', which is supposed to come from a specific moral world and to connect to a distinctive legal sensibility. This word would carry along with it all the specific meanings that are consubstantial with something that is called 'Islamic law'. In situations where many cultural systems are described as interacting, law would produce a 'polyglot discourse' (Geertz 1983: 226). Interpretive theory fundamentally conceives of law in holistic terms, that is, as one of the many reverberations of a larger explaining principle: culture (cf. also Rosen 1989). Accordingly, the laws that characterise societies carry along with them, throughout history, the same basic tenets.

However, cultural interpretivists fail to consider that law is not necessarily and integrally part of culture, and that culture is not a set of permanent pre-existing assumptions but something that is permanently produced, reproduced, negotiated and oriented to by members of various social settings.

* This chapter was originally published in *Theory, Culture and Society*, 24/2: 79–100 (2007).

The same pattern of argument holds true when the culturalist attitude is combined with text analysis. Messick (1993), for instance, associates the shape of Islamic cities with Yemeni Islamic lawyers' calligraphic style to demonstrate that Muslim societies were embedded in a system of textual domination. The text, here, is the *sharî'a*, something described as much more than Islamic law, a 'textual polity' including 'a conception of an authoritative text' and 'a pattern of textual authority' (Messick 1993: 6). Although texts are important in the study of law in literate societies, Messick, by focusing his attention on disengaged documents, loses sight of the phenomenon of law practice and its work of producing formalised records.

Most research considers human beings as rule-driven creatures, in societies dubbed Muslim in particular. Oussama Arabi (2001), for instance, states that Islamic law still determines the daily behavior of people in Muslim societies and constitutes a living reality in contemporary societies where it is implemented as the state's positive law. With regard to sexuality, for instance, Arabi seems to be implying that provisions identifiable in fiqh[1] treatises continue to influence today's common-sense and legal conceptions. Empirically speaking, it would be utterly hard to demonstrate this. Actually, according to Arabi, common sense considers that sexual relationships that go beyond simple flirtation belong to the category '*harâm*' (the forbidden) if they are not validated by a religious contract. The point is to know whether we can ground on the observation of the use of a contractual form the claim that a kind of internalised religious normativity still frames and determines the social.

Against incorporation theories, a praxiological approach shows that it is impossible to open the 'black box' of the authority of rules by substituting for it the other black box that makes of people the mere individual receptacles of cultural principles that are somehow consubstantial with them. Authority must be understood as the modality of an action (one acts with authority), an attribute of a person (someone has authority over others) or the quality specific to a norm (the authority of rules). It is always the predicate of something that somehow it accompanies. In Arabi's approach, rules are independent of practice. They are endowed with clear meaning and determine people's behaviour in a univocal way. They are invested with some intrinsic authority that proceeds from their belonging to the religious repertoire. This feature allows it to escape any hermeneutics. Whereas legal norms have an 'open texture' (Hart 1961), religious norms are rigid and a-temporal objects escaping contingency by virtue of their divine inspiration. To the contrary, I consider that rules are practical accomplishments and their authority a modality that is linked to people's public orientation to the force they recognise in them. Rules do not pre-exist their practice and their authority is not an intrinsic feature.

1 Usually, *sharî'a* is understood as Islamic law as revealed by God (in the *Qur'ân* or Koran) through His Prophet Muhammad (*Sunna* or Prophetic Tradition), whereas *fiqh* is the knowledge of this Law and the body of jurisprudence that originates in it.

Most literature on Islamic law tends to impose a structure on legal phenomena and activities, instead of looking at their operating process. For instance, Layish and Shaham (in the *Encyclopedia of Islam*, 2nd edn) give the Arabic word *tashrî* 'a religious signification on the ground of its etymology and ignore the fact it is used today to designate the notion of legislation in its most general sense. Starting from their pre-established knowledge of the etymological trajectory of the word, they impose on the legislative phenomenon a dimension that cannot be documented. Moreover, in their attempt to evaluate the transformations of *tashrî'*, they posit a distinction between legal orthodoxy and deviance that places the scholar in the situation of saying which rules are orthodox and of adopting an ironical stance vis-à-vis the many ways in which people deceive themselves when adhering to one or another conception of Islamic law. All this places the debate on a normative ground, while dodging the central question of how and what people do when they refer to the *sharî'a* in current contexts.

Islamic law can be the mere reference to Islam in a legal setting or it can be a legal system identified with the classical body of *fiqh*. In the latter case, there must be a substantial definition of Islamic law, the criteria of which are satisfied by the specific law on which we focus, so that it can be taken as a particular instance of a general model. This raises several questions about constitutive criteria, the paradigmatic model, relevant instances and the authority to constitute and certify the model. Literature on this issue drifts between different positions. Sometimes it claims that we must stick to people's utterances. However, while Islamic law is what people refer to as Islamic law, we should not consider that the use of the same word at different times necessarily means that the word refers to the same meaning and technical definition. Sometimes literature claims that people deceive themselves. Thus, for instance, the statement that, although Egyptian judges no longer use the word '*dhimma*' the *dhimma* system[2] is still in force in Egyptian law (Berger 2001). This is an ironic stance that assumes that scholars know better than the people engaged in a practice. It also contradicts the first assertion that we must stick to the words people use. Moreover, it is a metaphysical and deterministic position that claims that structures are permanent, even though people are no longer aware of them, and that people are determined by external constraints and neither produce nor transform anything, but only reproduce the past. The combination of these two positions makes the argument non-falsifiable.

B. Rephrasing the question

There is no reason to assume that what people refer to as Islamic law is identical to, or different from, the set of technical provisions that form the idealised model of Islamic law. The question is not relevant, because it is

2 The system of minority subjection and protection under classical Islamic law.

totally disembodied from actual practices; and it fails to address the phenomenon itself, that is, the practice of referring to Islamic law. For the question, 'What is Islamic law?' we should substitute the question, 'What do people do when referring to Islamic law?'

Legal actions, like all social actions, are irreducibly events or actions in a social order (Sharrock and Button 1991: 157). In law, as in any social activity, concepts, like words, are parts of what Wittgenstein calls 'language games' (1967: paras 7–24 *et seq.*). Wittgenstein specifically targets 'big concepts' that are often constructed as floating entities, totally decontextualised, and then projected back into the world as its inner nature, as 'something that lies *beneath* the surface' (1967: para. 92), independent of any instantiation or context of use. These remarks hold true with regard to concepts like 'Islamic law'.

There is no case to make something 'an instance of' something else (e.g. to make personal status in Egypt an instance of the larger 'model' of Islamic law). The main problem with any model construction lies in the idea of correspondence between the model and the data it is supposed to aggregate, between the general and the particular, between an abstract proposition and its concrete instances. In our case, Egyptian personal status law is supposedly an instance of an abstract Islamic legal system. Model building requires that the different instances of the model share some common characteristics that satisfy the postulates of identity and equivalence so that they can be measured accurately and ascribed to the general model. For instance, the characteristics of Egyptian personal status law may be measured so that their belonging or not-belonging to the general Islamic law model may be assessed. However, when referring to local situations as instances of a general model, researchers use implicit assumptions about both and hide the fundamental fact that the same word 'Islamic law' means very different things in various contexts. The result is that we know little about the properties of the underlying phenomena and take for granted the very basis of what we propose to explain.

Rather, we should ask how the members of any social group conduct the activities by which they identify and characterise something as an instance of something else (cf. Lynch 1991: 86ff.). In terms of Islamic law, this means to focus on how *people*, in their many settings, orient themselves to something they call 'Islamic law' and how *they* refer personal-status questions to the Islamic-law model. Such an attitude suggests that we focus on the methods people use locally to produce the truth and intelligibility that allow them to cooperate and interact in a more or less ordered way.

Egyptian personal status law can be categorised variously as an instance of Islamic law, Egyptian law, civil law or heterodox codified *sharî'a*. Rather than asking to which abstract category it actually belongs, we should ask what is the purpose and the mechanism of the categorisation itself (cf. Hester and Eglin 1997; Jayyusi 1984; Sacks 1974, 1995; Watson 1994). Attention must shift to the description of the phenomena and the properties they display. The consequence for social scientists is that their task is to observe and describe the methods used by the members of a society (ethnomethods) in their everyday life – including their professional life – to produce intelligibility, communicability and the capacity to be acted upon.

B.1 Re-specifying the sociological study of Islamic law

The study of Islamic law needs focusing much more on living phenomena and actual practices. Anthropological research has shown its willingness to engage in that direction. It turned away from scholastic conceptions of law, which would only be law in books, and turned to law as something encountered and lived by flesh-and-blood people (Mir-Hosseini 1993). It even sometimes attempted to capture the language of law in action in an Islamic setting (Hirsch 1998) and sought to explore the practical ways of legal reasoning (Bowen 2003). However, by concentrating on issues like power and gender, or by abstracting data from their context, it missed part of the phenomenon it set out to analyse. Our contention is that the whole issue of Islamic law needs a praxiological re-specification that can be argued around three central themes: the opposition between law in action and law in books; the 'missing what' of law-and-society and statistical-legal studies; the opposition between 'hyper-explanations' and description of situated activities.

C. Law in books and law in action

In *Marriage on Trial*, Mir-Hosseini states that 'from its inception, Islam has been both a political and a social order' (1993: 3–4), and Islamic law, 'the divine law', has constituted 'the backbone of Muslim society . . . ever since' (1993: 4). With reference to modern times, she describes *sharîʿa* as still forming 'the basis of family law, though reformed, codified and applied by a modern legal apparatus' (1993: 8). Opposing the theory of Islamic law to its practice, she adds that 'what characterizes the Shari'a perhaps more than anything else is the distance between the ideal and the reality' (1993: 8). She concludes that:

> . . . it is precisely because this Divine Will needs to be discerned by human intellectual activity, and, more importantly, because it is enforced by human courts, that it is bound to bear the influence of the time and environment in which it operates.
>
> (1993: 10)

By looking for the nature of law, Mir-Hosseini misses the phenomenon of the practice itself. In the core of the book, theory takes the form of a synthesis of applicable legal provisions, whereas practice is represented by 20 cases, duly summarised, and statistical data that supposedly provide the necessary basis for understanding the underlying patriarchal ideology of the *sharîʿa* model. However, even though she gives *sharîʿa* a meaning, a content, an ideological orientation, people do not seem to address it directly in the cases summarised by Mir-Hosseini. In other words, we suffer from a double bind: social actors remain external to the fundamental significance of the law they are practising; researchers who claim to have access to the meaning of the law have little grasp of its practicalities. This double bind is in part the result of the scholarly construction of a dichotomy between theory and practice.

Hirsch does not look for any substantial description of what is Islamic law and does not attempt to give it any trans- or a-historical meaning. When she uses the expression, it is generally to refer to *kadhi*s' conception or representation of it, not to ascribe it as an essentialist meaning. Actually, her bias stems from the marginal dimension of the legal setting in the design of her argument. Her analysis is neither about law nor about legal practices. It is about gender as observed from the vantage point of the Kadhi court. Law is not a topic in its own right, it is 'a symbol of both Muslim governance and its vulnerability in the postcolonial era' (Hirsch 1998: 136). There is something that is lost in this process, and this is the coherence of the legal setting in which all this happens, its recognisability for the participants, and the ways in which this recognisable coherence is produced.

Law as a social phenomenon cannot be reduced to the mere provisions of a legal code (law on the books). However, it would be misleading not to consider law on the books as an integral part of the practice of law. We must give credit to the natural attitude of people who do not experience reality as purely subjective and law on the books as purely formal. By merely opposing theory to practice and legal provisions to the 'living law', we fail to understand fully what, for instance, Egyptian personal status law is. We are more likely to gain such an understanding through the close description of people's orientation to, and reification of, legal categories as it emerges from their actual encounter with legal matters.

D. The 'missing what' of law-and-society and legal-statistical research on law

Describing her personal research experience in Iranian Courts, Mir-Hosseini says:

> One judge . . . assigned me the task of drafting court notes, the usual duty of the court clerk. This helped me a great deal to see the case from the court's viewpoint (or, more accurately, his), and I learned how to construct 'legal facts', how to translate the petitioners' grievances into court language, and how to discern the principles upon which the court operates.
>
> (1993: 18)

From a praxiological point of view, this statement sounds most promising. Indeed, praxiology advocates precisely that scholars pay closer attention to, and better describe, the modalities of the construction of legal facts and people's orientation to, and manifestation of, their understanding of the judicial setting, its constraints and its structure. However, Mir-Hosseini continues, '[L]ater this duty became cumbersome as it prevented me from paying full attention while following the disputes during that session' (1993: 18).

Hirsch's approach suffers from the same kind of bias, which is related to her focus on law as one strategic device among others through which power relationships are negotiated. In the sequence of her book, gender and power come first, language, as their vehicle, second. And law has an ancillary role, it is considered as an arena where conflicting narratives oppose each other. But law and the practice of law are not a bunch of mere narratives competing with other narratives, they also constitute an activity accomplished on a daily basis, of an overwhelmingly routine character, the place of production and reproduction of professional practices which are oriented to nothing but the accomplishment of the law.

Mir-Hosseini's use of the techniques of judicial statistics and case reports, and Hirsch's focus on discourse content and strategic uses eschew addressing law as a practical activity. This is the 'missing what' problem in the study of work. With regard to legal professions, this means that 'sociologists tend to describe various "social" influences on the growth and development of legal institutions while taking for granted that lawyers write briefs, present cases, interrogate witnesses, and engage in legal reasoning' (Lynch 1993: 114).

The problem with statistical data is that it largely erases the 'here and now' dimension of every case, that is, it obscures the necessarily situated character of every activity. The correspondence between statistical entries and the social reality thus codified so as to make it statistically relevant is, however, far from obvious. As a result, we fail to understand the two operations that are at the core of law: formulating legal categories and providing legal characterisations of facts. To paraphrase Michael Moerman (1974: 68), socio-legal scientists should describe and analyse the ways in which legal categories are used and not merely take them as self-evident explanations.

With regard to case reports, the problem is of a different nature.[3] Many studies have tried to capture some aspects of court activities through ethnographic observation, but very few attend closely to what is really done within this institutional setting. This is particularly true in studies that rely on participant observation and interviews. There is a real descriptive failing, which leads researchers to advance worldviews alternative to those of the actors or to remain insensitive to legal work as it is understood by its daily practitioners. Travers (1997) speaks of a descriptive gap. In order to bridge the descriptive gap and to fill the 'missing what', we must reorient ourselves

3 The use of case reports has also become a common method in political sciences (see, for instance, concerning the Middle East, Brown, 1997).

to the content of legal work, to its mainly practical character, and thus to its technicalities, situated character and specific modes of reasoning.

E. *Hyper-explanation vs. description of situated activities*

This last consideration leads to the question of macro- and dualistic explanations, what I call 'hyper-explanations'. Mir-Hosseini produces a historical sketch of Islamic law that allows her to examine the characteristics of *sharî'a* that are relevant to her study. She states that 'a historical perspective is essential to appreciate the current place of law in Muslim societies, and in particular to explore the dynamics of the changing relationship of law and society' (1993: 3). Although she claims that 'those who ardently argue for the rule of the Shari'a . . . tend to hold an idealized and totally ahistorical version of the development of the Islamic faith and its institutions', she asserts at the same time that 'Islamic law' has a 'nature' that is related to the 'nature' of 'Islamic civilization' (1993: 3). This paradox is strengthened when Mir-Hosseini claims that modernisation ended in 'the creation of a hybrid family law, which is neither the Shari'a nor Western' (1993: 11). In conclusion, she argues that there is a 'Shari'a model' according to which actual patterns of marriage and family structures can be evaluated and that is based on a patriarchal ideology (1993: 191 et seq.). Yet one wonders what models, patterns of marriage or ideologies look like outside their embodying practices. More important, we can also raise the issue of the explicative capacity of notions like patriarchy.

The same holds true when considering Hirsch. Although she seems clearly reluctant to engage in generalisations taking the form of cultural explanations, she advocates the substitution of other hyper-explanations like history, power, legitimation, ideology and globalisation. This is in particular reflected in her dealing with language as a medium that contributes to, and shapes, 'the gender-patterned production of accounts of conflict in relation to ideologies that link women to storytelling and men to authoritative speech' (Hirsch 1998: 222). Although concentrating on actual verbal interactions within Swahili Kadhi courts, her focus is on discourse content rather than on the discourse sensitivity to the context of its production and the constraints that result from its institutional embeddedness and organisation. It results in an overstatement of the strategic, reflexive and ideological dimensions of court interactions and an understatement of their institutional, conversational, contextual, procedural, technical and legal constraints.

II. The praxiological study of Islamic law: Egyptian cases

I turn now to actual Egyptian cases to show how the reference to Islam is practically achieved. In these contexts, the many people engaged in the production of a legally relevant description of facts to which legally relevant consequences are attached pay little attention to the question of 'Islamic law'. This does not mean that this or that legal provision has no history. Rather, it means that so long as a legal concept is used in a stable, unproblematic and unquestioned manner, any account of its theoretical and historical basis has no special relevance to its current uses. Conversely, exclusive attention to the theoretical and historical genesis of the concept leads to the disappearance of its contingent and situated character.

Personal status matters are organised in Egypt by, for example, Law No. 25 of 1920 and Law No. 25 of 1929, both amended by Law No. 100 of 1985, and Law No. 1 of 2000. In the absence of any statutory provision, Law No. 1 of 2000 stipulates that the judge must refer to 'the opinions that are prevalent in the school of imam Abû Hanîfa'.[4] In practice, many judges still make use of unofficial codifications compiling Hanafite-inspired legal provisions. Personal status has been subject to procedural rules that are common to all civil and commercial matters. Cases are adjudicated by specialised circuits within the courts. The personal-status circuit of the courts is competent with regard to financial (*wilâya 'alâ al-mâl*) and non-financial (*wilâya 'alâ al-nafs*) matters, including the granting of judicial divorce on the ground of harm, with regard to which Article 6 of the Law No. 25 of 1929 states:

> If the wife alleges that the husband mistreated her in such a way as to make it impossible between people of their social standing to continue the marriage relationship, she may request that the judge separate them, whereupon the judge shall grant her an irrevocable divorce if the harm is established and conciliation seems impossible between them. If, however, he [viz., the husband] refuses the petition and she subsequently repeats the complaint without establishing the harm, the judge shall appoint two arbitrators and he shall judge according to the provisions of Articles 7, 8, 9, 10 and 11.

In the following example, we can observe the form taken by a ruling in personal status matters:

Excerpt 1 (Case No. 858, 1998)

'In the name of God the clement, the merciful'
In the name of the people
Gîza Court of First Instance
for the Personal Status – Persons / First Circuit *shar'î*
Ruling

4 Sunni Islam is divided into four legal schools (*madhhab*): Hanafites (after Abû Hanîfa), Malikites (after Mâlik *b.* Anas), Shafi'ites (after al-Shâfi'res) and Hanbalites (after Ibn Hanbal).

At the *shar'î* session held publicly at the palace of the court on Tuesday 25/12/2000 m.[5] Under the presidency of His Excellency Mr . . . , President of the Court

And the membership of MM . . . and . . . judges

In the presence of Mr . . . , deputy of the prosecution

In the presence of Mr . . . , clerk

The following ruling was issued:

In the petition submitted by Mrs . . .

Against

Mr . . . Registered on the public roll as No. 858 of the year 1998 m., P.S., plenary of Gîza

The Court

After the hearing of the plea, the examination of the documents and the Prosecution's opinion, and the deliberation according to the law:

Considering that [it appears] from the facts of the case that the female petitioner introduced her petition in pursuance of a form deposed at the office of the clerk of this court . . . about which the defendant was legally notified, in conclusion of which she asked for a ruling [that would] divorce her, asking that it would be required from him not to oppose to her in her marital affairs and compelling him to [pay] the expenses [1]

In support of this, it is said that she is the wife of the defendant. . . . He kept on inflicting on her bad treatments . . . by assaulting her, insulting her and abandoning the marital domicile. . . . She asked her the divorce . . . but he did not accept. . . . [2] ['considering' 1 and 2 = petition]

Considering that . . . ['considering' 3 to 'considering' 7 = procedures followed by the court]

Considering that . . . ['considering' 8 to 'considering' 15 = examination of the legal grounds]

Considering that . . . ['considering' 16 = application of the law to the facts of the case]

Considering that . . . ['considering' 17 = expenses and accessory demands]

For all these reasons

The court rules the judicial divorce of the petitioner . . . from the defendant . . . in the form of an irrevocable divorce on [the ground of] harm, requires him not to oppose to her in her marital affairs and compels the defendant to [pay] the expenses and to [pay] 10 pounds for the attorney's retainer.

Clerk President of the Court

This structure reflects the actual procedural constraint under which the judge operates. One of his major tasks, as a professional routinely engaged in his occupation, is to publicly manifest the correct accomplishment of his job. At this procedural level, it is obvious that the judge orients himself exclusively

5 '*Milâdî*', i.e. AD.

to the technicalities of Egyptian procedural law. These technicalities may include some reference to provisions explicitly relating to Hanafite or Malikite law, but this is always through the provisions of Egyptian law, as eventually interpreted by the Court of Cassation:

> *Excerpt 2 (Case No. 858, 1998)*
> Harm is established through the testimony of two men or one man and two women, in pursuance of the prevailing opinion of the doctrine of Abû Hanîfa and in application of Article 280 of the By-law [organizing the courts] of the *sharî'a*[6]: 'Evidence belongs to two men or to one man and two women' (Cass., Civil, 28/2/1960 m., 11th judicial year, p. 181).

Most of the documents in any judicial file show this orientation of judges and other professionals to procedural correctness. This orientation proceeds from the general sequence of the trial in which every participant addresses in turn people who, at certain times, are not physically present in the courtroom, although they constitute silent auditors to whom the members of the trial turn beyond their direct and immediate verbal exchanges. This notion of the 'overhearing' audience (Drew 1992) can be extended to absent people to whom a document like the ruling is addressed (Dupret 2004). The potential overruling that an appeal might eventually produce is directly taken into consideration by the participants and translates into the very careful attitude they adopt vis-à-vis the procedures they are required to follow. These procedural constraints must not be considered as elements imported from a foreign, ancient or external legal system. Rather, they represent the direct, obvious, real and practical dimensions of a daily, bureaucratic routine of people engaged, in today's Egypt, in various legal, professional activities.

To illustrate the point, I reproduce a conciliation report written by the Arbitration and Conciliation Committee of Gîza in a case of unilateral divorce at the wife's request (*khul'*). This conciliation attempt is imposed by virtue of the new procedure settled by Article 20 of Law No. 1 of 2000. This document reflects the mainly bureaucratic and routinised nature of the practice of personal status, even though it originates from an explicitly religious institution, al-Azhar.[7]

> *Excerpt 3 (Case No. 180, 2000)*
> In the name of God the clement, the merciful
> al-Azhar al-sharîf — Concerning: Report in Case No. 180
> Department of Islamic Research — of the Year 2000 introduced
> General Office of Preaching — by Mrs . . .
> and against . . .

6 Law No. 1 of 2000 integrally reiterates this provision.
7 Al-Azhar is an old and famous mosque in Cairo, home of one of the most prestigious universities of the Muslim world.

Religious Information
Preaching Area of Gîza, Arbitration and Conciliation Committee

Report

His Excellency Mr Counsellor . . . , Court of North Gîza, First *shar'î* Circuit, Plenary, North Peace be upon you, God's clemency and His benediction

The honourable court has appointed us to arbitrate in the petition No. 180 of the year 2000 introduced by Mrs . . . against . . .

Execution of the warrant

1– The wife appeared before the Arbitration and Conciliation Office of the Preaching Area of Gîza and it was proceeded to record her words in writing and orally and to hear her. Many sessions were held concerning her. It appears from them that an agreement and a conciliation between her and her husband is impossible, given that her husband did not appear despite his knowledge of these sessions. The wife reported through her words that she had faced humiliation, slander, insult and assault to her honour from her above-mentioned husband. He so pronounced calumniating words, as to cause psychological harm to the children and to her hating him and her wanting to divorce in a unilateral way (*mukhâla'a*) in order to preserve the future of the children. She said: I fear not to respect God's limits with him (*allâ uqîm hudûd allâhi ma'ahu*).

2– We proceeded to send telegrams to the husband and he did not appear on the premises of the Arbitration and Conciliation Committee of the Preaching Area of Gîza until the writing of this report.

Opinion of the two arbitrators

After the examination of the documents of the case, the accompanying documents, the wife's words and what is asked from the husband, the impossibility of cohabitation and marital life between them appeared manifest. We bring this forward to your Excellency. It belongs to the justice of the court to adjudicate in the manner that is deemed adequate.

Peace be upon you, God's clemency and His benediction

First arbitrator Second arbitrator

Beyond the attempt to conciliate the spouses, to which this report testifies, the structure of the document reveals at least two things. First, the report is an accomplishment in itself, in which the arbitrators produce all the features that manifest their acting in their capacity and their mastering of the procedural and technical aspects that make it possible to produce a report from the ad hoc office of al-Azhar. Second, this report is part of a global procedure. It mentions that it belongs to the more encompassing procedure that is followed in the trial of a case that was submitted to the arbitrators by the court, asking them to perform the action required by the law.

Besides the constraining effect of procedural rules, legal issues must be addressed by the many people engaged in the judicial process. These issues mainly consist in giving a factual substance to some formal legal definitions.

In the case of judicial divorce on the ground of harm, two questions must be dealt with: what counts as harm? What is the cause of this harm? The two questions appear to be closely related to each other, and all the participants in the judicial process orient to them.

As for the harm itself, the statutory provision defines it broadly. Article 6 speaks of the wife alleging that her husband mistreated her in such a way as to make it impossible for people of their social standing to continue the marriage relationship. Hence, it is up to the judge to characterise the facts under review so as to fit them into the definition of Article 6. Here, the judge is constrained by the definitions given by the Court of Cassation, as appears explicitly in the following excerpt of the ruling:

> *Excerpt 4 (Case No. 701, 1983)*
> Considering that, as it emerges from the text of Article 6 of Decree-Law No. 25 of 1929 concerning certain provisions on repudiation, the Egyptian legislature requires, in order for the judge to rule for judicial divorce on the ground of harm, that the harm or the prejudice comes from the husband, to the exception of the wife, and that life together has become impossible. The harm here is the wrong done by the husband to his wife by means of speech or action or both, in a manner that is not acceptable to people of same status, and it constitutes something shameful and wrongful that cannot be endured (Cassation, Personal Status, Appeal No. 50, 52nd Judicial Year, session of 28 June 1983; its standard is here the non-material standard of a person, which varies according to environment, culture and the wife's status in the society: Cassation, Personal Status, Appeal No. 5, 46th Judicial Year, session of 9 November 1977, p. 1644). The harm also has to be a specific harm resulting from their dispute, necessary, not susceptible of extinction; the wife cannot continue marital life; it must be in the capacity of her husband to stop it and to relieve her from it if he wishes, but he continues to inflict it, or he has resumed it (Cassation, Personal Status, Appeal No. 5, 47th Judicial Year, session of 14 March 1979, p. 798; Cassation, Personal Status, Appeal No. 51, 50th Judicial Year, session of 26 January 1982).

Here again, the Court's formal definition does not totally extinguish the uncertainty the judge faces when characterising the facts. This does not mean, however, that the judge's work is problematic or arbitrary. On the contrary, the categories to which the judge refers have, for him, an objective nature, even though it is his characterisation that objectifies them. Moreover, the legal process of characterisation is thoroughly supported by the sociological process of normalisation, that is, the operations through which the judge routinely selects some of the features of a case resembling a common, normal, usual type of case. It is to these 'normal' categories, which have, beyond their legal definition, a common-sense dimension, that the judge, as well as the prosecutor, the attorney, the victim, the offender and the witnesses orient themselves.

In the case of 1983, the wife mobilised two types of grounds in order to substantiate the category of harm: (1) the husband's alleged impotence and, (2) the violence from which she allegedly suffered. Neither impotence nor violence is explicitly mentioned in Egyptian law. However, on the one hand, impotence is traditionally assimilated with either permanent illness (Article 9 of the 1920 Law) or harm (Article 6 of the 1929 Law), while violence is considered as the exemplary type of harm; on the other hand, Hanafite law recognises impotence as a ground for marriage dissolution (Shaham 1997: 125), and this is confirmed in our case by the judge:

> *Excerpt 5 (Case No. 701, 1983)*
> Abû Hanîfa and Abû Yûsuf permitted separation on the ground of a permanent defect that impedes intercourse between the man and the woman, if he is impotent, emasculated or disabled, because the goal of marriage is the protection of procreation, so that, if the man is not capable of this, it becomes impossible to implement the provision of the contract and there is no good in upholding it. Its upholding despite this [constitutes] a harm for the woman the prolongation of which cannot be accepted and which can only be resolved by separation (The Personal Status of imam Abû Zahra, p. 414, para. 297, ed. 1957).

However, this reference to Islamic law is made so as to substantiate a positive-law provision, that is, Article 6 of the 1929 Law. Impotence and violence are not presented as Islamic-law provisions that must be directly implemented by the judge, but as two forms of the harm from which the wife suffered and on the basis of which the judge grants a judicial divorce according to Article 6 of the 1929 Law. The judge seeks to substantiate the legal category of harm, and what counts as harm for him is not totally dependent on statutorily defined[8] or Islamically defined[9] provisions, even though they can play an important role. What counts as harm varies also according to the judge's conception of 'normal harm', that is, the manner in which he typically characterises a certain type of behaviour he encounters in the performance of his routine activities. As mentioned above, what counts as harm for the judge includes, for example, his knowledge of the typical manner in which a wife may suffer prejudice, the social characteristics of given classes of male offenders and female victims, the social and physical features of the settings in which such a situation can take place. The judge's conception of harm functions reflexively: he orients to a conception which he thinks he shares with, and

8 The 1920 and 1929 laws.
9 The above-mentioned stipulations of Abû Hanîfa and Abû Yûsuf.

which will be confirmed by, other people participating in the judicial process, while those other people bear on the judge's conception, which they are asked to confirm, and produce reports that in turn serve as the basis for the judge's final ruling.

> *Excerpt 6 (Case No. 858, 1998)*
> It is established in the [Court of] Cassation's jurisprudence that 'the harm committed by the husband is either positive or negative. Positive harm consists in the evil inflicted by the husband toward his wife by [means of] blows and insults, which is not authorized by Islamic *sharî'a* and from which the wife suffers. As for negative harm, it consists in the husband's neglect of his wife. This is the most severe harm, the harm that dishonours the wife. It suffices that it happens because of the husband, against the wife, only once, to entitle her to ask for a divorce on the ground of harm' (Cass., 31/3/1984 m., p. 287, Majallat al-qadâ', 1984 m.).
>
> The criterion for harm in the sense of Article 6 of Law 25/1929 m. is personal, not material, and its assessment is what makes the prolongation of marital life impossible. [Its criterion] is objective, left to [the discretion of] the judge [adjudicating on] the substance, and it varies according to the environment of the two spouses, their cultural level, and their social milieu (Cass., 1/11/1978 m., p. 1174).
>
> Harm is established through the testimony of two men or one man and two women, in pursuance of the prevailing opinion of the doctrine of Abû Hanîfa and in application of Article 280 of the By-law [organizing the courts] of the *sharî'a*: 'Evidence belongs to two men or to one man and two women' (Cass., Civil, 28/2/1960 m., 11th judicial year, p. 181).
>
> Article 6, although it makes judicial divorce on the ground of harm conditional upon the judge's inability to conciliate the spouses, does not design any precise way [to follow] for the conciliation attempt between the two spouses. The court henceforth proposed conciliation to the two parties. The husband accepted and the wife refused. This is considered an [expression of] the inability of the court to conciliate the two spouses as required by Article 6 (Cass., 14/47, 30th judicial year [sic!],[10] p. 906).

In the case of 1983, two evidentiary techniques are mobilised in order to establish the types of prejudice that result in the harm. With regard to the husband's impotence, the forensic physician is asked to give a medical report, while the husband's violence is established through the oral testimony of witnesses. The latter technique is one of the few sections of the ruling in

10 The 30th judicial year corresponds to 1962 and 1947 corresponds to the 15th judicial year.

which reference is made to Islamic law, although here again it is mediated by positive-law mechanisms, that is, the Court of Cassation's jurisprudence:

> *Excerpt 7 (Case No. 701, 1983)*
> Considering that Hanafî doctrine requires, in order to accept the testimony (*shahâda*) regarding the rights of believers, that it be congruent (*muwâfaqa*) with the petition (*da'wâ*) with regard to what is stipulated in it (*fî-mâ tushtarit fîhi*). The contradiction [of the petition by the testimony] is not acceptable. The congruence is complete when what the witnesses testify to is exactly what the petitioner has claimed; the congruence is implicit when he has testified to part of the case. This is accepted as an agreement. The judge considers what the witnesses testified to as evidence of what the petitioner claimed. The congruence need not be literal; congruence in meaning and intention suffices, whether the expressions are the same or different. (Cassation, Personal Status, session of 23 November 1982, published in the Judges' Review; Appeal No. 2, 53rd Judicial Year, session of 20 December 1983.)

Accordingly, the court decided to collect the testimonies of the witnesses designated by the petitioner and the defendant. Although these testimonies are written documents,[11] they tend to reproduce *verbatim* the parties' exact wording and they allow us to get closer to the interactional details of the practice of judging. These can be read as follows:

> *Excerpt 8 (Case No. 701, 1983)*
> [1]
> 1– The court called the petitioner's first witness and he said
> 2– My name is . . . **oath**
> 3– Question: What's your relationship to the two parties
> 4– Answer: My workplace is close to the post office in which the petitioner works
> 5– Q: What are you testifying to
> 6– A: The petitioner is the defendant's wife by virtue of a legal marriage contract there were disputes between them and I saw the petitioner's husband whom I know although I don't know the place of his residence he was addressing to her words in front of the post office in which she works calling her I heard him addressing her as you bitch you filthy and other words of this kind for nearly two years and one month ago he called the police against her because there was between them something I don't know
> 7– Q: For how long have you known the petitioner's husband

11 Legally, testimonies made in front of the court are considered written testimonies.

8– A: For nearly two years
9– Q: Does he live in your neighborhood
10– A: I don't know
11– Q: For how long has the defendant addressed bad words to the petitioner
12– A: For nearly two years
13– Q: What are the words he's addressed to her
14– A: He told her you bitch you filthy and words of this kind and this was in front of the post office
15– Q: Did any harm affect the petitioner because of this
16– A: Yes, she broke down while working at the post office
17– Q: Anything else to say
18– A: No . . .
[3]
35– The defendant's first witness was called. He said:
36– My name is . . . **oath**
37– Q: What's your relationship to the two parties
38– A: The defendant lives with me at home
39– Q: What are you testifying to
40– A: The petitioner is the defendant's wife by virtue of a legal marriage contract and the defendant lives with me and he's lived in my home for one year and eight months and nothing like a misunderstanding happened between them and he didn't assault her and he didn't hit her and he didn't insult her and the policeman came and took the defendant and locked him in the station
41– Q: Did you see the defendant assaulting the petitioner
42– A: No
43– Q: Did you hear the defendant insulting the petitioner
44– A: No
45– Q: The petitioner's two witnesses reported that he insulted her and hit her in front of her workplace
46– A: No it didn't happen
47– Q: Anything else to say
48– A: No . . .

Even though testimonies are supposed to be transcribed in the witnesses' own words, they clearly appear to have been at least partly reformulated by the judge (and his clerk). This is why the witness is always reported to have begun his testimony by stating that the petitioner and the defendant are spouses 'by virtue of a legal marriage contract'. In addition to this rewriting or editing process, the overall stereotypical nature of the organisation of the testimony and the pre-allocated sequence of turns in the production of the testimony are noteworthy. Both depend on the institutional context in which these testimonies are given. As noted in a seminal study of courtroom interactions, 'the talk in each stage of court hearings shares the feature that although it occurs in a multi-party setting . . . the parties who may participate are limited and predetermined' (Atkinson and Drew 1979: 35). Moreover, whatever is done in this context is necessarily managed by the participants within the constraining framework of this pre-allocated turn-taking organisation. In other words, unlike ordinary conversations, turn order in judicial settings is fixed, as is the type of each speaker's turn.

Within this system of turn allocation, both the judge and the witnesses are oriented to the production of information that may be legally relevant, and to the credibility of this information. On the judge's side, the credibility of the information provided by each witness is tested by questions directed at the credibility of the witness himself. This is why the interrogation always begins with a question about the witness's 'relationship to the two parties' (turns 3, 37). This credibility can be further investigated by asking the witness to produce a first account of his testimony (turns 5, 39) and then assessing the reliability of this global narrative by asking the same witness to confirm his statements piecemeal (turns 7–14, 41–44). Some of the judge's questions are clearly directed at challenging the witness's version of the facts by confronting him with another witness's testimony (turn 45: 'The petitioner's two witnesses reported that the defendant had hit her and insulted her'). Clearly, the judge also seeks to extract some elements of information – nature of demeanor (insulting and hitting: turns 41, 43), temporal dimension of the demeanor (for how long?: turn 11), content of the demeanor (words used by the husband: turns 13, 16), responsibility (who did it?: turns 11, 41, 43), prejudicial nature of the demeanor (what effect on the wife?: turn 15) – that are the constituting features of the legal category of harm. Indeed, together, the spare parts of this query for information are in congruence with the many conditional elements of the notion of harm as defined, in the ruling and according to the Court of Cassation, as:

> the wrong done by the husband to his wife in the form of speech or action, or both, in a manner that is not acceptable to people of same status, and it constitutes something shameful and wrongful that cannot be endured.

At the same time, the witness attempts to establish his credibility by offering some elements of information that can reasonably be considered to qualify him as a reliable witness – the nature of his perspective (turn 4: workplace; turn 38: neighbourhood), duration of his witnessing (turns 8, 12: nearly two years) – or which appear as very plausible – exact wording of the insults (turn 14: 'bitch' and 'filthy'), effects of these insults (turn 16: her breaking down at the post office). With regard to the content of his testimony, the witness clearly orients to what appears to him as the constitutive element of the harm, either denying or confirming it having occurred. Interestingly, the witness who denies the existence of any harm directly orients his first global narrative, the elements of which were not elicited by the judge, to the husband having neither insulted nor hit her. Accordingly, one may conclude that the normal conception of harm is made of either blows or insults, or both, in a manner largely independent of any formal legal definition.

If we turn now to the practical ways in which members of the judicial setting orient to the issue of causation and agency in the production of harm, we observe that, although Article 6 of the 1929 Law deals with harm for which the husband is deemed responsible, whereas Article 9 of the 1920 Law deals with harm resulting from the husband's permanent defect, for which he cannot be deemed responsible, however, in the case examined here, the judge merges the two sources of harm and mentions only the statutory reference of Article 6. Moreover, we see that, for the people engaged in judicial procedures, causation takes many forms that are directly linked to common-sense conceptions. These conceptions depend on commonly shared assumptions and vary according to the position people occupy within the judicial procedure. In the case under scrutiny, people orient to an institution such as marriage in terms of its normal goals. This teleological approach to marriage is clearly manifested in the petitioner's request and in the judge's ruling:

> *Excerpt 9 (Case No. 701, 1983)*
> Petitioner: The petitioner is the wife of the defendant in pursuance of a valid legal marriage contract; she was married to him and discovered suddenly that her husband the defendant had a constitutional defect, that is, he was totally incapable of having marital relations with her, which therefore made it impossible for her to procreate and this put her life in trouble and made her psychologically sensitive, and her life became deeply sad as it became clear that this kind of marriage would not realize the aims of marriage.
>
> Ruling: Considering that . . . the forensic physician has established that the defendant . . . is affected by psychological impotence. . . . Abû Hanîfa and Abû Yûsuf permitted separation on the ground of a permanent defect that impedes intercourse between the man and the woman if he is impotent, emasculated, or disabled, because the goal of marriage is the preservation of procreation, so that, if the man is not capable of this, it becomes impossible to implement the provision of the contract and there is no good in upholding it. Its upholding despite this [constitutes] a harm for the woman the lasting of which cannot be accepted and which can only be resolved by separation. . . .

The many parties to the case commonly consider the absence of marital relationships and the inability to procreate an incongruity that disturbs the normal course of a marriage. This is precisely what must be accounted for. A causal factor – here impotence – is invoked so as to remedy this incongruity.

Impotence is elevated to the rank of the main causal source, from which all other factors are derived.

Besides this teleological conception – the cause of harm is the element that forecloses the realisation of the goals of marriage – harm causation is considered in terms of successive integrated factors. This means that events are presented as necessarily following each other. In our case, the argument proceeds as follows: the wife risks committing infidelity, because of antipathy between her and her husband, because marital life has become unbearable, because the wife is compelled to live under moral duress, because of the blows, insults and false accusations that she must suffer, because of her husband's bitterness, because of his impotence. In this causal argument, Islam and Islamic law may play a role, but it is only one among the many different reasons why people abide by the rule. This is reflected in our case in the presentation of the petitioner's request in which her motives are exposed:

> *Excerpt 10 (Case No. 701, 1983)*
> For the same abovementioned reason the defendant's reproductive impotence and his inability to realize the aims of marriage led him to express his anger in revenge and hostility against the petitioner, by insulting and hitting her and finally by accusing her of dishonesty and telling the police that the petitioner, who is his wife, had stolen Egyptian £1500 and jewels (a golden bracelet, a necklace and a ring), falsely, aggressively and wrongly, so as to compel her to live with him under moral duress. Then, he denounced her for asking him to give back her marital belongings. The pursuance of marital life has become impossible, for there is antipathy and dislike between them and she is still a young person and she fears infidelity for herself and she fears God Almighty.

Explicitly 'Islamic' considerations are few. Moreover, they are generally mediated by reference to law books and case-law. In that respect, we must be concerned only with the way in which the judge (as also the Public Prosecutor, the forensic physician and the attorney) orient to the provisions of Egyptian law, including those rules that originate in classical Islamic *fiqh*. In our cases, impotence and violence are not characterised by the parties as Islamic-law provisions per se.[12] Rather, we observed the ways in which the parties refer to impotence so as to exhibit the workshop level of their practices, which are publicly and accountably made up of considerations for the institutional setting, procedural correctness and legal relevance.

12 This is an assumption that can be justified only because scholars know in advance that these are grounds for divorce in classical Islamic *fiqh*.

III. Conclusion

Many scholars claim that, despite major transformations in law and adjudication in Egypt during the last two centuries, it is still an Islamic judge who issues Islamic rulings in the field of personal status law, the last stronghold of Islamic law. I argued that such claims must be challenged on two different levels. On the first level, these claims fall short of any satisfactory definition of what is specifically Islamic that would make this law an Islamic law and its provisions something better characterised by their Islamic rather than their national Egyptian dimension. On the second and more fundamental level, my contention is that these claims are sociologically irrelevant, for they eschew the praxiological dimension of adjudication. Instead of assuming that there exists something called an Islamic personal status law to which judges necessarily conform, it would be better to examine and describe judges' actual daily activities and practices, through which they manifest their legal knowledge, their formal and practical legal training, and the routinised nature of their activity in the field of personal status law. Thus scholars should not presume the Islamic nature of rulings on the basis of their genealogical connection to the provisions of an earlier legal system, for this would be to adopt an ironic position by which scholars tell judges what is Islamic and what is not in their daily judicial activities. Instead, any ascription of an Islamic dimension and authority to rulings should proceed from the judges' personal characterisations and orientations, to which only a close scrutiny of actual interactions and utterances bears witness. In other words, there is no valid preconceived model to the yardstick of which one can evaluate actual judicial practices. The Islamic nature of rulings is something that is instantiated and realised by the actual written and oral performances of judges.

At the very place where it is supposed to be massive and overwhelming, that is, in personal status law, references to Islamic law are conspicuous for their paucity. This suggests that the issue of Islamic law in contemporary Egyptian law does not proceed from what the scholarly tradition generally claims. Reference to Islam is occasional; moreover, it is always mediated through the use of Egyptian law's primary sources, that is, legislation and case-law. Henceforth, this reference takes place in the banality and the routine of a judge's activity, which consists mainly in legally characterising the facts submitted to him. By so doing, the judge is obviously more interested in manifesting his ability to judge correctly – according to the standards of his profession, the formal constraints that apply to its exercise, the legal sources on which he relies and the norms of the interpretive work his activity supposes – than he is to reiterate the Islamic primacy of the law he implements. There is no doubt that, if asked, the same judge would underscore the conformity of his activity and the law he applies with Islamic law. However, such an attitude would only be retrospective, a posteriori and justificatory. In the course of his work, the judge does not orient himself to the necessity to assess the Islamic dimension of any object, even in this domain of law where the Islamic genealogy of rules seems most evident. The close description of the modes of usage of, and reference to, legal rules, some of which have an Islamic genealogy, shows us the extent to which law is a practical accomplishment, rather than an archaeological search for the Islamic pedigree of the norm.

References

Arabi, O. (2001) *Studies in Modern Islamic Law and Jurisprudence*, The Hague: Kluwer Law International.

Atkinson, J.M. and P. Drew (1979) *Order in Court: The Organization of Verbal Interaction in Courtroom Settings*, London: Macmillan.

Berger, M. (2001) 'Public Policy and Islamic Law: The Modern *Dhimmî* in Contemporary Egyptian Family Law', *Islamic Law and Society* 8(1): 88–136.

Bowen, J. (2003) *Islam, Law and Equality in Indonesia: An Anthropology of Public Reasoning*, Cambridge: Cambridge University Press.

Brown, N. (1997) *The Rule of Law in the Arab World*, Cambridge: Cambridge University Press.

Drew, P. (1992) 'Contested Evidence in Courtroom Cross-examination: The Case of a Trial for Rape', in P. Drew and J. Heritage (eds) *Talk at Work: Interaction in Institutional Settings*, Cambridge: Cambridge University Press.

Dupret, B. (2004) 'Intention in Action: A Pragmatic Approach to Criminal Characterization in an Egyptian Context', in B. Dupret (ed.) *Standing Trial: Law and the Person in the Modern Middle East*, London: I.B. Tauris.

Geertz, C. (1983) *Local Knowledge: Further Essays in Interpretive Anthropology*, New York: Basic Books.

Hart, H.L.A. (1961) *The Concept of Law*, Oxford: Oxford University Press.

Hester, S. and P. Eglin (1997) 'Membership Categorization Analysis: An Introduction', in S. Hester and P. Eglin (eds) *Culture in Action: Studies in Membership Categorization Analysis*, Washington, DC: University Press of America.

Hirsch, S. (1998) *Pronouncing and Persevering: Gender and the Discourses of Disputing in an African Islamic Court*, Chicago: University of Chicago Press.

Jayyusi, L. (1984) *Categorization and the Moral Order*, Boston, MA: Routledge and Kegan Paul.

Layish, A. and R. Shaham (EI) (1954–2005) '*tashrî'*', in *The Encyclopedia of Islam*, 2nd edn., Leiden: E.J. Brill.

Lynch, M. (1991) 'Method: Measurement – Ordinary and Scientific Measurement as Ethnomethodological Phenomena', in G. Button (ed.) *Ethnomethodology and the Human Sciences*, Cambridge: Cambridge University Press.

Lynch, M. (1993) *Scientific Practice and Ordinary Action: Ethnomethodology and Social Studies of Science*, Cambridge: Cambridge University Press.

Messick, B. (1993) *The Calligraphic State: Textual Domination and History in a Muslim Society*, Berkeley: University of California Press.

Mir-Hosseini, Z. (1993) *Marriage on Trial: A Study of Islamic Family Law*, London: I.B. Tauris.

Moerman, M. (1974) 'Accomplishing Ethnicity', in R. Turner (ed.) *Ethnomethodology*, Harmondsworth: Penguin.

Rosen, L. (1989) *The Anthropology of Justice: Law as Culture in Islamic Society*, Cambridge: Cambridge University Press.

Sacks, H. (1974) 'On the Analyzability of Stories by Children', in R. Turner (ed.) *Ethnomethodology*, Harmondsworth: Penguin.

Sacks, H. (1995) *Lectures on Conversation*, vols I and II, Oxford: Blackwell.

Shaham, R. (1997) *Family and the Courts in Modern Egypt: A Study Based on Decisions by Sharī'a Courts, 1900–1955*, Leiden: Brill.

Sharrock, W. and G. Button (1991) 'The Social Actor: Social Action in Real Time', in G. Button (ed.) *Ethnomethodology and the Human Sciences*, Cambridge: Cambridge University Press.

Travers, M. (1997) *The Reality of Law: Work and Talk in a Firm of Criminal Lawyers*, Aldershot: Ashgate Dartmouth.

Watson, R. (1994) 'Catégories, séquentialité et ordre social', in B. Fradin, L. Quéré and J. Widmer (eds) *L'Enquête sur les catégories*, Paris: Ed. de l'EHESS (Raisons pratiques, no. 5).

Wittgenstein, L. (1967) *Philosophical Investigations*, trans. G.E.M. Anscombe. Oxford: Blackwell.

Chapter 6

State of equalities

Law, marriage and citizenship in the Islamic Republic of Mauritania[1]

Satyel Larson

The question of *kafāʾa* or 'equality of birth' in Islamic law can be posed in a number of ways, and I shall do so three times throughout the course of this paper. After introducing *kafāʾa* and the problems around which this paper has been organised, I will first pose the question of *kafāʾa* doctrinally as an instance of a discursive production of a legal norm in Islamic law.[2] Then I will pose it empirically in order to illustrate two instances of *kafāʾa* in practice in postcolonial Mauritania. Finally, I will pose it a third time in a way that will, I hope, expose a relation between legal norms and practices in an Islamic context.

Kafāʾa is in a strict legal sense the concept of equality of marital partners developed by Sunni Muslim jurists that together with an appropriate dower (*mahr, ṣadāq*) render a marriage suitable.[3] In Arabic, the literal meaning of

1 I would like to thank Professors Baber Johansen, Marianne Constable and Adam Gearey for their generous and helpful comments on earlier drafts of this paper. I am indebted to Dr Zekeria Ould Ahmed Salem for directing my attention to his influential work on citizenship in Mauritania. I was fortunate to have in Nima Bassiri a superb and thoughtful reader.

2 A note on transliteration and translation: In general, I have followed the system of transliteration outlined by the *International Journal of Middle Eastern Studies* (*IJMES*) for transliterating Modern Standard and Classical Arabic. I have provided the transliterations with vowels (*tashkīl*) where I thought it may help to disambiguate the original text. However, so as not to encumber the reader, I have not voweled every word. Unless otherwise noted, all translations are mine, and I have tried to the greatest extent possible to preserve the intentions, effects and meanings of the original texts.

3 In Islamic law, marriage is the foundation of an affinity to an agnatic family that gives the marital partners the mutual right to inherit from one another. Marriage is instituted through the conclusion of an oral or written marriage contract (*nikāḥ*) that simultaneously renders licit sexual relations between a woman and a man, and the gaze upon the 'shame-zones' (*ʿawra*), areas of the body which were forbidden to the gaze prior to the conclusion of the marriage contract. The marriage is rendered legally valid when an adult woman or her guardian (*walī*) and an adult man consent to the marriage, which is duly witnessed by at least two people. Whereas in the Hanafi, Hanbali and Shafi'i *madhāhib* (schools of Islamic law, singular: *madhhab*) the offer and acceptance of marriage must take place in the same meeting and in the presence of two adult males, in Maliki law the presence of two witnesses

kafā'a is equality, or 'a position in which one thing is equal to another thing' (Luwīs Malūf 1954: 690). Traced to its consonantal root, it also connotes sufficiency or satisfaction as a means of balance, for instance, in weight.[4] Jurists and legal scholars confer a technical sense to *kafā'a*, and it is this technical meaning that has been translated into English as the suitability or equality of marriage partners with respect to certain aspects of the partners' identities, such as religion, freedom, lineage, morals, profession and piety. The meaning of the doctrine of equality (*kafā'a*), itself a formal, abstract standard to measure social identity, requires further interpretive schemas at multiple levels.

While I accept the fitness of the translation (i.e. equality, suitability), the three attempts to understand *kafā'a* in this essay are attempts to give a richer and more specific meaning to the doctrine and practice of equality as it mediates power as well as the ideas of nation and state in the postcolonial Islamic Republic of Mauritania, where authoritative interpretation of the law is not limited to state institutions and where knowledge of the law produces privilege and cultural capital. In order to give *kafā'a* a fuller meaning in this context, I will examine how the specific conditions of equality before the law are and have come to be practised and understood through the institutionalisation of national identity and the law of personal status. The question of legal equality positions the formal, abstract and universal identity of the Muslim citizen as the bearer of equal rights against the culturally and biologically defined identities (ethnic, tribal, racial, caste) of particularised legal subjects also bearing equal rights.

By filling out the complex meanings of *kafā'a*, I will effectively illuminate the conceptual parameters of this paper. First, I will show how *kafā'a* is an overlooked aspect of contemporary Maliki juridical practice of the family in the modern era of reformed, state-regulated Islamic law.[5] While fewer highly developed doctrinal and theoretical accounts of *kafā'a* exist in the juridical treatises of Maliki jurists than in the treatises of, say, Hanafi jurists, non-binding advisory legal opinions (*fatwā*, sing.; *fatāwā*, plural) and cases issuing from the territory that is now the Islamic Republic of Mauritania, a region that has historically and loyally followed Maliki jurisprudence (*fiqh*), show how *kafā'a* is either invoked (for instance, by matrimonial guardians) in an attempt to circumscribe the autonomy of the adult woman or her male guardian, or is forgotten (for instance, by spouses) in order to maintain matrimonial practices that govern the drawing up of the marriage contract.

is recommended, provided the marriage is given sufficient publicity. See Khalīl ibn Isḥāq al-Jundī (1980), 90; and Dawoud Sudqi el Alami and D. Hinchcliffe (1996).

4 Aḥmad ibn Muḥammad Fayyūmī and 'Abd al-Karīm ibn Muḥammad Rāfi'ī, *Kitāb al-miṣbāḥ al-munīr fī gharīb al-sharḥ al-kabīr li-l-Rāfi'ī* (1980).

5 For a historical discussion of the relation between the theory and practice of *kafā'a* in the late Middle Ages, see Zomeño (2001), 87–106.

The two cases of *kafā'a* I examine illuminate both how contemporary jurists, lawyers and courts in Mauritania continue a legacy of extensive juristic disagreement (*ikhtilāf*) among Maliki jurists on the issue of *kafā'a*, and how the specific interpretations of *kafā'a* map out the political terrain of Mauritanian society and mediate the question of the nation.

I will additionally demonstrate how measures of equality before the law are based on the repetition of the memories of founding moments, and imagined historical situations and traditions. Lastly, I will discuss how these measures of equality are doubly situated in that they reflect competing normativities and institutionalisations of group life that are determined by varying modes of temporally oriented, imagined communal identities or based on divergent modes of belonging. The difference between precolonial custom (viz. caste and ethnic identities) and the postcolonial nation-state (viz. citizenship) best illustrates the double situation of the measures of equality before the law. Each of these forms of imagined identity are grounded in practices that have distinct relations to time and which conceive and limit the identity of the postcolonial subject of Islamic family law.

I. What is *kafā'a*? The doctrine of *kafā'a*

Kafā'a is the doctrine of equality or parity in marriage first set forth in classical Sunni Islamic jurisprudence (*fiqh*), under which a woman may not contract a marriage with a man whom the male agnative relatives of the woman deem to be of unequal social standing to her and, through her, to them. A marriage that does not meet the requirement of *kafā'a* is the object of judicial sanction and lack of *kafā'a* is ground for annulment (*faskh*) of the marriage contract (*al-nikāḥ*).

Kafā'a may be the only situation in which Islamic law concerns itself with race (Lewis 1990: 128–9). Unlike the laws of Nazi Germany or Apartheid South Africa, it does not proscribe marriage between races, but rather gives the family as represented by the male relatives a legal possibility for opposing an 'unsuitable' marriage. It gives power to the father or guardian (*walī*) to oppose a marriage contracted without his consent, or to annul a marriage that has already been contracted through deception, as long as there is neither child nor pregnancy.

The doctrine of *kafā'a* finds antecedents in the law of Kufa, and pre-Islamic and tribal customs, which imposed a certain degree of social equality between spouses.[6] While various Qur'anic passages discuss the permissibility or

6 Ziadeh (1957), 509; Linant de Bellefonds (2008); Musa Ali Ajetunmobi (1984), 86–101; Schacht (1964), 182: 'The degrees of equality by birth (*Kafā'a*), which is demanded only of the man, among the free Muslims are: members of Ḳuraysh, the tribe of the Prophet; other Arabs; and non-Arabs (with subdivisions of these degrees)'; and Coulson (2005), 49.

prohibition of marriage according to diverse paradigms such as degrees of consanguinity and suckling as well as religious identity and morality,[7] and while reports of the sayings of the Prophet Mohammad (*Ḥadīth*) narrate discussions about the qualities that a man should look for in a wife and the desirability of equality in marriage,[8] the doctrine of *kafā'a* is not explicitly sanctioned by the Qur'an and indeed may contradict Qur'anic passages about the equality of all believers (Ziadeh 1957: 509 and Linant de Bellefonds 2008).

Kafā'a reveals an attitude toward marriage in which marriage is as much an alignment between two families as it is an alignment between two people. It is used to determine whether an alignment between two families will be beneficial beyond the two individuals being married and aims to protect the family of the woman from misaligning itself with a family that it considers unequal and unsuited to it. A man can marry beneath his social status without creating a misalliance, but lack of *kafā'a* of the future spouse of a woman is deemed harmful to the honor of the woman and her family. The rule is unidirectional insofar as it prohibits a woman from contracting a marriage to a man of inferior social status. Only the man's status is measured and it has to be equal to or better than the status of the woman's male relatives.[9]

According to the doctrine of *kafā'a*, the woman gains her fundamental value or meaning and is given her identity in the marriage contract, not through any intrinsic, particular value that she herself may hold, but rather only insofar as she represents, and is represented by, the men of her consanguineal

7 On Qur'anic passages about marriage, see Abdullah Yusuf (1998), chapter/verse: 2:221; 4:3–4, 20–5, 34–5, 128–30; 5:5; 7:189; 23:6; 24:3; 24:26, 32–3; 25:54; 30:21; 33:37, 50–2; 53:27–38; 60:10.

8 See Mohammed Muhsin Khan, *Ṣaḥīḥ Al-Bukhārī* (1994), chapter 60, The Book of *Nikāḥ*, Hadith 1835, 889: 'Narrated Abu Huraira, *raḍiya Allahu 'anhu*: The Prophet, *ṣalla Allahu 'alayhi wa sallam*: "A woman is married for four (things), i.e., her wealth, her family status, her beauty and her religion. So you should take possession of (marry) the religious woman (otherwise) you will be a loser".' Also see Al-Imam Hafiz Al-Baris Al-Allamah Jamaluddin Abi Muhammad Abdullah bin Yusuf al-Hanafi Al Zai'ali, *Naṣbul Al-Rayah* (no publication date) vol. 3, 196–7. The Prophet said: 'Women are not to be proposed (to) and married except by their equals', and 'Select (fit) woman (in respect of character) for your seeds and marry (you) your equals and give (your daughters) in marriage to them'. Quoted in Zaleha Kamaruddin (2004), 34–5.

9 Interestingly, in an equation, it might look something like the algebraic law of transitivity: $M \geq F$ where $F = m + m + m$ to ∞; therefore, $M \geq m + m + m$ to ∞. Thus while the doctrine seems to give adult women a certain amount of social mobility insofar as a woman, unlike a man, can marry into a class above the one she was born into, the unidirectionality of the social mobility indicates the woman's mediating function in the social exchange of marriage, since she does not elevate the status of her husband if she marries beneath her class. Since the woman is first associated with the status of her father and then with that of her husband, it seems then that it is ultimately the social identity of the father (both symbolic and real) that is at stake, as notions of honor and shame attach to him through the act of the daughter's marriage.

male forbearers. Of course, since personal attributes such as beauty, age and virginity help to determine the dower, and since a proper dower is an element that renders a marriage suitable, it may be said that particular characteristics of the woman play an indirect role in determining *kafā'a*.

There is a difference between the four Sunni schools, and differences within each school itself, as to what defines this equality and what grants this value – and as to whether the equality and the value are defined in terms of genealogy (*nasab*), piety (*dīn*) and the historical depth of the family's adherence to Islam (*bayt*), nobility or social prestige (*ḥasab*), race, liberty (*al-ḥurriyya*), profession or wealth.[10] The notion of *kafā'a* is practically irrelevant in Shi'i law, except in the case of marriage between a non-Muslim man and Muslim woman (Al-Hasan ibn Yusuf ibn al-Mutahhar al-Hillī 1991: 140). Literature on *kafā'a* attributes this difference between the schools, as well as the relative degree of sophistication of the doctrine, to the social climates in which the schools developed; it remains less developed in the Maliki than it does in the Hanafi doctrine. Indeed, the Hanafis have an elaborative hierarchy of professions that determine the equality of spouses.[11]

If the doctrine of *kafā'a* took root more firmly in classical Hanafi jurisprudence than it did in classical Maliki jurisprudence, the branches of those roots are even more visible in twentieth-century codifications of family law throughout the Islamic world in countries that have historically followed the Hanafi school of law (*madhhab*). Whereas Syria, Jordan and Iraq have incorporated *kafā'a* articles into their Codes of Personal Status, the doctrine of *kafā'a* is nearly absent – or expressed in a less obvious way – in the corresponding Maghrebi codes in Algeria, Morocco, Tunisia and Mauritania. For example, Chapter Four, '*Kafā'a*', of the Syrian Code of Personal Status (*Qānūn al-aḥwāl al-shakhṣiyya*[12]) devotes seven articles (26–32) to the regulation of *kafā'a*.[13]

10 For discussions of what determines equality in *Kafā'a*, see Johansen (1996), 76; Coulson (2005), 49, 94; Ziadeh (1957), 509; and Linant de Bellefonds (2008).

11 Coulson (2005), 94. Farhat Ziadeh concurs: 'A review of early authorities on Muslim law reveals that Malik had nothing to say about *kafa'ah* in *al-Muwaṭṭa* whereas Abu Hanifah, Abu Yusuf, and Shaybani (d. 189 A.H.) recognized it. Malik is reported to have expressly authorized the marriage of non-Arab men to Arab women, and to have said that lineage (*sharaf*) and honor (*ḥasab*) should not stand in the way of a previously married woman in marrying herself off to whomever she wishes, while these considerations are material to the Hanafi doctrine of *kafa'ah*' (Ziadeh 1957: 505).

12 Syria, and Muhammad Fahr Shaqfah, *Majmū'at qawānīn al-aḥwāl al-shakhṣiyya al-nāfidha fī Sūrīya ma' al-uṣūl wa-l-bayyināt: wa-tashmal Qānūn al-Aḥwāl al-Shakhṣiyya* (A Collection of the Laws of Effective Personal Status in Syria with the Sources and Explanations, including the Code of Personal Status) (1996) 22, hereafter referred to as *Syrian Code of Personal Status*.

13 See Syria, *Syrian Code of Personal Status*. These seven articles specify that the man must be equal to the woman ('*Yushtaraṭu fī lūzūmi al-zawāji an yakūna al-rajulu kufu'an li-l-mara'ati*') Art. 26; that *kafā'a* is determined by Syrian local custom (*'urf al-bilād*) Art. 28; and that a marriage contract should be annulled (*faskh*) if lack of *kafā'a* on the part of the husband is discovered after the conclusion of the marriage contract, the pregnancy or birth of a child notwithstanding, Articles 30 and 32.

One possible reason for the legal regulation of parity between spouses in the Hanafi doctrine, and the lack of such a developed doctrine in Maliki *fiqh*, may be found in the relationship between *kafāʾa* and institution of the matrimonial legal guardian (*walī*). In Maliki doctrine, the *walī* historically plays a greater legal role than he does in Hanafi doctrine.[14] In the classical Maliki doctrine, the *walī*'s presence and consent are necessary components of the adult woman's marriage contract, rendering *kafāʾa* less necessary and, perhaps, redundant.[15] This is because it is the duty of the *walī*, in giving his consent to the marriage, to respect the equality of the partners in a marriage alliance and to ensure that the woman's family will not misalign itself through a marriage contract. In Hanafi doctrine, however, the woman who has reached the age of puberty may contract her own marriage without a guardian. Her autonomy in selecting a marriage partner purportedly lends greater risk to the possibility of a misalignment and the necessity for legal redress in the event of such a misalignment (Johansen 1996: 76).

However, while the secondary literature on the doctrine would absent *kafāʾa* from Maliki doctrine and practice (Coulson 2005: 94; Ziadeh 1957:

14 Thus, the Syrian and Jordanian codes of personal status have incorporated this right of the guardian and permit him to intervene on the grounds of lack of *kafāʾa* to annul a marriage contract. See Syria, *Syrian Code of Personal Status*, Articles, 27, 29, 32; Jordan, and ʿIzzat Ghayth, 2001, *Qānūn al-Aḥwāl al-Shakhṣiyya: qānūn muʾaqqat raqm (61) li-sanat 1976. Silsilat al-Tashrīʿāt al-qaḍāʾiyya, 5.* Amman: Dar Qindil (Referred to as Code of Personal Status), Articles 21–2. While contemporary codes of personal status in the Maghreb that have historically followed Maliki doctrine have abolished matrimonial constraint (*jabr*) and require that the adult woman give her express consent to the marriage, the guardian is still a socially necessary component in the marriage contract. See Charrad (2001), 138–9, 160, 163, 224, 231; Ziba Mir-Hosseini (1991), 146–7. While the Code of Personal Status of Mauritania lists the guardian of both the legally adult woman (18 years) and the minor as one of the four constitutive elements to effect a legal marriage (Article 5), the guardian only continues to play a legal role in the marriage of the minor in the Tunisian (Articles 6–9) and Moroccan (Articles 13, 20, 22) Codes of Personal Status. See *The Moroccan Family Code (Moudawwana)* of 5 February 2004 (unofficial translation) www.hrea.org/moudawwana.html; The Tunisian Record of Personal Status, Tunisia (2007), *Majallat al-aḥwāl al-shakhṣiyya*. [Tunis]: *Manshūrāt al-Maṭbaʿa al-Rasmiyya li-l-Jumhūriyya al-Tūnisiyya*; and Mauritania (2001), Loi N° 2001-052 *portant Code du statut personnel/Qānūn raqm* 2001-052 *yataḍamman Mudawwanat al-Aḥwāl al-Shakhṣiyya*, in Arabic: www.mauritania.mr/index.php?niveau=6&coderub=4&codsoussous=175&codesousrub=11&codsoussous1=176 or French: www.mauritania.mr/fr/index.php?niveau=6&coderub=4&codsoussous=176&codesousrub=11&codsoussous1=178. Articles 24 and 25 of the 2004 Moroccan Code of Personal Status give the woman who has reached 18 years old the *de jure* power to contract her own marriage without a guardian. According to Linant de Bellefonds (2008), however, diminutions in the role of the guardian in Morocco have been accompanied by the introduction of attenuated forms of *kafāʾa* previously unknown to classical Maliki law.

15 See the chapters on marriage (*Kitāb al-Nikah*) of leading Maliki jurists: Khalil Ibn Ashaq al-Jundi (1980) 89–121; in Arabic/French: *La Risala, ʿAbd Allah ibn ʿAbd al-Raḥman Ibn Abi Zayd al-Qayrawani*, Bercher (1968), 173–93; and Malik Ibn Anas (1989).

503–7, 515–17; and Linant de Bellefonds 2008)[16] classical and modern,[17] and while its existence in contemporary personal status codes is attenuated,[18] the work of Yahya Ould al-Bara who has studied the vast corpus of Mauritanian *fatwās* on *kafā'a* (see Yahya Ould al-Bara 2001), as well as two cases of *kafā'a* in Mauritania in the late-twentieth century, bring to light *kafā'a* as an overlooked aspect of Maliki doctrine and practice, and call for a renewed interest in looking to adaptations of *fiqh* in specific localities and in a distinct social phenomenon, as well as to the legal literature that is studied and produced (decisions, non-binding advisory legal opinions – *fatāwā*, cases – *al-masā'il*, collections of cases – *al-nawāzil*), at the so-called margins of the Islamic world.[19] If we consider this legal literature as an important part of the development of the *sharī'a*, we may transform, broaden or deepen our understanding of the development of *kafā'a* in Maliki doctrine while reassessing or reimagining the kind of Islamic legal norms that could have historically existed and that could have impacted multiple social, economic and political relations.

According to Maliki jurists, the doctrine of *kafā'a* was originally addressed to women to prevent them from marrying non-Muslims, and then spread to ethnic difference, levels of employment, and class status between nobles and non-nobles, as is the case in Mauritania (Zekeria Ould Ahmed Salem 2003: 37–53). The founder of the Maliki school, Malik Ibn Anas (d. 179/796), never mentions *kafā'a* in his *Muwaṭṭa'*, nor specifies genealogical nobility as a requirement of *kafā'a* in Sahnun's *Mudawwana*, where he quotes Qur'anic verse 49:13 and states that 'All Muslims are equal'.[20] Nevertheless, local jurists

16 Amalia Zomeño's article (2001), 92 above, discusses the expansion of *kafā'a* in Maliki doctrine and its subsequent theoretical articulations after Malik Ibn Anas in the *furū'* works of Ibn Rushd, Ibn Juzayy, Ibn Mājishūn, Khalīl ibn Isḥāq al-Jundī, Ibn Mughīth and several other prominent Maliki jurists, whose works all 'reflect a lack of agreement with regard to the theoretical criteria which must be included in the evaluation of the *kafā'a* doctrine'. However, while the classical doctrine reflects the expansion of various juridical opinions on *kafā'a*, Zomeño finds only one case concerning *kafā'a* in Ahmad ibn al-Wanshari's voluminous collection of approximately 6000 *fatwās*.

17 For further discussion on the complicated question of the relationship between modern state family law reform of classical Islamic doctrine in the Arab-Islamic world, see Welchman (2004).

18 So that, for example, in Mauritania, Article 15 of the personal status code insists that the value of the dowry (*ṣadāq*) is fixed by parity. Article 44 states that the status of being afflicted by a serious illness (*al-iṣāba bi-maraḍ makhūf*) is a provisional or temporary obstacle (*al-mawāni' al-mu'aqqata*) to marriage, and Article 45 states that it is not permissible for a Muslim woman to marry a non-Muslim, and that a Muslim man may not marry a woman if she is not of the 'People of the Book', i.e. Jewish or Christian.

19 For responsible inquiries into how Islam and Islamic law are not monolithic phenomena, and how they adopt and are adopted into local custom and practice in Africa, and how Africa is considered and considers itself a marginal Islamic space, see Levtzion and Pouwels (2000); Fischer (1970); and Hunwick (1999), 72–99.

20 '*Ahlu al-Islami kulluhum ba'ḍuhum li-ba'ḍin akfā*'', Mālik ibn Anas, and Saḥnūn (1970) *Al-Mudawwanah al-kubrā*, 6 vols (Baghdad: Maktabat al-Muthannā).

in Mauritania introduced genealogical nobility in their adaptation of *kafā'a* to the point that it became moored in the local imaginary and represented in mythical litigation narratives. One of the oldest of these narratives is the legend of the fourteenth-century mythical war between 'black' (*Idawffal*) and 'white' (*Idashirghra*) tribes. The war began when a Maure scholar wanted to marry his young daughter to a young educated, pious man who belonged ethnically to the Peuls, but who had spent a long time with a Maure tribe.[21]

For at least three centuries in Mauritania, *kafā'a* has been situated between a tribal ideology and the rule of *fiqh*.[22] I understand tribal here to mean the political and social expressions of ethnicity as forms of power, alliance and collective identity. As noted above, social and customary differences in particular localities such as Medina and Kufa may account for the level of elaboration of *kafā'a*. According to Yahya Ould al-Bara, while juridical norms are most often invoked in *kafā'a* and in relation to marriage, there are social and political reasons that explain why the Islamic legal literature has privileged a restrictive reading of *kafā'a*. In a social optic where the tribe is of central importance, particular local values (genealogy, endogamy, *aṣabiyya*[23]) mix

21 This myth is narrated by Youra Ould Ahmed a Mauritanian *faqīh*, in Yahya Ould al-Bara (2001), 446.

22 A note on the use of tribe and ethnicity as categories of analysis: I recognise the major problems that inhere with the use of the words 'tribal', and 'ethnicity', their archaism and connection to racist essentialism (i.e. the classification of people, generally non-Anglo Europeans, by race as a biological category), and the colonial enterprise. I feel, however, that I must use the language of tribe and ethnicity in this essay for two reasons. First, the categories of tribe and ethnicity are primary analytics in contemporary scholarship of Mauritania. In order to address claims made by scholars who work on Mauritania, I must first reiterate the claims and describe the categories of analysis used. Second, one of the main issues in this essay is the way that collective identity, articulated through forms of belonging (racial, ethnic, tribal, caste, national), becomes the site of a power struggle at the social, political and legal levels. Thus while I am critical of the uses and effects, both productive and repressive, of these categories of identity, I think that they are appropriate for this essay. For helpful critiques of the use of the concept of tribe and ethnicity in Africanist and Mauritanian scholarship see Villasante Cervello and de Beauvais (2007); and Amselle and M'Bokolo (1985).

23 See Ibn Khaldun, *Muqaddima I*, 326 for a social – as opposed to a legal – analysis of the relationship between Saharan patrilineal genealogy (*naṣab*) and the structural corporation of agnatic solidarity (*'aṣabiyya*). The general rule between *'aṣabiyyāt* is the competition and hierarchy between them for social distinction and status, which eventually results in the power of one over all others: 'The tribal spirit is composite and results from the mixing of several clans, one of which is stronger than the others. This is the origin of social tribal organization and superiority over men and dynasties. The key to success is the clan that dominates the whole tribe tallies with the temperament that is in the process of gestation. The temperament results from the mixing of the elements. As we have seen, no mixing can take place if the elements are in equal proportion. One of these elements must be superior to the others in order to achieve mixing. In the same way, one of the clans must be stronger to unify the others and fuse them into a single corporate spirit (*'aṣabiyya*).'

with local interpretations of Islam, such that Islamic law is interpreted and instrumentalised through genealogical and endogamous ethics (Yahya Ould al-Bara 2001: 441). The anthropological structures of Maure marriages are such that the preferred alliance is between brothers' children (*awlād ʿamm*) and preferably with the female paternal parallel cousin, that is, the daughter of the brother of the father. This category of marriage is simultaneously a classificatory genealogy, as an entire tribe is ideally descended from one apical male ancestor (see Bonte 2006: 98–122). I will return to the importance of classification and its attendant exclusions as a form of danger and power later in this essay. For now, I would like to underscore this preferential choice of ideal marriage as that which establishes *kafāʾa* between individuals, families and agnatic solidarities (*ʿassabiyyāt*)[24] in Arab Maure marriages in Mauritania.

Mauritanian and Maliki *fuqahāʾ* have taken positions on this. The Maliki Egyptian jurist, Khalīl ibn Isḥāq al-Jundī (d. 776/1374) whose obscure yet concise *Mukhtaṣar* (abridged manual of legal treatises[25]) has become the main source of jurisprudence in many areas of law in contemporary Mauritania, and who introduced the Malikite doctrine in Mauritania and was well known and being widely studied there by the sixteenth century (Mohamed El Mokhtar Ould Bah 1981: 36, 43–72), wrote 'Matrimonial equivalence is religion and status' (*Al-kafāʾatu [hiya] al-dīnu wa-l-ḥālu*) (*Khalīl ibn Isḥāq al-Jundī* 1980: 103). Commentaries on the meaning of this, notably in the glosses of the Libyan Maliki scholar Muḥammad ibn Muḥammad al-Ḥaṭṭāb (d. 954/1547),[26] and the Egyptian Maliki glossator Muhammad ibn Aḥmad ibn ʿArafah al-Dasūqi (d. 1230/1815)[27] imply that there is consensus that 'status' (*al-ḥāl*) refers to the physical condition of being healthy and free from vulgar deformities (. . . *al-ḥālu ʾay al-salāmatu min al-ʿuyūbi*[28] and *al-murādu*

24 Two in-depth and concise analyses of the historicity of the political domain in Mauritania are Marchesin (1992) 51–4; and Bonte (2006), 109–11.

25 *Mukhtaṣar* is both the title of Khalil's manuscript, and reference to a genre of didactic, utilitarian oriented writing which began to appear with increasing frequency in the tenth to eleventh centuries in Arabic literature, philosophy, religious science, history and philosophy. The *mukhtaṣar* condenses and epitomizes lengthier works in order to relieve 'the educated readers from all the lengthy discussions, chains of transmitters and endless appendices; they offered them the essentials; the specialised work became more accessible'. The genre of the *Mukhtaṣar* was particularly important in the field of law as it permitted lawyers to be trained quickly. Khalil's *Mukhtaṣar* represents the 'termination of a series of abridgments, of which the *Mudawwana* is the beginning . . .' This genre, intended to concentrate many ideas into as few words as possible, inspired and perhaps necessitated lengthy commentaries (*sharḥ*) and supercommentaries (*ḥāshiya*) rendering somewhat redundant the attempts at abridgement. Arazi (2009).

26 Muḥammad ibn Muḥammad Ḥaṭṭāb, Zakarīyā ʿUmayrāt, Khalīl ibn Isḥāq al-Jundī, and Muḥammad ibn Yūsuf Mawwāq (1995), vol. 5, 106–7.

27 Muḥammad ibn Aḥmad ibn ʿArafah Dasūqī, Muḥammad ibn Aḥmad ʿIllaysh, Aḥmad ibn Muḥammad Dardīr, and Khalīl ibn Isḥāq al-Jundī (1980), vol. 2: 226.

28 *Ibid.*

bihi an yusāwīhā fī-l-ṣiḥḥati 'ay sālimān min al-'uyūbi al-fāḥishati[29]). The discussions of what constitutes religion (*al-dīn*) turn on the idea of righteousness and the question of what to do if the man is sinful (*fāsiq*) and drinks alcohol. The discussion of matrimonial parity (*kafā'a*) in al-Dasūqi's text extends beyond religion and status, to freedom (*al-ḥurriyya*), nobility (*ḥasab*) and a proper dower (*mahr al-mithl*).

While neither the texts of Khalil, nor al-Dasuqi and al-Hattab mention genealogy, ethnicity or lineage (*nasab*), these are the elements that, in addition to nobility or caste and the role of the *walī*, are most significant for this discussion of the meaning of status (*al-ḥāl*) as a measure of *kafā'a* in Mauritania. Ibn Rushd/Averroës (d. 595/1198) observes in *Bidāyat al-Mujtahid*, describing how guardians (*awliyā'*) are one of three necessary conditions of the marriage contract (*shurūṭ al-'aqd*), that disagreement on the matter of guardians who attempt to prevent their wards from marrying (*fī 'aḍl al-awliyā'*) arises between jurists around the question of which exact criteria (piety, freedom, lineage, health, wealth, proper dower) establish *kafā'a* (Ibn Rushd/Averroës 1995: 960–3). A survey of Maliki *fiqh* on this subject reveals differing opinions, ranging from piety alone, to wealth, health, freedom, proper dower and piety inclusively.[30] In the following section, I will examine how contemporary jurists, lawyers and courts in Mauritania continue this legacy of extensive juristic disagreement (*ikhtilāf*) among Maliki jurists on the issue of *kafā'a*, and in the final section, I will discuss how these disagreements mediate questions of law and the nation.

II. What is *kafā'a*? Two cases of *kafā'a*[31]

To illustrate the invocation of *kafā'a* in the Islamic Republic of Mauritania, I will now recount Mauritanian scholar Zekeria Ould Ahmed Salem's account of two present-day personal status cases in which the marriage between people of different castes and ethnicities is contested by individuals belonging to

29 Ibn Rashid in *Ḥaṭṭāb*, *op.cit.* 106.

30 See Zomeño (2001), 92. Zomeño's summary of the various criteria establishing *kafā'a* for Maliki jurists is helpful on many accounts. I would point out however that Zomeño seems to misread Ibn Rushd on the matter of slavery as a criterion of *kafā'a* and forgets to include wealth in her summary of his criteria for *kafā'a*. While Zomeño claims that Ibn Rushd states that slavery does not determine *kafā'a*, in *Bidayat al-Mujtahid*, he writes that 'There is no disagreement in the school that freedom is a measure of *kafā'a*, because of the established sunna giving the female slave a right to choose [to remain in a marriage contracted before she was granted her liberty] once she is liberated' (*'ammā al-ḥurriyyatu falam yukhtalif al-madhhabu 'ānnahā min al- kafā'ati likawni al-sunnati al-thābitati litakhyīri al-'āmati 'idhā 'utaqat.*) Ibn Rushd (1995), 962.

31 These cases are originally reported in their entirety in French in Zekeria Ould Ahmed Salem (2003), 47–51. My recounting of the two cases here, while not a strict translation, remains as close to the original text as possible.

historically nomadic tribal elites who have held power since the seventeenth century in the territory that has now become the republic of Mauritania.[32] In the final and subsequent part of this essay, I will represent the different levels of juristic argumentation and analysis of the meanings of *kafāʾa* presented by the two cases as they mediate the underlying question of the relationship between the grounds of law and the postcolonial nation-state. As I will explain further on, it is important to keep in mind that the cases are heard in the 1990s, after the publication of the first pluralist, democratic *and* Islamic 1991 Constitution, but before the first codification and promulgation of a Code of Personal Status in 2001 (*Qānūn raqm* 2001-052 *yataḍamman Mudawwanat al-Aḥwāl al-Shakhṣiyya*). It is important, from the point of view of the possible effects and functions of codifying classical Islamic law, to question the relationship between the absence of a codification of personal status law by the state, the court's acceptance of *kafāʾa* as a justiciable cause of action, and the particular tribalist and statist readings of *kafāʾa*.

These two cases have several points in common beyond their historical and geographical proximity. Both occur in the largest urban centre in Mauritania, the capital Nouackchott, in the mid-to-late 1990s; and both concern the contestation of the validity of a marriage based on the lack of equality of one of the spouses after the consummation of marriage. One is an inter-caste marriage and the husband is a local entertainer (*ighyuwa*), a profession that historically belongs to an occupational caste composed of musicians, poets, artisans and craftsmen. The other is an interethnic marriage in which the husband is a descendent of a slave. Furthermore, both cases are originally heard by state courts, which rely primarily on the norms of the *shariʿa* developed in Mauritania, although constitutional norms are also invoked in the first case. That case is decided by the State Court of Appeal of Nouakchott, while the second case is rejected by the State Court of First Instance, and is picked up and decided by private, non-state Mauritanian jurists (*fuqahāʾ* plural, *faqīh* sing). Finally, both produce personal status legal norms through their interpretations of the *Mukhtaṣar* (abridgement) of the Maliki Egyptian jurist Khalil ibn Ishaq al-Jundi, and in particular, of his phrase, '*Kafāʾa* or matrimonial equivalence is religion and status/condition' [*Al- kafāʾatu al-dīnu wa-l-ḥālu*].

Case I. Judgment number 57/92 of the Court of Tevragh Zeina and its appeal

The defendant, the young Y. Ould N., was an artist belonging to the Maure ethnic group and to the caste of griots (*igawen/ighyuwa*), which is situated at

32 Marchesin writes, 'The political and military hegemony of the Bani Hassan, whose language *Hassaniya* was imposed on the Berber speakers, was in effect in the 17th century. (*L'hégémonie militaire et politique des Bani Hassan dont la langue, le hassanya, s'impose aux berbéphones, est effective au XVII siècle*') (1992), 26.

the base of the pyramid of castes in Mauritanian society. Born in 1964, he already knew before the age of 30 a certain success and fame with Mauritanian youth in Nouakchott. In 1988, he became affiliated with a young adult woman, A. Mint T.E. who belongs to the tribe of *Shurfas* (pl. of *sharif*, descendants of the Prophet Mohammad) – and hence, to a noble family that, using a different terminology, may be described as part of the nascent middle class. The relationship infringes upon the general rule of endogamy observed by Mauritanian society.

After having tried in vain to separate the two lovers by exerting various tenacious pressures on the young woman, her family lived with the alliance as a serious catastrophe and source of social shame and familial decline. The case culminates in 1991 with the birth of a child, doubly illegitimate insofar as he was born out of marriage and was also the fruit of a forbidden love. The case, until this point purely social and cultural, took a juridical turn when the couple, in an attempt to make the alliance less insufferable to the woman's family, as well as to the eyes of society and the law (in theory, the Sharīʿa punishes the crime of fornication and illegitimate marriage[33]), produced a document proving a marriage beginning in 1988. The father of the woman, her guardian, had intervened and separated the two spouses to give her in marriage in January 1989 to a cousin of the family. According to a local Imam, this arranged marriage hardly lasted ten months, when the young woman fled to 'remarry' Y. Ould N. for the second time. The spouses lived like this for three years in difficult conditions until the very tenacious father of the woman, D. Ould T.E. brought them before a court in Tevragh Zeina (Nouakchott) in order to annul the second marriage.

On 16 June 1992, the Court of First instance in Nouakchott gave a verdict annulling the marriage for the following reasons: the marriage was secret and therefore not valid Islamically; the two spouses willingly concealed the marriage from the father, legal guardian (*walī*) of the woman. The act of marriage itself presents procedural problems: the marriage was performed by an unknown person who did not declare his identity, it is devoid of customary formulas, the witnesses were not cited, and so forth. The Court of First Instance insisted that it is not because a Muslim woman is divorced that she can do without a guardian; rather, on the contrary to what is believed, Malik Ibn Anas never permitted that (Zekeria Ould Ahmed Salem 2003: 47).

Following the judgement of annulment, the spouses immediately appealed and the case was sent to the '*chambre civile*' of the Court of Appeal of Nouakchott,

33 The connection between maintaining the family as the only unit with the right to sexual reproduction and licit sexual relations – and the principle of crimes against persons committed in acts of adultery (*zinā*) in Islamic penal law (*ḥudūd*, quite literally meaning limits or boundaries), is quite interesting. For more on *Zinā*, see *Islamic Penal Code of Iran* (1986), 39–47; *The Offence of Zinā* (Enforcement of Hudood) Ordinance, 1979; and Butti Sultan Butti Ali Muhairi (1996).

which decided the case a little less than a month later on 7 July 1992. The appeal was heard just one year after the adoption of the new pluralist and Islamic Constitution (12 July 1991) and only six months after the first pluralist elections in the country on 24 January 1992. The couple was defended by two lawyers, one of whom, Mohammad Chein was not picked by chance. Mr Chein, belonging to a family of entertainers (griots), was also President of the Bar of the Association of Mauritanian lawyers. The father was represented by three lawyers, amongst whom was Mr Ichidou, a former political militant well known for his liberal positions and his engagements in favour of human rights. The arguments of his plea, however, suspend his personal engagements for the benefit of his client and for a particular conception of personal status in Islamic law as it is applied in Mauritania.

Before the Civil Court, Mr Chein, the lawyer for the two spouses underscored the regularity of the marriage and the validity of the act without separating the Islamic juridical repertory from his defence. He emphasised that his client properly contracted the marriage in a mosque and not in a 'nightclub'. Then he cited Khalil: 'If the father persists in his refusal to marry his daughter, she can separate from him in the marriage procedure'.[34] Mr Chein then referred to texts that interpret *kafā'a* in the sense of a 'democratisation' of matrimonial relations. According to him, *kafā'a* or matrimonial equivalence does not concern caste or social status but only the religious quality of being a Muslim. Finally he invoked the Constitution of July 1991 (Article 1, line 2) that declares: 'The Republic guarantees all Mauritanians equality before the law and does not distinguish between origin, race, sex or social class'.[35]

The lawyers for the father, for their part, invoked the importance of the legal guardian (*walī*) and cited a number of *hadiths* as well as elements of the *sīra* (life of the Prophet Muhammad), which insist on the point of equivalence (*kafā'a*) without which the marriage is not valid. Mr Ichiddou, in particular, affirmed the lack of application and validity of the Constitution, which according to him was not a divine law in this particular case. He argued that the laws of the *shari'a* and positive laws in usage have far more substantive import in the law of personal status. He then cited texts taken from the Khalilian tradition to support his argument. Finally, he added that the only witnesses of the act of marriage – which itself presented a number of procedural inadequacies – were (*Zounouj*) 'Noirs', that their identification was insufficient, that the woman was barely 21 years old when she married Y for the first time and that she was consequently influenced and constrained (*mujbara*).

34 Zekeria Ould Ahmed Salem (2003), 48: citing Khalil: 'If the father persists in his refusal to marry a daughter, she may dismiss him from the marriage procedure. (*Si le pére persiste dans son refus de marier une fille elle peut l'écarter de la procedure du marriage.*)'.

35 1991 Constitution of Mauritania: *'Taḍmanu al-jumhūriyyatu li-kāffati al-muwāṭinīn al-musāwāata amāma al-qānūni dūna tamyīzin fī-l-aṣli wa-l-iʿrqi wa-l-jinsi wa-l-makānati al-ijtimāʿiyyati.'*

The Court of Appeal rendered the following decision:

> Considering that the parties are in agreement on the fact that there was an act of marriage, even if one of them wants to annul it; considering that the act of marriage was accomplished by the most simple form as stipulated by Khalil and the fact of the saying of the Prophet: "*Three things will be taken seriously even if meant in jest: marriage, divorce and the freeing of a slave*"; considering that the spouses went to the mosque to be married, giving thus the illuminating proof of their good faith and of their desire to avoid committing religious crimes [. . .]; considering that the brevity of the formula is not a sufficient motive for the annulment of the marriage, but rather, on the contrary, if we refer to Khalil and the interpretation given by El-Hattab [. . .]; considering that the marriage cannot have taken place in secret since, on the one hand, it was concluded in a mosque and, on the other, nothing indicates that the act intimated to the witnesses to keep it a secret; considering that the young woman, whether non-noble or noble, can in both cases dispense with a guardian. If she is considered non-noble, her guardian is not constrained to decide, namely because in this case another Muslim can give her in marriage, and, if she is known as 'noble,' her guardian cannot be consulted once that which Khalil calls '*ett'oul*' happens, that is to say the fact that a long period has passed between the consummation of the marriage and its contestation by the father.
>
> Considering the argument advanced by the lawyers of the defense according to which Y. Ould N. does not fulfill the conditions of *kafā'a*, it must be said that Khalil was clear and precise in affirming: '*Kafā'a* is religion and status.' Considering that the majority of commentators of Khalil see in the term 'religion' the reference to Islam and, in the term '*al-ḥāl*' the reference principally to the state of health that must be equivalent in quality to that of the spouse. This is what we can conclude from the commentaries of Ibn Bashīr, Ibn Shās and others, and even in the case where *kafā'a* would not be fulfilled in particular cases, it is totally possible to pass it because Khalil expressly said that the guardian as well as the woman can exempt it; without even considering that the dominant opinion is that the condition of *kafā'a*, is that it is religion. And this is Islam [. . .] and all Muslims are equal on this regard according to the Qur'an [. . .]. All this, knowing that the observance of the conditions of the guardianship and of *kafā'a* in marriage assume that the guardian is capable of protecting his ward against concupiscence, because even a second of loss of strength cannot be tolerated, and that marriage is always preferred. Now in this particular case, the father D. Ould T.E., has not clearly proven such a capacity since, according to his own declarations, he did not have knowledge of the first marriage of his daughter until

after she became pregnant; and he did not have knowledge of their second marriage until three years after they were married. Now, from two things, one: either he knew about the marriage and accepted it, or he did not. With this last hypothesis, he neglects his family and does not have the capacity to take care of them, in which case we would encourage A (the young woman) to live within the confines of marriage. The goal of marriage is to lighten the punishment of the final judgment.

Considering that the annulment of the first judgment in favor of the annulment of the act of marriage is very defendable from the point of view of Maliki texts after the précis of Khalil [. . .]; considering that the confirmation of a judgment of annulment is not supported by the texts and that it cannot result but in acts of loss and debauchery [. . .]; for these reasons and in reference to the text of Khalil, the Court decides:

1. To admit the appeal against the judgment number 57/92 of the court of Tevragh Zeina on June 6, 1992 and the recognition of the validity of the marriage between A. Mint T.E. and Y. Ould N.
2. Refusal of the demand of the D. Ould T.E. to maintain the first decision of the annulment of the marriage.[36]

Case 2: A private reading of kafāʾa

The second case epitomises the perspective of partisans of a racial and tribal notion of *kafāʾa* as it is revealed in the judicial arena through a private *fatwā*.

This case was set in motion in 1996 when two young people, a brother and a sister, joined a religious revival movement (*al-Jamāʿat al-daʿwa wa-l-tabligh* also known as the Tablighis) which had been spreading widely in Mauritania for several years. One of the ancestors of the brother and the sister was an exceptionally prestigious religious figure, Sheikh Mohammad El-Ḥafedh (from the eminent marabout tribe, *Idawali*, belonging to the class of the 'people of the book'), who is known for introducing the Tijaniyya brotherhood in Mauritania and West Africa. At the *Jamāt al-dawa wa-tabligh* meetings, the brother and sister met a young man, a descendent of a slave (*ḥaratīn*: quite literally, freed man or second freedom, i.e. from *ḥurr thannī*), and began a friendship with him. Later the brother, legitimate legal guardian of his sister, married her to the young 'haratin' man. Upon hearing news of the marriage, the collateral cousins of the siblings attempted to file a case before a court of first instance in order to have the marriage annulled. The cousins claimed that the marriage should be annulled for the social non-parity

36 See Zekeria Ould Ahmed Salem (2003), 48; '*(D)ans trois choses, la plaisanterie est sérieuse: le mariage, le divorce et l'affranchissement de l'esclave.*'

(*kafā'a*) between the young woman and her husband who was a descendant of slaves.

Despite the efforts of the members of the tribe to have the marriage annulled in state court, they did not succeed in bringing the case before the court. They then decided collectively to compose a *fatwā* that would shift the dispute from the scene of the state judiciary to the private sphere. An impressive assembly of illustrious jurists (*fuqahā'*) of the tribe composed a 42-page document that treated in detail the pertinence of their recourse to annulment. Produced before judicial and political authorities, this '*über-fatwā*' put forward three main arguments that showed how *kafā'a* could be interpreted in contradictory ways.

The first argument centred around the importance of the co-extensiveness of local custom and convention (*'urf*) in the practice and understanding of Islamic law. According to this line of thought, while the court's rejection of the demand to annul the marriage rested on the fact that the Prophet Mohammad married one of his cousins to a former slave (Zayd ibn al-Harithā), this marriage between a noble woman and a man descended from slaves was not jurisprudentially legitimate since *fiqh* in general, and *kafā'a* in particular cannot be abstracted from tradition and customs according to time and place. In Mauritania, the *fatwā* argues, the practice of marriage between a descendent of slaves and a girl descending from a noble, illustrious person is not known or admitted by local customary practice (*'urf*).

The second argument used by the opponents of the marriage in the *fatwā* focused on the definition of *kafā'a* in terms of religion and status or situation of the person (*al-ḥāl*). The *fatwā* proclaims that the religious movement of the *Tablighis*, where the two young people met, constitutes a blameable innovation (*bid'a*) and that it is closer to a sect than to the religion of Islam as it is practised in Mauritania, according to the admitted Maliki doctrine. Therefore, the condition of 'religion' as a measure of *kafā'a* is not met.

Moreover, the *fatwā* claims, the '*ḥāl*' of the young man does not make him a suitable marriage partner for the woman since, according to the *fatwā*, *ḥāl* indicates four things: genealogy, occupation, material riches, and the qualities of a prestigious family. Concerning the family of the young man, it argues, it is evident that the family is not very prestigious because the young man's ancestors were reduced to slavery. According to this, his genealogy is 'polluted or contaminated by a subordinatio'. On all these levels the spouse must have at minimum the same status and condition as his wife in order to be her pair or equal. The young man, furthermore, is poorer than the young woman that he married since the extended family to which the young woman belongs is wealthy.

The *fatwā* dwells on 'the interest of the claimants in the cause', that is, the interest of the tribe of the young woman in taking up a judicial measure to annul the marriage on grounds of *kafā'a*. The arguments taken from Islamic jurisprudence and from a particular conception of *kafā'a* are as follows: it is not the woman that determines the *kafā'a* of her future husband, but all those who might carry the prejudice of a disreputable alliance at the level of social shame that would affect all the adult male members of the tribe. For this reason, the guardianship of the woman is given to them, and this justifies their interest in the cause of annulling an improper marriage that is devoid of the *sine qua non* condition of Muslim marriage, which is *kafā'a*.

Despite their effort to popularise the cause and build a case based on these particular interpretations of *kafā'a*, the cousins did not obtain a matter of cause before the court. It seems important to note, however, that the state court did not reject the case due to a lack of justiciability of *kafā'a* (i.e. reject the case because the court does not recognise *kafā'a* as a valid cause of action) or due to its finding lack of *kafā'a* between the marital partners. The court did so rather because they would not establish race or ethnicity as a criterion governing the determination of *kafā'a*. The court's decision not to hear the case does not invalidate the doctrine of *kafā'a* as a socio-legal norm, but rather calls into question the specific interpretation of *kafā'a* set forth by the would-be plaintiffs. In refusing to grant jurisdiction for the want of lack of equality, it upholds equality as a value in determining marriage alliances. I will return to this issue shortly. The epilogue of this case happened in the private legal realm, outside the judicial system. Refused by the courts, the cousins of the young woman, after having exhausted all means and using all political pressures at their disposition, finally proposed a 'friendly arrangement' to the young man: they offered him a modest sum of 1,400,000 Ouguiyas, (about $5,500) to divorce his wife and restore their honor (Zekeria Ould Ahmed Salem 2003: 50–1).

III. What is *kafā'a*?; contextualising *kafā'a* in postcolonial Mauritania

European Enlightenment accounts of law's origin figure the people *qua* nation as both source and *telos*, subject and object, of the law. Through their general-yet-particularly located will, the people harness a universal, self-constituting and auto-generative force that founds the law. Modern jurisprudence of positive law, while shifting the focus from the people towards official technologies of propositional codes and constitutions, continues a tradition of thinking the law's origin according to the principle of self-constitution and self-generation, assuming that there is no law prior to positive law, and that the law always has a moment that founds it and to which future moments must return for legitimation and justification.[37]

37 It has been argued that postmodern critiques of both Enlightenment thought (i.e. Rousseau, Montesquieu, Hobbes) and modern legal positivism (i.e. Kelsen, Austin, H.L.A. Hart) incorporate the very religious and metaphysical assumptions that they were hoping to overcome. See Carter (1990).

One paradox of such foundationalist narratives is that despite this general self-constituting, self-legitimating and universalising condition, law has to be *particularly* founded so as to be determined and determining in specific places at specific times. It has to issue from a bound place, and yet not be bound by it, remaining intensely particular and uninhibitedly universal. The place of the people, the law and their codes since the Treaty of Westphalia, has predominantly, though certainly not exclusively, been the territorial nation. In an age of rights, codes and constitutions, law has extended its reach most intensely and most frequently in, over and through the nation. The particularities of a nation elevated to the status of the universal form the content of its law. Reciprocally, law continuously forms the nation, linking and mediating between its universal and particular dimensions, between its claims to inclusiveness and its force of exclusion.

Literature on law and the modern nation reveals a sweeping spectrum of values, concepts and prognostications concerning the possible or impossible unfolding and overcoming of the universal-particular, territorialised-deterritorialised and civilised-barbaric dynamics that separately and jointly constitute law and nation. For example, E.J. Hobsbawm famously prophesied the impossibility of the nation and nationalisms, as they remain persistently linked to the very particularities that are repeatedly unable to form them absolutely (Hobsbawm 1992). Others like Benedict Anderson, assert that the end of the era of the universalising force of the imagined community of the nation, whether constituted by or in opposition to particularly or ethnically founded myths, is 'not remotely in sight' (Anderson 1991: 3). While it is not within the scope of this essay to canvass the historical or philosophical trajectories of the literature on the nation and nationalism, the remaining discussion connects the role of Islamic law in the postcolonial Mauritanian context to the persistent issues (universal-particular, territorialised-deterritorialised and civilised-barbaric) raised in debates about the nation. The problem of the relation between Mauritania as a nation and *kafā'a* as a doctrine and practice of personal status law centres on the problem of 'particular universals'. It is a relationship of complementarity in which Mauritania and *kafā'a* mutually compensate for their intrinsic inadequacies – that is, the intrinsic inadequacies of the particular universals that effectively define and sustain both. This leads to the question of the relation between personal status law and the nation-state, each remaining unresolved without the other, their duality being mutually dependent. How, in other words, is the irresolution of Mauritania's identity as a multi-ethnic nation overcome or resolved by *kafā'a*, and the irresolution of *kafā'a's* identity as a doctrine and practice of matrimonial equality overcome or resolved by Mauritania? And is their mutual resolution ever absolute? Does it, for example, take on a pure form, like that of the state?

Personal status law holds a considerable place in Mauritania and touches on the fundamental question of the nation (*la question nationale*), which was first posed after independence as a question of how to Mauritanianise the law (*Mauritanisation de la justice*) (Mohamed Yahya O. Abdelwedoud 2001: 141–54) – that is, how to unify the disparate elements of the postcolonial nation. The national question became critically transparent in the 1989 pogroms, when non-Maure Mauritanian nationals (i.e. Halpulaar/Toukalour, Wolof, Soninké, Fulbe, Bambara) were expelled from Mauritania into Senegal. The Mauritanian government, dominated by Arab Maure nomadic elites complied with the violence, expulsion and dispossession of its own citizens based on ethnicity. While Mauritanian authorities asserted that those expelled were not Mauritanian citizens, the refugees themselves, together with international humanitarian organisations charged the Mauritanian government with ethnic cleansing by forced migration: the government deliberately manufactured refugees in order both to purge Mauritania of its non-Maure population, and expropriate the property and land they left behind.[38]

This violence, reflective of exclusionary (ethnocentrist) state practices, deeply traumatised Mauritania and in turn, made ethnicity and personal status into *the* question-problem of law and the nation. Personal status in Mauritania crystallises around questions of equality and value, the relations between different ethnic and social groups, as well as the relations of inequality, difference and exploitation at the heart of identity groups.

The 1991 Constitution, following the aftermath of the 1989 Mauritania–Senegal events, introduced an article declaring that no citizen will be discriminated against based on race or ethnicity. The two cases above reveal that this constitutional-democratic principle of the equality of all citizens challenges the principle of equality of the doctrine of *kafāʾa*. It was of course Aristotle (d. 322 B.C.) who pointed out in Book Five of his *Politics*, that while democratic justice in Athens implies equality, it is not for everybody, only for those who are equal (Aristotle 1941: 1233). Equality of marital partners thus has a very different meaning if equality is originarily exclusive, based on the idea of intrinsic and insuperable inequalities. Moreover, without governing criteria that determines the interpretation and limits of equality, *kafāʾa* has very little meaning. How is *kafāʾa* in particular, and democratic equality more generally, both a challenge to and an instance of discrimination? How does and can a doctrine of equality determine what is equal without falling into inconsistency or without looking outside itself for its meaning? What then is the function of *kafāʾa*?

In the Mauritanian context, the interpretations of *kafāʾa* operate according to at least two measures of equality, both of which reveal Islamic law as a

38 Marion Fresia work offers an excellent ethnographic account of the Mauritanian refugees on the Senegalese River Bank: Fresia (2009); Park, Baro and Ngaido (1991), 2; Fleischman (1994), 13–16; Doyle (1989), 14; and BBC News, 'Mauritania's Victims of the Race Divide' (2001).

means of contesting and producing the identity of the nation. In the two cases above, Islamic law, rather than providing a universal warrant for a unified national law, signifies cultural capital representing particular interests striving to control productive resources and maintain relations of social hierarchy. The strife involved within the nation to determine its identity plays out as a theatre of interpretations of the law. At least two measures of equality are at work in the two cases: on the one hand, a formal measure based on an abstract universal notion of the citizen and member of the nation-state, as the legal subject who bears rights; and on the other hand, a formal measure based on the abstract notion of a particular subject, of a subject granted rights based on his or her place in a rigidly demarcated social hierarchy – as a member of a tribe or caste.

The two cases show both the enveloping and the limiting function of *kafā'a*, while reflecting and producing the contending fantasies of what the nation is, or what the nation should be according to the conflicting visions of the jurists, guardians and marital partners who represent the state, historically nomadic elites and marginalised minorities, respectively. *Kafā'a* in the *fatwā* of the inter-ethnic case is a limit classification that sanctions the destruction of the matrimony of non-equals. Cruel and exclusionary, the measure of matrimonial equivalence is a technique to reproduce normatively the social hierarchy as a barrier that maintains cultural and material capital in the hands of distinct elite groups. Aiming to arrest the potential flux of the identity of the non-Maure post-colonial subject, the *kafā'a* of the *fatwā* presupposes equality as the measure of diversity according to the degree of distance from or proximity to a principle of identity (i.e. as difference between self and other), emphasising difference as monstrosity ('free from vulgar deficiencies'), evil (the blameable innovation of the Tablighis), danger ('contaminated or polluted') or error. In the *fatwā*, *kafā'a* becomes a classification that internalises the frontiers of the national space at the heart of that space itself, thus making possible the modern notion of the 'internal enemy', the non-parity of Mauritanian nationals, and the expulsion of citizens based on ethnicity. The *fatwā* of the inter-ethnic case seeks the coherence of the nation through the production of an internal alterity in which the nation forms its identity through the exclusion of that which remains integral to it (viz. the non-Maure Mauritanian citizen). It gives a private reading of Islamic law and *kafā'a*, based on the repetition of customary matrimonial practices and of a past prior to the law. It presents a particular and fixed legal subject petrified both by categories of social identity and by the model of the family and tribe as an extended patrilineage based on agnatic kinship ties.

Kafā'a as a measure of belief, on the other hand, as presented by the Court of Appeal, has an enveloping function, a power and a safety, which unifies the not-equal (caste) in the equal (national), leaping over and confounding the barriers between properties as unmediated diversity (or as difference within a commonality): the Court of Appeal states, apropos of religion: '[A]ll Muslims are equal on this regard according to the Qur'an.' This is the image of equality issuing from the inter-caste case – an image that emerges from the perspective of the state – that gives a public reading of Islamic law and *kafā'a*, and presents a universal legal subject based on the idea of the equality of citizens. Since both cases attempt to transform the idea of the nation-state by relying on the sources of the Maliki doctrine of Islamic law, we cannot look to the latter to explain the difference in the two cases, but must rather inquire further into the public and private spaces of Mauritania.

What I will try to do now, then, is to show how Mauritania as a nation provides a ground, a location for *kafā'a* as a doctrine and practice of Islamic law. Then, I will reverse the perspective, and show how *kafā'a* as an instance of Islamic law locates Mauritania as a nation.

A. Mauritania as a condition of kafā'a: national identity as the essence of law

Mauritania's identity as a nation is not violated by its relation to *kafā'a* since the nation appropriates *kafā'a* as an instance of self-affirmation, both in its private and public readings which attempt to identify particular fantasies of nation with society itself. A desire to represent one form of belonging to the exclusion of all others animates the readings of *kafā'a* and the relationship between the various kinds of equalities and belongings (ethnic, gendered, familial, linguistic, national) affirm and constitute Mauritania as a nation. It is precisely the inclusion of the various belongings and equalities that give law its particular Mauritanian content. Paradoxically, the completeness of Mauritania as a nation contains its own relatedness to law.[39] Given the ethnic, social and political histories and the co-existence of multiple origins of Mauritania, equality is the accommodating condition of the nation's self-affirmation.

The story of the conflicting interpretations of *kafā'a* here is integral to that of the modern nation of Mauritania. In its identification with local history, practices and myths – with genealogy, birth, death and memory – it acquires location in a rigidly demarcated national territory, which it clings to as its epitome. While nomadic elites in Mauritania have a biological conception of history, a cyclical notion of time and a tribal concept of territory – such that the nation, far from representing a monolithic space, is associated with necessary solidarities and reciprocities in the harsh environment of the Sahara (Marchesin 1992: 26–30) – the nation-state that incorporates them conceives of history and territory, including the space beyond the Sahara and the incorporation of the Senegal River valley, as the founding of a new time

39 For a discussion of how the nation and other communities can be defined through the political nature of resistance against immanent power, see Nancy (1991), 4.

and space that leaps over the tribal territories and biological boundaries and homogenises them.

Thus, while *kafāʾa* may seem to issue from time immemorial, from custom, historical traditions and founding myths before the law (as I suggested in part I), it also issues from a national time, a time simultaneous to the *nascere* of the nation. Its origins may be chronologically and geographically distant from contemporary law but that distance can only be perceived from the national post-colonial space. Thus, *kafāʾa* is about repeating origins that predate Islamic law, but which establish Islamic law as the appropriate emblem with which to characterise the specifically Mauritanian quality and originality of *kafāʾa*. Equality becomes pre-originary, not only in its capacity to index a pre- or extra-Islamic moment, but in its power as a first cause – a founding power that establishes Islamic law as the terms by which the nation defines equality, and thus defines itself. It attempts to found two different measures of equality by presupposing a pre-existing inequality in the interethnic case, and a productive equality in the inter-caste case, both of which spring, generate and enfold their own origins.

B. Kafāʾa as a condition of Mauritania: law as the essence of national identity

What first stands out in the comparative account of the two cases I offer is the absolute disagreement about the meaning of *kafāʾa* between the Court of Appeal in the first case and the *fuqahāʾ* in the second. While for the Court, individual status concerns a discourse on the equality of citizens, for the *fuqahāʾ* it refers to an 'anarchy of minor differences': genealogy (family, ethnicity and rootedness), and the level of belonging within a certain class, understood either as a social hierarchy (tribe, caste, historical relationship to freedom–dependant, protected, profession), or as a degree of authenticity and purity.

The Court of Appeal says that *kafāʾa* is religion and status, where status means good health. The first principle observed by the Court of Appeal is that marriage is a legal relation that cannot be submitted to social factors such as social caste, or an institution based on oppressive classifications and exclusionary practices. The state no longer validates the power of the kin group or the power of the patrilineage over individual choice. Equality for the court is based on an abstract universal religious identity (Muslim) and an abstract biological normativity (health, 'free from vulgar deficiencies'), which is granted to the citizen, an abstract juridico-political subject limited only by a territorial concept of political sovereignty. Where *kafāʾa* stipulates religion uniquely in terms of Islam and status in terms of health, all healthy Muslim male Mauritanians are abstractly equal as marriageable subjects before the law. The court interprets *kafāʾa* as a measure of difference occurring after the founding of the Republic and law – so that the terms of legal equality must be integral to the state as an Islamic Republic. If the state is constituted by religion – as proclaimed by the 1991 Constitution[40] – it is the abstract quality of religiosity that is constitutive of the citizen, the legal subject, before the law. Interpreting *kafā'a* for the court is a method for measuring the present in reference to a past historical situation that is *coextensive* with the founding of the law of the nation-state. Equality before the law is therefore measured in relation to the founding of an imaginary ideal future of a homogeneous nation governed by central rule, insofar as that founding is conceived as a radical break with the temporalities, practices and political logics of the past.

Kafā'a for the Court of Appeal thus attempts to constitute Mauritanian society, in its aggregation of society's disparate elements by incorporating a religiously derived universalism with the particularity of the territorial assertion of a centralising government; but *kafā'a* does so by also transcending the diverse and particular within the territory. The *kafā'a* of the court attempts to occupy and homogenise the space of the nation through a juridical apparatus that must deliver to the Mauritanian citizen a deracinated, universal subject and a law orienting itself towards the universal. The simultaneity of the two understandings of *kafā'a* unfolds in the state's struggle to deracinate the doctrine from its tribal roots, which emphasise the particular, the racinated, the heterogeneous, the 'blood and soil'. As I will elaborate in just a moment, it is this impossible oscillation between an assumption of the universal and an emphasis on the particular that is the very tension between nation and state, which *kafā'a* attempts to mediate.

In the second case, the *Tablighi* case, the principle observed by the *fuqahā'* is that marriage is a legal relation that can be submitted to specific social factors such as ethnicity and caste. *Kafā'a* means religion in terms of an orthodox understanding of the discourses and practices of the Maliki doctrine, and status in terms of 'genealogy, occupation, material riches, and the qualities of a prestigious family'. The *Tablighi* husband is not the equivalent of the spouse in terms of religion (his interpretation of Islam is inauthentic – a 'blameable innovation' – rendering his status as a Sunni Muslim unorthodox and untrue) or status. Born into a family descended from slavery, his blood is 'polluted or contaminated by a subordination'.

The *fuqahā'* interpret *kafā'a* as presupposing a natural or biological inequality that is *prior to* legal norms, social institutions, society and the state. The norm (*kafā'a*) is then instituted *a posteriori* to measure the *a priori* equality among those who belong to a particular collective identity and the inequality of those who do not belong. Belonging is defined by a quasi-biological concept of pure blood, where equality is measured by a person's distance or proximity to an ideal origin defined by agnatic blood relations. The young man's blood is condemned, 'polluted' or 'contaminated', by a historical oppression.

40 'Islam is the religion of the State and the people'. See 1991 Mauritanian Constitution.

Social identity through the body becomes a sign that bears the mark of its origin. Both try to ontologise socially determined conditions of the body (what constitutes health, racial or class purity, etc.) as abstract equivalences to be read or measured before the law. In this way, the Mauritanian *fuqahā'* seem to be engaging in what Mary Douglas calls pollution behaviour, 'which condemns any object or idea likely to confuse or contradict cherished classifications' (Douglas 2006: 45), posing a constant danger to the power of the kin group.

In this way, *kafā'a* reconstructs the status of the man in his reproductive capacity as a marriage partner such that his sexuality is a performance of social relations. The danger of mixing blood is related to his status, a socio-biological category determined before his birth. *Kafā'a* for the *fuqahā'* is thus a method for measuring the present in reference to a past historical situation that is prior to the law, and which prepared the ground for legal life. Indeed, their notion of *kafā'a* is a topographic genealogy of the field of social relations from which the noble Maure family can measure its relation to another *geneā* (*nasab*)[41] for the marriage at hand. Equality before the law is thus measured in relation to an imagined ideal past insofar as that past is said to exist before the law.

The disagreement in the two cases on the meaning of religion and status (*al-ḥāl*) in *kafā'a* conceals a deep agreement on the value of founding or of origin itself. The distinction between *equal* and *unequal* maps on to the division between civilisation and barbarism, reason and simulacrum, cosmos and chaos. In other words, the question of the origin, or of the founding of the measure of equality, is itself one form of the question of ethics. Both interpretations, that of the Court of Appeal and that of the jurists of the *über fatwā* agree that, insofar as it is stipulated that a condition of equality must be met in order for a marriage to have legal validity and for a legal social exchange to occur, the measure of equality is the same: an imagined historical situation. In both cases, *kafā'a* is claimed to re-enact a historical, contingent situation – in one case the founding of the nation, in the other the founding of a tribe.

The nation and the tribe, however, operate according to different temporalities. Citizenship and the nation vie here with the contained familial-tribal bond and status. Both, however, unify and transcend, and join together groupings, marking what is common to them. The equality of castes and tribes is isomorphic and prior to the equality of citizens. While the member of the tribe and the tribe itself is conceived of over and against the barbarian without, while excluding proximates within (women, slaves, occupational groups

41 The definition of *nasab* in the *Hans Wehr Arabic-English Dictionary* is: lineage, descent; origin, parentage; genealogy, noble descent; kinship, relationship, affinity; and relationship by marriage.

and so forth), the citizen and the nation are conceived of in opposition to the barbarian without, while continually constituting themselves in opposition to customary and traditional identities within. What is particular and localised, what is difference in rank and status, must give way to a common citizenship tied to a territorial sovereign. In both, the claim is reduced to an assertion of belonging and commonality as against an idea of a perceived threat or danger. But, the particular has its revenge: for while citizens are supposed to be related by law, law has an operative common existence within the order of the nation. The law constitutes that existence and mediates between the citizenry making up the nation. Equality between citizens certainly cancels what is particular and makes all subjects formally equal before the law – this is often the paradigm of the human *par excellence*, the paradoxical bearer of human rights necessarily tied to a particular soil. However, and here is the essential quandary, equality between particulars ultimately institutes and reproduces in a strict sense the particular bodies which are read as signs of ethnicity, caste, genealogy, class, profession and so forth – bodies that bear the mark of the pure or impure blood of their origin.

In the end, the nation's attempts to produce the general conditions of democratic equality reproduce the marks of inequality in equal measure. In this light, it is possible to reconsider *kafā'a* as an analytic of the socio-political nature of the power relations that inhere in interpreting the law. As an analytic, *kafā'a* allows us to see how a discourse and practice of equality migrates between and is grasped by the state, as an image of the nation, and society. The consequence of this is that the more the state generalises its law of equality, the more it forces particular equalities to name the particular inequalities it is attempting to resolve. The more Mauritania through the force of its state law enacts universal equality, the more it reproduces, sustains, and perhaps even embeds in greater measure, the wide-scale inequalities that it cannot through any lawful means resolve. This must give us pause to wonder whether the law and with it the democratic state are the mechanisms by which universal equalities can be achieved.

IV. Conclusion: revitalising *kafā'a*, translating citizenship

By way of a conclusion, I offer a brief analysis of how the encounter between *kafā'a* and citizenship in the legal arena is mutually transformative. I would suggest that the cases at hand illuminate not only how a normative model of democratic state law of the equality of citizens revitalises and transforms the 'traditional' Islamic doctrine of *kafā'a*, but also how the model of citizenship is translated and transformed in the process.

This paper has analysed how the liberal democratic model of citizenship, expressed by Article 1 and by the 'right to equality' in the Constitutional Preamble, has been translated in Mauritanian state courts and private legal practices, as well as particularistic resistances (tribal, ethnic and caste based) to such translations. It has simultaneously examined particular translations of Islam as a source of law. At the heart of this inquiry has been the question of the very translatability of the democratic model of universal equality – and of Islam – as it is articulated, understood and practised by lawyers and state-appointed judges in Mauritanian state courts, as well as by non-state private Islamic jurists (*fuqahā'*).

As we have seen, the 1991 Constitution, following the aftermath of the 1989 Mauritania–Senegal events, introduced an article guaranteeing all Mauritanians equality before the law, declaring that no citizen will be discriminated against based on 'sex, race, ethnicity or social class (*al-makāna al-ijtamā'īya*)' and stating that the law intends to punish all 'particularistic propaganda of racial or ethnic character' (Art. 1). Relying on secular liberal models of democratic citizenship that understand citizenship primarily as a legal status denoting a community of shared law in which all members are equally protected by the law, the 1991 Constitution explicitly reflects the influence of the Constitution of the French Fifth Republic in its dedication to liberal democratic principles and inalienable human rights. The Constitution also proclaims adherence to the principles of the 1789 Declaration of the Rights of Man, 1948 Universal Declaration of Human Rights and the 1981 African Charter on Human and Peoples' Rights. At the same time, the new constitution re-emphasised its commitments to Islam as 'the religion of the people and the state' (Art. 5) guaranteeing the 'rights attached to the family as the basic unit of the Islamic society' and declaring for the first time the 'precepts of Islam' as 'the sole source of law' (Preamble, *al-dībāja*).

Thus, at least two measures of equality are at work in the two cases: on the one hand, a formal constitutional measure based on an abstract universal notion of the citizen and member of the nation-state, as the legal subject who bears rights; and on the other hand, an equally formal customary and quasi-Islamic measure based on the abstract notion of a particular subject, of a subject granted rights based on his or her place in a rigidly demarcated social hierarchy – as a member of a tribe or caste.

While some scholars and legal practitioners have prophesied the disappearance of traditional customary or religious legal forms under the twofold pressures of state and transnational law, these cases in Mauritania suggest that the normative model of democratic equality paradoxically revitalises customary and religious traditions of equality in and outside the official legal system. *Kafā'a* is revitalised in a number of ways, the first of which is through the court's recognition of *kafā'a* as a justiciable cause of action. In both cases, the Court of First Instance is the plaintiffs' first venue of choice. By allowing *kafā'a* as a cause of action, and by ruling on *kafā'a*, the judiciary permits *kafā'a* as a traditionally Islamic legal form to continue not only to have social value, but also to gain legal validity within the juridical apparatus of state law and its institutions.

In this light, it seems important to repeat that the state court did not reject the Tablighi case due to a lack of justiciability of *kafā'a* (i.e. reject the case because the court does not recognise *kafā'a* as a valid cause of action) or due to the lack of matrimonial equivalence between the marital partners, but did so rather because they would not establish race or ethnicity as a criterion governing the determination of *kafā'a*. In other words, in the Tablighi case, the court's decision not to hear the case does not invalidate the doctrine of *kafā'a* as a legal norm, but rather calls into question the specific interpretation of *kafā'a* set forth by the would-be plaintiffs. In refusing to grant jurisdiction for a case attempting to base matrimonial equivalence on racial or ethnic grounds, and by limiting the specific criteria that determine the validity of *kafā'a* to the religious quality of being a Muslim in good health, the Court effectively revitalises matrimonial equivalence (*kafā'a*) as a social value in determining marriage alliances, while transforming the specificity of its social significance and the form of its cultural entrenchment in order to reflect new national commitments to democratic equality and social cohesion.

The second way in which *kafā'a* is revitalised is through its translation as a democratisation of Islamic equality. In the Appeal of the first case, the democratic model of liberal citizenship wherein all citizens are equal before the law revitalises and transforms the doctrine of *kafā'a*, filling out the specificity of its national contours while renewing its democratic meaning. When the lawyer for the young couple invokes Article 1 of the Constitution declaring the equality of all Mauritanians before the law, and argues that *kafā'a* means a democratisation of matrimonial relations such that 'matrimonial equivalence does not concern caste or social status, but only the religious quality of being a Muslim', he effectively reconfigures *kafā'a* through the lens of a new notion of Islamic citizenship. The decision of the Court of Appeal revitalizes *kafā'a* in this light, emphasising the Qur'anic and *sharī'a*-based nature of its jurisprudence. Relying on specific interpretations of Islamic jurisprudence that define 'religion' and 'status' in the broadest possible ways, the Court decides that the sole conditions of *kafā'a* are health and Islam, and that 'all Muslims are equal on this regard according to the Qur'an'. Thus, particular interpretations of Islamic law in general and Maliki *fiqh* in particular are revitalised in the name of democracy.

Finally, citizenship itself becomes Mauritanian. The terms of legal equality must be integral to the state as an Islamic Republic such that the criteria governing the determination of *kafā'a* become the equality of all *Muslim* citizens. Where *kafā'a* is now a matter of the equality of Muslim citizens, the secular liberal model of citizenship is transformed such that religion, and specifically Islam, is reinforced as the very criteria governing citizenship. Paradoxically, it is the secular model of equality of citizens before the law that revitalises and democratises *kafā'a*, which reciprocally reconfigures and reasserts citizenship according to the religious criterion of being Muslim.

When the state is constituted by religion, it is the abstract quality of religiosity that becomes constitutive of the citizen, the legal subject before the law. In this way, the principle of the equality of all believers becomes a tenet of Mauritanian citizenship and democracy.

References

Aḥmad ibn Muḥammad Fayyūmī and ʻAbd al-Karīm ibn Muḥammad Rāfiʻī (1980) *Kitāb al-miṣbāḥ al-munīr fī gharīb al-sharḥ al-kabīr li-l-Rāfiʻī*, Beirut: Dār al-Qalam.

Al-Hasan ibn Yusuf ibn al-Mutahhar al-Hillī (1991) *Mukhtalaf al-Shīʻa fi Aḥkām al-Sharīʻa*, Qom, Iran: Islamic Sciences Research Center, Vol. 7.

Al-Imam Hafiz Al-Baris Al-Allamah Jamaluddin Abi Muhammad Abdullah bin Yusuf al-Hanafi Al Zai'ali (no publication date) *Naṣbul Al-Rayah*, Beirut: Al-Maktab Al-Islami, Vol. 3: 196–7.

—— (2004) *Islamic Family Law: New Challenged in the 21st Century*, Zaleha Kamaruddin (ed.), Malaysia: Research Centre, IIUM, Vol. 2.

Amselle, J.-L. and M'Bokolo, E. (eds) (1985) *Au Coeur de l'Ethnie*, Paris: Editions La Decouverte.

Anderson, B. (1991) *Imagined Communities: Reflections on the origins and spread of nationalism*, London: Verso.

Arazi, A. (2009, 2nd edn.) '*Mukhtaṣar*'. *Encyclopaedia of Islam*, P. Bearman, Th. Bianquis, C.E. Bosworth, E. van Donzel and W.P. Heinrichs (eds), Brill Online. University of California UC Berkeley CDL. Available HTTP: www.brillonline.nl/subscriber/entry?entry=islam_COM-0792 (accessed 19 April 2009).

Aristotle (1941) *The Basic Works of Aristotle*, R.P. McKeon (trans. 2001), New York: Random House.

BBC News, 'Mauritania's Victims of the Race Divide'. Available HTTP: http://news.bbc.co.uk/2/hi/africa/1515054.stm (accessed 29 August 2001).

Bercher, L. (1968) *La risâla; ou, Epître sur les éléments du dogme et de la loi de l'Islâm selon le rite mâlikite*, Alger: Editions populaire de l'armée, Bibliothèque arabe-française, vol. 3, 173–93.

Bonte, P. (2006) '*Individuals, factions and tribes among Moorish societies*', in D. Chatty (ed.), *Nomadic Societies in the Middle East and North Africa: Entering the 21st century*, Netherlands: Brill.

Butti Sultan Butti Ali Muhairi (1996) 'The Islamization of Laws in the UAE: the case of the penal code', *Arab Law Quarterly*, Brill.

Carter, A. (ed.) (1990) *Post-Modern Law: Enlightenment, revolution and the death of man*, Edinburgh: Edinburgh University Press.

Charrad, M. (2001) *States and Women's Rights: The making of postcolonial Tunisia, Algeria, and Morocco*, Berkeley: UC Press.

Coulson, N.J. (2005) *A History of Islamic Law*, Edinburgh: Edinburgh University Press.

Douglas, M. (2006) *Purity and Danger: An analysis of concepts of pollution and taboo*, London: Routledge.

Doyle, M. (1989) 'Blood Brothers', *Africa Report* (New York) Jul–August.

El Alami, Dawoud and Doreen Hinchcliffe (1996) *Islamic Marriage and Divorce Laws of the Arab World*, London: CIMEL, Kluwer Law International.

Fischer, A.B. (1970) *Slavery and Muslim Society in Africa: The institution in Saharan and Sudanic Africa and the Trans-Saharan trade*, London: Hurst & Co.

Fleischman, J. (1994) 'Mauritania's campaign of terror', *Human Rights Watch/Africa*, 13–16 April.

Fresia, M. (2009) *Les Mauritaniens Réfugiés au Sénégal. Une anthropologie critique de l'asile et de l'aide humanitaire*, Paris: Harmattan, Connaissances des hommes.

Hobsbawm, E.J. (1992) *Nations and Nationalism Since 1870: Programme, myth and reality*, Cambridge: Cambridge University Press.

Hunwick, J. (1999) 'Islamic financial institutions: theoretical structures and aspects of their application in Sub-Saharan Africa', in J. Guyer and E. Stiansen (eds), *Credit, Currencies and Culture: African Financial Institutions in Historical Perspective*, Stockholm: Nordiska Afrikainstitutet, 72–99.

Ibn Khaldun, *Muqaddima I*, 326.

Ibn Rushd/Averroës (1995) *Bidāyat al-Mujtahid wa-Nihāyat al-Muqtaṣid*, 3 vols, Beirut: Dar Ibn Hazm, 3: 960–63.

'Izzat Ghayth (2001) *Qānūn al-Aḥwāl al-Shakhṣiyya: qānūn mu'aqqat raqm (61) li-sanat 1976. Silsilat al-Tashrī'āt al-qaḍā'iyya*, 5, Amman: Dar Qindil.

Johansen, B. (1996) 'The valorization of the body in Muslim Sunni law', *Princeton Papers, Interdisciplinary Journal of Middle Eastern Studies*, Spring, vol. IV.

Khalīl ibn Isḥāq al-Jundī (1980) *Mukhtaṣar Khalīl*, Cairo: Dār Iḥyā' al-Kutub al-'Arabīyah, 103.

Khalīl ibn Isḥāq al-Jundī (1980) *Mukhtasar: Maliki Law: Being a summary from French Translations of the Mukhtasar of Sīdī Khalīl, with notes and bibliography*, R.H. Huxton (trans.), Hyperion, 89–121.

Levtzion, N. and Pouwels, R.L. (2000) *The History of Islam in Africa*, Athens: Ohio University Press.

Lewis, B. (1990) *Race and Slavery in the Middle East*, New York, Oxford: Oxford University Press.

Linant de Bellefonds, Y. (2008) '*Kafā'a*.' *Encyclopaedia of Islam*, P. Bearman, Th. Bianquis, C.E. Bosworth, E. van Donzel and W.P. Heinrichs (eds), Brill Online. Harvard University. Available HTTP: www.brillonline.nl/subscriber/entry?entry=islam_SIM-3772 (accessed 3 May 2008).

Luwīs Malūf (1954) *al-Munjid; Mu'jam lil-lugha al-'Arabiyya*, Beirut: Catholic University Press.

Mālik ibn Anas, and Saḥnūn, *Al-Mudawwanah al-kubrā*, 6 vols, Baghdad: Maktabat al-Muthannā.

Malik Ibn Anas (1989) *Al-Muwatta of Imam Malik ibn Anas: the First Formulation of Islamic Law*, Aisha Abdurrahman Bewlwy (trans.), London: Kegan Paul International.

Marchesin, P. (1992) *Tribus, Ethnies et Pouvoir en Mauritanie*, Paris: Karthala.

Mohamed El Mokhtar Ould Bah (1981) *La littérature juridique et l'évolution du malikisme en Mauritanie*, Tunis: Publications de l'Université de Tunis, Faculté des lettres et sciences humaines de Tunis, vol. 19: 36, 43–72.

Mohamed Yahya O. Abdelwedoud (2001) 'Le Système Mauritanien Aprés L'Indépendance', *Revue Juridique et Politique Indépendence et Coopération*, Institut international de droit d'expression française, and Editions juris Africa, Le Vésinet: EDIENA, May–August, 55(2): 141–54.

Mohammed Muhsin Khan (1994) *Ṣaḥīḥ Al-Bukhārī*, Riyadh: Maktaba Dar-us-Salam, Chapter 60, The Book of *Nikāḥ*, Hadith 1835, 889.

Muhammad Fahr Shaqfah (1996) *Majmūʿat qawānīn al-aḥwāl al-shakhṣiyya al-nāfidha fī Sūrīya maʿ al-uṣūl wa-l-bayyināt: wa-tashmal Qānūn al-Aḥwāl al-Shakhṣiyya* (A Collection of the Laws of Effective Personal Status in Syria with the Sources and Explanations, including the Code of Personal Status), Dimashq: Mu'assasat al-Nuri, 22.

Muḥammad ibn Aḥmad ibn ʿArafah Dasūqī, Muḥammad ibn Aḥmad ʿIllaysh, Aḥmad ibn Muḥammad Dardīr, and Khalīl ibn Isḥāq al-Jundī (1980) *Ḥāshiyat al-Dasūqī ʿalá al-Sharḥ al-kabīr*, Cairo: Dār Iḥyā' al-Kutub al-ʿArabīyah, Vol. 2: 226.

Muḥammad ibn Muḥammad Ḥaṭṭāb, Zakarīyā ʿUmayrāt, Khalīl ibn Isḥāq al-Jundī, and Muḥammad ibn Yūsuf Mawwāq (1995) *Mawāhib al-Jalīl li-sharḥ Mukhtaṣar Khalīl*, Bayrūt, Lubnān: Dār al-Kutub al-ʿ Ilmīyah, Vol. 5: 106–7.

Musa Ali Ajetunmobi (1984) 'An Analytical Survey of Kafa'ah (Equality in Islamic Marriage) at the Dawn of Islam', *Journal of Arabic and Religious Studies* I: 86–101.

Nancy, J.-L. (1991) *The Inoperative Community*, Minneapolis: The University of Minnesota Press.

Park, T.M., Baro, M. and Ngaido, T. (1991) *Conflicts Over Land and the Crisis of Nationalism in Mauritania*, Prepared for USAID and the Land Tenure Center, University of Madison–Wisconsin, 2 February.

Schacht, J. (1964) *An Introduction to Islamic Law*, Oxford: The Clarendon Press.

Villasante Cervello, M. and de Beauvais, C. (eds) (2007) *Colonisation et Heritages Actuels au Sahara et au Sahel: Problemes conceptuels, etat des lieux et nouvelles perspectives de recherché (XVIIIe–XXe siecles)*, Paris: L'Harmattan.

Welchman, L. (ed.) (2004) *Women's Rights and Islamic Family Law: Perspectives on reform*, London: Zed Books.

Yahya Ould al-Bara (2001) *Fiqh, société et pouvoir {Texte Imprimé}: étude des soucis et préoccupations socio-politiques des théologiens-légistes maures (fuqahā) à partir de leurs consultations juridiques (fatāwā) du XVIIème au XXème siècle*, Anthropology doctoral dissertation, Paris: EHESS, 2 vols.

Yusuf, A. (1998) *The Meaning of the Holy Quran/Abdullah Yusuf*, Beltsville, MD: Amana Publications.

Zekeria Ould Ahmed Salem (2003) 'Droit du Statut Personnel et equivalence citoyenne en République Islamique de Mauritanie', in *La Pensée: Exploitation Extrême et Travail Forcé*, Paris, vol. 336, Octobre–Décembre, 37–53.

Ziadeh, F. (1957) 'Equality (*Kafā'ah*) in the Muslim law of marriage', *American Journal of Comparative Law* 6(4) (Autumn): 509.

Ziba Mir-Hosseini (1991) *Marriage on Trial: A Study of Islamic Family Law, Iran and Morocco Compared*, London: I.B. Tauris & Co, 146–7.

Zomeño, A. (2001) '*Kafā'a* in the Mālikī School: A *fatwā* from fifteenth-century Fez', *Islamic Law: Theory and practice*, R. Gleave and E. Kermeli (eds), London: I.B. Press.

Codes and regulations

Constitution of Mauritania (1991). Available HTTP: www.mauritania.mr/index.php?niveau=5&coderub=4&codsoussous=74&codesousrub=11 (accessed 8 April 2011).

Islamic Penal Code of Iran (English Translation 1986), Sayyid Ali Raza Naqva (trans.), Islamabad: Iran Pakistan Institute of Persian Studies, 39–47.

The Offence of Zinā (Enforcement of Hudood) Ordinance, 1979. Ordinance No. VII of 1979. Available HTTP: www.pakistani.org/pakistan/legislation/zia_po_1979/ord7_1979.html (accessed 9 February 1979).

The Moroccan Family Code (Moudawwana) of 5 February 2004, unofficial translation. Available HTTP: www.hrea.org/moudawwana.html (accessed 8 April 2011).

The Tunisian Record of Personal Status, Tunisia (2007) *Majallat al-aḥwāl al-shakhṣiyya*. [Tunis]: *Manshūrāt al-Maṭbaʿa al-Rasmiyya li-l-Jumhūriyya al-Tūnisiyya*.

The Mauritania Record of Personal Status (2001) Loi N° 2001-052 *portant Code du statut personnel/Qānūn raqm* 2001-052 *yataḍamman Mudawwanat al-Aḥwāl al-Shakhṣiyya*, Available HTTP in Arabic: www.mauritania.mr/index.php?niveau=6&coderub=4&codsoussous=175&codesousrub=11&codsoussous1=176 or French: www.mauritania.mr/fr/index.php?niveau=6&coderub=4&codsoussous=176&codesousrub=11&codsoussous1=178.

Chapter 7

Entrepreneurs and morals

*Gül Berna Özcan**

> We repudiate all morality that is taken outside of human, class concepts . . . We say: morality is that which serves to destroy the old exploiting society and to unite all the toilers around the proletariat.
>
> Lenin (1921, USSR leader, communist thinker)

> Don't break anyone's heart, even if he is an unbeliever
> To break the heart of a man is equal to hurting God.
>
> Yesevi (twelfth-century poet, Sufi philosopher)

> Out beyond ideas of wrong-doing and right-doing there is a field. I'll meet you there.
>
> Rumi (fourteenth-century poet, Sufi philosopher)

I. Introduction

In the twelfth century the Mogul ruler, Akbar, argued that morality can be guided by critical reasoning. Akbar stipulated that morality would be above religion and beyond faith as part of the human capacity to reason and intelligence. While supporting Akbar's wisdom, Amartya Sen (2000: 35) went further by questioning the sceptical view that the scope of reasoning is limited by cultural differences and refuted two common views: that reliance on reasoning and morality is a western way of thinking and approaching issues; and that people in different cultures may systematically lack basic sympathy and respect for one another. Reasoning, Sen argued, plays a crucial role in cultivating moral imagination and creating a better world. The relativity and cultural disharmony in moral sense is also being challenged by other scholars. For example, Wilson (1997) in his substantive work on the moral sense illustrated the depth and importance of morality in human action, showing its universality and existential role in social encounters. The common premise put forward by different scholars is that morality is a formidable

* PhD reader in International Business and Entrepreneurship, the School of Management, Royal Holloway, University of London (g.ozcan@rhul.ac.uk).

undercurrent in all human actions and shapes the principles and boundaries of economic relations, the scope of transactions, and an individual's deliberation about self-worth, justice and virtue. However, accepting the universality of moral reasoning does not presuppose a moral uniformity or a preordained pre-eminence of a singular morality. Norms and values are subject to biological and behavioural evolutionary changes (Ben-Ner and Putterman 1998). Our moral sense, as illustrated by Wilson, has evolutionary, developmental and cultural origins. In a recent work, Hallpike (2004) showed that the evolution of moral comprehension is an outcome of individuals' capacity to perceive and comprehend moral problems and this is largely acquired through participation in group life (Hallpike 2004).[1]

This chapter examines entrepreneurs' inner worlds in relation to their business activities and moral dispositions within the changing contours of faith and values. Moral harmony is an invisible yet a formidable part of market and state building. Similarly, a moral void, confusion and polarisation bring societal upheavals and conflicts. We draw our examples from newly independent states of Central Asia where there has been a massive shift from Soviet to capitalist relations during the past two decades. The emergence of new markets and entrepreneurial classes brought about massive changes to the region. However, the transition from the vassal Soviet satellite statehood to independent nation states proved to be much harder than anticipated by all parties, local and international actors alike. The state building process not only requires national identity formation and power consolidation but also societal moral harmony. In order to forge this, as the past experience of modern western nation states illustrate, the state uses its coercive power to eliminate opposing groups and impose uniform moral harmony and unity in many realms of life (language, religion, identity, etc.). The state has been subject to new pressures in recent years. In particular, the need for moral harmony in nation building and in reinforcing the legitimacy of central power has become the fundamental concern for the emerging states of post-Soviet Central Asia.

Central Asian entrepreneurs face profound anxieties that mainly stem from three sources: extreme information asymmetries, weak legal regimes, and highly erratic institutions. They also face moral dilemmas about wealth accumulation within impoverished post-Soviet countries that have no strong social references for legitimating business success. Property rights remain blurred, formal contracts matter little, and the market is manipulated by powerful political elites. Racketeering and violence exercised by self-governing syndicates deepen the penetration of disguised interest groups in the market.

1 C.R. Hallpike in his book, *The Evolution of Moral Understanding*, identifies the lack of consensus about the nature of morality among contemporary philosophers and puts forward a strong case in support of evolution of moral comprehension. He develops four fundamental non-reductive aspects of morals (utility, the social order, virtue and human status).

In the face of these pressures, entrepreneurs search widely for moral references that might justify their actions, protect their positions and legitimate their pursuit of profit seeking.

Looking at entrepreneurs' worlds through a prism of morality leads to many interesting and challenging questions. As the three quotes at the beginning of this section suggest, Central Asia, once the home of a tolerant pragmatic Sufi tradition and the hub of the Silk Road trade, became a decaying backwater in the Middle Ages with little economic growth and innovation. Both Russian colonial expansion throughout eighteenth and nineteenth centuries and subsequent Soviet power consolidation in the region imposed by non-titular groups, that is, Russians and European settlers, brought deep societal changes such as cultural Russification, modernisation and collectivisation. There are shades of the long waves of cultural and ideological transformations in today's moral understanding and culture; sometimes exerting itself through overlapping coexistence or disruptive changes. The influences of Shamanism, Buddhism, Christianity and Islam have different effects and shades in the daily lives of Central Asians. They are often disguised and mixed with the influences from two centuries of Imperial Russian modernisation followed by Marxist scientific determinism, intensified Russification and collectivisation. The historical disruption and societal turmoil brought by colonisation and later Soviet social engineering not only created confusion over moral standards but also led to deep changes to an individual's moral standing vis-à-vis the state and society. This process on the one hand dissolved prevailing societal structures through spatial displacement and re-distribution of wealth, and on the other hand enforced new group identities and encouraged the transformation of clan relations.

In this essay, I aim to illustrate the importance of morality in entrepreneurs' lives by looking at the formative lines of massive ideological waves of faith and world views. By using a combined method of empirical observation and secondary literature review, that is, relevant scholarly work as well as literature, poetry, and dictums, I develop a proxy setting to examine the moral positioning among entrepreneurs in three analytical categories: the core morality of doing business, understandings of the virtue of duty, and ideas of justice and the greater good. This analysis is built on the contours of each ideological wave and its ethical world with moral proxies rather than claiming its exact shape of moral standing. There are naturally many overlaps and heterodox moral positions in each sub-set defined here; as it is hard to argue that moral purity or homogeneity even under a dominant ideology, regime rule or single time period. However, for the simplicity of abstraction, I will identify domineering moral positions today and their corresponding entrepreneurial dimension in this examination.

Based on new empirical studies with male entrepreneurs in Kazakhstan, Kyrgyzstan and Uzbekistan, the chapter examines the variety of moral positions entrepreneurs take in handling their everyday businesses. In analysing this evidence we point out three major patterns of moral disposition set in waves of faith, ideology and world views. These are Soviet rationality, Sufism, and utopian Islam. This paper presents the nature of these moral positions in relation to the ethics of running business. Three categories are used as proxies for exploring the essence of morality and business: a core morality of doing business, the virtue of duty for businessmen, and the quest for justice and a greater good.

A. Morality, markets and entrepreneurs

There is an idealised, benign notion of free markets in liberal economic theory that focuses on the self-interested individual and on liberty. For example, in Morals by Agreement, Gauthier (1986) suggests that a perfectly competitive market is a morally free zone, an arena of social life in which moral evaluation has no role to play. The fundamental notions of liberty, impartiality and optimality of perfectly competitive markets form the basis of a morality-free zone. Similarly, Milton Freedman emphasised that markets promoted freedom in two ways: (1) in market systems participation in economic actions is itself an exercise of freedom, and (2) markets guarantee a separation of powers that is necessary for political freedom. Political freedom is threatened if those who direct the coercive apparatus of the state gain control of the means of livelihood as well. These analysts recognised grave dangers when a single group monopolises the two main sources of social power. Where markets accomplish the economic tasks of allocation and distribution without relying on a centralised bureaucracy they prevent such concentration of power (McMahon 1981: 273).

Other scholars put forward convincing arguments against the rather abstract view of the market as a morally free zone. These studies emphasise that markets are not amoral and value-neutral spheres and that morality should be seen as an integral part of human action and transactions in the market (McMahon 1981; Kuran 1998; Sen 1985; Wilson 1997; Zak 2008). Hausman (1989) argued that not just the intentions of individuals but the outcomes of perfectly competitive markets would be subject to moral criticism and assessment.

In one of the earliest such studies, Barnard (1938) argued that business frequently presents situations in which owners and managers must violate their personal moral codes. From this perspective Barnard proposed a distinction between public and private morality. In a popular work, Albert Carr (1968) argued that 'bluffing' is a part of doing business; questioning the need, or even the notions, of honesty and integrity for business. Carr's argument is not only interesting in that it offers a sense of moral compartmentalisation but it also sheds some light on entrepreneurial motivation and risk taking. Bluffing, imagination and opportunism go hand-in-hand with entrepreneurial initiative and rent seeking, but not utter frankness or the search for certainty. In defending himself against the criticism that he is condoning unethical behaviour, Carr insisted that an executive who acts according to prevailing business practices is guilty of nothing more than conformity; he is merely playing the game according to the rules (Carr 1968).

There is a common belief that business is inherently problematic from the moral point of view. One position, exemplified by McMahon (1981), is that the morals of doing business might as well be different from all other ethical ideals of civilised relationships. From time immemorial, there has been widespread scepticism about the moral climate of business and the moral character of business people in different theological contexts and cultures. Even just the notion of wealth accumulation by a small number of people, not to mention the numerous scandals, abuses and unlawful practices, has always drawn attention to immorality or the unjust character of business owners in contrast to wage earners, peasants and small property holders. At the time of a deep financial crisis, precipitated through miscalculation, fraud and greed, these views resonate even more strongly than a decade ago. Until recently, liberal economics looked invincible while its rival, the Socialist command economies, all crumbled throughout the 1980s and the 1990s. The recovery is expected to come from new entrepreneurs, morally sound, innovative and hardworking types.

Behavioural economics offers a promising tool to analyse morality in entrepreneurship. Timur Kuran's work is illuminating in many ways. According to Kuran (1998: 242) we have inherited a moral capacity, and the values that form our moral systems are rooted partly in our biological evolution and partly in social processes exhibiting inertia. One can identify values which form clusters called moral systems or moralities. This can be interpersonal or intrapersonal. Interpersonal values consist of the judgements we make about the preferences of others and it is them that produce moral conflict. Intrapersonal values encompass the judgements we make about our own preferences. The state of having values which cannot be satisfied within the prevailing physical and financial constraints may be called moral overload. This condition generates moral dissonance, psychological discomfort stemming from the feeling that one's personal values remain unfulfilled or compromised beyond desirable levels (Kuran 1998: 232). One can claim that entrepreneurs, as individuals but more importantly as economic actors who deal with the allocation of scarce resources to maximise their gains in everyday life, encounter more intensive moral dilemmas than others. This may be especially the case in the post-Soviet context.

We can see a two-dimensional moral axis for entrepreneurs. The first one represents inner judgements and moral convictions, with pure altruism at one end of the axis and entirely self-regarding motives at the other end. Entrepreneurs live in constant conflict between these two positions. The second dimension represents the relationship between inner judgement and action. At the one end of this continuum are actions that accord with moral ideas; at the other extreme are deceit, dissembling and dishonesty. The problem for entrepreneurs is that they often have to act opportunistically and disguise their real motives and intentions. Information asymmetries provide specific advantages and privileges that can enable the 'squeezing out' of competitors. Entrepreneurs often hide their business intentions for speculative purposes or to protect their gains. Other practices that verge on the dishonest can be imitating the products or ideas of others without considering that these strategies amount to unfair competition. Specific problems comes out of the post-Soviet context. Some entrepreneurs believe in collective ownership and communism but do business for profit. This leads to moral dissonance. At the personal level an individual might believe in communist norms, but acts as a self-serving capitalist to survive. There are two related moral issues: a contradiction within the core beliefs of the 'inner self' and a belief that one is being dishonest in one's dealings with others. The scientific materialism of communist ideology and the vision of a timeless purity of Islamic fundamentalism can both lead to similar situations of moral discomfort, guilt and shame.

In realistic human conditions, however, incentives to cheat, free ride and steal necessitates an enforcement body, namely a government or a god-given order (Pfleiderer 1896). Yet, the coercion of the state and self-regulatory groups distort the liberal and liberating provisions of the idealised market even further in post-Soviet transition. A multiple-layered moral compass is more likely to emerge among entrepreneurs in their day-to-day business dealings. Based on societal and individual moral convictions entrepreneurs can hold many moral positions, sometimes even temporarily in contradiction with one another, as opposed to a neat linear notion of private and public morality. The moral convictions of their decisions in market dealings swing within the bi-polarity of altruism and egoism like a pendulum. The centre of gravity is the base of their ideological world standing. In the following sections we will illustrate the most visible elements and exemplary cases of these positions of central gravity: Soviet rationality, Sufi traditions, and utopian Islam.

II. The moral gravity of entrepreneurship: three categories for central Asia

In order to apply our concept of moral conviction to the behaviour of Central Asian entrepreneurs, we use a typology that categorises positions. We assess entrepreneurs based on their reported or observed stances in relation to their business practices, their perceived sense of duty, and their sense of justice. Here we will provide illustrative cases from our extensive field work among entrepreneurs of Central Asia. A survey of 183 entrepreneurs was carried out between 2004 and 2007 through face-to-face interviews. This survey revealed many aspects of an emerging entrepreneurial class and its position between the state-market axis. I published my extensive findings in a monograph, *Building States and Markets: Enterprise Development in Central Asia* (Özcan

2010). The arguments and the case studies in the following section are based on the data and interviews of this survey. The three cases below correspond to a general pattern of entrepreneurial positions I observed in my sample. To illustrate the real life circumstances we will tell the story of one entrepreneur within each category.

A. Paradoxes of Soviet rationalism

Even after around two decades of separation from Russia, the current generation of Central Asian entrepreneurs over the age of 40 retain a Soviet mind-set that inhabits a moral space that includes traditional regional and nomadic beliefs. This has created a hybrid of Turko–Mongolian traditions and Marxist–Leninist ideology. Older businessmen were educated in Soviet universities, trained and apprenticed to state enterprises and associate personal, societal and technical advancement with Russian culture and language. In the process of being Russified and Sovietised, many lost their native identity and culture, but the majority retained a strong spiritual link with their nation, clan and community. They express concepts of principled and rational living in terms of scientific determinism and try to explain the change in their lives thus. A cold rationality of survival is at the core of their moral being. However, that has to co-exist with a passion for family and ancestral lineage. Their moral flexibility is facilitated by their strong sense of realism and the necessity to be rapid adapters to radically changing circumstances.

Although Central Asians were rarely recruited into the Moscow-centred Soviet elites, thorough socialisation of the population, through schooling, workplace integration, the press and party bureaucracy succeeded in transforming the region. That transformation was partly successful, as remnants of Asiatic culture were occasionally apparent. While those remnants fostered suspicion among non-Asian Soviet citizens, they provided the foundation for some adaptability to the post-Soviet liberal economy and search for new identity. Those adaptations, however, made frequent reference to underlying notions of Soviet rationalism and a deterministic understanding of the market (Alexander 2007; Payne 2001).[2]

Atheistic ideals and communism, blended with shamanism and tribalism of ancestral lineage, co-habited reasonably well in Kazakh and Kyrgyz societies. The former was public and the latter was pushed to the private sphere; often relegated to the status of irrational traditions. In their late conversion to Islam, the Kazakh and Kyrgyz peoples incorporated the naturalism of centuries of nomadic traditions into Muslim rituals and developed a pragmatic attitude

2 See Alexander (2007) for an extensive debate on this. A Kazakh professional who trained and worked in the Soviet era states, 'I tell them the market is like the law of gravity'.

towards the teachings of Islamic law. Compared to a tendency to ritualise adherence to Islam among the settled and agrarian peoples of the Fergana Valley and elsewhere in the region, the Kazakh and Kyrgyz people followed Islam selectively, blending it with their animism and pantheism. Shamanistic and celestial celebrations were also maintained more easily as part of nationalistic and folk culture under communism, divorced from church-based monotheistic religions.

Entrepreneurs who are most influenced by this blending of Soviet rationalism and the surviving elements of ancestral nature religion are more likely to have the following traits in relation to business and morality (see Table 7.1 for a comparison):

I. Core morality of doing business: they believe that business is a means to survive and the change of the regime is a consequence of dialectic materialism. Life is seen through the prism of determinism but sacred lineage and family and tribal relations form an exception. Care for others is limited to these lineages and veneration is reserved for the progenitors of their clan.
II. The virtue of duty: an entrepreneur's duty is to survive and serve the needs of their extended family. The law of nature applies: whoever is stronger will survive; this often takes on a predatory character. In order to achieve success and manage to survive one can be ruthless and bend the rules when necessary.
III. Justice and greater good: there appears to be a bounded sense of justice for the clan and the family. However, they tend to be open to new ideas and curious about the world. There appears a continuing moral dissonance with formative Soviet teaching. There is a commitment and individual responsibility to friends and family. These entrepreneurs often have faith in and expectations from the capitalist life style as a form of personal advancement.

Case Study 1: Aybek: the ex-physician taxi man[3]

We were sitting in a small rundown Suzuki minibus covered in dust with fellow passengers waiting in front of the Ak Tilek market in the town of Karakol, near the eastern end of Issyk-Kul in Kyrgyzstan. Ak Tilek was established in 1987 as part of the Perestroika programme's aim to loosen state control and encourage cooperative and entrepreneurial activities. From 100 traders in those early days the market expanded to 1,000 traders in 2004 as unemployment in the town grew exponentially. Mostly poor and rural people shopped there. Unbranded items ranging from foodstuffs to second-hand clothes were sold on open stalls. Many brought small items to

3 See Özcan (2010: 201–2).

sell to make ends meet for the day. A few jars of jam, a few cups of pickled vegetables, several kilogrammes of apples and other goods were on display. It was mostly women, but some men and children dressed in many layers of clothes were waiting for buyers. It was dusty, noisy and cold. Porters were pushing their carts with a singing tone '*jol ver, jol ver*' (open the way).

Aybek, in his 40s with hazel eyes and a black moustache dominating his round face, was wearing a dark leather waistcoat and a hat. Fond of Pushkin and Tolstoy, he preferred to talk in Russian. He was deeply nostalgic about the Soviet era; yet saw the inevitability of economic changes and their consequences too. He was educated and lived briefly in Moscow before rising in his profession as the chief physician of a hospital in Karakol. Soon after the dissolution of the USSR, however, hospitals, as with other public institutions, began having financial problems and failed to maintain basic services. There were shortages of much essential medical equipment; even electricity. Salary rises remained way below the inflation rate. In the mid-1990s, he was earning as little as 30 USD a month. This forced him to seek other income-generating jobs to survive. There was nothing to do. He felt depressed for weeks. Gradually, he came to accept the state of turmoil and decided to establish a business to help his income. After several trading jobs, he began running a shuttle taxi service with two minibuses and a car. He owned the vehicles, hired the drivers and supervised their daily routine.

While talking, the minibus began filling up with massive shopping bags and other trading items including a small lamb. Since he had no office space we had to carry on our talk in his vehicles. He took us to his second minibus which was next in line. The driver left us alone and only a couple of old peasants with their bags and a young girl with a beautiful round face framed by ruby earrings were there. They all looked uninterested. Aybek looked unsettled and spoke in Russian about his moral stance:

> My main aim is to survive and keep the family together. This business has been doing well so far. You never know, things might change . . . Everything looks calm and stable right now as if it has always been. But, since the end of the Soviet Union, we have been going downhill . . . and the future remains uncertain.

Aybek looked around with some displeasure and avoided communication with his fellow customers. He praised the Soviet system and complained about the new Kyrgyz state. When we came close to finishing our conversation we left our seats to fellow passengers carrying bags. Before departing, Aybek looked out over the bustling market place. While bitterly smiling, he sighed:

> During the Soviet Union life was good for professionals like me and I miss those days. You know, when I was a chief medic, if someone told

me that I would run a taxi service in front of a dirty bazaar one day, I would have only laughed . . . Well here I am . . .

B. Attractions of Sufism

As Islam melded with Central Asian culture, traditions from Buddhism, animism, the naturalist religion of Tengri (celestial god in old Turkic) and mystical sacred lineages were incorporated into Islamic ritual. One widespread heterodox Islamic faction, Sufism, was especially adept at accommodating pluralism while promoting peace, balance, harmony and divine love. Sufis are attractive to Central Asians also because of some similarities between the rituals of shaman priests and the ways miracles and prophecies are employed. Ancestor cults and the spirits of early nomads are associated with veneration of Sufi saints and their shrines have become places of popular respect and worship (Mélinkoff 2003; Privratsky 2001).

In his pioneering work, first published in 1951, Sabri Ülgener explored the morals and mentality behind the economic dissolution of the Islamic world in the Middle Ages and compared this moral and economic descent to the rise of the west, which witnessed increased entrepreneurial activities and overseas expeditions and the emergence of dynamic capitalist enterprises. Ülgener (1991, 2006) illustrated that the intolerant moral and ethical values and increased mysticism and fanaticisms in Islam eventually hindered enterprise growth by condemning the pursuit of wealth, shaming risk taking, and eventually perpetuating economic laxity. This moral and formative ideological decay, which took place over several centuries, subsequently limited market expansion and inhibited the growth of capitalist enterprises along the Silk Road and in the Ottoman Empire. Consequently, prolonged feudal and semi-feudal relations led to the traditional markets mostly being controlled by a narrow group of artisanal and rentier classes along with despotism and political dissolution. Eventual shrinkage in capital, production and trade brought about the isolation of markets, ambiguous morals for business, and introverted communities.

Although Sufism is hardly intact as a belief structure or institution in the region, Sufi ethics has survived and is especially apparent in master–apprentice relations and associated traditions. Some Sufi groups are resurgent, offering spiritual guidance, arbitrating disputes and offering new networks that invariably extend material opportunities. They tend to be more pragmatic in applying religion to their lives. Businessmen occasionally join such groups, identify with a spiritual leader, and are likely to display the following traits:

I. Core morality of doing business: they see business as part of a moral responsibility that they have to accomplish in the world through their labour. Hard work in this world is a preparation for the afterlife. Working is also a form of reaching God and seeking blessing.

II. The virtue of duty: their virtue is based on the principle of serving God in a search for harmony and upholding family values. The old Sufi master–apprentice tradition is reflected in the workplace. This requires obedience to hierarchy and seniority. Learning a business or a craft from a master or elder is preserved as a form of passing good moral attainments and work discipline from older generations to the new ones, from one believer to another.

III. Justice and greater good: they do not have a compartmentalised morality of communism or fundamental Islam. At the very core there is humanism and universality but it is also open to interpretation as well as various ideas and influences. Therefore, it is both pragmatic and non-monolithic.

Case Study 2: Ali: the humanist multi-tasker[4]

At the age of 43, Ali was upbeat about business, family life and his achievements. He began as an apprentice at the age of 16 to a Jewish master leather worker, for whom he worked 12 years in Tashkent. His master became an inspiration and role model in life for him. Over the years his business grew into a small shopping centre in a newly acquired site employing 82 people in eight stores. He later followed some links to Jewish businessmen in the USA and sold semi-processed leather for a few years to them. Then he traded garments and foodstuff between Turkey and Uzbekistan for a couple of years and later brought construction material from China. He was pragmatic, non-doctrinal and argued that Uzbeks needed to learn how to establish and run businesses from other countries like China and Turkey.

After entering into a large courtyard surrounded by a single storey building where eight different businesses were located (a hairdresser, internet cafe, dry cleaner, billiard room, café-restaurant, home appliances store, watch repairer, and barber), we were met by Ali's secretary who took us into a meticulously clean and orderly room with a desk, table and bookshelves full of files. Ali came to greet us, dressed in white well-ironed trousers and a colourful shirt. He was short, looking fit and smiling with big round dark eyes. The business life and serenity of order he built around his modest courtyard had more to it. This was a world within a world; a shelter. Ali was a man of principles, ideals, duties and he claimed to have higher values beyond making money and enjoying a good living. It was easy to follow his Khorezm dialect.

4 See Özcan (2010: 205–7).

> It is not enough that you are good. Your workers have to be good, well behaved and disciplined too. The master-apprenticeship relations are important. They need to respect their elders, have a good social and spiritual discipline. They also should know the business well . . . If you don't satisfy your customers they won't come back.

Ali stressed the importance of recreation, travel and learning, and above all a spiritual depth. According to him, there are three respectable spaces in life and we should approach them with purity: God's realm (mosque and cemetery), family (home), and enterprise (work place). In the harmony of these three divine realms, there exists a humanistic and tolerant view of the world.

While obsessively organised and disciplined, Ali had many liberal and pragmatic ideas along with a Sufi-style Islamic adherence. He did his deeds and adhered to Islam. Yet, he did not believe in orthodoxy. He had a deep affection for the Jewish faith and praised his old Jewish master. Ali's desk had a large PC, many files and books. He had several photos of his well-groomed children and Russian wife and he was very proud of his family. Ali first met his wife at a Japanese art exhibition in Tashkent. He was not only impressed by her looks but also by her taking notes while looking at the items on exhibit. For him marrying a woman of a different faith and race was even a blessing. He claimed that children from mixed marriages are better looking and smarter.

'The more you know the less you lose'.

Ali first proudly took us around and showed his large courtyard and shops, and later explained his new business ideas and plans. He was exuberant and believed that he could open more businesses and create more opportunities for others and even generate work for up to 3,000 people. He was planning to develop the bakery business further by exporting new machinery that would provide novelty and productivity. He joked with a confident smile on his face: 'I often lose in chess but usually win in business.'

C. Utopian Islam

Aside from Sufism, various forms of modern, fundamental, utopian Islam are having an increasingly strong influence. This is most visible in the Fergana Valley of Uzbekistan, where, despite the government's efforts to suppress Islamic groups, resurgence of religion continues to be a binding force. However, Islam is expressed in diverse ways, often with a local flavour. Social groups, known as '*jamaats*', fill the vacuum left by the state by delivering public goods and welfare provisions. New empirical evidence shows that even in towns most loyal to the government, local representatives of state organs tolerate Islamic groups as they alleviate the state's poor economic performance, mediate between corrupt institutions and ameliorate local service delivery.[5]

Some such groups are organised in the Sufi fashion, others are aligned to political Islam or religious utopian sects. They aim to carve an autonomous realm in the market for their own benefit to avoid the state, seek cultural authenticity and to protect their wealth. Mutually beneficial networks help to exchange capital, goods and business opportunities. These businessmen and communities utilise Islam to foster trust and legitimise their business and group behaviour (Özcan and Çokgezen 2006). The twin promise, worldly and spiritual, has considerable appeal to ordinary people, many of whom try to survive on marginal incomes from agriculture and small trade.

While entrepreneurs from professional classes and in major urban centres display mostly non-theological morality, the more agrarian and rural characteristics of people in the Fergana Valley are comfortable with a balance of religion and political authority. Political opposition, protest against exclusion or suppression, finds different expressions among social groups in power politics. For example, as studied by Ilkhamov (2006), the Akromiya movement led by small business leaders in the Fergana Valley is not just a religious movement proselytising good morals but also a business solidarity platform and an attempt to establish a self-governing rule in order to insulate businessmen and their local communities from the negative effects of corruption and authoritarian rule.

Entrepreneurs who are influenced by the teaching of fundamentalist Islam wish to construct a different realm for themselves. Contrary to common perceptions in the West about fundamentalist Islam, these individuals pursue their path peacefully and consciously. An imagined pure Islamic society, they believe, would bring material wealth, spiritual richness, and inner calm to them and their community. As in other such groups, they search for justice not liberty (Kuran 1989, 1996). These groups are more likely to have the following traits:

I. Core morality of doing business: they see business as part of the duty of a Muslim and link it to the paternal or family continuity of trade or craft. One has to conduct oneself as if an omnipotent and omnipresent God is watching. Carrying out the mater craftsmen tradition and paternal lineage of business preserves order with responsibility and obedience.
II. The virtue of duty: their virtue is based on the principle of serving God and helping to re-establish the perfect order by going back to their interpretation of 'original Islam' under the Prophet Muhammad. The

5 Alisher Khamidov, who carried out extensive empirical research on Islamic groups in the Fergana Valley, observes that despite the suppressive policies carried out against Islamic groups by the central government, the local government functionaries tolerate and even benefit from the charity and welfare provision of Islamic business groups and their social arm: '*jamaat*'.

duty of an entrepreneur is to maintain the craft or business as a living and a way to be a good Muslim.

III. Justice and greater good: political tyranny leads to moral suffocation. Within fundamentalist Islam, entrepreneurs see their future within the fraternity of groups and paternal lineage rather than state institutions or a broader society. The outside world is troubling and distressing until liberation which will emerge under perfect Islamic order.

Case Study 3: Osman: the bewildered silk weaver[6]

Osman, tall by Uzbek standards with hazel eyes and a restless spirit disguised in an ill-fitting dark suit, accompanied us to his home in the suburbs of Namangan. A tall gate took us into an open porch surrounded by rooms and a wide open garden. My two assistants, Osman and I sat on the floor around a low table symmetrically and colourfully decorated with Fergana nuts and fruits; grapes, apples, pistachios, pomegranates, almonds, candies, etc. Two young girls around 12, veiled and looking down at the ground, brought tea bowls. They shyly avoided our eyes but secretly watched behind the curtains. We saw no adults from the family. After breaking his Ramadan fast, Osman was eager to talk and the girls brought in a delicious soup. Then came the Uzbek pilau, the master dish of Uzbek dining, rice with meat, raisins, chickpeas and grated carrot. Each colourful bowl of pilau was topped with a succulent piece of baked quince.

Osman came from a typical artisan-merchant family that was common in the Valley. His father was a silk weaver, as his eight brothers were all involved in silk production, dying, weaving and marketing. He was an atheist until the age of 20 when, doing his military service on the cold Kazakh steppe, he fell ill. The Army sent him back home where he remained bedridden for a year. Recovery was slow and he claimed that during that period he had many thoughts and reflections on life and God. After his recovery, he came into contact with Islamists who preached the purity of Islam. It felt good to believe and to 'start again'.

Osman believes in Islamic salvation through the teachings of Prophet Muhammad; and striving for purity and the fundamentals of Islam. Like most of his fellow Fergana folk, he is neither an extremist preacher nor a militant. His approach to work, life and religion had signs of Wahabi teaching although he simply explained that he had been attending mosque meetings where he learned Arabic in the 1990s.

> A devout man in the Muslim faith would not touch unlawful substances and would not take another's share. A man without faith can do anything and get lost in life. If you are faithful, you know what is at stake. I work

6 See Özcan (2010: 212–14).

with people who have this faith and I do my trade and business with such men. I get my blessed share. In this village we don't lock our doors we just close them . . .

During the Soviet era, the Namangan silk factory employed around 3,000 people. One of his brothers served eight years in prison for weaving silk at home, a prohibited pursuit of personal wealth. During those years they used to steal materials from the factory and weave at home. Their silk patterns and the quality of weaving done at home was always better then the factory ones which lacked care, patience and attention. The bothers then used to sell the woven goods to black market traders in Samarkand and Bukhara.

Osman explained the miracles of silk and emphasised how maintaining family traditions was his duty to his father and generations of grandfathers, how silk is blessed by god and how he is a 'slave of god' pursuing a craft that has such sanctity. Osman produced a treatise on silk and in which he had written the following:[7]

> Women wore silk to look pretty but the skin health and healing is the essence of silk. If you wear one hundred per cent silk, bugs don't get close to you, and even if you don't wash you don't get ill.
>
> If there was another more significant fabric then Allah would have dressed all heavenly people with that fabric but the Koran says: . . . They all will be dressed in pure silk in heaven.
>
> I am proud of choosing my father's profession, being a national atlas weaver . . .

Osman, in common with many other artisans I met, has a deep resentment about the policies of the Tashkent government. According to him, laws come

7 Osman wrote this for a national festival of artisans and won an award. His pamphlet on silk contains the following information on how local silk cloth, atlas, is produced:

1. 1,500–2,000 units of silk caterpillar eggs, which amount to 1 gram, are placed into incubator to turn them into caterpillars.
2. The silk caterpillar is looked after for 28–30 days and nights with mulberry leaves. By this time the caterpillar is 5 years old and at the last in 3–4 days it will start to turn into a cocoon.
3. Cocoons are submitted to warehouses where they are sorted and stored.
4. Cocoons are processed into silk in special workshops.
5. The raw silk is milled in the silk-mill and reeled.
6. The raw silk is boiled in soda and the sericin is washed out.
7. The processed silk is winded and then warped.
8. The die maker prepares the warp for painting. The silk is dipped into the die according to the pattern and design of the fabric.
9. The artisan weaves the Atlas fabric in an eight-pedaled weaving loom.
10. The fabric is decorated and presented to the buyer.

from above with no prior deliberation for people concerned. The only role expected from them is to cheer, clap and bend down to whatever comes from the government. Artisans face deep problems and have a tough time surviving in the Fergana Valley. Despite several government initiatives to protect traditions and train artisans, the region is entirely cut off from the world. There is no tourism and with the decline of local merchant traditions and physical isolation, artisan families are increasingly at the mercy of large traders who often have a bad reputation for being opportunists. Many such merchants come from Samarkand and Bukhara where there is a bigger market and international tourism. While we were chatting the girls brought in towels and Osman initiated the final course by pealing and slicing apples and dividing the watermelon. He then dismantled the sweet, glassy red seeds of pomegranate with patience. At the end of the long and slow chatty meal, our casual togetherness was ritualised and evolved into friendly bonding and Osman felt comfortable enough to show us his hidden underground workshop.

Where we dined, Osman later told us, was his sister's house. We crossed the street to another big mud brick house with a large garden on a slope. Ten to fifteen kilometres out of the city centre this suburb was new, built in the northern hills of Namangan in 1996, and it followed local architectural traditions with single houses surrounded by tall walls and spacious gardens; quite different from the usual fully circled Uzbek gardens. Osman's atelier was next to his house dug under several basement floors with many small rooms connected to one another. There were at least 10 large Soviet-made spinning machines, dye material and other items. His atelier was protected from outside intruders through several floors beneath the entrance in a maze-like basement. But, despite his treatise on silk, the materials were bright red and white nylon. Harsh economic circumstances intensified competition and low incomes fuelled the demand for cheap products. The colourful shades of adras and atlas are giving way to cheap Chinese imports and lowering the quality of local production. But, sadly and more profoundly, a centuries-old craft and artisanal tradition, together with sophisticated artistic forms and values, was slowly fading away. Silk was what god prized, the craft was his ancestors' legacy, but Osman was spinning nylon thread in a disguised workshop to earn his livelihood. Osman summarised his sentiments with a sad look:

> If you don't hope and take sadness lightly in the face of the problems we have here, you cannot endure. Life becomes a pain, sour . . . I often act silly and take it lightly to survive . . . We have a saying: a man can get used to even his grave within three days.

Early the following morning, we departed from the Namangan guest house built for high ranking Soviet bureaucrats out of granite and marble, yet with little charm compared to Osman's suburb. He insisted the night before that we should have breakfast in his home before leaving the town. Most of his family had just

Table 7.1 A typology of entrepreneurs' moral dispositions

	Core morality of business doing	*Virtue of duty*	*Justice and greater good*	*Moral dissonance*
Soviet rationality ***Disjointed***	– Survivalist – Consequence of rational laws – Straight forward opportunism	– Surviving and adapting – Preserving the family and sacred lineage – Continuity of family lineage	– Materialistic and flexible – Indifferent or lacks enthusiasm for greater moral goods – Predatory in character	Medium
Sufism ***Normative***	– Responsibility as a human being – Accomplishing the world by labour – Pragmatism	– Serving good – Hard work, search of an harmony between divine and worldly – Respecting the master	– Seeking both material and divine return – Humanistic – Universal goodness	Low
Orthodox Islam ***Utopian***	– Duty of a believer in search of perfect order – Preserving family lineage – In search of blessed and fair share – Uncompromising search for autonomy	– Living as god sees it – Establishing perfect Islam – Maintaining paternal traditions, family trade or craft	– Seeking a fair and just society for Moslems – Hard work to serve worldly and divine – Loyalty to Islamic world and fraternity	High

gone to sleep after finishing their Ramadan meal before the crack of the dawn. He was overjoyed by our return and watched us drink tea and eat our breakfast. For him, we were a novelty, maybe a hope, in isolated and mundane Namangan.

III. Conclusion

The examples provided here of different moral paths illustrate the pervasiveness of longstanding societal overtures against the forced convergence of Soviet engineering that aimed to eradicate the past by building a timeless future. As the Soviet regime collapsed, there emerged a moral void and many people searched for a new direction to compensate for their worsening conditions. They needed to be able to cope with the burdens of increasing corruption and the authoritarian regimes that presided over the ruthless process of economic re-allocation (Özcan 2010: 217).

As a response, three patterns of moral disposition arose based upon naturalistic shamanism, Sufi harmony and utopian Islam. In relation to the core morality of conducting business, virtue, justice and the greater good, these three patterns are associated with radically different moral dispositions: pragmatic, normative and utopian.

The points of each moral standing in relation to core morality, virtue and justice relate to entrepreneurial choices. The three patterns of thinking lead to different levels of pragmatism, normative and utopian stance with varying degrees of moral satisfaction, guilt and dissonance. The highest moral dissonance is observed among the ones who are guided by a utopian-style Islam.

The desirability of institutions that lessen cultural or moral diversity is important and indeed the function of the state is to converge and co-opt these positions under a web of institutions and legal frameworks. As Kuran (1998) pointed out, conflicting interpretations of the world may breed cognitive dissonance. Numerous sociologists, most notably Emile Durkheim (1933), have suggested that nation building requires a convergence of values. Scholars have also argued that the homogenisation of individual values contributes to social stability and economic cooperation by reducing violence and conflict. Therefore, as Timur Kuran argues (1998: 262), conflicts between individuals leading to moral diversity can be socially costly to manage. One group of moral entrepreneurs will institute a moral escape; another will pursue moral reform. Even if trying to resolve the same problem, the groups may become rivals.

The process of building states and markets in Central Asia requires the promotion of harmonious moral regimes. Yet, deepening moral confusion in the weakness of intellectual and political leadership towards a lawful and fair society is likely to continue to play at the hands of authoritarian regimes.

References

Alexander, C. (2007) 'Soviet and post-Soviet planning in Almaty, Kazakhstan', *Critique of Anthropology*, 27(2): 165–81.

Barnard, C. (1938) *The Functions of the Executive*, Cambridge, MA: Harvard University Press.

Ben-Ner, A. and Putterman, L. (eds) (1998) *Economics, Values and Organization*, New York: Cambridge University Press.

Carr, A. (1968) 'Is business bluffing ethical?', *Harvard Business Review*, January–February: 145–53.

Durkheim, E. (1933) *Division of Labour in Society*, Macmillan Company.

Gauthier, D. (1986) *Morals by Agreement*, Oxford: Oxford University Press.

Hallpike, C.R. (2004) *The Evolution of Moral Understanding*, Prometheus Research Group: www.prometheus.org.uk

Hausman, D. (1989) 'Are markets morally free zones?' *Philosophy and Public Affairs*, 18(4): 317–33.

Ilkhamov, A. (2006) 'The Phenomenology of "Akromiya": Separating facts from fiction', *China and Eurasia Quarterly*, 4: 39–48.

Kuran, T. (1989) 'On the notion of economic justice in contemporary Islamic thought', *International Journal of Middle East Studies*, 21(2): 171–91.

Kuran, T. (1996) 'The discontents of Islamic economic morality', *American Economic Review*, 86(2): 438–42.

Kuran, T. (1998) 'Moral overload and its alleviation', in A. Ben-Ner and L. Putterman (eds) *Economics, Values and Organization*, New York: Cambridge University Press, 231–66.

McMahon, C. (1981) 'Morality and the invisible hand', *Philosophy and Public Affairs*, 10(3): 247–77.

Mélinkoff, I. (2003) 'Ahmad Yesevi and Turkic popular Islam', *Electronic Journal of Oriental Studies*, 6(8): 1–9.

Özcan, G.B. (2010) *Building States and Markets: Enterprise Development in Central Asia*, Hampshire: Palgrave Macmillan.

Özcan, G.B. and Çokgezen, M. (2006) 'Trusted markets: the exchanges of Islamic companies', *Comparative Economic Studies*, 48(1): 132–55.

Payne, M.J. (2001) *Stalin's Railroad: Turksib and the building of socialism*, Pittsburgh: University of Pittsburgh Press.

Pfleiderer, O. (1896) 'Is morality without religion possible and desirable?', *The Philosophical Review*, 5(5): 449–72.

Privratsky, B.G. (2001) *Muslim Turkestan: Kazak religion and collective memory*, Surrey: Curzon Press.

Sen, A. (1985) 'The moral standing of the market', *Social Philosophy and Policy*, 3; reprinted in E.F. Paul, F.D. Miller, Jr. and J. Paul (eds), *Ethics and Economics*, Oxford: Blackwell.

Sen, A. (2000) 'East and west: the reach of reason', *The New York Review of Books*, July 20: 33–8.

Ülgener, F.S. (1991) *The World of Ethics and Mentality of Economic Dissolution* [*Iktisadi Çözülmenin Ahlak ve Zihniyet Dünyası*], Istanbul: Der Yayınları.

Ülgener, F.S. (2006) *Mentality and Religion – Islam, Sufism and economic ethics of disintegration period* [*Zihniyet ve Din – Islam, Tasavvuf ve Çözülme Devri Iktisat Ahlakı*], Istanbul: Der Yayınları.

Wilson, J.Q. (1997) *The Moral Sense*, New York: Simon and Schuster.

Zak, P.J. (ed.) (2008) *Moral Markets: The critical role values in the economy*, Princeton: Princeton University Press.

Chapter 8

Religion, politics and the dilemma of national identity in Pakistan

*Tasneem Kausar**

Introduction

Understanding the mysteries of the creation and mutation of religious and political identities in a pluralistic society is a challenging and pressing task. Identities are neither stable nor permanent; they are subject to historical process of transformation. It is this process of invention and re-invention that will be addressed in this essay; indeed, it would appear that – in the context of Pakistan – the identities of the 'pre-terrorism age'[1] are presently subject to complex forms of re-alignments. The question of 'identity' in Pakistan has always been fraught. Religion played a crucial role in the creation of the country; as it did in the foundation of the Israeli state. However, while religion as a source of identity has helped integrate the identities of multi-ethnic Jewish communities (see Ben-Rafael and Sharot 1991: chapters 2, 8 and 10; see also Reed 1978), religion in Pakistan has largely failed to create a sustained notion of national identity, despite what was achieved at independence in 1947.

Pluralist societies require integrating processes whereby ethnic, cultural, regional and linguistic differences are downplayed and a common identity asserted (Ben-Rafael and Sharot 1991: 170; Ortega y Gasset 1930: 169–171). With the creation of Pakistan in 1947, the Indian sub-continent witnessed a unique event. Religious identity was effectively mobilised to create a country defined by Islam. In order to understand this process, and taking the sovereign nation as our reference points, we can make an analytical distinction between

* Associate Professor of Law at Pakistan College of Law; LLB (Pakistan College of Law), LLM. (Yale Law School, USA), MA. (Punjab University). This article was presented at the Conference organised by The British Academy on Religious and Political Identities in Monotheistic Cultures, held in Istanbul, Turkey in August 2007.
I would like to dedicate my article to my daughter Zarrmein and all the children of Pakistan with a wish that they will have a better understanding of their identity as Pakistanis then the earlier generations.

1 Author makes an arbitrary division between the time period before 9/11 and after 9/11. It is the world before the event of 9/11 that has been labelled as the pre-terrorism age.

internal and external factors. Scholars have tended to stress the internal factors in the creation of Pakistan, in particular the homogeneity of the religion shared by the different Pakistani peoples. This tends to sideline the equally important external factors – the most important of which was the 'common fear of Hindu dominance'.[2]

Over-emphasis on religion as the primary cause of integration has not just been a scholarly preoccupation. This paper examines the role of religious identity in Pakistan, and, its integrative and disintegrative relationship with other ethno-political identities. It focuses on four phases of Pakistani history: the creation of the nation, the cessation of East Pakistan, the Islamisation of the Zia regime and the recent military rule of General Musharraf. It is argued that the creation of a state and its preservation[3] are two distinct phenomena. The continuous deployment of religious identity as national identity has created a problematic myth: Pakistan and Islam are synonymous. Moreover, the failure to understand the distinction between the creation of the nation and its preservation has led to religion becoming a primary prescription for many of the nation's problems and a deflection of debate over matters of democratisation and modernisation; in particular, the creation of a satisfactory system of sharing economic benefits and political power (Brass 2005: 30–31, 40–41 and 45–46).

Arguably, the drift from Jinnah's vision of Pakistan as a liberal welfare state began early. The early militarisation of Pakistan shaped the Pakistani identity, nation and state and has continued to do so for more than 40 years. It is concluded that unless Pakistan's objectives are redefined to focus on economic prosperity and popular participation in governance, reforms which the military have consistently obstructed or blocked, the state will continue to turn to Islam as a national unifier and a symbol of national identity.

2 Bharat Verma (2006). The author writes that: 'In 1950s, Hans J. Morgenthau, the then Director of Center for the Study of American Foreign Policy at University of Chicago, in his book The New Republic had observed, "Pakistan is not a nation and hardly a state. It has no justification, ethnic origin, language, civilisation or the consciousness of those who make up its population. They have no interest in common except one: fear of Hindu domination. It is to that fear and nothing else that Pakistan poses its existence and thus for survival as an independent state." During the same period, another American scholar Keith Callard in his book Pakistan-a Political Study commented, "the force behind the establishment of Pakistan was largely the feeling of insecurity".' See also von Tunzelmann (2007) (commenting that after the elections of 1937, Jinnah suddenly transformed from an electoral failure into the champion of free Islam against Hindu dominance).

3 See Rafiqul Islam (1985) 219 (enumerating factors essential for creating state such as desire of self-determinism, homogeneity of people, separatist demands must be based on gross human rights abuse, promise of minimum and reasonable political stability, economic viability, etc.); Cohen (2002) 109 (mentioning that when security, economic parity, human services, justice and basic necessities are not provided the states can fail).

I. Two nation theory: Muslim nationalism in undivided India

The point at which the Muslims of India became conscious of the differences that existed between them and the Hindu majority is perhaps open to debate. However, it was the identification and articulation of this difference that led ultimately to the separatist agenda. Scholars have attributed 'the two nations theory' to Muhammad Ali Jinnah – a defence of common belonging on the grounds of religion as well as culture (Qureshi 1974: 127–29).

Within this fraught historical field, there are further arguments between scholars regarding the origins of Muslim nationalism (see Ikram 1997; see also Qureshi 1974). However, in the context of the Pakistan movement, three years stand out: 1906, 1930 and 1940. It was in 1906 that the demand for political participation on the basis of a separate religious community was made by establishing a new political party, the All India Muslim League. In the same year, the Muslim League made a claim for seats in the legislatures on the basis of separate Muslim constituencies. Religious affiliation had become an issue in the British period. Scholars have suggested that when Muslim dynasties ruled over India, the religious affiliation of their subjects was not their main concern (see Riaz 1987: 11–13). The merger of religious and political identities in the Indian sub-continent had its primary basis in the introduction and development of representative institutions in British India (Gaborieau 1985: 7), where political alignments were sought to be adopted on the basis of religion (Gaborieau 1985: 7).

This politicisation of a separate identity of Muslims emerged more forcefully, when in 1930, Dr Iqbal presented a structured idea of a separate Muslim state as an extension of the religious identity of Indian Muslims.[4] Dr Iqbal was convinced that a natural correlation existed between the religion and state in Islam (see Hakim 1992: 54, 55; see also Hakim 1983: 1640). The creation of an Islamic state was the only way to preserve Islamic society and an Islamic way of life in India (see Neufeldt 1981: 178). In this process, religion was an adhesive that united and bound together the political aspirations of the Muslims of India. Consequently, in 1940, Muhammad Ali Jinnah, while formally announcing the demand for Pakistan, stated the crux of Muslim nationalism:

> The Hindus and Muslims belong to two different religious philosophies, social customs, literatures. They neither intermarry, nor dine together and they belong to two different civilizations which are based mainly on conflicting ideas and conceptions.
>
> (Ahmad 1970: 380)

4 In the 1930s Presidential address of All India Muslim League in Allahabad, a demand was forwarded from the forum of All India Muslim League whereby the Muslims of India claimed a separate state.

This emergence of a profound religious identity and nationalism, in the form of two-nation theory, was accepted as theoretically sound and practically feasible only by Indian Muslims themselves and their very few foreign supporters,[5] since both in theory and practice, it challenged many already existing stable perceptions of nationhood.[6] Returning to the point made earlier, the factors responsible for the emergence of Muslim nationalism can be seen to be internal as well as external to the religious ideology. Internal factors have received a great deal of attention from researchers and scholars of the Independence movement.[7] It is popularly believed that Muslims of India united to seek separation from the Hindu majority because of the perception that the ideological differences between the two religious systems were almost impossible to reconcile (Ahmad 1952: 469; Gaborieau 1985: 8). Internal factors thus stress expressions of common belief and ritual which bound the Muslims of India together despite ethnic, economic or linguistic differences.

External factors relate to those circumstances and events that were not intrinsically present in the schematic characteristics of religious or cultural identity. From this perspective, Muslim nationalism can be seen as a reaction against Hindu political identification. It is necessary to generalise a little; to place our discussion in context. Modern considerations of the factors responsible for forming and preserving nations refer to factors such as religion or ideology; common ethnicity; cultural, especially linguistic homogeneity; and common economic interest (Deutsch and Foltz 1966: 3; Ward 1966: 18). The relative influence of each of these factors varies considerably in actual historical experience (Syed 1980: 578).[8] Our analysis can be clarified in the following way:

Thesis I: The integration of religious and political identities is a reactive phenomenon.

Thesis II. In the absence of circumstances justifying a reactive response to a hostile ideology, it may not be possible to transform religious identity into political identity.

5 For example, British writer Beverly Nichols (1944) and the British Labor M.P. Woodrow Wyatt (1952).

6 See Gaborieau (1985) 8 (referring to factors responsible for forming and preserving nations, enumerates agents such as religion or ideology, common ethnicity, cultural or language or economic interest). See Gareth and Wright Mills (1958) 177–178 (mentioning that Max Weber while noting the common factors for creating state, commented that even though any one of them might suffice to generate sense of nationhood, none of them can be relied upon to produce a nation); Ortega y Gasset (1930) 169 (saying that it is the state which makes the nation, not nation the state); see also Emerson (1962) 96 (quoting Lord Acton: 'a nationality should constitute a state is contrary to the nature of modern civilization').

7 Almost all major writers on this topic, such as Muhammad Ali, Ishtiaq Hussain Qureshi, S.M. Ikram, etc., have considered the religious, cultural and linguistic differences of Muslims and Hindus as a basis for their separation.

8 See *supra* footnote 6.

In the context of the discussion of Islamic identity and the two nations theory, it seems that thesis II is more compelling than thesis I; that Hindu–Muslim antagonisms animated the creation of the independence movement rather than the 'natural' homogeneity of Indian Muslims. Indeed, barring the small urban elite, the over-whelming rural Muslim masses did not share any internally common characteristics of race, language or culture. The one factor that they had in common was dislike of Hindu-dominion, a glimpse of which was had during the brief period of Congress Ministries in 1937–39.

This is not to dismiss the political force that the perception of a shared identity had. Pakistan did come into being as a Muslim nation – and in such a way that involved a massive migration[9] of population. Although migration was in part a response to massacres and genocide, it can perhaps also be seen as evidence of mass popular commitment to the 'idea' of Pakistan.[10] At the same time, the 'common belonging' thesis can be overdone. In 1971 Bangladesh achieved its independence from Pakistan. Although the Bengalis had been ardent supporters of the creation of Pakistan, a common identity as Muslims was clearly not enough to hold the nation together.[11]

So, 'Muslim nationalism' was a reaction to Hindu nationalism. Historians have arguably established that Hindus took the lead in Hindu–Muslim separatism.[12] On the other hand, the primary focus of Muslims at least up to 1940 has been to secure the political rights of their community. It was not until 1940 that Indian Muslims were formally declared to be a 'nation'. The repeated failure of Congress to cater to the interests of Muslims in India, shifted the political focus of All India Muslim League, and directed it towards religion as a focus for oppositional energies to Congress. Hence, antagonism and reaction are the two persistent themes in the tense relationships between Hindu and Muslim nationalism in undivided India (Spear 1963: 36).

9 It was considered to be the largest migration of a population at a singular point of time in the recent history. According to one estimate more than one billion people (of all religions) migrated at the time of partition.

10 The count of dead was approximated to be between the figures of four to five hundred thousand.

11 Maulvi Abdul Haque of Bengal has been reported to have been the main author of the Lahore Resolution of 1940 whereby the claim of independent country with the name of Pakistan was made.

12 Majumdar (1963) 39–41 (referring to the beginning of the Hindu nationalism, he noted that in 1870, the 'National Society' was founded to promote unity and national feelings among the Hindus. When objection was taken to the use of the word 'national' for a Hindu organisation, it was asserted by the organisers of the National Society, *Hindu-Mela*, that 'the Hindus certainly form a nation by themselves, and as such a society established by them can very properly be called a national society').

There is another external factor that can be seen as central.[13] During the course of the independence movement, at least until 1940, the awareness of the political status of Muslim identity was much stronger at the level of the elite than the masses (Qureshi 1969: 22). It was the failure of this elitist politics which compelled the Muslim elite to mobilise the masses and spread 'Muslim nationalism' as an integrated religious and political identity of Indian Muslims. Congress, on its part, could not understand the apprehensions of the Muslim minority.[14] Furthermore (and ironically) the Muslim League had very little support amongst the ulema of India,[15] perhaps due to its secular leadership (Binder 1963: 183–207). Therefore, it became more a matter of political expediency for the Muslim League to show a religious face in order to gather support from the Islamic factions of society. The use of religion brought the ethnically divided Muslims of India political power and recognition, a significant outcome, as they had been marginalised since the fall of the Moghul Empire.

In brief, Muslim nationalism became the vehicle for the achievement of Pakistan. This nationalism was uni-dimensional since it singularly focused on religion and disregarded factors of geography, ethnicity and local tradition. With one stroke, it separated Muslims from the people with whom they had resided for generations and made them kin to those with whom they had never interacted due to the difference of ethnicity and language.

II. Pakistan, national identity crisis and Bengali nationalism

Pakistan was created on 14 August 1947. During the last days of the campaign for Pakistan, nationalistic symbols[16] (such as language, dress, etc.) with religious connotations were adopted and used successfully. The deployment of religious identity to achieve the goal of Pakistan, suspended for the time being, the ethnic and linguistic identities of the people of the newly created state of Pakistan. Nevertheless, history from 1947 to 1971 witnessed the disintegration of this newly acquired national identity due to the ethnic, linguistic and demographic differences as well as political disagreements.

13 See text at page 189.

14 Congress refused to incorporate the 14-point demand of Muslims in Nehru Constitution, rejected the Communal Award and declined to include Muslim Leaguers in the ministries in the Congress-dominated provinces. For detailed examination of the role of the Congress in alienating Muslims, see Moon (1962); Dwarkadas (1966).

15 Muslim League received the support of Islamic factions when finally *Jamiat-ulema-i-Islam* was organised in 1945.

16 For example, Quiad-e-Azam Mohammad Ali Jinnah always appeared in public meetings dressed in a *sherwani*, the national dress of Indian Muslims, and the Muslim League made great efforts to promote the Urdu language as the main language of Indian Muslims as against Bengali, since Urdu was similar in script to Arabic, whereas Bengali was written in Hindi-like script, i.e. *devnagri*.

At the time of its creation Pakistan was composed of two parts: East Pakistan and West Pakistan. When examining the integrative 'adhesives' present in both parts of Pakistan, one is provided with an interesting lead for analysis. East Pakistan, now known as Bangladesh, bore the potential of a nation state. It was and is culturally, ethnically, linguistically and territorially homogenous. In contrast, West Pakistan was and is quite heterogeneous in character. It has multiple cultural and regional traits. It has at least four provincial languages,[17] various dialects and many cultural streaks. Furthermore, various component groups in West Pakistan had strong cultural and linguistic affiliations with groups outside the national boundaries.[18]

Given the heterogeneity of Pakistan, how could a sense of national identity be sustained in the absence of visible external threats to the Muslim nation? Although the invasion of Pakistan has been a constant feature of Pakistan's history, in the immediate post-Independence period there was no eminent threat. Although the two-nation ideology had provided a compelling founding idea, it lost some of its relevance in the post independence period. Although there would not have been any Pakistan, if Bengalis, Punjabis, Sindhis, Pathans and Balochs would not have chosen their Muslim identity over and above their ethnic and linguistic identities, this religio-political identity required further development so that it would address the regional and cultural diversity of the new nation.

One must be mindful that individuals are members of various social groups, identifiable on the bases of religion, family, tribe, caste, region and language. A multiethnic state cannot afford to ignore its multiple identities (Wendell and Freeman 1974). In Pakistan's case, it was taken for granted that the religious national identity of being a Muslim would always prevail. However, bonds of a shared religion and a shared history of the Independence movement proved too weak to hold the country together. Although ethnic differences or similarities do not necessarily lead to balkanisation (Rafiqul Islam 1985: 219; Cohen 2002: 109), many analysts have held the separation of East and West Pakistan can be traced to its ethnic divisions (Oldenburg 1985: 711).[19]

The argument that the Bengalis had strong reasons to separate from Pakistan – as people ethnically different, shut off from political power and furthermore

17 These include Punjabi, Sindhi, Pushto and Balochi.

18 For example, the people of North West Frontier Province (NWFP) are culturally as well as linguistically, aligned with the people of Afghanistan. It is in the context of this alignment that after the fall of Kabul, a very large number of Afghan refugees entered Pakistan and settled predominantly in NWFP.

19 Separate ethnic identification may operate as a necessary internal condition to begin with, but not a sufficient one, or else every multiethnic state would naturally lead to fragmentation. Besides, if the political system is seen as an independent variable itself with the multiple sets of strategies, policies and influences as external factors, one may arrive at a better understanding of changing national identities integrate or disintegrate (Nordlinger 2002: 45–47).

economically exploited – has been widely accepted. However, the staunch support of Bengalis for Pakistan in 1946–47 is enough evidence to prove that the Bengali Muslims considered the religious differences more significant than the racial characteristics or linguistic differences. In spite of their ethnic affinity, the Bengali Muslims did alienate from Bengali Hindus in 1947. Bengali Muslims supported the idea of a separate Muslim state and voted for Pakistan with a large majority. Religion as a principal source of Bengali Muslim identity retained its importance during the pre-Pakistan as well as post-Pakistan era at least for the masses.[20]

Political factors, and the economic disparity between East and West Pakistan[21] created the conditions for the disintegration of the nation. The elections of 1954 and 1970[22] proved the closure of religious differential, as the political parties who went to the polls with religious agendas performed miserably. In East Pakistan, the Awami League won on the basis of a programme of regional autonomy, and in the West, the People's Party of Pakistan (PPP) won by presenting a socialist manifesto.[23]

In this speculative understanding, the cessation of East Pakistan was in part the result of a failure to recognise what the meaning of Pakistan would be in the absence of a 'Hindu-Muslim dichotomy'. After the creation of Pakistan, there was no modern interpretation of Shari'a to provide the basis for a Pakistani Constitution acceptable to all political groups. The pre-1947 ideal of an Islamic welfare state never materialised.

Bengali nationalism grew in response to the changing nature of ethnic-group interactions. It aimed at changing the 'dominant-subordinate' relationship between East and West and the distribution of power within society with demands for language rights and economic equality. In the same way that the Pakistan of 1947 came out of the failure of Hindus and Muslims to accommodate each other, the Bangladesh of 1971 was a product of the inability of East and West Pakistanis to share power equally and freely.

III. Post-1971 Pakistan: mainstreaming religious identity

The cessation of Bangladesh in 1971 left Pakistan a territorially homogenous unit, not 'a religious geography carved out of history' (Qureshi 1973, quoting

20 The fact that Bangladesh, though severed from Pakistan, did not reunite with India or Indian West Bengali Hindu majority has been an evidence of the sustainability of two-nation theory and Islamic identity (Qureshi 1973: 570).

21 See further Oldenburg (1985).

22 The 1954 elections were held only in East Pakistan, whereas 1970 elections were held in both East and West Pakistan.

23 It may be noted, however, that both these parties had equal claims to Islamic ideology and none of them posed to be secular in its political ideology.

from *The Times* 1971). To compare Pakistan of 1947 with Pakistan of 1972 is somewhat misleading but nevertheless essential. The political problems of these two periods remain identical: the search for national identity, consensus upon a new constitution and the role of the military are the central themes.

The post-1971 history of Pakistan witnessed a fresh attempt to integrate religio-political identities. In this period, Islam was used as a focus for recovery from the 1971 defeat in Dhaka. The then government spent energy in establishing the power structures not only internally but also internationally, so that Pakistan could be taken as a key member of the Islamic *Ummah* (Ritcher 1979: 547).

However, the creation of a polity is a process inherently different from its preservation. What had been useful in creating Pakistan proved less so for its continuity. The real problem of post-1971 Pakistan has not been the use of religion but its misuse and overuse. During 1971–87, Pakistan experienced many attempts at artificial implantation of the integration processes with full concentration upon the internal factor of religion as the basis of identity as well as legal and political agendas. This part of the paper will review this mainstreaming of religion in post-1971 Pakistan.

My position regarding this period is that the religious identity of the people of Pakistan has never been subjected to a democratic 'test'. There has never been a serious democratic attempt to gauge popular inclinations, favourable or unfavourable to religious identity. Without such assessment, the attribution of religious identity to Pakistani people is questionable. Indeed, the continuous failure of Islamist political parties in elections, suggests that it was an international desire to see a 'religious Pakistan' as a cold war partner and to prop up the 'Islamicist' military dictatorship of President Zia that sustained the religious identity of the nation. There is little evidence of a sustained 'organic' and democratic commitment to an Islamic identity.

A. Constitutionalising religious identity

If the ambiguities of the Muslim League's demands, during the Independence movement had irritated its opponents, the unambiguous language in which Jinnah spoke for the separation of state and religion,[24] at the first meeting of the Pakistan's Constituent Assembly on 11 August 1947 would have utterly confounded the followers of the 'Islamic state ideal' (Jalal 1995: 73, 77). However, unsatisfied and unsure of the wisdom of Jinnah, the definition of Pakistan on religious lines started right after the demise of Jinnah in 1948. The first recorded political move to incorporate Islam in the state apparatus

24 Jinnah declared: 'You are free; you are free to go to your temples, you are free to go to your mosques or to any other place of worship in this State of Pakistan. You may belong to any religion or caste or creed – that has nothing to do with the business of the State.'

was through the Objective Resolution of 1949, which outlined the aims and objectives for future constitution of Pakistan. In retrospect, it can be concluded that this document was the outcome of intense pressurising by the Ulema who started mobilising the public to hold the government accountable for backing off from its commitment to 'make Pakistan a fortress of Islam' (Binder 1961: 85; Nasr 1993: 261, 267).

The Resolution had two significant clauses: first, it stated that sovereignty lies with Allah; and second, the document asserted that Muslims of Pakistan would live their lives in accordance with the teachings and requirements of Islam as set out in the Holy Quran and the Sunnah. Although the document has been described as 'carefully imprecise' (see Smith 1971), it could not mask the tensions between traditionalists and modernisers. Who was to speak for the nation? In ensuing struggle, one of the most significant sources of Islamic information which keeps the religion of Islam 'modern', that is, Ijtehad was almost swept aside. This empowered the clergy and their claims that they alone could interpret the Quran and Sunnah for the ignorant citizens of Pakistan. It almost seemed like an attempt to shift the power base towards those who had protested against the very origin of the country of Pakistan, that is, the Ulema.

The Objective Resolution was passed by the Constituent Assembly of Pakistan in March 1949, but was only made a substantive part of the Constitution of Pakistan by General Zia-ul Haq in 1985.[25] The year of its pre-ambler formulation and its much later incorporation into the main text of the 1973 Constitution suggests that the military leadership of the 1980s wanted to procure the maximum from the introductory but recessive, shift of power base that the Objective Resolution had caused.

Pakistan's struggle to become a complete Islamic state was still deemed to be incomplete. In later years Pakistan continued to debate the 'Islamic state' ideal, leaving the country polarised between religious and secular factions. The 1956 Constitution labelled Pakistan as an Islamic Republic, a title that was retracted with the Constitution of 1962. The 1973 Constitution again made Pakistan an 'Islamic Republic'. This frequent label-changing indicated a serious struggle between religious identity and territorial identity. This, in turn, led to an internal dualism between ethno-Islamism and the ethno-nationalism. Within the ethno-Islamic framework, a citizen was considered to be a Muslim first and then Pakistani. This points towards a pan-Islamic sentiment, as witnessed during the Soviet invasion of Afghanistan and (in more recent years) the Pakistani stances upon Afghanistan, Iraq, Lebanon and Palestine issues. On the other hand, if a citizen is Pakistani first and Muslim second, then her primary identification will be ethnic because she may be a Pakistani Punjabi, Sindhi or Balochi. Therefore, within the

25 Presidential Order No. 14 of 1985, Article 2-A (with effect from 2 March 1985).

ethno-national framework the internal dualism oscillates between ethnicity and nationality, which requires that the external factors, mainly distribution of power and economic disparity, be seriously addressed. Furthermore, this political adoption of religious identity over and above ethno-national models posed a further challenge inside Pakistan, due to the multiplicity of religious identities. This was the problem confronted by Pakistan during the sectarian divide of the 80s and 90s discussed later in this paper.

B. The Islamic Constitution of 1973

The 1973 Constitution can easily be seen as the most religiously oriented constitution of the country. It contains a number of provisions, which mention 'Islam' or 'Muslim' in one manner or another. Of Pakistan's three constitutions, only the 1973 Constitution, in its original form, has been recognised by commentators as a democratic document due to its creation by a duly elected parliament, and the procedure which led to its adoption.[26] However, the changes and amendments introduced without popular mandate and through authoritative military regimes have considerably destroyed its democratic credentials.[27]

The Constitution of 1973 was created by a parliament that was elected in the 1970 elections. In this first ever general elections, the PPP was pitched against the Muslim League and Jamat-i-Islami, the two leading political parties emphasising religious identity and agendas. The slogan 'Islam is our religion; Socialism is our economy; Democracy is our politics' was the one with which PPP mobilised the masses and scored an astounding victory (Ahmed 1973; Syed 1991: 582). Though people voted for the PPP in the name of social and economic rights, however, within months of establishing government, the PPP built a grand political alliance with all those religious and semi-religious parties, which had bitterly opposed PPP in elections. If

26 Newberg (2002) 138–40 (commenting that while the process that led to the 1973 constitution was full of acrimony and power politics, '[n]onetheless, a new constitution was written and approved by a directly elected [National] Assembly for the first time since independence. . . . [While] no party or faction was fully satisfied by the governance structure created by the constitution, . . . it received unanimous approval from the National Assembly.').

27 Since 1973, the resilience of both Pakistan and its Constitution have been tested by several events, including:

(1) General Zia's 1977 military coup;
(2) Presidential Order of 1985, of important General Zia-sponsored amendments to the 1973 constitution;
(3) unstable and short-lived democratic governments in Pakistan throughout the late 1980s and 1990s; and
(4) General Musharraf's 1999 military coup and his sponsorship of yet more amendments to the 1973 constitution.

the people of Pakistan had wanted Pakistan to be an orthodox theocracy, they could in fact have voted for the parties with religious programmes (see Nasr 1993: 261), especially where some of those parties had Islamic socialism as the basis of their manifestos and at least in theory, could have delivered a progressive Islamic state. However, the Constitution drafted under the alliance with religious parties created a document that sufficiently pushed into motion the mainstreaming of religious identity in Pakistan. The concrete manifestation of this can be seen in Article 260[28] which provided the constitutional definition of the 'Muslim' (and 'Islam', by implication).[29] Previously constitutional provisions concerning Islam had not taken such a specific form. For example, Article 31, the principle of policy, whose subject matter is the 'Islamic way of life', references 'the fundamental principles and basic concepts of Islam', the 'meaning of life according to the Holy Quran and Sunnah', and 'Islamic moral standards', but gives no precise or controversial content to these ideas.[30] Furthermore, Article 2 of the Constitution declares that 'Islam shall be the State religion of Pakistan' (Constitution of Islamic Republic of Pakistan, 1973, Article 2).[31] Other constitutional

28 This article was inserted into the 1973 constitution in 1974 through a constitutional amendment.

29 Constitution of Islamic Republic of Pakistan, Article 260(3). In its present form, this article states:

> **260.** In the Constitution and all enactments and other legal instruments, unless there is anything repugnant in the subject or context, –
> (a) "Muslim" means a person who believes in the unity and oneness of Almighty Allah, in the absolute and unqualified finality of the Prophethood of Muhammad (peace be upon him), the last of the prophets, and does not believe in, or recognize as a prophet or religious reformer, any person who claimed or claims to be a prophet, in any sense of the word or of any description whatsoever, after Muhammad (peace be upon him); and
> (b) "non-Muslim" means a person who is not a Muslim and includes a person belonging to the Christian, Hindu, Sikh, Buddhist or Parsi community, a person of the Quadiani Group or the Lahori Group (who call themselves 'Ahmadis' or by any other name), or a Bahai, and a person belonging to any of the Scheduled Castes.

30 *Government of N.-W.F.P. v. Said Kamal Shah*, P.L.D. (1986) S.C. 360, 474 (presenting a contemporary demonstration of the Islamic legal implications that might arise by a specific reliance on the Qur'an and Sunnah, instead of other sources of Islamic law, in a dissenting opinion Justice S M H Quraishi says: It must, however, be noted that Muhammaden Law as understood and interpreted in the above cases by the Courts is based on the juristic principles (Fiq-h) [sic] as expounded by the scholars of legal thought in Islam. But here, in a matter arising under Article 203-D of the Constitution we are concerned with the question whether the law is repugnant to the Injunctions of Islam as laid down in the Holy Qur'an and the Sunnah of the Holy Prophet. A law may not be in conformity with the juristic opinion of one or the other of the Schools but that would not render the same repugnant for the purposes of Article 203-D unless the repugnancy is clearly brought out as against some specific Injunction either in the Qur'an [sic] or the Sunnah.).

31 Constitution of Islamic Republic of Pakistan, 1973, Article 2.

articles require that the President, the Prime Minister[32] as well as most members of the Parliament be Muslim.[33]

The 1973 constitution also created certain institutions to channel the application and interpretation of Islam: the Council of Islamic Ideology and the Shariat Court. The 'Council of Islamic Ideology' (Constitution of Islamic Republic of Pakistan, 1973, Art. 227-31) was created to ensure that 'all existing laws shall be brought in conformity with the Injunctions of Islam as laid down in the Holy Quran and Sunnah . . . and [so that] no law shall be enacted which is repugnant to such injunctions' (Constitution of Islamic Republic of Pakistan, 1973, Art. 227(1)). The real import of this Council came into the limelight during General Zia's regime when it was used in conjunction with the Shariat Court to create an Islamic State of Pakistan by testing the vires of all existing and future laws of the country.

The Shariat judicial courts were not present in the original Constitution of 1973 and were later inserted in 1979 by General Zia-ul Haq who came to power after the successful coup d'état of 1977. Religion was the foundation on which General Zia attempted to build a structure of support for his otherwise unconstitutional rule. He introduced reforms designed to create a Nizam-i-Islam (Islamic Order) (Gustafson and Ritcher 1981: 166) in Pakistan. The establishment of Shariat courts was central to the reforms. The Shariat judicial system was designed to operate in parallel with Pakistan's long-standing mainstream judicial system, which had the usual common law system. Importantly, the original jurisdiction of the Federal Shariat Court was defined in the Constitution. It was given the power to examine and decide the question whether or not any law or provision of law was repugnant to the Injunctions of Islam, as laid down in the Holy Quran and Sunnah of the Holy Prophet (Constitution of Islamic Republic of Pakistan, 1973, Art. 203-D(1)-(3)(b)). Further, if any law or provision of law is held by the Court to be repugnant to the Injunctions of Islam, such law or provision shall, to the extent to which it is held to be so repugnant, cease to have effect on the day on which the decision of the Court takes effect (Constitution of Islamic Republic of Pakistan, 1973, Art. 203-D).[34] Hence, a significant merging of Shariah and the modern state system was formed under General Zia's military rule.

32 Although no article of the Constitution requires the Prime Minister to be Muslim specifically, however Article 91 used to mention that the 'National Assembly shall . . . elect . . . one of its Muslim members to be the Prime Minister', but this explicit requirement was eliminated by changes made to the 1973 constitution in 1985. While the Prime Minister is required, before assuming office, to take an oath – part of which includes a declaration that the Prime Minister is a Muslim – there is nothing in the 1973 constitution stating any consequences for mendacity vis-à-vis this oath. See Id. Art. 91(3), Third Schedule [art. 91(4)].

33 There are specified seats for non-Muslim minorities on the basis of separate electorate.

34 Ibid. at Art 203-D.

C. The process of Islamisation and the referendum of 1984

General Zia came to power in 1977 in a military coup. During his 11-year rule, he gained international support, mainly from the US, by using the Soviet invasion of neighbouring Afghanistan as an argument that Pakistan required a strong and stable government under his leadership. As for domestic political support, General Zia looked to Muslim groups and parties (see Nasr 1993: 262–265). For their appeasement, Zia declared Pakistan an Islamic state and embarked on a path of promoting Islamic practices in the social sphere and in the legal system. However, the same parties and religious groups that Zia relied upon to support his rule, had not done too well earlier in the elections of 1970 and 1977 (Nasr 1993: 262–265). The discussion that follows in this section revolves broadly around the policies of the Zia regime that gave Pakistan its unparalleled religious identity. I will argue that there was no democratic or popular basis for the religious policies of the Zia regime, and therefore, the Islamic face of Pakistan presented during this period cannot be truly reflective of the identity of the people of Pakistan.

During his reign, General Zia contemplated significant and ambitious Islamic reforms in Pakistan. His programme contemplated modifications in Pakistan's legal, economic, educational and social systems. General Zia's agenda of Islamism was a demand for legalism since a broad-based Islamic programme could not have been enforced in a state that was not Islamic itself. Therefore, beginning with the Constitution, some crucial changes were made. Through a 'repugnancy clause' in the form of Article 2-A, the Objective Resolution, was made a justiciable provision of the Constitution. Furthermore, Shariat Courts were grafted onto the judicial system of the country, criminal laws were amended, newer Islamic criminal laws in the form of Hudood Ordinances of 1979 were enforced, and evidence laws were also Islamised to change the competency and quantum of testimony in civil and criminal matters (Kennedy 1990: 62–77). Above all, a universal process of Islamisation of laws was commenced under the collaborative initiative of the Council of Islamic Ideology and the Federal Shariat Court. All major and minor laws were examined to asses the vires of those laws in the presence of Article 2-A, the 'repugnancy' provision of the Constitution (Kennedy 1990).

Within the economic system, Islamisation was done by establishing 'Islamic Banks', calling for abolition of riba (usuary), and introducing a mandatory collection of Zakat (social welfare tax) against the bank holdings of Sunni Muslims. The Islamisation agenda of General Zia also mandated educational reforms by extablishing new institutions to promote Shariah education by enhancing the importance of Arabic in the curricula, and by contemplating the wholesale redrafting of textbooks to incorporate Islamic pedagogy. Social reforms were introduced through stressing the sanctity of Ramzan, the encouragement of purdah (veil), and stricter enforcement of bans on gambling and drinking. These Islamic reforms had a very prominent public profile and were portrayed as leading Pakistan in the direction of becoming 'truly Islamic'.

Hence, General Zia bestowed upon Pakistan, an unparalleled religious identity. Never before had there been such an involvement of religion in every aspect of life, public or private. This brings us to the questioning of the validity of this representation of Pakistan under Zia's regime.

General Zia enjoyed a form of personal rule, until 1981 when he inaugurated the Majlis-i-Shoora, an appointed advisory body that replaced the elected national assembly. When General Zia inaugurated the Majlis-i-Shoora in 1981, he announced that its main tasks were to accelerate the process of Islamisation in the country and to create conditions congenial to the establishment of an Islamic democracy.[35] President Zia viewed the role of his appointed Shoora as an intermediate step to the eventual development of what he called an Islamic democracy (Korson and Maskiell 1985: 591–592).

Interestingly, in Zia's Islamic democracy, political parties and their political manifestos had no place. The Islamic Ideology Council, in support of military regime, declared all political parties un-Islamic. With Parliament already dissolved, political parties declared 'defunct' and hence banned, General Zia called for a referendum in December 1984. In the referendum, people were asked to vote on a single issue: 'whether they supported the process initiated by the Government for the Islamisation of all laws in accordance with the Holy Qur'an and Sunnah and whether they supported the Islamic ideology of Pakistan'. General Zia further manipulated the terms of the referendum to provide a vote of confidence for his leadership and gave an interpretation of a 'yes' vote on the referendum as constituting an endorsement of his Islamisation policies and an extension of his Presidency for a further five years.[36] By incorporating multiple consequences into a single question, the government presented voters with a choice of voting for Zia or against Islam.[37] Despite General Zia's claims of a fair and free referendum, the entire exercise was rather a one-sided affair.[38] The referendum of 1984 was followed by a non-party-based general election in 1985, in which, however,

35 The other two tasks assigned to the appointed Majlis-i-Shoora were, first, to offer 'opinion and wisdom' to the administration on important national and international matters; and second, to assist in overcoming the economic and social difficulties of the people. On these tasks of Majlis-i-Shoora, see further Korson and Maskiell (1985) at 590.

36 Some voters who resolved this dilemma by marking the *yes* column of their ballots 'Islam *yes*' and *no* column 'Zia *no*' had their ballots declared invalid.

37 During the referendum campaign weeks, the controlled media exhorted the people to vote 'yes'; to oppose the referendum or to advocate a boycott was declared a crime and, hence, illegal. The offence of boycotting the referendum was made punishable with three years imprisonment.

38 On the referendum of 1984, see further Waseem (1989) at 410.

Jamaat-i-Islami was registered as the only eligible party to contest elections; other candidates were expected to contest individually without any party affiliations. Since the elections did not involve any political party or political manifestos, it is almost impossible to read the electoral tilt. The government created under those elections did not present any independent policy but continued to tow General Zia's line. Neither the referendum of 1984, nor the general elections of 1985 could bring the required legitimacy of the policies of Zia's regime.

D. Religious sectarianism of the 1980s and 1990s

The rise of the sectarian divide between the Sunnis and Shi'as of Pakistan in the 80s subjected the nation's sense of identity to further strains. The emergence of the sectarian divide broke that myth of homogeneity of religious identity in Pakistan. The sectarian split extended beyond sporadic clashes over doctrinal issues between Sunnis and Shi'as, and metamorphosed into a political conflict around the mobilisation of religious-group identity to achieve political power and viability. Sectarianism in the Pakistani context refers specifically to organised and militant religio-political activism, the specific aim of which was to promote the socio-political interest of the particular Muslim sectarian community. Militant discourses promised empowerment to the sectarian community, in tandem with greater adherence to Islamic norms in public life (Ahmed 1992: 230–240).

This prominence of religious-group sectarianism presented a new phase in the career of religious identity in Pakistan. This time the demand was not for an Islamic state only but for the 'correct form' of the Islamic state where religious minorities would be marginalised. This sectarianism was tied to Islamism in that the defining identity was elaborated in terms of Islam. Sectarianism in Pakistan displayed far more concern for religious orthodoxy than Confessionalism in Lebanon, and Protestant and Catholic politics in Northern Ireland, but the fundamental direction of their politics were not dissimilar (Nasr 2000: 171–190) from these other expressions of extremism.

There are a number of theories as to why sectarianism flared up in Pakistan. Some see Iranian desires to exert control over Pakistani politics as the main driver in sectarian divisions (Nasr 2000: 171–190). This understanding can be developed in two different ways. Some analysts have argued that the ideological force of the Iranian revolution, combined with the fact that the first successful Islamic revolution had been carried out by the Shi'as, emboldened the Shi'a community and politicised its identity within Pakistan. Others have suggested a rather different account of Iranian influence. According to these analysts, the emergence of a Shi'a state inspired the Pakistani Sunnis so much that they started conceiving afresh the ideal of establishing a Sunni Islamic State in Pakistan. In whatever way we approach the influence of the

Iranian revolution, other important factors relate to the domestic religious and political context. Since General Zia's reforms[39] were based on strict Sunni interpretations of Islamic law (rather than Islamic universalism), the Shi'as viewed them as interferences with their religious freedom and a threat to their socio-political interests. These grievances fed into the violent clashes between the Sunni majority and Shi'a minority (Zaman 1998: 689–716).

Alongside the domestic context, we need to keep in mind the significance of the Soviet–Afghan war of the eighties. The Iranian revolution and the Afghan conflict were redefining the terms of the Cold War. The need to sustain an anti-Soviet alliance led western powers to ignore or even support the universalisation of religious identity in Pakistan. The unpopular and despotic military regime thus received little criticism from the US and their western allies. However, except for its utility in the Soviet–Afghan war, such a strong and universal religious identity was in no one's interest, a fact so thoroughly proven by the events of 9/11 and later (Zaman 1998).

E. Integrating religious and political identities: a comment on Zia ul Haq regime

During the Zia era, therefore, Pakistan continued to suffer a 'real' identity crisis. Although this time, the appended hardcore religio-political identity of Pakistan was in line with the script of a broader world scenario. Two important inferences could be drawn from the analysis made in this part of the article. First, no process has been initiated to assess democratically the inclination of the people of Pakistan, which consequently makes the entire attribution of religious identity to the Pakistani people a highly questionable assumption, especially in the light of counter-indicators such as the referendum of 1984. Second, the attachment of religious identity to Pakistan has served the interests of military regimes, and the interests of western powers. Under Zia's rule the image of religious identity was stretched to such a point that it became a religious identity of universal import. However, what Pakistan really needed was a territorially tailored identity to accommodate its otherwise ethnically plural society. This could not be developed since the ruling civil-military oligarchy continued to define the state's identity through mixing religious and militarist nationalism. Sectarianism further revealed the tensions inherent in the vision of a nation united under Islam.

39 Shi'as made their position clear when in 1980 General Zia sought to implement Sunni laws of inheritance and collection of *zakat*, which the state was charged to collect in the name of Islam. Faced with the strong Shi'a protest and significant external pressure, the government capitulated. It recognized Shi'a communal rights and thus gave legitimacy to their sectarian posturing.

IV. Pakistan, religious identity and post-9/11 world

Although the period from 1988 to 1999[40] can be marked as democratic, the military continued to dominate Pakistani politics. It set Pakistan's ideological and national security agenda, and repeatedly intervened to direct the course of domestic politics. Hence, Pakistan was prevented from developing a consistent system of government, with unrelenting political polarisation between civilians and the military, and between Islamists and secularists. This semi-democratic period ended when General Musharraf seized power in October 1999. The Musharraf regime has both experienced and shaped the impact of the post-9/11 transition upon the religious identity of Pakistan.

A. The Musharraf regime: distancing religious identity from national identity

In the context of religious identity, the Musharraf regime presents a phase that is distinct from the earlier periods. The pre-Musharraf periods of Pakistan's political history can be easily classified as one uniform phase on the basis of at least three common characteristics. First, in all previous political periods of history, Pakistan has had authoritarian military regimes; second, these regimes have used religion profusely as a common denominator in national identity; third, all these regimes had especially used a pan-Islamic interpretation of religious identity.

The Musharraf regime, however, has been different. When Musharraf took over in 1999, his military government needed a new ideology. As we have seen, the military regime of Zia had extensively used religion. Musharraf, on the other hand succeeded the semi-democratic period of the 1990s, which followed the massive Islamisation of the 1980s. The 1990s governments of Ms Bhutto and Mr Nawaz Sharif did not interfere with the already existing Islamisation of General Zia and continued with existing Islamic policies. When Musharraf took over government, the political utility of religion in Pakistan was at its lowest ever. Musharraf's emphasis on taking up a moderate approach towards religion reflected the lack of support for a religion-based politics amongst the masses who repeatedly showed themselves to be more interested in economic reforms and social justice.

Moreover, Musharraf's option to use religion politically was further reduced by the events of 9/11. One of the main dynamics of the post-9/11 world had been a suspicion of pan-Islamism, and the unfortunate identification of Islam

40 The reason for passing over the entire period of alternated democratic governments of Ms Benazir Bhutto and Mr Nawaz Sharif has been that both of their tenures had hardly any effect on the identity crisis of the country. Pakistan continued its disproportionate focus on religious identity as the primary political identity, defined and developed mainly through military leadership.

with terrorism and violence. The decision to ally with the US-led coalition made it necessary for the Musharraf regime to break away from this religious identity of pan-Islamism. Thus in terms of religio-political identity, the Musharraf government can be contrasted to Zia's. During the Zia regime the religious parties and the military had been the leading architects of the religious identity of Pakistan. In the aftermath of 9/11, for the first time, there has been a 'real' clash of interest between the religious parties and the military. At last the military leadership appears to be denouncing the Islamism that is so bound up with Pakistani political identity.

B. 'Pakistan First' – a paradigm shift: from pan-Islamism to globalism

The Musharraf regime invented a new slogan: 'Pakistan First'[41] to denote an ideological departure from the previously held religious identity. 'Pakistan First' attempted to redefine Pakistani identity on three primary lines. First, Pakistan's identity should break free from the stagnant religio-political elements based on pan-Islamism. Second, the identity of Pakistan must be defined in terms of the territorial reality of Pakistan with the commitment to preserve the state. And third, the preservation of the state lies in opting to side with the US and her allies.[42] The 'Pakistan First' ideology was further supplemented by an 'enlightened moderation'[43] doctrine that called for the adoption of a new approach to religion, stressing tolerance, openness, revolt against taboos and acceptance of western cultural values.

Comparing 'Pakistan First' and 'enlightened moderation' with the universalistic religio-political ideology of the 1980s, reveals that although they are quite distinct positions, the methods of their implementation have been the same. The universalistic religious identity of Pakistanis was a military attribution, just as this latest moderation had been conferred upon the people of Pakistan by a military ruler. There is another fundamental problem. Musharraf's 'Pakistan First' impressed upon people the need to identify with globalism, as represented by the culture and values of the West. The demands of pan-Islamism and globalism, in the context of Pakistan, are common in the sense that they both have considerably ignored the demands attached to the territorial reality of Pakistan.

41 President Musharraf's Speech on 19 September 2001 available at www.americanrhetoric.com/speeches/pakistanpresident.htm (last visited on 11 October 2007).

42 Ibid. For further comment on Musharraf's 'Pakistan First' theory, see Shafqat Mehmood, *Pakistan Comes First*, available at www.jang.com.pk/thenews/columnists/shafqat/shafqat21.htm (last visited on 21 October 2007).

43 Pervez Musharraf, *Time for Enlightened Moderation* (2004) available at www.presidentofpakistan.gov.pk/EnlightenedModeration.aspx (last visited on 12 October 2007).

C. Rejection of attempts at disintegration between religious and national: electoral success of religious parties in 2002

Ever since the creation of Pakistan, religious parties have struggled to establish a foothold in the country's mainstream politics. The 'liberal lobby' always boasted that religious groups had never been able to muster double-digit figures in terms of seats in any general election (Murlidhar Reddy 2002). Ironically, the general elections of 2002 proved an exception to this rule. In the 2002 elections, the Mutahidda Majlis-i-Amal (MMA), a political alliance of religious parties, came to power. Their success and popularity can be explained as a popular reaction against the US invasion of Afghanistan, and the failure of leadership in the mainstream political parties in the 2002 elections (Moreau and Hussain with Hirsh 2002: 39). Just as the Muslim League in undivided India highlighted the external factor of 'fear of Hindu dominion' to transform the religious identity into a political aspiration, the interpretation of 'war against terrorism' as 'war against Muslims' has helped religious parties to success in elections.[44]

At the time of the formation of this religious parties alliance, it was proclaimed that they should struggle to 'protect the Islamic identity' of the country and promote the basic objectives of the creation of Pakistan. Most of these successful religious parties initiated their demand for converting Pakistan into an Islamic state soon after independence in 1947. Although they were unable to generate popular support for their mission, the ruling elite (particularly the military) did initiate a process of giving the Pakistani state an Islamic identity for reasons of their own political expediency. The official measures taken to Islamise Pakistan in the first three decades have been more of cosmetic exercises, whereas the electoral success of 2002 did raise speculation as to how these Islamic parties' world-view would affect the spectrum of 'national identity' in Pakistan.

V. Complexity of the national identity issue faced by Pakistan

Why did Musharraf's 'Pakistan First' fail as an identity slogan for the people of Pakistan? This question is particularly important since two arguments have already been made in the paper: first, the religious identity of 1947 needed to be transformed into a more territorially designed political identity;[45] and second, the people of Pakistan did not politically support the pan-Islamic

44 For detailed results of the 2002 parliamentary elections, see www.heraldelections.com (last visited on 10 October 2007). See further Moreau and Hussain with Hirsh (2002) 39–40 (noting that among others a notable factor in this political victory has been the passivity of the otherwise secular voters, though the religious parties have made these electoral gains without dramatically increasing the share of votes traditionally won by them).

45 See text on page 20.

version of religious identity bestowed by Zia.[46] Therefore, the chances of success for Musharraf's identity doctrine should have been quite bright since 'Pakistan First' created an impression of being a territorially oriented identity and 'enlightened moderation' cuts deep into the Islamic universalism adopted during the Zia regime. The creation and growth of an identity, however, is not a mechanical but an organic process. In fact, Musharraf repeated Zia's mistake. He tried to implant an identity upon the people of Pakistan. Musharraf's vision of 'enlightened moderation' for Pakistan was fraught with contradictions in regards to its domestic, regional, and international policies. Furthermore, this 'enlightened moderation' was not followed by any democratisation of the country.[47]

Furthermore, the current attachment of a non-religious identity on Pakistan is ever so more important due to its timing in world history, particularly when capitalism, in the guise of an ideology, is asserting its need to be transnational. These are the times when, globally, the choice has been reduced between acceptance and rejection, which further cuts deeper into the chance for 'moderation' to evolve as an ideology. Following this upon the basis of arguments developed in this paper, it is submitted that instead of predeterminism, chance must follow the democratisation process since the formation and change of identity is a process that can neither be planted nor uprooted. Hence, reliance must be placed upon leaving this organic process intact, and upon allowing the democratisation of the society and people of Pakistan. This will offer a possibility of the evolution of moderate forces which will in return shape a national identity for Pakistan in which a balance between the religion and politics will be struck; a realisation of Jinnah's vision of Pakistan, as stated in July 1947 (Khan 1985):

> Religion is there and religion is dear to us . . . . but there are other things which are very vital, our social life, our economic life, and without political power how can you defend your faith and your economic life?
> (Ahmad 1970: 380)

References

Ahmad, J. (1952) *Speeches and Writings of Mr. Jinnah, Vol. I*, Lahore: Shaikh Muhammad Ashraf, 469.

Ahmad, J. (1970) *Historic Documents of the Muslim Freedom Movement*, Lahore: Publishers United, 380.

46 See Part-III, Section C, last paragraph.

47 So far, Musharraf has only confirmed a commitment to his indispensability in pursuance of his claim that his presence is vital for the protection of the national interest of Pakistan. However, the events following the dismissal of the Chief Justice of Pakistan in March 2007 have clearly proved that Musharraf's interpretation of national interest is itself a threat to Pakistan's national interest.

Ahmed, F. (1973) 'Swing to the right', *Pakistan Forum*: 24(9).
Ahmed, M. (1992) 'Islam and the state: The case of Pakistan', in M. Moen and L. Gustafson (eds), *Religious Challenge to the State*, Philadelphia: Temple University Press, 230–240.
Ben-Rafael, E. and Sharot, S. (1991) *Ethnicity, Religion and Class in Israeli Society*, Cambridge: Cambridge University Press, Chapters 2, 8 and 10.
Binder, L. (1961) *Religion and Politics in Pakistan*, Berkeley: University of California Press, 85.
Binder, L. (1963) *Religion and Politics in Pakistan*, California: University of California Press, 183–207.
Brass, P.R. (2005) *Language, Religion and Politics in North India*. Available HTTP: <Backinprint.com>30–31, 40–41 and 45–46.
Cohen, S.P. (2002) 'The nation and the state of Pakistan', *Washington Quarterly*: 25(3): 109.
Constitution of Islamic Republic of Pakistan, 1973.
Deutsch, K.W. and Foltz, W.J. (eds) (1966) *Nation-Building*, New York: Atherton Press, 3.
Dwarkadas, K. (1966) *India's Fight for Freedom*, Bombay: Popular Prakashan.
Emerson, R. (1962) *From Empire to Nation*, Boston: Beacon Press, 96.
Gaborieau, M. (1985) 'From Al-Beruni to Jinnah: Idiom, ritual and ideology of the Hindu-Muslim confrontation in South Asia', *Anthropology Today*: 1(3): 7.
Gareth, H.H. and Wright Mills, C. (trans. and eds) (1958) *Max Weber: Essays in Sociology*, New York: Oxford University Press, 177–8.
Government of N.-W.F.P. v. Said Kamal Shah, P.L.D. (1986) S.C. 360, 474.
Gustafson, W.E. and Ritcher, W.L. (1981) 'Pakistan in 1980: Weathering the Storm', *Asian Survey*: 21(2): 166.
Hakim, K.A. (1983) 'Renaissance in Indo-Pakistan: Iqbal' in M.M. Sharif (ed.), *A History of Muslim Philosophy*, Vol. II, Pakistan: Royal Book Company, 1640.
Hakim, K.A. (1992) *Fikr-e-Iqbal*, Lahore: Mahmood Printing Press, 54, 55.
Ikram, S.M. (1997) *Modern Muslim India and the Birth of Pakistan*, Lahore: Institute of Islamic Culture.
Jalal, Ayesha (1995) 'Conjuring Pakistan: history as official imagining', *International Journal of Middle East Studies*: 27(1): 73–77.
Kennedy, C.H. (1990) 'Islamization and Legal Reform in Pakistan 1979–89', *Pacific Affairs*: 63(1): 62–77.
Khan, A. (1985) *Islam, Politics and the State: The Pakistan Experience*, London: Zed Books.
Korson, J.H. and Maskiell, M. (1985) 'Islamization of Pakistan and Social Policy', *Asian Survey*: 25(6): 590.
Majumdar, A. (1963) *Advent of Independence*, Bharatiya Vidya Bhavan (Bombay): 39–41.
Mehmood, S. (2007) *Pakistan Comes First*. Available HTTP: www.jang.com.pk/thenews/columnists/shafqat/shafqat21.htm (accessed 21 October 2007).
Moon, P. (1962) *Divide and Quit*, Berkeley: University of California Press.
Moreau, R. and Hussain, Z. with Hirsh, M. (2002) 'A big vote for Jihad', *Newsweek*, 21 October 2002: 39.
Muralidhar Reddy, B. (2002) 'Rise of the right', *Frontline*: 19(22) available HTTP: www.flonnet.com/fl1922/stories/20021108004205000.htm.
Musharraf, P. (2004) *Time for Enlightened Moderation*. Available HTTP: www.presidentofpakistan.gov.pk/EnlightenedModeration.aspx (accessed 12 October 2007).

Nasr, S.V.R. (2001) 'Islamic opposition to Islamic state: The Jamaat-i-Islami, 1977–88', *International Journal of Middle East Studies*: 25(2): 261, 267.
Neufeldt, R.W. (1981) 'Islam and India: The Views of Muhammad Iqbal', *The Muslim World*: 71(3,4): 178.
Newberg, P.R. (2002) *Judging the State: Courts and Constitutional Politics in Pakistan*, Cambridge: Cambridge University Press, 138–40.
Nichols, B. (1944) *Verdict on India*, London: Jonathan Cape.
Nordlinger, E.A. (2002) *Conflict Regulation in Divided Societies*, Cambridge, MA: Center for International Affairs, 45–7.
Ortega y Gasset, J. (1930) *The Revolt of the Masses*, New York, 169–71.
Oldenburg, P. (1985) 'A place insufficiently imagined: language, belief and the Pakistan crisis of 1971', *Journal of Asian Studies*: 44(4): 711.
President Musharraf, Speech on 19 September, 2001. Available HTTP: www.americanrhetoric.com/speeches/pakistanpresident.htm (accessed 11 October 2007).
Qureshi, I.H. (1974) *The Struggle for Pakistan*, Pakistan: University of Karachi Press, 127–9.
Qureshi, S.M. (1969) *Jinnah and the Making of a Nation*, Karachi: Council for Pakistan Studies, 22.
Qureshi, S.M. (1973) 'Pakistani nationalism reconsidered', *Pacific Affairs*: 45(4): 570.
Rafiqul Islam, M. (1985) 'Secessionist self-determination', *Journal of Peace Research*: 22(3): 219.
Reed, D. (1978) *Controversy of Zion*, Dolphin Press. Available HTTP: www.vho.org/aaargh/fran/livres/reeedcontrov.pdf (accessed 12 October 2007).
Riaz, S.H. (1987) *Pakistan Naguzeer Tha (Pakistan was Inevitable)*, Karachi, 11–13.
Ritcher, W.L. (1979) 'The political dynamics of Islamic resurgence in Pakistan', *Asian Survey*: 19(6): 547.
Smith, D. (1971) *Religion, Politics and Social Change in Third World*, Princeton: Free Press.
Spear, P. (1963) 'The Political Evolution of Pakistan', in S. Rose (ed.), *Politics in Southern Asia*, London: Macmillan, 36.
Syed, A.H. (1980) 'The Idea of a Pakistani Nationhood', *Polity*: 12(4): 578.
Syed, A.H. (1991) 'Pakistan People's Party and the Punjab', *Asian Survey*: 31(7): 582.
The Times (London), 20 December 1971.
Verma, B. (2006) *Pakistan's Faultline, Indian Defence Review*: 20(4). Available HTTP: www.bharat-rakshak.com/SRR/index.php (accessed 7 October 2007).
Von Tunzelmann, A. (2007) *Indian Summer: The Secret History of the End of an Empire*, Toronto: Picador.
Waseem, M. (1989) *Politics and the State in Pakistan*, Lahore: Progressive Publishers, 410.
Ward, B. (1966) *Nationalism and Ideology*, New York: Norton, 18.
Wendell, B. and Freeman, W.E. (1974) *Ethnicity and Nation Building*, Los Angeles: Sage Publications.
Wyatt, W. (1952) *Southwards from China*, London: Hodder and Stoughton.
Zaman, Muhammad Qasim (1998) 'Sectarianism in Pakistan, the radicalization of Shi'i and Sunni identities', *Modern Asian Studies*: 32(3): 689–716.

Chapter 9

Theorizing Islam without the state

Islamic discourses on the minority status of Muslims in the West

*Alexandre Caeiro**

I. Introduction

Discussions about the necessity of creating a 'European Islam' have become ubiquitous throughout the continent today. State actors and public intellectuals across the political spectrum frequently emphasise the need to adapt Islam to the West in order to counter the threat of terrorism, prevent the radicalisation of young Muslims, facilitate the integration of immigrants and render Islam compatible with European secularisms. Although they rarely take part in these public discussions, orthodox Muslim scholars committed to the Islamic legal tradition (*fiqh* or shari'a) have over the past decades been debating similar issues in the global spaces of Islamic normative debate which they inhabit. This article deals with these debates, focusing specifically on the attempts by Islamic scholars to theorise a distinctive 'European' or 'Western Islam' through what is called a Muslim jurisprudence for minorities (*fiqh al-aqalliyyat* or minority fiqh).[1] *Fiqh al-aqalliyyat* is a new construct in the Islamic legal tradition closely associated with the fiqh councils based in the West, namely the European Council for Fatwa and Research and the Fiqh

* Research Fellow, Erlangen Zentrum für Islam und Recht in Europa EZIRE, Friedrich-Alexander-Universität Erlangen-Nürnberg.

1 I distinguish here between descriptive and normative uses of minority fiqh. By descriptive uses I mean the understandings of the rights and duties under Islamic Law of Muslims living as minorities in predominantly non-Muslim lands. In this regard, instances of *fiqh al-aqalliyyat* occur whenever Muslim minorities have sought guidance under the shari'a. The problems they have faced, and the juristic opinions these problems have elicited, constitute *fiqh al-aqalliyyat* in this descriptive sense. The focus of this paper is, however, on the normative uses of *fiqh al-aqalliyyat*. These refer to the call voiced by Muslim actors to devise a new system of Islamic normativity (fiqh) that suits the specificities of Muslim minorities. As I argue below, this call is thoroughly a modern one, engaging a wide number of contemporary Muslim scholars and activists. The extent to which this discourse draws on, selects and ignores the opinions found in the Islamic fiqh heritage is left here as an open question.

Council of North America.[2] It finds one of its most regular social expressions in the live fatwa sessions conducted by websites such as www.IslamOnLine.net, a prominent Arabic–English Internet portal with headquarters in Doha.[3] Although an attempt to understand the practical orientations of the construct must also therefore study the fatwas that are issued in its name, in this paper I approach *fiqh al-aqalliyyat* from a third angle: as the subject of specific theoretical reflection by Muslim scholars and public intellectuals. A significant number of books and articles arguing for and against minority fiqh have been published in Arabic since the early 2000s.[4] These texts have so far received little attention from social scientists, perhaps because of a tendency to view these kinds of writings as apologetic texts seeking – in the best tradition of Islamic legal theory (*usul al-fiqh*) – to provide theoretical bases for already existing social practices (and therefore of limited theoretical interest in and of themselves).[5] In contrast to these views, I treat the elaborations on *fiqh al-aqalliyyat* here as discursive interventions into larger debates on Muslim identity and the integration of Islam in Europe – debates which in turn connect variously with discussions in the Muslim majority world about the viability of tradition, the prospects of reform, and the dynamics of religious authority. In this paper I seek to unpack the debate on whether or not European Muslims require a new system of Islamic normativity specifically designed for life as a minority living in a predominantly non-Muslim polity, and the particular conceptions of Islam and of Europe that underlie this debate.[6] Given the diversity of trajectories, interests and sensibilities of the Muslim actors participating in the minority fiqh discourse, the question of what actually constitutes this construct arises with a certain urgency: what precisely underlies the vivid terminological dispute about the legitimacy of a 'minority fiqh' – a dispute which has blurred the conventional dichotomies

2 On the ECFR see Caeiro (2004 and 2010) and Rohe (2004); on the FCNA see DeLorenzo (2000) and Karman (2008).

3 On IslamOnLine see Gräf (2008).

4 Many of these writings are listed in the bibliography.

5 See on this point al-Azmeh (1988). Some orthodox Muslim scholars have reached similar conclusions. As 'Abd al-Majid al-Najjar (2003: 45–8) notes, *usul al-fiqh* emerges counter-intuitively not before but after fiqh has dealt with real cases. For a different attempt to make sense of Muslim writings on *fiqh al-aqalliyyat* see March 2009.

6 Many of the texts arguing for or against minority fiqh are responses to particular fiqh issues such as the permissibility of political participation in non-Muslim countries, the status of the marriage of a married woman who converts to Islam while the husband does not, or the uses of interest-bearing mortgages to buy property. I have dealt with the latter in an earlier article (Caeiro 2004). The hypothesis I am pursuing now in this article is that the debates on minority fiqh, even when they take as their starting point particular fiqh issues as those mentioned above, are actually debates about how to understand the viability of the Islamic legal tradition (what continuities and changes are necessary for it to remain a living and coherent tradition?), and how to conceptualise the contemporary secular West and the kinds of freedoms and constraints that it places upon Muslims.

between 'traditionalist' versus 'reformist' actors?[7] And what is at stake in discussions of minority fiqh as 'just another branch' (Qaradawi 2001) or a 'special kind' ('Alwani 2003) of Islamic normativity?

I will argue here that writings on minority fiqh are – as the name indicates – predicated on a commitment to the Islamic legal tradition, and on an understanding of the minority condition as posing a particular challenge to the viability of that tradition. I then show that the kinds of commitments to fiqh as well as the understandings of the appropriateness of the minority condition to describe the situation of Muslims in Europe actually vary widely even amongst minority fiqh advocates. This variation seems to reflect the fact that Muslim actors writing on the topic come from different social and intellectual backgrounds;[8] if they write mostly in Arabic, they nevertheless address different audiences and respond to divergent concerns.[9] The starting points of their reflections range from the continuation of an interest in non-Muslim minorities under Islamic states (Qaradawi 2001), to a contextual engagement with Islam debates in Western public spheres ('Alwani 2003), to a critical approach to human rights discourses ('Atiya Muhammad 2007). I conclude by suggesting that it is perhaps in the relatively open-ended nature of the minority fiqh discourse, liable to different appropriations by various actors, that resides the interest and appeal of the discourse.

II. The emergence of *fiqh al-aqalliyyat*

It seems appropriate to start by providing a sense of the contexts in which the discussion on minority fiqh takes place. The transnational circulation of

7 In the writings of contemporary Muslim scholars the very use of the expression '*fiqh al-aqalliyyat*' has become fraught with implications. Muslim scholars who write today on '*fiqh al-aqalliyyat*' are assumed to be in favour of the political participation of Muslims in the West, the use of interest-bearing mortgages to buy a house, and the permissibility of staying in a marital relationship with a non-Muslim husband for the married woman who converts to Islam – in other words, they are assumed to agree with the fatwas issued by the European Council for Fatwa and Research (ECFR) under the guidance of Qaradawi. Those scholars who write on Muslims in the West from a fiqh perspective but who nevertheless do not wish to be associated with the particular approaches of the ECFR use terms such as '*fiqh al-darura*', '*fiqh al-nawazil*', or '*qadayya al-jaliyat al muslima fi-l-gharb*'.

8 Qaradawi and Alwani are traditionally trained ulama who have earned doctorates in fiqh from Al-Azhar, while Bishri and al-Najjar, although qualified in fiqh, are more eclectic Muslim/Islamist intellectuals. They all seem to share, however, an emphasis on Islam's comprehensiveness, a hallmark of the Muslim Brotherhood paradigm.

9 Qaradawi's work on *fiqh al-aqalliyyat*, to give just one example, has been presented at the Muslim World League's 4th General Islamic Conference in Saudi Arabia (April 2002); it has been discussed in front of a transnational audience on Al-Jazeera's *al-sharia wa-l-haya* (14 September 1997; 2 May 1999); it is widely available for a general readership in Egypt; and has been presented by Qaradawi to gatherings of Muslims on the occasion of his visits to Europe – and in his meetings with European state officials.

the discourse is in this regard quite striking. Its most famous advocates live in locations as different as the United States (Taha Jabir al-'Alwani and Salah Sultan), France ('Abd al-Majid al-Najjar and Al-'Arabi al-Bishri), and the Gulf countries ('Abd Allah Bin Bayyah in Saudi Arabia and Yusuf al-Qaradawi in Qatar).[10] Similarly, some of the most vocal contestations of the construct have originated in continental Europe (Tariq Ramadan), the United Kingdom (Asif Khan), Egypt (Salah al-Sawi) and Syria (Sa'id Ramadan al-Buti). *Fiqh al-aqalliyyat* has thus seemingly given rise to global – and often impassioned – debates. Although this transnationalism draws to some extent on the traditional cosmopolitanism that characterises the universalistic traditions of Islam, the task at hand is to avoid ahistorical and reified notions by providing a situated account of the scope and limits of this cosmopolitanism.[11] The current article seeks to lay the grounds for such an account.

Minority fiqh has become an established topic of study and research in several Islamic institutions of higher education across the West.[12] In addition to the Arabic texts on minority fiqh which circulate in a variety of media forms,[13] translations of the books by 'Alwani and Qaradawi have appeared in English and French, targeting mostly the Muslim youth born or educated in the West.[14] While elite study groups convening in London, Paris, Rotterdam or the San Francisco Bay Area have debated the pros and cons of minority fiqh,[15]

10 Interestingly, all of these advocates of minority fiqh are themselves migrants: 'Alwani was born in Iraq, studied at Al-Azhar and moved to the US in the early 1980s; Qaradawi is Egyptian by birth and education; Bin Bayyah was a Minister in his home country Mauritania before moving to Saudi Arabia to teach; al-Najjar is Tunisian, and lived in the Gulf before settling in France around the turn of the century. The Algerian-born al-Bishri has been based in France for two decades.

11 See on this point Zaman (2005).

12 The list of institutions offering courses on minority fiqh includes the Institut Européen des Sciences Humaines in France (IESH); the ALIM (American Learning Institute for Muslims); the IIIT and the Graduate School of Islamic and Social Sciences (now Cordoba University) in the United States; the European Academy of Islamic Studies (East London); and the Abu Zahra in the UK, etc. Fiqh of minorities is also an area of research at Malaysia's International Institute of Advanced Islamic Studies (IAIS), Saudi Arabia's Al-Imam Muhammad Ibn Saud Islamic University, Dar al-'Ulum in Cairo, Batna University in Algeria, etc.

13 'Alwani's book has been published by Nahdat Misr in Cairo and is available at www.islamonline.net. Bin Bayyah's treatise was published by the Global Wasatiyya Centre in Kuwait as well as the Global Centre for Renewal and Guidance in the UK. The lectures on which the book was partly based are available in an 18-CD set from Alhambra Productions in the US.

14 Significantly, Qaradawi's book has also been translated into Bosnian, while 'Alwani's treatise has come out in Russian and there are plans to translate it into Chinese (see IIIT, 'Chinese Scholars, IIIT Look into Possibilities of Joint Research', at www.iiit.org).

15 In June 2005, a talk on 'The Jurisprudence (Fiqh) of Muslim Minorities' by the imam of al-Muntada al-Islami Mosque (West London) Haitham al-Haddad was held in London. At the time of writing the speaker was completing a PhD on minority fiqh at the School

larger Muslim audiences attending the great Islamic meetings of the Diaspora have become increasingly familiar with its principles and techniques.[16] Although the discussion is framed in the language of the fiqh tradition, the participants who have actively engaged in this debate in the West are not limited to the traditional interpreters of that tradition, the ulama.[17] Muslim preachers, social scientists, media professionals and activists have also made significant contributions to the discourse. Western policy-makers and academics are also paying increasing attention to (and sometimes actively encouraging) these inter-Muslim debates.

Unsurprisingly, perhaps, for a concept which deliberately attempts to construct borders in a global religious field (Bowen 2004), minority fiqh has also attracted considerable attention in the Muslim majority countries of the Arab world.[18] In the Muslim world state and non-state actors alike participate in the production and dissemination of minority fiqh – including in its most

of Oriental and African Studies (SOAS). In Spring 2008, a study group met at London's Regent Park Mosque around Kamal Hussein (also known as Abu Zahrah) to critically engage reformist approaches to Islam, including those related to *fiqh al-aqalliyyat*. Email discussion groups and internet forums announced both events widely. In 2001 'Abd Allah Bin Bayyah (a member of the ECFR) gave a series of lectures on fiqh al-aqalliyyat at the Zaytuna Institute in California. A five-part lecture entitled 'The Need For A Minority Fiqh' by US scholar Ali at-Tamimi is available on YouTube. In the mid-2000s the Islamic University of Rotterdam invited Sa'id Ramadan al-Buti to discuss the idea of minority fiqh.

16 Minority fiqh has become a regular topic in events such as the Annual Convention of the Islamic Society of North America (ISNA) since the 1990s, typically through panels involving scholars affiliated to the Fiqh Council of North America (Ihsan Bagby, Zulfiqar Ali Shah, Jamal Badawi, Yusuf Ziya Kavakci, etc.). Likewise, the 'Rencontre Annuelle des Musulmans de France' organized by the Union des organisations islamiques de France (UOIF) at the Bourget has included discussions on fiqh al-aqalliyyat since the late 1990s (involving mostly 'Abd Allah Bin Bayyah and local members of the ECFR).

17 In an explicit attempt to widen the scope of voices in the debate beyond the circle of the traditional scholars a conference on 'Fiqh Today: Muslims as Minorities' was organised in 2004 by the Association of Muslim Social Scientists (AMSS) in association with the International Institute of Islamic Thought (IIIT), the London-based Muslim College, and the British Muslim monthly magazine Q-News. Anas S. Al-Sheikh Ali used his Opening Remarks to criticise the 'knowledge by remote control' of many of the scholars issuing fatwas for Muslims in the West, calling for the 'full participation' of social scientists in the construction of a *fiqh al-aqalliyyat*. Proceedings of the AMSS are forthcoming from AMSSUK Publications, see www.amssuk.com/docs/pdf/Fiqh%20for%20Minorities%20Conference%20Review.pdf. The conference found wide echoes both in the media. See 'Jam'iyyat ulama al-ijtima'iyyat al-muslimina fi Britania tundhdhimu mu'tamaran hawla fiqh al-aqalliyyat', *Al-Sharq Al-Awsat*, 17/2/2004 and the conference report in IslamOnLine by Adul-Rehman Malik, 'Fiqh Today: Muslims as Minorities', www.islamonline.net/servlet/Satellite?c=Article_C&cid=1162385854362&pagename=Zone-English-Euro_Muslims%2FEMELayout.

18 The interesting question of how to explain the overwhelmingly Arab dominance in the current debate (in comparison to the relative lack of engagement by South Asian or Turkish scholars despite the importance of their respective Diasporas) cannot be dealt with here.

official circles. Several Arab states have been directly involved in the financing of the minority fiqh project, such as the ruling family of Dubai (Sheikh Hamdan Rashid's Maktoum Foundation funds the ECFR) and the Ministry of Religious Affairs in Kuwait (which sponsors a newly established Global Wasatiyya Centre active in the West) and Qatar (which has published a treatise on minority fiqh in its Kitab al-Umma series). Publishing houses in Cairo and Beirut – the powerhouses of Arabic publishing – as well as in Amman, Doha and Kuwait City have invested the discourse. In Egypt, the investment in this discourse by representatives of state Islam and of the Islamist opposition provides one illustration of the porosity of the boundaries between the two camps.[19] Meetings of Muslim scholars organised by the Saudi-backed Muslim World League have since the 2000s regularly included the presentation and discussion of papers establishing the contours of a distinctive 'minority fiqh'.[20] The recently established International Union of Muslim Scholars (Ittihad al'Alami li-l-Ulama al Muslimin) has a special committee that deal with the issues of minorities and publishes books on the subject. The London-based Arabic newspaper *Al-Sharq Al-Awsat* has contributed much to stimulating the debate amongst Arabic-speaking Muslims at home and in the Diaspora. The satellite TV station *Al-Jazeera*, particularly in the weekly talk-show *al-shari'a wa-l-hayat* (Islamic Law and Life), has provided another privileged venue for debate on the topic.[21]

As several of the previous examples suggest, many of the actors engaging with minority fiqh are linked to the scholarly networks established around Yusuf al-Qaradawi, the 'global mufti' (Gräf and Skovgaard-Petersen 2009) who chairs the ECFR and author of a widely read and taught book on *fiqh*

19 In addition to regularly attending the sessions of the European Council for Fatwa and Research, scholars from Al-Azhar also participated in a 2003 Cairo conference on *fiqh al-aqalliyyat* organised by IslamOnLine for its media muftis. The conference, which targeted mainly the fatwa editors of the website, was attended by two members of the ECFR educated at Al-Azhar and living in the West (Salah Soltan and Hussein Halawa) and a professor of comparative fiqh from the millenariam Islamic university ('Atiya Fayyad). A summary of the meeting is available at www.islamonline.net/arabic/Daawa/2003/08/article09.shtml. More recently, a lawyer with connections to the Muslim Brotherhood published a book on the topic in Cairo ('Atiya Muhammad 2007).

20 See, for a recent illustration, 'Al-mu'tamar al-'alami li-l-fatawa: hadithu "an al-zaman wa-l-makan wa haya" li-riqaba "al-fatwa" wa fiqh "al-aqalliyyat"', *Al-Sharq Al-Awsat*, 19/01/2009. Qaradawi's work on *fiqh al-aqalliyyat* was presented at the Muslim World League's 4th General Islamic Conference in Saudi Arabia (April 2002). See also the article of Sano Koutoub Moustapha, 'Towards a Comprehensive Method in Handling Issues of Muslim Minorities', *Journal of the Islamic Fiqh Academy*, 16th Issue, Vol. 1 (2006).

21 Episodes of Al-Shari'a wa-l-Hayat devoted to *fiqh al-aqalliyyat* or to fiqhi perspectives on Muslims in the West have been aired with relative frequency since the programme's foundation in 1996. For the importance of *al-shari'a wa-l-hayat* amongst Arabic-speaking Muslims in Europe see for example Roald (2001).

al-aqalliyyat (Qaradawi 2001).[22] The interest on *fiqh al-aqalliyyat*, however, seems part of a broader global Muslim concern with the future of Islam in the West – a concern that has galvanised and perplexed public opinion in the Arab world at key moments (the wars in Bosnia and Kosovo; the terrorist attacks in Madrid and London; the recurrent European debates on veiling) and with relative intensity since 9/11 and the rise of Islamophobia. This concern with Muslim minorities mobilises figures as different as the state Mufti of Egypt Ali Gumu'a,[23] the constellation of actors and networks involved in the discourse on the *maqasid al-shari'a*[24] and *tajdid al-islam*,[25] the drafters of *The Amman Message*,[26] and the international Islamic fiqh councils based in Saudi Arabia.[27] It often appears to be predicated upon a de-politicised understanding of terrorism as stemming from inappropriate understandings

22 More specifically on Qaradawi's role and activities in Europe see Caeiro and al-Saify (2009).

23 See IslamOnLine, 'Egypt's Mufti Urges Integration Protocol for Muslims in the West', www.islamonline.net/English/News/2004-01/13/article08.shtml.

24 Work on the *maqasid* is often what leads Muslim scholars to engage in minority fiqh in the West as in the East: 'Alwani, Qaradawi, Jamal al-din 'Atiya Muhammad, 'Abd al-Majid al-Najjar, and Muhammad Brich all fall under this category. Many of these thinkers sometimes appear to use *fiqh al-aqalliyyat* and *fiqh al-maqasid* interchangeably.

25 As Professor Muhammad al-Mansi of Dar al-'Ulum told me, 'to speak of *fiqh al-aqalliyyat* is to speak of *tajdid al-fiqh*' (personal communication, Cairo, 25 May 2010). Mansi began teaching a course on *fiqh al-aqalliyyat* which he devised himself in 2008. Similarly, the current Minister of Religious Endowments of Egypt singles out in a recent publication Muslim minorities as one of the areas of jurisprudence where the need for *tajdid* is most pressing (Zakzouk 2007: 28).

26 Note in this regard the necessity felt by the drafters of the Message to include in this Islamic declaration against terrorism a sentence enjoining Muslims in the West towards 'good citizenship' (The Amman Message, pp. VIII, 90).

27 The minority fiqh construct has also given rise to (largely autonomous) debates and local appropriations in places like India, Singapore and South Africa. The ways in which these local debates inter-relate with those I study here are outside the scope of this paper. See inter alia Yoginder Sikand's review of Taha Jabir al-Alwani's *Towards a Fiqh for Minorities* published in two parts in the Indian Muslim magazine *The Milli Gazette*, 16–30 April 2004 and 1–15 May 2004; Noor Aisha Binte Abdul Rahman (Assistant Professor at National University of Singapore), 'Muslim Resurgence and the Case for Minority *Fiqh* in Singapore', paper presented at The Sacred in a Global City: Symposium on Religion in Singapore (10 March 2007), National Museum of Singapore, 10 March 2007; Shaykh Moegamat Igshaan Taliep (Vice-Rector of the International Peace University South Africa), 'Muslim Participation in South African liberal democracy: an usul al-fiqh approach', online at www.ipsauniversity.com/index.php?option=com_content&view=article&id=128:muslim-participation-in-south-african-liberal-democracy-an-usul-al-fiqh-approach&catid=54:papers&Itemid=111 (accessed 23 January 2009); and Na'eem Jeenah, 'Political Islam in South Africa and its contribution to a discourse of a *fiqh* of minorities', paper presented at Islamic Civilisation in Southern Africa conference, organised by the University of Johannesburg, Awqaf South Africa and OIC Research Centre for Islamic History, Art and Culture (IRCICA), University of Johannesburg, 1–3 September 2006.

of Islamic norms.[28] The global nature of the *fiqh al-aqalliyyat* debate thus confirms the existence of a specifically Muslim public space (Mandaville 2001; Eickelman and Salvatore 2004) while reminding us that globalisation leads not only to the collapse of old frontiers but also to the establishment of new boundaries. Advocates of minority fiqh have to work through the disjuncture arising out of their various geographical locations (in other words, their operation in a global field), on the one hand, and their own commitment to setting symbolic boundaries (designing a fiqh for minorities), on the other.[29]

III. The concept of minority, citizenship, and the law

Advocates of minority fiqh seek to 'restore the role of sharia in modern life'.[30] This commitment to the Islamic legal tradition, as Qasim Zaman (2002) has shown, is in many ways constitutive of the otherwise heterogeneous body of the ulama. In the writings of minority fiqh advocates, as I hinted above, this commitment is accompanied by a view of the minority status as constituting a distinctive political problem for the Islamic tradition. Accordingly, the concept of 'minority' has given rise to quite wide-ranging debates: on what grounds can the status of minority be legitimised? How should the minority condition itself be understood – in terms of numbers, power differentials, legal rights, or states of mind? Does this status accurately reflect the reality of Muslims in Europe? Is the distinction majority-minority *natural* to Muslim legal thought *and* to the workings of European secular democracies – or is it the product of a political imagination which tends to view European Muslims as *less than* normal citizens?

Practitioners of minority fiqh vary in their understandings of the historical specificities of the presence of Muslim minorities in the West. Some argue that the current minority situation is unprecedented (Ibram 2002), mirroring the claims made by a number of Western social scientists.[31] Others point to the

28 Alternatively one might read the connections that are established between the need to establish a minority fiqh and the terrorist threat as an attempt to pre-empt an understanding of terrorism as stemming from religious interpretations. If this is the case, one might still consider the risk of performative contradiction that strikes Muslim discourses which explicitly connect the two. For an explicit postulation of the link between 'the need' for fiqh al-aqalliyyat and the necessity to contain the terrorist threat see 'Alwani (2003: xviii).

29 Muslim scholars based in the Islamic world such as Qaradawi or Bin Bayyah face of course a particular predicament: if their call for devising a new fiqh for minorities by integrating knowledge of the reality of Muslim communities in the West works to disqualify competing Muslim voices in the Muslim world, it also seems to undermine their own authority to speak on these issues, not least in the eyes of Muslims in the West. As far as I am aware they have not yet openly addressed this seeming paradox in their writings.

30 Quotations of 'Alwani are taken from the English text published by the IIIT in 2003, except when the Arabic text published in the ECFR's *Majalla* (to which 'Ajil al-Nashmi responds) differs significantly from the English version. All translations are mine.

31 Yusuf Ibram is a Moroccan scholar based in Zurich and a member of the ECFR.

fact that although Muslim minorities have historically existed and have in many ways been a condition for the expansion of the religion, their incorporation into the juristic tradition of fiqh has been limited due to historical contingencies.[32] According to the latter line of reasoning, the contemporary necessity for elaborating a minority fiqh is variously related to the current centrality of minorities in Islam ('Alwani 2003: xiii; see also Nielsen 2002 and Ramadan 2003); the connectedness of the modern world ('Alwani 2003: xiii; Bin Bayyah n/d); the need to dispel talk of civilisational clashes; the unprecedented level of penetration of modern state power into individual lives; and the possibilities offered by the institutionalisation of minority rights under international human rights regimes ('Alwani 2003: xii; Bin Bayyah n/d; 'Atiya Muhammad 2007).

One of the most common starting points for the reflection on a Muslim jurisprudence for minorities has been the question of the religious status of Muslims living in non-Muslim lands. Critically engaging the fiqh tradition on this question, Muslim scholars have asked whether emigration from and residence outside traditional Muslim lands is forbidden (*haram*), discouraged (*makruh*), permissible (*mubah*), encouraged (*mandub*) or obligatory (*wajib*) – the five gradings that have historically defined the system of Islamic normativity. Yusuf al-Qaradawi draws on two different structures of justification to legitimise the Muslim presence in the West. In a number of fatwas and other texts, he has argued from within the fiqh tradition that Muslims living in non-Muslim nations are not required to emigrate to Muslim lands: Qaradawi stresses here the universality of Islam and refers to the Qur'an (21: 107; 25: 1). This universality usually requires, in a second moment, a redefinition of the *dar al-islam/dar al-harb* binary; Qaradawi preferring to use *dar al-'ahd* (the domain of truce) or the non-committal 'non-Muslim lands'.[33] Historical memories of

32 al-Najjar explains the relative lack of theorisation of minorities in fiqh by reference to the small number of Muslims living as minorities historically, and to the fact that by the time Muslim minorities acquired a certain importance the gate of *ijtihad* had already been closed (2003: 45–8). One Muslim explanation of the closing of the gate of *ijtihad* represents it as the result of attempts by the ulama to preserve the authenticity of the shari'a from political interventions (Bin Bayyah, n/d).

33 *Dar al-Islam* (The Domain of Islam) refers to the territories where the population is Muslim and/or shari'a is applied. It is classically opposed to *Dar al Harb* (The Domain of War), a non-Muslim space where the safety of Muslims could not be guaranteed and which was considered to be at war. Intermediate spaces where Muslim safety was expected were deemed Domains of the Truce. While the terms used to describe the West may vary ('Alwani speaks of '*dar al-da'wa*'), all practitioners of minority fiqh share a refusal to categorise the West simply in terms of *dar al-harb*. As Nielsen has argued elsewhere (1992: 86), the point to be made here is not that the distinction between Muslim and non-Muslim lands has become irrelevant; clearly, the very idea of *fiqh al-aqalliyyat* is an attempt to re-imagine this distinction in a 'globalised context' governed by 'international treaties'. Having said this, it is also evident that the distinction between Muslim and non-Muslim contexts turns out to be significantly less clear than in the past; in fact, its relative importance becomes a matter of debate and contestation among competing Muslim actors.

Mecca before the Hijra and of the first Companions' stay in Abyssinia are typically mobilised. In relative continuity with the classical fiqh discussions (Abou El Fadl 1994), the permissibility of residing outside Muslim lands is then made *conditional* solely on the safeguarding of religion.

Elsewhere (including in his treatise on *fiqh al-aqalliyyat*), Qaradawi's defence of the possibility of living outside Muslim countries has been more overtly pragmatic: the Muslim presence in the West is a fact that is not only 'permissible' but 'necessary' for spreading the Islamic message, welcoming converts, receiving Muslim migrants, and politically defending the causes of the *umma* (Qaradawi 2000, 2001; see also al-Nashmi 2005). This reasoning, which Qaradawi is careful to relate to the discursive tradition of the shari'a by naming it the '*fiqh* of priorities' (*fiqh al-awlawiyyat*), stands in contrast with the previous mode of argumentation in so far as it does not seek to relate itself directly to the founding texts or the established juridical schools, but seems to depend instead upon contextual assessments of changing social conditions (*fiqh al-waqi'*). In this sense, Qaradawi's justification of the choice to live under minority status appears symptomatic of his impetus to politicize fiqh, that is, to render the Islamic legal tradition accountable to changes in underlying power relations. This politicising impetus, which Qaradawi seems to share with all reformist actors, be they conservative or liberal, may also explain some of the larger Muslim debates and contestations around minority fiqh.[34]

Despite an acknowledgement of the different types of Muslim minorities in the 'West' and in the 'East' (Qaradawi 2001: 16–20),[35] the writings of Qaradawi and his peers often betray an Arab-centric view of Islam which suggests that the real addressees of minority fiqh are (Arab) Muslim immigrants in Western Europe and North America.[36] As Andrew March has recently pointed out, the focus on the 'West' in the writings on minority fiqh indicates a perception of a distinctive *liberal* challenge created by the secular nature of Western political regimes (March 2009: 36). The emphasis on geopolitical considerations – particularly the need to develop an active Muslim presence in the global decision-making centres of the West – further reinforces the symbolic exclusion of Muslims located at the European periphery. This may help to elucidate the relative lack of interest in minority fiqh among Muslim minorities outside Western Europe, and why the historical experience of

34 For a more specific critique of how advocates of minority fiqh politicise the Islamic tradition see Said Ramadan al-Buti (2007: 143–156).

35 Qaradawi's distinction between Muslim minorities in the West and in the East is remarkable because most authors engaged in this reflection assume 'Europe' (*al-Najjar*) or the 'West' (*'Alwani*) to be the geographical framework of minority fiqh.

36 The implicit assumption, common among champions of minority fiqh, that Muslims in Europe are immigrants serves as a reminder that advocates of minority fiqh are mostly of Arab ethnicity (and some are first-generation immigrants themselves).

Muslims in the Balkans – with the creative adaptations that Muslims in the region have devised to live Islamically under non-Muslim rule (Karčić 1999) – have remained largely outside the minority fiqh debate (in spite of the presence of the Bosnian *reisu-l-ulema* Mustafa Cerić among the members of the European Council for Fatwa and Research).[37]

Fiqh al-aqalliyyat for Qaradawi and his peers is perhaps best understood then as the starting point for a general theory of Islamic law for Muslim minorities which builds on their *conditional legitimation*.[38] It is an attempt to 'preserve the identity of Muslims' in the absence of the Muslim state. In moving away from the problematics of the state by virtue of the minority status (and thus reiterating its relevance in Muslim majority lands), practitioners of minority fiqh deliberately seek to shift religious authority and moral responsibility away from the state and towards the community – and its authorised scholars (Bin Bayyah n/d; Qaradawi 2001; al-Najjar 2003; al-Bishri 2004). This move depends also upon a fictional account of the legal primacy of the shari'a in Muslim majority countries, an account which purports to ignore the ubiquitous role of 'man-made laws' in the legal reasoning of contemporary Muslim states.[39] Acknowledging the relative loss of the self-evident character of Islam in a minority setting ('Alwani 2003: 13; al-Najjar 2003: 48; see also Roy 1999), advocates of minority fiqh seek to counter the double threat posed by 'assimilation' and 'isolation' through the interpellation of Muslims – including 'forgetful' Muslims – as believers subject to the Divine Will (shar'). Writings on *fiqh al-aqalliyyat* are to a large degree concerned with defining this Will and the demands it makes upon Muslims living in the West. Some authors go one step further and remarkably recognise that the existence of a Muslim minority in the West is not simply given, but requires prior disciplining: for these writers ('Alwani 2003: 25; al-Bishri 2004: 204), it is the role of Islamic leaders and institutions in the Diaspora

37 Although Mustafa Cerić's project for establishing a 'European Isla' based on the Bosnian experience and on a centralised structure of religious authority resonates in part with the aims of the *fiqh al-aqalliyyat* school, Cerić himself has publicly declared he does not 'believe in the fiqh of minority because [he does] not accept to be treated as a half-way Muslim' (2004). Even if Qaradawi's treatise on minority fiqh has been translated into Bosnian, possible reasons for the relative lack of interest in the concept in the region include the reliance upon the language of traditional fiqh and to the connotation that the term 'minority' carries in the context of the ex-Yugoslavia. Obviously, many Muslims in countries like Albania, Bosnia or Turkey do not consider themselves as 'minorities'.

38 For a perceptive analysis along these lines of the ECFR's fatwa on residing outside Muslim lands see Peter (2006: 450–2).

39 'Abd al-Majid al-Najjar, a cosmopolitan Tunisian intellectual living in France, bases his call for establishing minority fiqh on the claim that Muslims in Europe are subject to 'man-made laws' (al-Najjar 2003: 60–1). While this claim functions as a rhetorical strategy, the erasure of the legal transformations of the Muslim world in the twentieth century is rather striking for someone educated at Tunis's al-Zaytuna.

to persuade Muslims living in non-Muslim countries that they actually form a minority community.[40]

If, as I have been trying to suggest, minority fiqh seeks to institute a relation of power – delineated by Islamic legal orthodoxy – that can restore the role of the shari'a in the life of Muslims denaturalised as minorities, it does so within a specific understanding of the political nature of Western societies (and of the place of Muslims therein). Secularism, for many of the Muslim authors considered here, is a distinctively Western development arising out of tensions within Christianity. Part of the difficulties of establishing Islam in Europe relates to the hegemony of a secularist understanding of religion as a private matter of inner faith (al-Najjar 2003: 53). In this political-theological framework, positive law functions both as the terrain and the boundary of Muslim claims. Muslims living as minorities are thus urged by minority fiqh advocates to respect the Constitution and the laws of the countries they settle in by virtue of an implicit contract.[41] Despite an occasional reference to the legal authority that Muslims as citizens of European democratic nation-states also hold (al-Bishri 2004: 203), the understanding of Muslims in Europe as simple addressees of the Law seems to be widespread amongst minority fiqh advocates.[42] This vision reposes in turn on a perception of weakness which is further underscored by the regular emphases on *taysir* (lenience) and *darurat* (necessities). At the same time, calls for the state recognition of Muslim 'religious, cultural, social, economic and political rights' (Qaradawi 2001), including Muslim Family Laws, try to extend the legal pluralism of Western societies.[43] The fact that these claims are often framed

40 The ideas that Muslims can become 'alienated from their roots' ('Alwani 2003: xv) or be 'unaware of their identity' (Qaradawi 2001) are predicated upon a racialised understanding of Muslim-ness. Although scholars such as Alwani are acutely aware of – and even sensitive to – the perceived contradiction between understandings of freedom of religion in the West and the traditional condemnation of apostasy in Islam ('Alwani 2003: xix–xx), exit conditions from the Islamic religion remain un-theorised in minority fiqh.

41 Muslims are also urged, in at least one instance, to 'love' Western countries: Salah Sultan's emphasis on affect – on the need for Muslims in the West to 'love', show 'gratitude' and 'affection' to their new countries (Sultan 2008) – ironically mirrors the liberal state's insistence on *romanticising* citizenship.

42 The most intriguing case is al-Najjar: although he recognises that laws in Europe are 'established on the basis of collective cooperation' (al-Najjar 2003: 54–5), he goes on to claim that Muslim minorities have neither the power to change these laws nor even in some cases the right to claim to change them (al-Najjar 2003: 63). It is precisely this kind of reasoning that led the Union des organizations islamiques de France (UOIF) to refrain from participating actively in the demonstrations against the French headscarf ban in public schools in 2003 and 2004. According to the UOIF's Muslim critics – particularly the Muslim youth organisations – this sensitivity to the politicisation of legal discourse in France precluded the realisation that French Muslims were citizens, not (neo-)colonial subjects.

43 I do not discuss here the extent to which claims for recognition of Muslim family law are politically realistic. This might vary significantly from one European country to another.

in a language of *equal* rather than *special* rights signals a relative familiarity with tensions within liberal political thought: Western Muslims are urged to strive for recognition 'as a minority amongst other minorities' and to establish legal forums for settling personal status like other religious groups.

Calls for legal recognition seem to presuppose both a secular-liberal regime (where such rights, as Qaradawi is keen on noting, are 'guaranteed by the Constitution') *and* a critique of liberal strategies of exclusion (which prevent the Muslim holders of such rights to effectively access them).[44] Two decades of controversy regarding the visibility of Islam in Europe have made Muslim actors acutely aware of the difference between the religious freedom granted by European laws, and the social and political obstacles which prevent its actual realisation – a difference between the 'formal' and 'actual' equality familiar to critics of liberal legalism (Brown 1995; see also 'Atyia Muhammad 2007). It is arguably the realisation that Muslims need to fulfil certain previous conditions in the social field (including the acquisition of a specific cultural capital) in order to be able to have access to the formal equality promised by the Law (al-Bishri 2004: 204) that partly drives the enterprise of minority fiqh.[45]

So far the main response of minority fiqh advocates to this conundrum has been to reaffirm the necessity of applying the existing (European) laws. Muslims are thus enjoined to 'stand up for their rights' ('Alwani 2003: 29) while Islamic institutions are urged to disseminate the knowledge necessary for Muslims to make use of the legal possibilities available to them. This reliance upon law is partly related to the traditional fiqh misgivings concerning political participation in non-Muslim regimes. It draws both upon a long tradition of Muslim legalism (Diamantides 2006) and upon a more recent history of penetration of cosmopolitan norms and Human Rights discourses in the Islamic world (Johnston 2007). But the primacy of Law should also be seen in a wider postcolonial context. As Comaroff and Comaroff (2007: 141–6) have argued, the current prevalence of zones of law and disorder dialectically feeding into each other often results in a 'fetishisation' of the former. Law appears to become the privileged language of a very wide range of actors since it promises a 'ready means of commensuration' in the face of difference, heterogeneity and fragmented subjectivities.

44 See 'Alwani (2003); al-Bishri (2004); and 'Atiya Muhammad (2007). I borrow the concept of 'liberal strategies of exclusion' from Mehta (1990) and Peter (2010).

45 The realisation that law does not guarantee equality does not seem to apply when the law in question is Islamic Law. Qaradawi states in his treatise on the status of non-Muslims in Islam: 'Although man-made laws and constitutions speak of equal rights and obligations for their citizens, their realization in practice is thwarted because of the prejudices . . . upon which laws can have no impact, and because the people either have no sense of the laws' sacredness or do not believe in submitting to legal authority. Islamic laws are, however, an exception' (Qaradawi 1985: 14).

In the case of minority fiqh, the reliance upon law has rendered Muslim practitioners vulnerable to at least two different critiques – each bearing distinct political import. The first, voiced by figures such as the imam of Bordeaux Tareq Oubrou, criticises minority fiqh for 'misconstruing the legal status of Islam in Europe'.[46] While Oubrou may mean a number of different things by this claim, one of them appears to be the following: the attempt to make Islamic norms compatible with European legal systems partly through the state recognition of Muslim family law seems to the French–Moroccan scholar to be unrealistic and even counterproductive.[47] Although Oubrou's 'sharia de minorité' also started off as an attempt to achieve a 'double legality' – shariatic and French – (Oubrou 2004: 206), the politicisation of law witnessed in recent integration debates in France (particularly during the headscarf affair) persuaded Oubrou of the need to reconcile Islamic norms not with 'French law' but with 'French culture' instead. Although the distinction between law, shari'a and culture is central to the Islamic Reformist traditions where minority fiqh practitioners draw inspiration, 'culture' has remained largely outside the integration process attempted by the institutions engaged in minority fiqh.[48] Oubrou's project depends on a recognition of the cultural dimensions of historical fiqh (as well as the existence of shared cultural norms in France – to be measured ideally by sociological surveys). Placing culture at the centre of the hermeneutical exercise allows Oubrou to bridge the gaps between Islamic norms and French calls to integrate/assimilate Muslims. It also seems to open up a hermeneutical field which has wider implications than the simple invocation by advocates of minority fiqh of *'urf* (custom) as a normative source for issuing fatwas.

The second – and politically more radical – kind of critique, articulated most notably by Tariq Ramadan, attempts to reformulate European Muslims less as a *docile group* and more as a *resisting or dissenting community* through an emphasis on 'citizenship' instead of 'minorityness' (Ramadan 2003; see also Mestiri 2004). In seeking to displace the legal imaginary which serves as the symbolic boundary of minority fiqh (and arguably of much of the current Muslim social-political activism in Europe), Ramadan wants to refashion Muslim activism within an ecumenical ethical horizon open to a greater range of political claims – and where Muslims see themselves as (at least)

46 Oubrou, personal communication, Bordeaux (2005). For an attempt to contextualise Oubrou's sharia de minorité, see Caeiro (2006).

47 I do not discuss here whether Oubrou is right or not in this assessment. For a recent discussion of Muslim demands for state recognition see Williams (2008) and Bano (2008).

48 As I argue elsewhere, integration in institutions such as the European Council for Fatwa and Research has tended to be understood in legal rather than cultural terms (Caeiro 2009). Alwani comes closest to echoing Oubrou's call when he writes intriguingly of the 'polemical relationship between legislation, whether divine or man-made, and cultural traditions and conventions' ('Alwani 2003: xiv).

potentially part of the 'ethical majority' (Ramadan 2003). The political possibilities unlocked by Ramadan's critique have started to be recognised by the members of the ECFR themselves. Responding in part to this criticism, Qaradawi's own understanding of the situation of Muslims in the West has started to move away from the emphasis on minorityness towards a stress upon citizenship (Qaradawi 2007) – although it may still be too early to see what is precisely at stake in this move.

These and other Muslim critics of minority fiqh have thus argued that the status of minority is not a natural category but rather the product of a specific political imagination which seeks to contain Muslim agency. Mohamed Mestiri (International Institute of Islamic Thought-France) considers that *fiqh al-aqalliyyat* consolidates categories that are foreign to the practices of democratic politics. For Ajil al-Nashmi (see below), the concept of minority presupposes a 'nationalist framework' which does not correspond to contemporary post-national Europe (or the US). In so far as Western nation-states are 'secula'', and both citizens and immigrants ruled by a 'social contract' on the basis of 'needs and necessities' (al-Nashmi's way of describing the neutrality of the liberal state), the minority condition is deemed inappropriate to think of the Muslim predicament (al-Nashmi 2005: 20).[49] Other writers like Jamal al-Din 'Atiya have started to think of minority fiqh in the context of the institutionalisation of minority rights in international law. His use of fiqh interchangeably with law, even in non-Muslim contexts, highlights the hybrid nature of the discourse. Muslim scholarly debates about the minority status have thus tried to articulate two different universes of reference. While Muslim scholars are now involved in the contestation over the proper limits of legal pluralism, their engagement with the problematics of minority rights in a world increasingly governed by cosmopolitan norms is seemingly only starting.

IV. The prophetic Sunna, the commitment to the *fiqh* tradition, and affective reason

Writings on *fiqh al-aqalliyyat* presuppose, as I have shown above, specific understandings of Europe as a distinctive political space. As engagements with the Islamic legal tradition, however, they also appear in many ways to carry their own context. The minority fiqh discourse often reads as lists of legal maxims (*qawa'id fiqhiyya*) providing hermeneutical and methodological guidelines for muftis dealing with questions from Muslims in the West.[50] A

49 al-Nashmi also questions the relevance of the status of minority for fiqh: in so far as fiqh is a method of extraction of rules considerations of power or number are not relevant. 'Minority' in this view is incommensurable with the term – fiqh – which it purports to qualify (al-Nashmi 2005: 22–3; see also al-Buti 2007: 181–7).

50 Writings on minority fiqh bear strong resemblance to the traditional *adab al-mufti* genre: they articulate a number of themes familiar to that literature, such as the gravity of issuing

set of these guidelines relates to the structures of religious authority. The often-repeated call for exercising 'collective ijtihad' (Mahdi n/d; Qaradawi 2001; Ibram 2002: 70–1; 'Alwani 2003: 33; Sultan 2008) is an attempt to unify the various – and sometimes contradictory – fatwas of Muslim scholars, as well as a way of coming to grips with the complexity of Western societies, where 'good and evil appear mixed in complicated ways' (al-Najjar 2003: 61–2; see also al-Bishri 2004: 204). The emphasis on taking the context (*al-waqi'*) into consideration is another regular leitmotif (Qaradawi 2001: 44–6; Sultan 2008: 42–7), taken to its radical conclusion by 'Alwani's call for incorporating social scientists into the fiqh reflections ('Alwani 2003: 3, 33–6; see also Badawi in 'Alwani 2003: ix; and Ramadan 2009).[51] This emphasis, often accompanied by a less than subtle effort to exclude scholars based outside Europe (and not affiliated to the institutions committed to minority fiqh) from participating in the discussions (Halawa n/d; Mahdi n/d), should be seen as an attempt to modify the capital required for speaking in the name of Islam (Peter 2006). It is therefore perhaps not surprising that it should have elicited sarcastic responses from excluded Muslim scholars, who prefer to emphasise instead the importance of knowledge of the Islamic texts and its disciplines (al-Buti 2007).

A second set of guidelines invoked by the advocates of minority fiqh deal directly with hermeneutical questions. These guidelines typically stress the objectives of the shari'a (*maqasid al-shari'a*),[52] the understanding of priorities (*awlawiyyat*) and the consideration of the collective requirements over the individual needs of Muslim minorities. This insistence on the values and principles of the shari'a over its historically constituted norms appears as a condition for various kinds of strategic thinking, laying the ground for the emergence of what has been called a 'public Islam' (Eickelman and Salvatore 2004). Understandings of the 'common good' are thematised as preconditions for conveying Islam's universal message. A striking example is provided by Salah Sultan, who wonders what would happen if 'the Muslims took upon themselves the mission of eradicating the illiteracy of 23 million Americans': 'How many of them could become Muslims or think good of Islam and Muslims or at least stay neutral' (2008: 40–1).

fatwas, the danger of following people's whims or submitting to the desires of the rulers, the contrast between the reticence of the pious predecessors regarding issuing fatwas and the current facility and haste in which so-called muftis respond to questions. The vitality of the *adab al-mufti* tradition under changed conditions is further demonstrated by the fact that criticisms of minority fiqh are also played out in the field of the etiquette of the mufti (al-Buti 2007). On the *adab al-mufti* see *inter alia* Masud (1984); Caeiro (2006).

51 The emphasis on devising a 'realistic fiqh' may be seen as an attempt to overcome the 'pessimistic consciousness of the tension between ideal and actuality' which Kerr attributes to traditional Muslim scholars (Kerr 1966: 1).

52 On the *maqasid al-sharia* see Johnston 2007.

The lists of principles are extensive, perhaps because minority fiqh advocates seek to contain the elements of arbitrariness and subjectivism inherent in the emphasis on upholding the *maqasid* of the shari'a (as their critics have repeatedly pointed out). The principles do not eliminate these arbitrary elements altogether but they succeed in many cases in rendering clearer the intended direction of the *ijtihadi* reasoning.[53] Because they are sensitive to the politics of authenticity enacted by those who criticise *fiqh al-aqalliyyat* as a regime of exceptions for 'Westernised Muslims' (Khan 2004; al-Buti 2007; see also Ramadan 2003), most of the authors considered here rhetorically emphasise that minority fiqh is not a 'fiqh of concessions' but an authentic fiqh bound by the rules of the universal shari'a (Qaradawi 2001; 'Alwani 2003: 4; al-Bishri 2004: 205).[54]

Writings on minority fiqh have not only provoked wide-ranging debates within Muslim public spheres; they have also given rise to some controversy within the ranks of those scholars committed in principle to the idea of devising specific rules for Muslims in the West by virtue of their minority status. Below I focus on an exchange between two members of the European Council for Fatwa and Research, Taha Jabir al-Alwani and 'Ajil al-Nashmi. The exchange is remarkable because it highlights the diversity of understandings of minority fiqh in those institutions most closely associated with the project.[55] The context of this discussion is the European Council for Fatwa and Research. Qaradawi's first use of the expression *fiqh al-aqalliyyat* – in the late 1990s – was part of an attempt to legitimise the ECFR in the Muslim world,[56] and various theoretical attempts to ground minority fiqh have been

53 al-Najjar attends to the need to weigh conflicting goods: forbidding evil (*mafsada*) and promoting interests (*masalih*) are two kinds of acts valued in and of themselves, but when an evil and an interest are simultaneously present al-Najjar enjoins Muslim jurists to pay attention to the short- and long-term effects of each (al-Najjar 2003: 61–2): but how is one to distinguish the situations in which the evil is only temporary and the corresponding *maslaha* great in the future, from those where the *maslaha* is small and the evil so large that it will cause a *fitna* amongst Muslims in the future? How is the genuine interest (*al-maslaha al-haqiqiyya*) to be identified without falling into arbitrariness? al-Najjar does not seem to provide an answer.

54 'Ajil al-Nashmi's perception of Taha Jabir al-'Alwani's characterisation of *fiqh al-aqalliyyat* as a 'rigorous' rather than 'concessionary' fiqh ('Alwani 2003: 4) as an attempt to make life difficult for Muslim minorities, denying them the possibilities of legitimate derogations offered by the Islamic tradition (al-Nashmi 2005: 28), totally misses this point. On the exchange between 'Alwani and al-Nashmi see below.

55 The internal diversity of opinion on this issue explains the adoption of a descriptive rather than normative understanding of *fiqh al-aqalliyyat* by the ECFR: 'The final opinion of the Council on the Fiqh of minorities is that it means: the juristic rulings concerning the Muslim who lives outside the Islamic land' (Resolution 12/5).

56 In his introduction to the ECFR's First Collection of Fatwas, Qaradawi wrote that the ECFR does not pose itself as a 'competitor to the established fatwa bodies in the Muslim world' [the MWL's Islamic Fiqh Academy and the Fiqh Committee of the OIC]; rather, according to Qaradawi, it complements such bodies through a specialised focus on what

closely connected with the efforts to guide and redirect the ad hoc nature of the work of the European fatwa council (al-Najjar 2003; see also 'Alwani 2003: 14). The ECFR's bi-annual scientific magazine (*al-Majalla al-'Ilmiyya*) has done much to foster the debate, publishing research papers and also occasionally responding to external criticism against *fiqh al-aqalliyyat*.[57] A full day of discussion was devoted to the topic at the ECFR's 12th ordinary session held in Dublin in December 2003/January 2004. Taha Jabir al-'Alwani's paper on *fiqh al-aqalliyyat* was presented and discussed.[58] This and other papers on the topic were published in the corresponding issue of the *Majalla* (issues 4/5, 2004), which was to a large extent devoted to efforts at grounding *fiqh al-aqalliyyat*. In his response paper (presented at a later meeting of the ECFR and published in the 7th issue of the *Majalla*), the Kuwaiti scholar 'Ajil Nashmi offers a very critical – and at times remarkably ungenerous – reading of Alwani's text. Here I describe and then interpret the controversy, all the more noteworthy since – as al-Nashmi himself points out – both scholars studied together the same subjects (*usul al-fiqh*) under the same scholars at Al-Azhar in the early 1970s.

Although al-Nashmi disagrees with 'Alwani on a range of different issues, the core of al-Nashmi's critique of 'Alwani's treatise focuses on the assessment of the place of the Sunna in the extraction of Islamic norms. al-Nashmi's disagreement with 'Alwani on this count over-determines some of al-Nashmi's reactions to unrelated claims made by 'Alwani. This debate sheds light also on what is at stake in the discussion of whether *fiqh al-aqalliyyat* is just a branch of fiqh – like the fiqh of medicine, economic or politics (Qaradawi 2001; see also al-Najjar 2003: 50) – or whether it requires a new fiqh methodology (*usul al-fiqh*) – as claimed by 'Alwani (2003).

The status of the Sunna has arguably been at the centre of Muslim responses to modern challenges to religious authority (Brown 1996). Muslim scholars associated with the Islamic Revival – including those who advocate minority fiqh – have typically tried to navigate between the modernist attempts to dismiss Prophetic narrations in favour of the Qur'an, on the one hand, and the traditionalist reliance on the Sunna as the unsurpassable model for practical action on the other. Muslim Revivalists have sought to emphasise the complementariness of the two sources even as they recognise the ontological primacy of the Qur'an. In contrast to many of the controversial discussions

he called for the first time (as far as I am aware – a Muslim 'fiqh for minorities'. If fatwas change according to place, time and circumstances, 'what greater difference is there', Qaradawi rhetorically asks, than that between 'a Muslim and non-Muslim land'? (Qaradawi in ECFR [1999] 2002: X).

57 See the issue 12–13, 2008: 11–13.

58 Unlike the other North American members of the ECFR (Salah Sultan and Jamal Badawi), Alwani does not regularly attend the meetings of the European fatwa council. His paper on *fiqh al-aqalliyyat* was presented and discussed in absentia for health reasons.

in the Muslim world which deal directly with concrete issues related to the place of women in society, Islamic criminal laws, and questions of economics, the practical implications of the exchange between 'Alwani and al-Nashmi are mostly implicit. To put it briefly, Taha Jabir al-'Alwani argues, in his treatise on minority fiqh, that the Qur'an takes precedence over the Sunna. While this claim appears at first sight conventional for reformist actors keen on reviving the practice of ijtihad, the repeated emphasis which 'Alwani places on this hierarchization of the Islamic sources is – as al-Nashmi himself notes – quite remarkable (2003: 18, 19, 20). On closer look, this claim represents a break with Alwani's previous writings, which mainly stressed the 'complementariness' of the two major sources in Islamic legal thought.[59] In *Towards a Fiqh for Minorities*, however, 'Alwani seeks to marginalise the Prophetic Sunna to the rank of mere auxiliary: 'The Sunnah revolves around the Qur'an and is closely tied up with it, but never surpasses or overrules it' ('Alwani 2003: 18–19). While fiqh practitioners have always recognised that the Qur'anic text – as 'the direct word of God Almighty, the eternal and absolute miracle' which 'cannot be allegorically read or interpreted' – is ontologically different from the Prophetic Sunna ('Alwani 2003: 18), they have not concluded with him that jurists cannot derive new rulings from the Sunna alone. For 'Alwani, however, the normative authority lies exclusively upon the Qur'an – and specifically upon what he calls its 'higher principles'.

There is a particular representation of the Sunna underlying 'Alwani's call for 'a review of the relationship between the Qur'an and the Sunnah' ('Alwani 2003: 19); this is a representation of the Sunna as 'intolerant' which occasionally resurfaces in 'Alwani's writings.[60] 'Alwani's Quranic-centred methodology, based on two crucial Quranic verses (Al-Mumtahanah 8–9 and al-Ma'idah 8), seeks to establish 'kindness and justice' as the two higher principles of Islam governing Muslim relations with the Other ('Alwani 2003: 26–7).

In assuming that 'tolerance' and 'justice' can be transculturally defined by standards outside a specific tradition (Islamic or otherwise), 'Alwani's vision seems to rest on certain a priori philosophical–political commitments – a method that has long been part of the Islamic reformist discourse and strategy.

59 In an article originally published in 1995, 'Alwani argued explicitly for the complementary of the Qur'an and the Sunna: 'Both the Qur'an and the Sunnah represent sources of revealed knowledge that complement the natural universe . . . The Sunnah clarifies and elaborates on the Qur'anic epistemic methodology by linking the Prophet's example and the Qur'an's values so that these may be applied to the actuality of changing circumstances' (reprinted in 'Alwani 2005: 5).

60 This perception of the Sunna is revealed in passages like the following: 'Once the Qur'an establishes a certain principle, such as tolerance and justice in dealing with non-Muslims, the ruling of the Qur'an takes precedence' ('Alwani 2003: 20). Qaradawi provides an example of an account of the Sunna which shares with 'Alwani the effort to derive general principles from Prophetic narrations but ends up emphasising quite the opposite – the Sunna's 'tolerance, convenience, and ease' – see Brown (1996) 119–22.

Part of al-Nashmi's critique of 'Alwani has been of a hermeneutical nature: in the absence of the explanatory Sunna, which 'Alwani voids of normative content, what are the grounds – al-Nashmi asks (2005: 37) – from which one can understand the so-called higher principles of the Qur'an? 'Alwani's prudent silence on the sources of these guiding principles leaves him exposed to the critiques of those claiming to be solely driven by a commitment to the founding texts of the Islamic tradition in all their multivocity.

What is at stake here, I submit, is not a particular understanding of how Muslims should relate to the Other. It is not even a disagreement about the need to reform specific historical normative understandings or to revise certain fatwas. al-Nashmi is part of the large constellation of ulama who view *ijtihad* as a contemporary necessity. The fiqh he and his peers desire is a 'creative' one: al-Nashmi works within a complex temporality which simultaneously draws inspiration from the pious predecessors while interiorising the linear narrative of progress and reform. The Kuwaiti Muslim scholar makes sufficiently clear in his response paper that he does not seek to apply old fatwas to current situations (al-Nashmi 2005). Like most members of the ECFR, al-Nashmi also privileges the objectives of the shari'a over its historically constituted norms, and emphasises the need to adapt religious rulings to specific circumstances. Both 'Alwani and al-Nashmi belong to a school of thought which politicises – through references to the fiqh of priorities – the Islamic tradition. If, in the eyes of critics like al-Nashmi, 'Alwani's comments about the Sunna appear unacceptable, it is not only because their basis in certain *a priori* philosophical commitments makes them liable to characterisations of unbridled personal opinion (instead of reliance upon the founding texts). It is also – and mainly – because they are seen as symptomatic of a *conditional commitment* to the Islamic fiqh tradition. It is the threat that he perceives in this conditionality that underlies al-Nashmi's uncharitable reading of 'Alwani's text, and which explains why the critique is largely played out in the register of 'affective reason'.[61] In other words, it is less the content of Alwani's engagement with the Sunna than his way of doing so that seems to be at stake.

To be sure, 'Alwani is not what one would conveniently identify as a modernist; he openly criticises those Muslims in America who 'tend to apologize for those statements ["randomly" picked out by "Islam's detractors"] and dismiss them as ancient and irrelevant' ('Alwani 2003: xix). As a religious scholar, he naturally presupposes a 'true' Islam distinguishable from its historical understandings ('Alwani 2003: 25). For 'Alwani as for al-Nashmi, fiqh is also the terrain in which solutions to current problems are to be sought ('Alwani 2003: 34). 'Alwani's project, however, is also predicated upon a specific appraisal of the inherited fiqh which borders at times on an assertion of its contemporary irrelevance. It is perhaps because 'Alwani's remarks on

61 I borrow this notion from Hirschkind (2006) 133–7.

the Sunna are part of his larger critique of the fiqh tradition that al-Nashmi's rhetorical defence of the status of the Sunna needs to be so vigorous.

Many of 'Alwani's critiques of the fiqh tradition are shared by fellow members of the ECFR; but while the latter seek to minimise the impression of discontinuity, 'Alwani seems to deliberately wish to emphasise them.[62] The tradition of fiqh is equated with a 'mere collection of philosophical and polemic rules or linguistic and intellectual arguments' (2003: 12), in sum, a 'minor science' (2003: 12).[63] Past jurists were – in the eyes of 'Alwani – guilty of *imprecision* (they 'did not classify the sources of Islamic law in a precise way', 9), *introversion* and *parochialism* (they 'overlooked the universality of Islam', 9). Their approaches were 'confused' (18), 'simplistic' and 'unscientific' (4), and their theories mere reflections of a particular historical context – one furthermore characterised by the logic of 'conflict' (11) and a superiority complex.[64]

al-Nashmi's main aim in his response paper is to demonstrate the contemporary relevance of the Islamic fiqh tradition. He does this partly by recasting 'Alwani's reformist claims as unoriginal, and partly by showing (somewhat circularly) how they fall outside the tradition of the pious predecessors and the scholars of the past.[65] It is 'Alwani's attitude towards these scholars, however, that comes under the most severe criticism, justifying the irony and sarcasm with which al-Nashmi treats his fellow mufti. The lack of 'respect' that al-Nashmi perceives in 'Alwani's text is deemed incompatible with the discipline (2005: 49). It underlies al-Nashmi's subtle exclusion of 'Alwani from the circle of the *fuqaha* (al-Nashmi 2005: 17–18). This is not (only) an authoritarian argument against internal critique. It also signals a different relationship to the tradition of reasoning which both 'Alwani and al-Nashmi purport to share, albeit differently. As Hirschkind has shown in another context, excellence in fiqh requires not only mastery of the relevant sciences but a certain inner disposition. This is also why Muslim scholars setting the

62 The contrast between Alwani and Qaradawi or al-Najjar is in this regard striking: although they call for a new legal methodology (*usul al-fiqh*) for devising a minority fiqh – and often resort to a language that seems foreign to the fiqh tradition – al-Najjar and Qaradawi go to great rhetorical lengths to minimise the discontinuities with this tradition, which they repeatedly praise, while 'Alwani seeks on the contrary to deliberately emphasise ruptures.

63 Elsewhere 'Alwani (2005: iv) has criticised the 'fiqhi mentality' of Muslim communities.

64 For a similar account of fiqh as the historical product of Muslim hegemony and superiority in medieval times see the works of Wahid al-din Khan (as described in Zaman 2002: 181–3).

65 Thus the call for introducing the social sciences into fiqh is equated with the centuries-old insistence on understanding the social conditions of the mustafti (al-Nashmi 2005: 29–30); 'Alwani's call for a new type of *ijtihad* is condemned because the Sahaba were able to answer all kinds of question following the only method of *ijtihad* they knew (al-Nashmi 2005: 30–2).

conditions for issuing fatwas insist on the need for the mufti to be pious and to fear God (Caeiro 2006; Sultan 2008).

I have been arguing that the polemical discussion between al-Nashmi and 'Alwani is less about specific Muslim attitudes towards non-Muslims than about different kinds of commitment to the fiqh tradition. But what are the contexts in which these two positions are articulated? Clearly, the two Muslim scholars assess differently the possibilities for gradual reform – the necessity of which none of them really questions. These assessments, I suggest, appear in turn related to the positions that each scholar occupies in the Islamic religious field.

'Alwani's reform project – which borrows significantly from the Islamisation of Knowledge venture, with which he has long been associated (Abaza 2002) – views the 'crisis' of the Muslim world as first and foremost an 'intellectual crisis' ('Alwani 2005). This diagnosis of a modern intellectual crisis is not, however, a call for a return to a pristine Islam, since classical Islamic sciences, not least the fiqh tradition itself, are also deemed in dire need of reform. Rather, it is a call for a much more wide-ranging – if somewhat ambiguous – critique of Western and Islamic intellectual traditions. Minority fiqh for 'Alwani appears as a step in this wider reform agenda. His engagement with the minority status is in this sense quite self-consciously strategic: 'There is a need to propose and develop such principles to assist in revealing more of the purposes of the Qur'an. This should, in turn, help in building up fiqh rules for minorities as well as majorities' ('Alwani 2003: 20).

While the inscription of minority fiqh within a global reform agenda significantly raises the stakes of the debate, 'Alwani's reform project – like al-Nashmi's and the ECFR's – also depends upon the continuing viability of authority structures. How should one therefore understand 'Alwani's argument that Islam has no clergy or 'grand "ulamā" board' who can 'monopolize the sources of religious knowledge and the interpretation of religious dogma' ('Alwani 2003: xiv)? This claim, as al-Nashmi himself has pointed out, leaves the door wide open to all kinds of interpretations.[66] While 'Alwani himself is wary of the individualisation and assimilation of Muslims in the US which the fragmentation of religious authority engenders, the statement above suggests a greater sensitivity to the perceived weight of established traditions of reasoning than to the dangers of assimilation (and terrorism for that matter). It nevertheless leaves 'Alwani powerless in the face of conflicting religious advice: if 'ordinary people can select the scholar whom they wish to follow and pick from the "common law" the reasons, terms and restrictions' ('Alwani 2003: xiv), how can the ulama counter the 'sea of confusion' in

66 al-Nashmi argues that while there are clear preconditions for performing *ijtihad* and exercising religious authority, there is no evidence suggesting that one group cannot monopolise the interpretation of religious scriptures at any one point in time (al-Nashmi 2005: 24–5).

which Muslims find themselves when confronted with 'differences in opinion among jurists' ('Alwani 2003: 7)? If 'Alwani's discussion suggests that contrary to Qaradawi, al-Nashmi and many of his peers within the ECFR, 'Alwani locates himself within the margins of the Islamic religious field, it also appears to highlight a more general perplexity regarding the *intractability* of the problem of authority in contemporary Islam.

V. Conclusion

This chapter has attempted to provide an account of ongoing Muslim scholarly debates on the status of Muslim minorities living in the West. The vitality of the discussions notwithstanding, the terms of the debate on minority fiqh may appear in certain respects to be quite narrow. Advocates and opponents of *fiqh al-aqalliyyat* do not by and large seek to disrupt 'the immanent relationship between normative particularism [fiqh] and social behaviour' which is sometimes seen as one of the prime dimensions of functional pluralisation of Islamic knowledge (Mandaville 2007). In some ways it could be argued that they seek precisely to reaffirm this relationship. These Muslim voices nevertheless act in a social context where Islamic knowledge has been *de facto* resettled as one among various systems of authority, standing sometimes in open conflict, often in productive tension with each other. As a series of engagements with the Islamic legal tradition and with the reality of Muslims in the West, these transnational conversations are part of a wider global context marked by the proliferation of Islamic discourses on the 'objectives of the law' (*maqasid al-sharia*), 'moderation' (*wasatiyya*) and 'renewal' (*tajdid*). They echo the increasingly insistent voices calling for the 'integration' of Muslims in the West. Like the discourse on 'Islamic moderation', minority fiqh emerges as an internal critique and as a civic response to the fear of Muslim radicalisation and 'Islamic terrorism' – a response which simultaneously lends credence to, and seeks to redirect, the European debates and policies on the integration of Muslims.[67] The discourse seems furthermore to share with the wider integration debates in Europe a similar concern about the social consequences of religious interpretation. This concern is based upon a widespread ambivalence towards religion understood as the 'causally effective clause' (to borrow an expression from MacIntyre) of social action of people defined as 'religious' – in this case 'Muslim'. It provides in this regard a prime example of how 'the penetration of geopolitics into religious discourse

67 Taha Jabir al-'Alwani is the most explicit about the anti-terrorist import of *fiqh al-aqalliyyat*: 'The shattering events of September 11 have left everyone in a state of shock. Since then, Muslims and Americans have woken up to a new reality, the like of which has never been known before. Since then, the need has arisen, as never before, for a new fiqh dealing with the question of Muslim minorities in the West in particular' ('Alwani 2003: xviii).

impacts the politics of knowledge production' in contemporary Islam (Mandaville 2007: 112). If the relative success of the minority fiqh construct lies in the possibility it gives to a range of Muslim actors to engage and re-shape debates about the integration of Islam in Europe, its limits are related to the reliance upon a discursive tradition – fiqh – which is increasingly contested by Muslim and non-Muslim voices alike.

References

Abaza, M. (2002) *Debates on Islam and Knowledge in Malaysia and Egypt: Shifting Worlds*. New York, NY: Routledge Curzon.

Abou El Fadl, Khaled (1994) 'Islamic Law and Muslim Minorities: The Juristic Discourse on Muslim Minorities from the Second / Eighth to the Eleventh / Seventeenth Centuries', *Islamic Law and Society* 1 (2): 141–187.

al-Azmeh, Aziz (1988) 'Islamic Legal Theory and the Appropriation of Reality', in *Islamic Law: Historical and Social Contexts*, ed. Aziz al-Azmeh. London: Routledge, 250–265.

al-Bishri, al-'Arabi (2004) 'Muntalaqat li-fiqh al-aqalliyyat', *Al-majalla al-'ilmiyya li-l majlis al-ūrūbbī li-l-iftā' wa-l-buḥūth* 4–5: 201–218.

al-Buti, Said Ramadan, www.bouti.com/ulamaa/bouti/bouti_monthly15.htm (June 2001).

—— (2007) *Al-islam wa-l gharb*. Damascus: Dar al Fikr.

al-Najjar, 'Abd al-Majid (2003) 'Nahwa minhaj usuli li fiqh al aqalliyyat', *Al-majalla al-'ilmiyya li-l majlis al-ūrūbbī li-l-iftā' wa-l-buḥūth* 3: 41–64.

al-Nashmi, 'Ajil (2005) 'Ta'aliqat 'ala bahth 'madkhal ila usul wa fiqh al-aqalliyyat' li-l –ustadh al-duktur Taha Jabir al-'Alwani', *Al-majalla al-'ilmiyya li-l majlis al-ūrūbbī li-l-iftā' wa-l-buḥūth* 7: 15–63.

'Alwani, Taha Jabir al- (2003) *Towards a Fiqh for Minorities: Some Basic Reflections*. London and Washington: IIIT.

—— (2005) *Issues in Contemporary Islamic Thought*. Herndon, VA: IIIT.

'Atiya Muhammad, Jamal al-Din (2007) *Nahu Fiqh Jadid li-l-Aqalliyyat*. Cairo: Dar al –Salam.

Bano, Samia (2008) 'In Pursuit of Religious and Legal Diversity: A Response to the Archbishop of Canterbury and the "Sharia Debate" in Britain', *Ecclesiastical Law Journal* 10 (3): 283–309.

Bin Bayyah, 'Abdullah (n/d) 'Sacred Law in Secular Lands'. Two sets of CDs. Alhambra Productions.

Bowen, J. (2004) 'Does French Islam Have Borders? Dilemmas of Domestication in a Global Religious Field', *American Anthropologist* 106 (1): 43–55.

Brown, D. (1996) *Rethinking Tradition in Modern Islamic Thought*. Cambridge: Cambridge University Press.

Brown, W. (1995) *States of Injury*. Princeton, NJ: Princeton University Press.

Caeiro, A. (2004) 'The Social Construction of Shari'a: Bank Interest, Home Purchase, and Islamic Norms in the West', *Die Welt des Islams* 44 (3): 351–375.

—— (2006) 'The Shifting Moral Universes of the Islamic Tradition of Ifta'', *The Muslim World* 96 (4): 661–685.

—— (2009) 'Transnational 'Ulama, European Fatwas, and Islamic Authority: A Case Study of the European Council for Fatwa and Research', in van Bruinessen, Martin and Stefano Allievi, eds. *Producing Islamic Knowledge.* Abingdon: Routledge, pp. 121–141.

—— (2010) 'Transnational 'Ulama, European Fatwas, and Islamic Authority: A Case Study of the European Council for Fatwa and Research', in van Bruinessen, M. and Allievi, S., eds. *Producing Islamic knowledge: Transmission and Dissemination in Western Europe*. London: Routledge.

Caeiro, A. and al-Saify, M. (2009) 'Qaradawi in Europe, Europe in Qaradawi: The Global Mufti's European Politics', in Bettina Gräf and Jakob Skovgaard-Petersen, eds. *The Global Mufti: The Phenomenon of Yusuf al-Qaradawi*. London: Hurst, pp. 109–148.

Ceric̀, M. (2004) 'Keynote Speech', AMSS Conference 'Fiqh Today – Muslims as Minorities', London, 21 February 2004 (available online at www.rijaset.ba/en/index.php?option=com_content&task=view&id=98&Itemid=1, accessed 22 April 2011).

Comaroff, Jean and Comaroff, John (2007) 'Law and Disorder in the Postcolony', *Social Anthropology* 15 (2): 133–152.

DeLorenzo, Y.T. (2000) 'The Fiqh Councilor in North America', in *Muslims on the Americanization Path?*, Yvonne Yazbeck Haddad and John L. Esposito, eds. Oxford: Oxford University Press.

Diamantides, M. (2006) 'Towards a Western-Islamic Conception of Legalism', in Barshack, L., Goodrich, P. and Schutz A., eds. *Law, Text, Terror*. London: Glasshouse Press, pp. 95–118.

Eickelman, D. and Salvatore, A. (eds) (2004) *Public Islam and the Common Good.* Leiden: Brill.

Gräf, B. (2008) 'IslamOnline.net: Independent, interactive, popular', *Arab Media and Society*, January.

Gräf, B. and Skovgaard-Petersen, J. (eds) (2009) *The Global Mufti: The Phenomenon of Yusuf al-Qaradawi*. London: Hurst.

Halawa, Hussain (n/d) http://wasatiaonline.net/news/details.php?data_id=466, accessed 22 April 2011.

Hirschkind, C. (2006) *The Ethical Soundscape*. New York: Columbia University Press.

Ibram, Y. (2002) 'La procédure de la fatwa', in Mortanges, R. and Tanner, E., eds. *Muslime und schweizerische Rechtsordnung / Les musulmans et l'ordre juridique suisse.* Freiburg: Universitätsverlag Freiburg Schweiz.

Johnston, D. (2007) 'Maqasid al-Shari'a: Epistemology and Hermeneutics of Muslim Theologies of Human Rights', *Die Welt des Islams* 47 (2): 149–187.

Karčić, F. (1999) *The Bosniaks and the Challenge of Modernity – Late Ottoman and Hapsburg Times*. Sarajevo: El Kalem.

Karman, K.-L.J. (2008) *Rethinking Islamic Jurisprudence for Muslim Minorities: The Politics, and the Work of Contemporary Fatwa Councils*. PhD Dissertation submitted to the University of Aarhus, Aarhus (Denmark).

Kerr, M. (1966) *Islamic Reform: the Political and Legal Theories of Muhammad 'Abduh and Rashid Rida*. Berkeley, CA: University of California Press.

Khan, A. (2004) *The Fiqh of Minorities – the New Fiqh to Subvert Islam*. London: Khilafah Publications.

Mahdi, T. (n/d) 'Droit des minorités' (in two parts). Available online at http://taharmahdi.free.fr, accessed 22 April 2011.

Mandaville, P. (2001) *Transnational Muslim Politics – Reimagining the Umma*. Oxon: Routledge.

—— (2007) 'Globalization and the Politics of Religious Knowledge: Pluralizing Authority in the Muslim World', *Theory Culture Society* 24: 101–115.

March, A. (2009) 'Sources of Moral Obligation to non-Muslims in the "Jurisprudence of Muslim Minorities" (*Fiqh al-aqalliyyat*) Discourse', *Islamic Law and Society* 16: 1 (February).

Masud, K. (1984) 'Ādāb al-Muftī: The Muslim Understanding of Values, Characteristics, and Role of a *Muftī*', in Barbara D. Metcalf, ed. *Moral Conduct and Authority: The Place of Adab in South Asian Islam*. Berkeley, CA: University of California Press, 124–151.

Mehta, U. (1990) 'Liberal Strategies of Exclusion', *Politics & Society* 18 (4): 427–454.

Mestiri, M. (2004) 'From the Fiqh of Minorities to the Fiqh of Citizenship'; paper presented at the AMSS Conference 'Fiqh Today – Muslims as Minorities', London, 21 February 2004.

Nielsen, J. (1992) *Towards a European Islam*. London: Macmillan Press.

—— (2002) 'New Centres and Peripheries in European Islam?', in B. Roberson, ed. *Islam and the Shaping of the Current Islamic Reformation*, *Mediterranean Politics*, vol.7, no.3, pp. 64–81.

Oubrou, T. (2004) 'La sharî'a de minorité: réflexions pour une intégration légale de l'islam', in Frégosi, Franck, ed. *Lectures contemporaines du droit islamique – Europe et monde arabe*. Strasbourg: Presses universitaires de Strasbourg.

Peter, F. (2006) 'Islamism, Islamic Reformism and the Public Stigmatization of Muslims: A Study of Muslim Discourses in France', *Oriente Moderno*. n.s. 25 (3): 443–460.

—— (2010) 'Welcoming Muslims into the Nation. Tolerance Politics and Integration in Germany', in Jocelyne Césari, ed. *Muslims in Europe and the United States since 9/11*. London: Routledge, pp. 119–144.

Qaradawi, Yusuf al- (1985) *Non-Muslims in the Islamic Society*. Indianapolis, Indiana: American Trust Publications.

—— (2000) *The Priorities of the Islamic Movement in the Coming Phase*. London: Awakening Publications.

—— (2001) *Fi Fiqh al-Aqalliyyat al-Islamiyya: Hayat al-Muslimin wast al-Mujtam'at al-'Ukhr*. Cairo: Dar al-Shuruq.

—— (2007) 'al-Watan wa 'l-Muwātana: fi daw' al-Usūl al-ʿAqadiyya wa 'l-Maqāsid al-Sharʿiyya', Paper presented at the ECFR's 17th session in Sarajevo, May 2007.

Ramadan, T. (2003) *Les musulmans d'Occident et l'avenir de l'islam*. Paris: Sindbad / Actes Sud.

—— (2009) *Radical Reform: Islamic Ethics and Liberation*. Oxford: Oxford University Press.

Roald, A.-S. (2001) 'The Wise Men: Democratization and Gender Equalization in the Islamic Message: Yusuf al-Qaradawi and Ahmad al-Kubaisi on the Air', *Encounters* 7 (1): 29–55.

Rohe, M. (2004) 'The Formation of a European Sharī'a', in Jamal Malik, ed. *Muslims in Europe: From the Margin to the Centre*. Münster: Lit Verlag.

Roy, O. (1999) *Vers un islam européen*. Paris: Éditions Esprit.

Sultan, S. (2008) *Al-dawabit al-manhajiyya li-l-ijtihad fi fiqh al-aqalliyyat*. USA: Sultan Publishing.

Williams, Rowan (2008) 'Civil and Religious Law in England: A Religious Perspective', *Ecclesiastical Law Journal* 10: 262–282.

Zaman, M.Q. (2002) *The Ulama in Contemporary Islam: Custodians of Change*. Princeton and Oxford: Princeton University Press.

—— (2005) 'The Scope and Limits of Islamic Cosmopolitanism and the Discursive Language of the *'Ulama*'', in Miriam Cooke and Bruce Lawrence, eds. *Muslim Networks from Hajj to Hip Hop*. Chapel Hill and London: The University of North Carolina Press.

Zakzouk, M. (2007) *Objectives of Islamic Shari'ah and the Need for Renewal*. Cairo: Supreme Council for Islamic Affairs – Ministry of Al-Awqaf.

Chapter 10

Terror in the faculty lounge[1]

Addressing the politics of fear and the politics of difference in government security policies

Katherine E. Brown

1. Introduction

> 'Two held in terror swoop on campus'
>
> (Press Association, 15 May 2008)

> 'MGS seeks to unite all those Muslimahs[2] who have a strong interest either in promoting or pursuing education. This can be in any capacity, from those wishing to enter university from A Level's to adult learners wanting to go back to education . . . We believe that Muslim Sisters in the UK need to work together to achieve the standards of British Muslims'
>
> (Muslimah Graduate Society homepage 2008)

The aim of this chapter is to explore the dynamic relationship between two forms of politics in the UK: fear and difference. The way in which the politics of fear has co-opted the discourse of difference fundamentally undermines the development of multifaceted public identities, such as those based on religion. This debate is not just an issue of Islam within Britain, but also highlights the complex relationship in modern Britain between the citizen, human rights and the state. By way of example, the chapter addresses the securitisation of British universities and the challenges this presents to the development of civic-minded Muslim citizenship.

In contemporary British politics security dangers and fears are identified not so much as existential threats to the 'life of the nation' but as those which undermine the 'British way of life'. The UK security agenda has moved away from a 'military' external threat to 'homeland', such as those faced during

1 The analysis, opinions and conclusions expressed or implied in this chapter are those of the author and do not necessarily represent the views of the UK Joint Services Command and Staff College, the UK MOD, or any other governmental agency.

2 'Muslimah' is the feminine form in Arabic for Muslim, and is used here to denote that the focus is on Muslim women.

the Second World War,[3] towards an internal 'enemy within' which is perceived not to share 'our' values and customs. For example, Charles Clarke (MP) when introducing the 2006 Counter Terrorism Act said that:

> The government is determined to do everything possible to protect our citizens from those who seek to destroy our society, way of life and our freedoms . . .
>
> (Clarke 2006)

As a result of this security narrative, which also posits 'new terrorism' as motivated by extremist religious sentiments and carried out by a particular religious group targeting 'liberal ways of life', Afshar, Aitken and Franks argue that ordinary Muslims 'stand accused of being a threat to the West and its national security and insufficiently committed to the politics and values of their host communities' (2005: 262). This confirms a 'new racism' in Britain, 'which reconstitutes the discourse of "the Asian" through a foregrounding of "the Muslim": the latter having certain very particular pan-European and global connections' (Brah 1996: 169). Attention given to an emerging 'green peril' within and beyond UK borders has consequently provided the focus for a range of security policies covering ever more areas of social life (Ismail 2001; Ferguson 2004), including education. The shift in security policy matters and attendant rhetoric implicitly places 'the blame' for potential 'support for extremist sentiments' on multicultural policies in the past and on the sociological phenomena of multiculturalism. In February 2008 David Cameron, then leader of the opposition party, argued that 'we cannot continue with the multicultural apartheid' caused through the preservation of cultural differences and played out in education policies (www.conservatives.com). In particular students on university campuses are seen as vulnerable to the 'extremist message' because they exist outside of the 'common bonds' of community and nation and are exposed to foreign radicalising influences (Glees in Taylor and Smithers 2005; House of Representatives 2005). Such rhetoric prioritises 'fear' of the 'cultural other' in addressing security issues.

However, taking education as an example, such 'apartheid' may be more the consequence of poor implementation of multiculturalism and a failure to address the material conditions of minority groups than as a result of many cultures sharing educational and civic spaces. Research shows that across the education key stages Muslim children in Britain generally have lower levels of attainment than the national average, and lower levels than those of

3 Concerns about the 'defence' of the homeland remain but are no longer policy priorities, and various civil contingency acts and military roles endeavour to 'protect'. Please refer to Codner (2007).

white and some other ethnic groups (Department for Education and Skills 2006: 5). Detailed analyses of educational findings suggest that differences in achievement between various Muslim communities are linked to social class and length of stay in Britain (Department for Education and Skills 2003). In higher education, despite the differential acceptance rates between Muslims and whites with the same qualifications by British universities (40 per cent and 54 per cent) the proportion of Muslim children in higher education is slowly increasing (Anwar 2008). Stephen Twigg MP, in his forward to the Department for Education and Skills policy document, *Aiming High: Raising the Achievement of Minority Ethnic Pupils* (2003) argues that:

> for these pupils [Black and Pakistani], the achievement gaps remain unacceptably wide. They make it harder for them to go on to university or to access good jobs. And they increase the chances that those who miss out will disengage not only from education, but wider society.

The implications are clear, for the liberal state 'all children and young people should be able to achieve their potential' so that they make a positive contribution to society as active citizens (Department for Education and Skills 2003: 4, 7). Thus the apartheid to which Cameron refers emerges not then because of the politics of multiculturalism, but as a structural failure to enable equal access to the 'public sphere'. Policies and aspirations to improve access to the public sphere, although not always successful or far-reaching enough, are characteristic of the UK approach to multiculturalism and what Modood (2003) terms the 'politics of difference'.

In order to fully explore the relationship between these two forms of politics in the UK, of fear and difference, this chapter first outlines the rise of a religio-political identity among British Muslims as part of the 'politics of difference'; in particular it notes the emergence of 'British-Islam', which places emphasis on pursuit of education and 'active citizenship'. The paper then moves on to consider legal and policy changes to manage fear through the promotion of a secure British identity: in this context the current attempts by government to encourage British universities to 'spy' on Muslim students, and recent arrests of British students on terrorism-related offences are discussed. These two sections demonstrate an inherent contradiction in government policy towards a post-national and post-multicultural state and its attempts to manage fear. Specifically, it is argued that securitising the space of 'the university' runs counter to the effort to encourage pluralism and civic-minded Muslim citizenship.

II. The politics and policies of difference

Traditionally, the politics of difference asserts that minority groups have distinct cultures, experiences and perspectives which should be valued rather than triumphed over (Smith and Stephenson 2005). As part of this process the recognition and incorporation of different identities in the civic realm is required to facilitate group representation necessary to overcome systematic oppression faced by minority groups within 'the normal processes of everyday life' (Young 1990: 41). For Modood (2003) this demonstrates that 'equality' encompasses public ethnicity, where difference is acknowledged in both the public and private spheres. Public difference from a dominant culture and access to the public sphere is therefore negotiated and built through consensus rather than suppressed. To facilitate this, UK multicultural practices have always been 'laissez-faire' and under the New Labour Governments decentralised with responsibility devolved to the 'local' level (Cesari 2004; Jopkke 2004). Jack Straw summarises New Labour's approach towards multiculturalism in his championing of the Race Relations Amendment Act (2000) where he concluded 'full delivery of the Action Plan[4] can only be a start on the road to delivering a truly multi-cultural Britain, not just free from the scourge of racism, but where diversity becomes a cornerstone of our modern society' (BBC 2000). In the longer term, this vision encourages the uneven but ongoing transformation of political identities of minority groups in the UK, such that their 'coloured' migratory experience no longer defines them (Modood 2003).

Despite the aspirations of the 'politics of difference' the identity formation of migrant and minority communities in the UK has been marked by struggles against oppression which deny materially and symbolically the legitimacy of their difference. Their oppression has been primarily organised around racism stemming from the legacy of colonialism in immigration policy and popular politics (Fekete 2004). Initially, ethnic minority communities were engaged in the struggle against racism through the promotion of Black-ethnic identity. During the late 1970s and 1980s, acceptable difference to the dominant culture was re-negotiated to include 'racial' difference thereby allowing equal access to the public sphere and the state for 'non-White' citizens. This process is seen, for example, in the emergence of Race Relations Acts. However, this subsumed many differences under a 'black' identity, which was defined as the common experiences of oppression of non-whites. As a form of essentialism, it focused on the differences of groups from each other, and stressed the internal coherence of bounded groups of different 'others'. Consequently, this 'black' politics failed to incorporate adequately the layers and nuances of exclusion and identity among Britain's ethnic minority populations. For example, the different patterns of migration and

4 The Action Plan linked to the McPherson Report included 'initiatives aimed at monitoring staff in the public services, and highlighted the new emphasis on racial awareness training and the review of the National Curriculum to foster diversity' (Taylor 2000; Back et al. 2002: 447).

settlement between those emigrating from the Indian sub-continent and those from the Caribbean lead to different socio-economic vulnerabilities. Nor did it account for the variety of positions and activism adopted by different ethnic minority communities. In this sense it conflated the race riots in Brixton and Toxteth occurring in the 1980s with those protesting against Salman Rushdie in the 1990s (Glynn 2002).

However, in light of these failings, and following periods of self-identification, since the 1990s, recognition has been awarded through 'politics of difference' to a myriad of identities – some externally imposed, others self asserted – one of which is the increasing prominence of religious identities, including those based in Islam (Ranger 1996).[5] The importance of faith-based identities and communities were recognised in the inclusion of a question on religious affiliation in the 2001 census of the UK: the first time such a question was included for over a hundred years. The results of this census showed that 1.6 million individuals declared themselves to be Muslim, representing approximately 3 per cent of the population in Britain and Wales (National Statistics Office 2001). Indeed Muslim activists have campaigned for, and demanded, the inclusion of 'Muslim' identity – as opposed to 'Asian' identities – in politics for recognition and rights. Issues such as providing *halal* foods in schools, provision of prayer rooms in places of employment and protection from discrimination on the grounds of religion (as opposed to race) have entered into the public sphere. These issues are not ethnically 'Asian' – in that they do not affect Sikh or Hindu Asians in the same way.[6] This transformation of identity is further realised in the plethora of Muslim civic and civil society groups, such as the Muslim Parliament of Britain, An-nisa, the Islamic Society of Britain, the Young Muslim Society, Muslim Women's Help-line, Islamic Human Rights Commission, various *Shari'a* Councils, Mosque associations and locally arranged women's groups. The term 'British-Muslim' has been coined to indicate the dual focus of the identities among this group. As one Bangladeshi Islamist in Birmingham argued:

> A British identity is important and should be important for the Bangladeshi youth. On the other hand if they neglect their Islamic identity, it will be like assimilation . . . But you can't survive here in isolation; to live here you need to have both identities, British and Muslim. . . .
>
> (cited in Eade and Garbin 2005: 15)

5 Other factors have also led to the emergence of religiously focused identities, such as the abandonment of the myth of return among migrant families, the Salman Rushdie affair, and the French banning of the hijab in schools (Asad 1990; Brown 2006).

6 This is further notable as Sikhs and Jews are protected under the Race Relations Act whereas other faith-ethnic groups are not.

This combined focus has been demonstrated in a number of polls conducted in the UK since 2002 (ICM and The Guardian 2005; Blick et al. 2006; Choudhury 2007). Importantly, this new identity is contingent upon developments in national multicultural politics; it is self-consciously articulated in the public sphere, but it does not necessarily coincide with increased piety among Muslims (Lewis 1994: 176–8; Samad 2004).

Furthermore, these public identities are negotiated within the local as well as global contexts of everyday lives, such that at times this 'Islamic' identity and rights articulation is in tension with other positions held by groups and individuals. The census also revealed the differences within Muslim communities that resist homogenisation. The 'British Muslim' label is a convenient umbrella term that masks a variety of other identity positions: ethnicity, class and gender. For example, approximately 42 per cent of all British Muslims have a Pakistani ethnic heritage (National Statistics Office 2004). 'British Muslim', as an identity position vis-à-vis the state and other communities, is not static or timeless: the ways in which this is understood both by the groups themselves and by others has altered with the context in which they are rooted. Thus in the 'politics of difference' the incorporation and recognition of identities in the civic realm is an ongoing process.

Tensions between different aspects of public identities are visible in the determination of some Muslim groups to separate culture from religion. For these groups, those aspects of a culture which are perceived as oppressive from a rights perspective are denounced as non-Islamic. For example, as the coordinator of the nationally organised Muslim Women's Help Line (MWHL) said:

> Culture is engrained, the migrants brought their culture, but failed to bring or forgot their religious obligations beyond rituals.
>
> (2004)

She continued:

> The second generation are learning more, through Islamic societies (especially University based ones), and there is a change in thinking and a realisation of diversity. That they were only doing certain things because their parents did, not because it was Islamic.
>
> (2004)

As a result, traditions are changing, and culture is being redefined to include the customs and habits of Muslims from throughout the world. However, while managing the outside influences on the Muslim community, there are also attempts to portray/create a Muslim community which absorbs differences of race and ethnic heritage. Younger Muslims, it is argued, are attempting to rejuvenate their religious obligations and disentangle culture from faith. They are attempting to preserve their religious identity and prioritise it over their ethnic-cultural heritage. A theme often repeated in interviews in an attempt to separate out culture and religion is the suggestion that things 'occur that are forbidden in Islam'. In an interview Tahmina Saleem of the Islamic Society of Britain (2004) argued that violations of women's rights in Muslim communities 'are reflections of culture, not of Islam'. As with other Muslim groups it was clear that she considered that when violations occur of women's rights it is often because culture is confused with faith, because those perpetrators are not aware of the full range of rights afforded to women in Islamic jurisprudence (2004). For example, debates around women's access to higher education and marriage are seen to be renegotiated through this framework. Merali of the Islamic Human Rights Council argues that this debate between culture and religion is part of the search for suitable ethical codes and self-management in the modern context (Merali 2004). It is not possible to discuss the successes or failures of this attempt to separate religion from culture in this chapter; however, this new management of faith and culture suggests the beginning of positions which may accommodate new forms of discourse, identity and rights (c.f. Brown 2006). This negotiation has led to what many scholars are labelling as 'British Islam' and indicates attempts to reconfigure the consensus which identifies acceptable difference in the public sphere.[7]

A. British Islam, rights, and women's education

One way in which this management of faith and culture is occurring is in debates regarding the promotion of women's education. Increasingly as part of 'British Islam' there is an emphasis on rights of education, including for women. Some of the non-governmental organisations espousing a 'British-Islam' interviewed for this research found resistance among traditional representatives of Islam and Muslim communities to their redefinitions of Islam, faith and women's roles. For example the Muslimah Graduate Society said that some opposition was encountered to the idea of creating a female Muslim graduate society because 'women shouldn't be at university in the first place' (Muslimah Graduate Society 2004). However, the interviewee felt that such attitudes were changing and a product of culture rather than religion, thereby making a distinction between traditional religious practices and 'British-Islam'. Furthermore, more commonly noted among the interviewees were Muslim women's educational achievements and the rights afforded to them in Islam with regard to lifelong learning. For the editor of *The Revival* magazine, Sajid Iqbal (based in Manchester, this is a magazine which aims

7 Although some prefer to identify this as part of a European-wide development – 'Euro-Islam'. Please refer to Nielsen (1999); Klausen (2008); Cesari (2004).

to make Islam more relevant to young people), lifelong education was seen as both a right and a duty of all Muslims regardless of gender (2004). In nine of the ten interviews conducted among Muslim civil society groups a woman's right to education was explicitly stated and located in religious texts. Thus educational attainment was a necessary requirement of religious fulfilment. Indeed the Muslimah Graduate Society understands its work to support Muslim women in their quest for education in this way; the section on their website 'Women in Islam' lists the number of ways in which rights and citizenship are implicit and explicit in the holy texts of Islam. Through their activities the organisation not only promotes 'religious education' but also provides careers guidance and a further education hardship fund.

The right to education is also considered as a protection against violations of rights in marriage. It was seen as a survival strategy in a modern economy where the family may not be able financially to support an estranged wife. As one woman aptly argued 'A degree is a must, but not necessarily for a career but [sic] if you've studied then you could support yourself, just in case' (thirty-three-year-old South Asian housewife 1999). She continued:

> I'm educated, and I know I can get a job and support myself, so obviously I'm not bothered by it (leaving a marriage/domestic abuse) . . . I know I can cope on my own . . . But these women (wives from the Indian subcontinent) because they are not educated, and they haven't been to European countries or anywhere (before marriage), it's totally different to them, so what do they do if they leave their husbands? They've no-one to turn to, their family are in Pakistan, and nobody tells them how they can get income support and things like . . . and here she can't work or anything like that coz she's not educated . . . they're stuck with their husbands no matter what.
>
> (Thirty-three-year-old South Asian housewife 1999)

Thus education also provides British female Muslim citizens with the tools by which to guarantee and protect additional rights. Indeed, Afshar, Aitken and Franks argue that their British education, and the demands it makes of students to have enquiring minds, creates a new individualistic approach to identity, faith and belonging (2005: 268). This is a reciprocal relationship and according to Tariq Ramadan (2004), acquiring education is not simply placed as a religious duty, but being a 'good Muslim' also requires civic engagement, which demands knowledge of your political, social and physical environment. Engle and Ochoa (1988) argue that being a 'democratic citizen' means exercising independent judgement, where education cannot be limited to being socialised in unquestioning ways. Contrary to stereotypes about Islamic religious education, what was found in a number of interviews was an assertion of active research, with a questioning mind-set that challenged authority figures and sought practical application of knowledge. An example of this is found in the June 2008 'Urban Muslim Woman Event', which emphasises Muslim women's agency and independence as citizens, and promotes their involvement in decision-making forums. Thus vernacular 'British-Islam' requires participation in the politics of difference and enables them to participate freely in the public sphere.

However, a more contentious topic (than simply maintaining the right to education within Muslim communities) is the nature of that education and the setting in which it should take place. In the interviews I conducted, Islamic single-sex schools and the issue of Muslim girls' school uniforms in state schools were commonly referred to as ways of fulfilling educational rights. The debate surrounding school uniform centres on the right (or otherwise) of young Muslim women to wear in schools a hijab and jilbab,[8] which are linked to issues of identity, citizenship and rights (Dwyer 2001). Throughout the research, the hijab debate has been ongoing, frequently igniting fears that the hijab and face veils might be banned in the UK, as in France (Al Jazeera 2010). On a BBC *Panorama* programme a number of Muslim women were interviewed on a variety of issues including the *hijab*. They implied that their right to wear the *hijab* at school enabled them to pursue their educational rights (White et al. 2004). Furthermore, decisions to restrict schoolgirls from wearing either the jilbab, niqab or hijab are seen as violations on rights to education: for example, the case of Shebina Begum, where the school objected to her decision to wear a jilbab, and she claimed interference with her right to manifest her religion and right to education protected by the European Convention on Human Rights (*Begum v Denbigh High School Governors*, 2004; *R (On the Application of Begum) v Headteacher and Governors of Denbigh High School*, 2006). Although the House of Lords later held that it was not a violation of Article 9, the framing and discourse of this case demonstrates how central the 'politics of difference' is to the construction of Muslim women's rights in the UK. In light of the Muslim Council of Britain's report to Bernard Stassi on the French Government ban of the *hijab* in schools, the representative I interviewed argued that 'The right to wear religious symbols links with the right to participate fully in civil society and the right to express your identity' (Muslim Council of Britain 2003). In eight out of ten interviews conducted with UK-based non-governmental Muslim organisations about rights and citizenship, the *hijab* was referred to directly in relation to education. It appeared to function in two ways: firstly as a symbol of the right of Muslim women to express their religious identity in the public-political sphere; and secondly as a tool to access that sphere safely and legitimately (Muslim Council of Britain 2003; Iqbal 2004; Qureshi 2004). Thus while theological and traditional reasons about the hijab remain contested, the contemporary framing of the *hijab* demonstrates how 'British-Islam' is embedded in a political and civic culture.

8 A *jilbab* is a long loose-fitting overcoat.

Nevertheless, the adoption of veiling practices by Muslim women in the UK is often perceived as a marker of difference which is often linked to debates about radicalisation.[9] The perceived radicalisation of British Muslim university students, often personified/symbolised by students who wear Islamic dress, also draws on these debates. The decision by Imperial College London, on security grounds, to ban face veiling is symptomatic of this linkage (Garner 2005). A year later the Higher Education Minister, Mr Bill Rammell, supported Imperial College's decision stating that: 'Muslim students were entitled to ask for tolerance and consideration but there were limits to what they could and should ask for' (*The Guardian* 2006). Rammell places limits on the 'politics of difference' by claiming that Muslim students (and others) are 'unreasonable' in their expectations and demands vis-à-vis the liberal state (specifically here, in higher education institutions).

Thus, as the debates on *hijab* and access to higher education indicate, a form of identification among British Muslims emerges from the interaction with their socio-political environment and their religious beliefs. It particularly emphasises rights which encourage engagement with the public sphere where difference is recognised (Tarlo 2007). It is therefore contingent and flourishes within the continued development of the 'politics of difference' found in multiculturalism. However, alongside this move towards a political agency based on Muslim identity have been rising fears of a 'fifth column', which has thrown British multiculturalism into disarray. The perception of a 'multi-cultural' Trojan horse is reinforced by a political environment which prioritises the duty of government to 'protect' citizens (Modood 2003; Sparks 2003).

III. The politics and policies of fear

The politics of fear attempts to manage or eradicate threats to the state, and focuses on eradicating both existential threats to the nation and those which threaten the 'British way of life' via counter-terrorism discourses (Sparks 2003). Thus 'danger is not an objective condition. It [sic] is not a thing that exists independent of those to whom it may become a threat' (Campbell 1998: 1–2). The articulation of danger relies on threats being represented in terms that are vilified by a community not simply by stating existential threats to the territorial state (Campbell 1998). In the UK case, dangers which are perceived to stem from 'radical Islam' are often granted such characteristics, because 'radical Islam' is understood to be antithetical to the 'liberal way of life'. The 2007 *Building on Progress* policy review makes this linkage clear: support for extremist sentiments and parties indicates support for values and

9 The comments of Jack Straw MP regarding veiling as a 'visible statement of separation and of difference' provoked some outcry (BBC 2006b).

social norms that are counter to those that should be at the core of a modern British identity (Cabinet Office 2007: 89).

Thus, while most security-orientated legislation and policing activity focus on the criminal activities of terrorists, other security aspects focus on issues of identity and multiculturalism. For example, 'home-grown' suspected terrorists are seen to lack a strong link to 'British identity' and are apart from the commonalities that 'bind citizens together' (Her Majesty's Government 2007). These absences are seen to make the carrying out of terrorist activity conceivable for the individuals involved (Home Affairs Committee 2005: 52). One soft measure to counter this can be seen in the re-justifying of citizenship classes, which, whether occurring in schools or mosques, are now explicitly linked to counter-terrorism rather than seen as a measure to increase young adults' participation in civil society or to curb anti-social behaviour.

Current counter-terrorism measures have taken new forms to meet the changing needs of the post 9-11 and 7-7 security environment and are brought together in the Government's strategy: CONTEST and CONTEST 2. CONTEST contains four key elements: pursue, protect, prevent, prepare. Although these have existed since 2003, they are reiterated in the UK 2006 strategy for *Countering International Terrorism* (Her Majesty's Government 2006). These strands aim to tackle radicalisation of individuals, lessen the terrorist threat by disrupting terrorists' activities, reduce vulnerability of the public and key national services, and ensure that the UK is 'as ready as it can be' for the consequences of a terrorist attack (Her Majesty's Government 2006: 1–2). A fifth component concerning community cohesion and resilience is also envisaged in *Preventing Extremism Together* and in CONTEST 2 on 'winning hearts and minds' (Department for Communities and Local Government 2005, 2007; Her Majesty's Government 2009). This combination of elements ensures that many areas of socio-political life are incorporated within the remit of counter-terrorism, including legislation, policing and citizenship.

For the eradication of fear to be efficient in this framework, new legislation has been introduced. Justifications for changes in law are based on demonstrations that there is an immediate danger to 'the public' posed by a 'real' and 'serious' threat. The most significant change to the law is the anti-terrorist legislation put forward by the government in 2001 and 2006. The Anti-terrorism, Crime and Security Act (ATCSA) 2001 extends provisions of earlier laws by removing spatial and temporal restrictions on police counter-terrorism powers. It provides for the detention, pending deportation, of foreign nationals suspected of being terrorists; increases powers of arrest in certain areas; and protects critical national infrastructure. The Terrorism Act 2006 provides further consolidation by creating a number of new criminal offences, primarily relating to the preparation, encouragement and dissemination of publications pertaining to terrorism and related training offences. Charles Clarke, who was Home Secretary in 2006, said of the 2006 Act that:

> The Government is determined to do everything possible to protect our citizens from those who seek to destroy our society, way of life and our freedoms . . . These new measures will give our law enforcement agencies the additional powers they need to help prevent terrorism and prosecute terrorists.
>
> (Clarke 2006)

In this announcement key elements of security strategy are brought together: prevention, protection and prosecution. Charles Clarke also makes the clear distinction between 'our citizens' and 'terrorists'. (This distinction is discussed in more detail later.) Evidence of the success of this legislation is cited by reference to 'the hundred plus individuals waiting trial for terrorism related offences' (Clarke 2007). However, perceived failures led to demands for new legislation in the autumn of 2007 to improve the effectiveness of 'control orders', and to extend the detention of suspects without trial above the current limit (Branigan 2007).[10]

This legislation has two main effects: first it criminalises Muslim communities, and second it de-politicises the threat. Crime, deviancy and criminality have been securitised. While the definition of terrorism has expanded, encompassing 'serious disruption', the definition of a terrorist has narrowed to simply that of a criminal (Gearty 2005).[11] When this new legislation is combined with a wider moral concern (even moral panic) it helps creates the persona of the 'Islamic radical-criminal', who is not countenanced as 'British' (Campbell 1998). The Home Secretary, Jacqui Smith, stated this directly:

> Let us be clear – terrorists are criminals, whose victims come from all walks of life, communities and religious backgrounds. Terrorists attack the values that are shared by all law-abiding citizens.
>
> (Smith 2007)[12]

10 The indefinite detention without trial of suspects – as outlined in the 2001 Act – was deemed unlawful by the courts. New methods of controlling 'suspect' terrorists who cannot be prosecuted in the courts have been put in place known as 'Control Orders' (BBC 2005).

11 Including a wider range of criminal 'protest' activities – Animal Rights Activists are now labelled as 'terrorists' for example (Home Office and Northern Ireland Office 1998 para 3.17). See also, Anti-terrorism, Crime and Security Act 2001, s.21(1), and Walker (2002: 20–30).

12 It is also worth noting that the respected Islamic Scholar, the late Shykh al-Azhar Jad al-Haqq, 'Ali Jad al-Haqq' of Al-Azhar University, Cairo largely agrees. In 1995 he argued that 'those who [commit violence] are not Islamists and do not represent Islam. They are criminals who must be punished. Every individual who challenges public order and the State's authority and power must be punished. Such an individual is not an Islamist at all. Those who make mischief in the land are the enemies of God and his prophet [pbh]' in *Al-Jumhuriyah* 23 February 1995 p. 2. This is Egypt's main newspaper. Also at: www.algomhuria.net.eg/algomhuria/today/fpage.

The framing of terrorism as an attack on values is important in the understanding of the new threat. Terrorist activity is now understood as a consequence of irrational, unbounded and non-negotiable [religious] ideology as opposed to tangible discrete 'political causes' (Ruby 2002; Wiktorowicz 2005). The 2007 *Building on Progress* policy review argues that the current threat is 'from those who seek to cause the death and destruction in the name of a perversion of the faith of Islam' (Cabinet Office 2007: 8). Tony Blair also argued that extremism was not caused by 'flawed' multiculturalism but 'in the name of an ideology alien to everything this country stands for' (Blair 2006b).

However, the government is keen to stress that this is not a 'war against Islam'; rather the government asserts that certain 'perverted' or 'radical' forms of Islam may encourage terrorist activity. Jackson argues that it is typically asserted that 'Islamic terrorism' is motivated largely by religious or 'sacred causes' which helps build the 'widely accepted "knowledge" that certain forms of Islam are by nature violent and terroristic' (2007: 405). The Muslim Council of Britain fears that, as a result, there is a pending criminalisation of orthodoxy (2004). Such depictions of 'radical as terrorist' Islam denies the multiple ways in which Islam is lived and believed, and prioritises particular understandings of faith over others. As a result, there are 'Good Muslims' and 'Bad Muslims'; 'Good Imams' and 'Bad Imams'; and so on (Birt 2006). The 'Bad Muslim' is a radicalised male and is said to represent one per cent of all British Muslims (Saggar 2006). However, although this distinction suggests a degree of subtlety on the part of policy makers, nevertheless the overall impression is that there is something within 'Islam' that makes it uniquely prone to being used as a justification for violence. Overall, terrorist threats are seen to reside with those who adhere to the Islamic faith because they always remain susceptible to the 'terrorist' message. The media too reflects this characterisation, for example as *The Daily Telegraph* published, 'it is the black heart of Islam, not its black face, to which millions object' and 'all Muslims, like all dogs, share certain characteristics' (Cummins 2004a, 2004b). The changes in legislation and framing of the security threat make this demonisation tolerated where it would not be for other groups (Islamic Human Rights Commission 2006: 56).

As a result, contemporary terrorist threats are seen to lack any possibility of 'explanation or mitigating circumstance, and [is] isolate[ed] as well, from representations of most other dysfunctions, symptoms and maladies of the contemporary world' (Said 1988: 47). Understanding terrorism in this way established a need to reinforce the values which terrorism seeks to undermine. This can be seen in the new legislation to deal with the dissemination of material which might support or glorify terrorist activity. Counter-balancing this affirmation of the liberal state values is a 'hearts and minds' strategy aimed at preventing (Islamic) radicalisation which is seen as the first step on the way towards supporting terrorism (Department for Communities and

Local Government 2005, 2007; Kelly 2007). Consequently the 'eradication' of fear becomes forcefully linked to issues of identity and citizenship.

A. Citizenship, identity and education

The above mechanisms indicate how CONTEST is implemented and incorporated into a new judicial framework. However, the first major report from the Home Affairs Committee, asserted that the strategy should be 'more than a set of police and judicial powers: it must be part of an explicit broader anti-terrorism strategy' (2005: 3). This is to be achieved by overcoming experiences of isolation and developing a vision of 'British identity' (Home Affairs Committee 2005) in three ways: reiterating the international element of terrorism; highlighting that terrorism is partly a problem of controlling foreigners; asserting that terrorists are not genuine citizens (Wolfendale 2006; Bulley 2008) and establishing ways of linking citizenship to identity as a counter-point to extremism and radicalisation.

Debates in the Houses of Parliament indicate that early on, terrorism was seen to relate to non-citizens, for example David Blunkett stated:

> I think that we all accept that there is a compelling need for more effective powers to exclude and remove suspected terrorists from our country. We rightly pride ourselves on the safe-haven that we offer to those genuinely fleeing terror. But our moral obligation and love of freedom does not extend to offering hospitality to terrorists.
>
> (2001)

Implicit in this is an assumption that government and security services are dealing with international terrorism, and therefore the terrorists are foreign.[13]

However, although the origins of the Islamic-terrorist threat are conceived of as lying outside of the UK, through processes of globalisation the 'Islamist world' is also seen as residing within state borders. This is epitomised by the phrase *Londonistan* (Philips 2006; Jackson 2007; *Le Figaro* 2007). The attacks on London in July 2005 by UK nationals destabilised the division between 'our citizens' and terrorists. The threat has become internalised, seen as emanating from deviant (Islamic) groups operating within tolerant democratic societies and not only from Muslim-majority states (Adamson and Grossman 2004). Unsettling the discursive link between foreign and terrorist, leads to a focus on citizenship embedded in a

13 This is not dissimilar to events in Germany, where in 2002 the leader of the Christian Democrats made a pledge during election campaigning to expel '4,000 Islamic fundamentalists' from the country (Hooper 2002).

'British identity'. One participant at the *Listening to Muslim Women* event in Manchester said, referring to those July 2005 bombings:

> If we see what happened in the UK this summer, they were British-born. How can someone brainwash them? Because they feel isolated, they don't feel they belong to Iraq or Pakistan or wherever their parents were from and don't feel British either.
>
> (Raz 2006: 41)

This question of identity was explicitly raised in the Home Affairs Committee report *Terrorism and Community Relations*, which dedicated an entire section to the issue. It concluded that 'questions of identity may be inextricably linked with the reasons which may lead to a small number of well-educated and apparently integrated young British people to turn to terrorism' (2005: 52). David Blunkett argued, 'it is religious extremism which forces them to choose, separating them from their citizenship and demanding the impossible' (2003). Those who commit acts of terrorism, and those associated with them, are rhetorically stripped of their British citizenship because these acts demonstrate that they did not identify with the 'commonalities that bind citizens' together (Her Majesty's Government 2007).

In an attempt to strengthen the 'commonalities that bind', the government has implemented 'hearts and minds' and 'community cohesion' policies in order to articulate 'Britishness' as part of the counter-terrorism strategy (Department for Communities and Local Government 2005, 2007). The terms of reference for anti-terrorist activities have broadened to incorporate this new element, focusing now on counter-radicalisation (The Security Service 2006). So, the 2007 policy review states that:

> Terrorism itself may not be prevented by increased [community] cohesion, but lack of cohesion is considered to be a significant factor behind communities allowing extremist feelings to go unchallenged and for not condemning extremist views. Support for extremist sentiments and parties indicates support for values and social norms that are counter to those that should be at the core of a modern British identity.
>
> (Cabinet Office 2007: 89)

The multicultural model premised on a 'politics of difference' is now seen to have significant problems, namely minimal cultural contact between distinct different communities and conflict over material resources (Jopkke 2004; McGhee 2005). This 'weak integration', emerging from old multicultural polices, is said to lead to radicalisation and increased security threats in the form of 'home-grown' terrorism; this can be overcome through developing a 'meta-community'. Thus a new 'politics of difference' occurs, through emphasising the need for communities to be drawn together by a 'meta-community' united by 'civic renewal' and 'civic integration' to increase a sense of 'nationhood' (Cantle 2001, 2006; Joppke 2004). These common bonds based on a 'civic integration' agenda are premised on 'liberal' democratic principles and procedures, such that the 'liberal way of life' or 'British way of life' is prioritised and overcoming particular traditions and practices of 'other' different groups.

Tony Blair's speeches towards the end of his premiership insisting on a 'more hard-line' stance towards Muslim communities also reflects this troubling of British Muslim citizenship and identities formed under the 'politics of difference' (2006a; BBC 2006a; *The Scotsman* 2006). Muslim communities are held responsible for tackling signs of difference and non-cohesiveness (BBC 2006b, 2006a), a requirement articulated by Denis MacShane, MP for Rotherham, who demanded that Muslims must choose 'the British way' or the 'way of terrorists' (2006).[14] The special duty of Muslims to detect terrorists is emphasised because it is believed that:

> This new generation of terrorists is more discreet than its predecessors. They no longer gather at Mosques, where clerics rant against Western governments, or congregate with known militants. Instead they prefer to set up their own youth clubs, using back rooms in parents' houses to devise their schemes.
>
> (McGrory 2006)

More recently, universities have been identified as spaces where this 'new generation' of Muslims gather. This has resulted in Ministerial requests that academics 'spy' on Muslim students at British universities. Since April 2005 the issue of 'radicalism' on university campuses has emerged on an annual basis. In April 2005 Claude Moniquet[15] testified to the Committee on International Relations of the US House of Representatives, claiming that the expansion of radical Islam in Europe was helped by the presence of refugees in universities who fled their native country 'because of repression for their Islamist activities'. He continued 'in Universities we find cells of Islamist of terrorist movements such as the Muslim Brothers, Hezbollah or Hamas, Algerian, Moroccan, Tunisian or Turkish groups etc . . .' (House of Representatives 2005: 35). In July 2005 the Higher Education Minster, Mr Rammell, told university vice-chancellors that there would 'have to be a debate' about the role universities will play in confronting the 'evil ideology' that brought about the London bombings (Curtis 2005). At this time there were also

14 This is not the first time Denis MacShane MP has made such claims: in 2003 he demanded that it is 'time for the elected and community leaders of British Muslims to make a choice' between being British or Muslim' (*The Guardian* 2003).

15 Claude Moniquet is the Director General of European Strategic Intelligence and Security Centre – a think-tank based in Brussels.

reports that 'security services' had 'barred more than 200 foreign students from the UK' since 2001 'amid fear they could present a security threat' (Curtis 2005). By September 2005, the Education Secretary demanded a 'clamp down on student extremists' (Taylor and Smithers 2005). A report by Professor Glees of Brunel University argued that 'It is in this environment [university] that these groups can flourish without being detected' (cited in Taylor and Smithers 2005). In April 2006 Hizb-ut-Tahrir' members re-ignited the debate by protesting that the group was falsely accused of being a terrorist group. Their actions were part of a campaign to have them removed from the NUS 'no-platform' list but was reported as primarily about rising 'radicalisation' on British campuses. In reporting by *The Guardian* attempts were made to show how support for Hizb-ut-tahrir was widespread among Muslim students and their representative organisations (Federation of Student Islamic Societies; FOSIS) (Lewis 2006). FOSIS responded to *The Guardian* article by arguing that although many Muslim students disagreed with Hizb-ut-tahrir they supported its right to free speech and to exist. And, further, that such support did not demonstrate that FOSIS or other Muslim students are 'influenced by a hardcore of extremists' or that this 'represents a new and dangerous flirtation with radicalism' as *The Guardian* article suggested (Kahn 2006). By October that year, 'radicalisation' of students was once again reported as a 'growing problem at some UK universities' (Gardner 2006). This time 'Muslim sources' claimed that 'on certain campuses radical Islamist groups have secretly been recruiting new members, preying on those they regard as vulnerable' (Gardner 2006). London Metropolitan University's appointment of a 'respected moderate Imam' to 'tackle the problem' was seen as one of the ways in which universities are responding to public fears (Gardner 2006). However, this was not seen as sufficient, and later that month *The Guardian* gained access to a draft document by the Department for Education which announced that it would be providing universities with information about how to inform 'special branch' about suspicious activities of students of 'Asian appearance' (Dodd 2006). Ruth Kelly asserted that academic staff were not being asked to 'spy' but rather to monitor their students (Taylor et al. 2006; BBC 2006c). The document was released the following month, which aimed to give 'practical guidance' about tackling the promotion of 'extremism in the name of Islam'. The document asks academic staff to 'become more vigilant and take preventative action to tackle violent extremism' (BBC 2006d). It was not until July 2007 that the issue re-emerged when five British Muslim students were jailed for downloading and sharing 'extremist material'. The reporting was framed by the constant reference to their 'student' status (they were at Bradford University) (BBC 2007). With the new academic year, fears of 'radicalism' on campuses emerged in October 2007, when the Prime Minister announced he would update guidance to universities regarding extremism and affirmed the government view that they had a significant role to play in combating terrorism (Lipsett 2007). Jonathan Evans, head of the

UK domestic spy agency MI5, warned in November 2007 that there is evidence that extremists are grooming children and teenagers for attacks against Britain (Stringer 2008). In January 2008 the government reissued the advice it gives universities, this time confirming that although 'there is no single profile' 'they are likely to be young – generally younger than 30 – and male, although the number of women who support and participate in violent extremism is increasing' (BBC 2008a). And in February 2008, the five students convicted of terrorism offences the year before were released after a Court of Appeal decision, much to the disdain of politicians and the media. The Appeal court decision means that the prosecution team now has to demonstrate that the material was intended for terrorist use (*The Times* 2008). The Islamic Human Rights Commission said it hoped that the Appeal Court's judgement would stop the 'criminalisation of Muslim youth for downloading and reading material that is widely available to everyone' (BBC 2008b).[16]

This three-year concern with the perceived threat of radicalisation on British campuses and the responses by Islamic groups, university unions and other university representatives confirms inherent limitations in this policy.[17] The guidance by the government re-affirms trends away from the 'politics of difference' towards the 'politics of fear'. As universities respond to fears of 'radicalisation' on campus, Muslim community reactions are as yet unreported. Nevertheless, the *niqab* ban by Imperial College London and the promotion of a culture of 'monitoring' students is unlikely to encourage young Muslim (women) into higher education. Matthew Boulton College has also banned 'religious student groups' (Kahn 2006), thereby making what Werbner (2007) refers to as 'ethnic empowerment' virtually impossible, as this relies on 'autonomous ethnic spaces' that are now banned. Making universities 'unsafe' spaces for Muslim women, by subjecting Muslim women to the increased 'gaze' of security services and staff and by preventing them from observing religious dress, is likely to hinder their attempts to convince families and

16 This has not been the case as, in May 2008, a university student and member of staff were arrested for downloading an edited version of al-Qaeda's training manual from the US government website (Newman 2008). A spokesman for Nottingham University stated that: 'There was no reasonable rationale for this person to have that information . . . The police were called in on the basis of reasonable anxiety and concern' (cited in Newman 2008). He added that the edited version of the al-Qaeda handbook was 'not legitimate research material' in the university's view (cited in Newman 2008).

17 It is now in fact a five-year concern. The issue re-emerged following UCL graduate and former FOSIS president Umar Farouk Abdulmutallab's arrest in the US, Christmas Day 2009, for attempting to blow up an aeroplane. This led to the Centre for Social Cohesion to report that 'British university campuses are breeding grounds of Islamic extremism' (2010 p.v; see also Quilliam Foundation 2010). In 2010, recently graduated Roshonara Choudry, re-ignited the issue of radicalisation among university students, as 'despite' her first-class academic career, she attempted to stab to death an MP because he voted in favour of the war in Iraq (Reisz 2011).

communities of the appropriateness of higher education. As a result, attempts to reinforce the commonalities that bind, and the eradication of 'material' factors which hinder integration, such as through the promotion of higher education, are unlikely to succeed given the focus on the purging of danger in these security policies aimed at universities.

The focus on universities as sites of fear, and sites of recruitment to radicalisation, is one indicator of the broader trend of securitisation (Wæver 1995). Religion has become the over-arching frame and narrative in which Muslim communities in the UK has come to be viewed. In the securitised context, such an association of religion with danger generally, problematises the development of Muslim identities in the UK. In the process of securitisation, a Muslim student's identity and politics become reduced to a homogenising radicalised position, rather than being recognised as diverse and multifaceted. Thus the symbolic ways in which the 'meta-community' and 'civic integration' and the commonality of 'nationhood' are being articulated in security policy and institutionalised in practice, risks disenfranchising Muslim citizens.

IV. Conclusion

It is argued in this paper that the growing securitisation of Muslim students, and university campuses, implies that Islam is perceived as a threat to the 'British way of life' and the liberal state. In attempts to protect liberal democratic principles and procedures the government has identified a need to 'revitalise' citizenship based on the 'commonalities that bind' numerous communities into a 'meta-community'. However, the fundamental issue with the attempts to create such a 'meta-community' is the 'symbolic' terms on which commonality is created and institutionalised. Muslims are effectively locked out of this through the foregrounding of such initiatives in the politics of fear. In this sense, it is not so much the politics of difference as the fundamental problem of definition of the point of commonality that allows difference.[18] This foregrounding has led to an emphasis on the ethnic and religious minorities' cultural differences in the creation of the meta-community, and specifically a need for government to 'reach out' to minority youth and women and to eradicate 'radicalisation' in dangerous spaces – such as mosques and universities (McGhee 2005; Brown 2008). However, although acknowledging the importance of identity and citizenship in soft measures, the implementation of 'harder' security policies makes it increasingly difficult for some citizens to achieve the minimum liberal standards demanded through the 'squeezing' of public space (Adamson and Grossman 2004). In this chapter, policies promoting universities' surveillance of their Muslim students have

18 I would like to thank Dr Adam Geary for highlighting this point.

been examined as indicative of this squeezing effect. Furthermore, this squeezing of the public space runs contrary to multicultural policies premised on 'equal opportunity accompanied by cultural diversity in an atmosphere of mutual tolerance' (Roy Jenkins 1966 cited in Back et al. 2002). Consequently, such attention on 'unsafe spaces' has the potential to undermine efforts by Muslims living in the UK to engage as 'active citizens' and to create a vernacular Islam that promotes 'civic integration' and education. As Amnesty International argues:

> For many years the UK authorities have been undermining human rights, the rule of law and the independence of the judiciary in the name of combating terrorism. They have persecuted people labelled a "threat to national security".
>
> (2006)

The focus on an uncontrolled and unsurveyed Muslim student body functions within this security discourse as a way of delegitimising the 'politics of difference'. In this debate recurring imagery is apparent in the construction of danger and the way it is used to justify new security policies to the detriment of policies aimed at promoting the 'politics of difference'.

References

Adamson, F. and Grossman, A. (2004) *Framing Security in a Post-9/11 Context*, Background Report for the Program on Global Security and Cooperation, The Social Science Research Council. Available HTTP: www.ssrc.org/programs/gsc/gsc_activities/migration/backgroundpapers.page (accessed 3 June 2007).

Afshar, H., Aitken, R. and Franks, M. (2005) 'Feminisms, islamophobia, and identities', *Political Studies* 53: 262–83.

Al-Haqq, Shykh al-Azhar Jad al-Haqq 'Ali Jad (1995) 'Those who commit violence are not Islamists', *Al-Jumhuriyah* 23 February, 2. Cited in Tamir, M. (2000) 'Conflict and cooperation between the state and religious institutions in Egypt', *International Journal of Middle East Studies* 32: 3–22.

Al Jazeera (2010) 'UK minister rejects veil ban calls Immigration chief says copying French ban on face coverings would be "un-British".' *Al Jazeera English*, 18th July 2010. Available HTTP: http://english.aljazeera.net/news/europe/2010/07/20107181778114793.html (accessed August 2010).

Amnesty International (2006) 'United Kingdom: Human rights: a broken promise' (London, Amnesty International). Available HTTP: http://web.amnesty.org/library/pdf/EUR450042006ENGLISH/$File/EUR4500406.pdf (accessed 27 March 2011).

Anwar, M. (2008) 'Muslims in western states: The British experience and the way forward', *Journal of Muslim Minority Affairs* 28(1): 125–37.

Asad, T. (1990) 'Multiculturalism and British identity in the wake of the Rushdie affair', *Politics and Society* 18(4): 455–80.

Back, L., Keith, M., Khan, A., Shukra, K. and Solomos, J. (2002) 'New Labour's white heart: Politics, multiculturalism and the return of assimilation', *Political Quarterly* 73(4): 445–54.

BBC (2000) 'Government defends Anti-Racism Record', 23 February. Available HTTP: http://news.bbc.co.uk/1/hi/uk/653134.stm (accessed 27 March 2011).

BBC (2005) 'Control orders explained', 12 March. Available HTTP: http://news.bbc.co.uk/1/hi/uk_politics/4343081.stm (accessed 27 March 2011).

BBC (2006a) 'Muslims "must root out extremism"', 4 July. Available HTTP: http://news.bbc.co.uk/1/hi/uk_politics/5144438.stm (accessed 27 March 2011).

BBC (2006b) Straw's veil comments spark anger, 5 October. Available HTTP: http://news.bbc.co.uk/1/hi/uk_politics/5410472.stm (accessed 27 March 2011).

BBC (2006c) 'Kelly denies Muslims demonised', 16 October. Available HTTP: http://news.bbc.co.uk/1/hi/uk_politics/6053992.stm (accessed 19 January 2008).

BBC (2006d) 'Campus radicals "serious threat"', 17 November 2006. Available HTTP: http://news.bbc.co.uk/1/hi/education/6155916.stm (accessed 8 April 2011).

BBC (2007) 'Extremist students sentenced', 26 July. Available HTTP: http://news.bbc.co.uk/1/hi/uk/6917288.stm (accessed 22 January 2008).

BBC (2008a) 'Tackle extremism, academics urged', 22 January. Available HTTP: http://news.bbc.co.uk/1/hi/education/7200783.stm (accessed 27 March 2011).

BBC (2008b) 'Five students win terror appeal', 13 February. Available HTTP: http://news.bbc.co.uk/1/hi/uk/7242724.stm (accessed 18 February 2008).

Begum v. Denbigh High School Governors [2004] EWHC 1389 (Admin).

Birt, J. (2006) 'Good Imam, bad Imam: Civic religion and national integration in Britain post-9/11', *The Muslim World* 96: 687–705.

Blair, T. (2006a) 'Press Conference 4th July'. London: HMSO. Available HTTP: www.pm.gov.uk/output/Page4295.asp (accessed 27 March 2011).

Blair, T. (2006b) *Our Nation's Future: Multiculturalism and integration* (London: PM Office). Available HTTP: www.number-10.gov.uk/output/Page10563.asp (accessed 27 March 2011).

Blick, A., Choudhury, T. and Weir, S. (2006) *The Rules of the Game: Terrorism, community and human rights* (Democratic Audit, Human Rights Centre, University of Essex). Available HTTP: www.jrrt.org.uk/index.php?page=publication&showpublication=6 (accessed 8 April 2011).

Blunkett, David (2001) 'Anti-terrorism measures' Column 924 15th October 2001, House of Commons, Hansard. Available from: www.publications.parliament.uk/pa/cm200102/cmhansrd/vo011015/debtext/11015-06.htm#11015-06_spmin0 (accessed 7 April 2011).

Blunkett, D. (2003) 'One nation, many faiths: unity and diversity in multi-faith Britain', Heslington Address, York, 30 October. Available HTTP: http://press.homeoffice.gov.uk/documents/heslington.pdf?view=Binary (accessed 7 April 2011).

Brah, A.K. (1996) *Cartographies of Diaspora: Contesting identities* (London: Routledge).

Branigan, T. (2007) 'Brown sets out tougher plans in anti-terror battle', *The Guardian*, 4 June.

Brown, K. (2006) 'Realising Muslim women's rights: The role of Islamic identity among British Muslim women', *Women's Studies International Forum* 29: 417–30.

Brown, K. (2008) 'The promise and perils of women's participation in UK mosques: The impact of securitisation agendas on identity, gender and community', *British Journal of Politics and International Relations* 10(3): 472–91.

Bulley, D. (2008) '"Foreign" terror? London bombings, resistance and the failing state', *British Journal of Politics and International Relations* 10(3): 379–94.

The Cabinet Office (2007) *HM Government Policy Review – Building on progress: security, crime and justice*, London: Prime Minister's Strategy Unit, Cabinet Office. Available HTTP: http://webarchive.nationalarchives.gov.uk/20070402090122/cabinetoffice.gov.uk/policy_review/ (accessed 8 April 2011).

Cameron, D. (2008) 'Extremism, individual rights and the rule of law in Britain', Equality and Human Rights Commission Debate, 26 February 2008, London. Available HTTP: www.conservatives.com/tile.do?def=news.story.page&obj_id=142585 (accessed 27 March 2008).

Campbell, D. (1998, 2nd edn) *Writing Security: US foreign policy and the politics of identity* (Manchester: MUP).

Cantle, T. (2001) *Community Cohesion: A Report of the Independent Review Team* (London: Home Office).

Cantle, T. (2006) *Challenging Local Communities to Change Oldham*, The Institute of Community Cohesion, Coventry University. Available HTTP: www.oldham.gov.uk/cantle-review-final-report.pdf (accessed 27 March 2011).

Centre for Social Cohesion (2010) *Radical Islam on UK Campuses: A Comprehensive List of Extremist Speakers at UK Universities*, The Centre for Social Cohesion. Available HTTP: www.socialcohesion.co.uk/files/1292336866_1.pdf (accessed 27 March 2011).

Cesari, J. (2004) *When Islam and Democracy Meet: Muslims in Europe and the United States* (Basingstoke: Palgrave Macmillan).

Choudhury, T. (2007) *The Role of Muslim Identity Politics in Radicalisation (a study in progress)* (London: Department for Communities and Local Government). Available HTTP: www.communities.gov.uk (accessed 27 March 2011).

Clarke, C. (2006) *Powerful New Laws to Tackle Terrorism*. Available HTTP: http://press.homeoffice.gov.uk/press-releases/new-terrorism-laws (accessed 27 March 2011).

Clarke, P. (2007) *Learning from Experience – Counter Terrorism in the UK since 9/11, The Colin Cramphorn Memorial Lecture 24 April* (London: Policy Exchange). Available HTTP: www.policyexchange.org.uk/images/publications/pdfs/Learning_from_Experience_-_Jun__07.pdf (accessed 8 April 2011).

Codner, M. (2007) 'British defence policy – Rebuilding national consensus', *RUSI* 152(2): 18–22.

Cummins, W. (2004a) 'The Tories must confront Islam instead of kowtowing to it', *Sunday Telegraph*, 18 July.

Cummins, W. (2004b) 'Muslims are a threat to our way of life', *Sunday Telegraph*, 25 July.

Curtis, P. (2005) 'Minister urges action on campus extremism', *The Guardian*, Wednesday, 20 July 2005. Available HTTP: www.guardian.co.uk/education/2005/jul/20/highereducation.uk (accessed 18 August 2006).

Department for Communities and Local Government (2005) *Preventing Extremism Together.* Working Groups August–October 2005 Report, London: Department for Communities and Local Government.

Department for Communities and Local Government (2006) *Engaging with Muslim Women: a report from the P.M.'s event, 10th May 2006* (London: Department for Communities and Local Government, Women and Equality Unit).

Department for Communities and Local Government (2007) *Preventing Violent Extremism – Winning Hearts and Minds* (London: Department for Communities and Local Government, www.communities.gov.uk).

Department for Education and Skills (2003) *Aim High: Raising the achievement of ethnic minority pupils.* Available HTTP: www.education.gov.uk/publications/standard/publicationdetail/page1/DfES%200183%202003 (accessed 8 April 2011).

Department for Education and Skills (2006) *Ethnicity and Education: The Evidence on Minority Ethnic Pupils aged 5–16* (Research Topic Paper: 2006 edn). Available HTTP: http://publications.teachernet.gov.uk/eOrderingDownload/DFES-0208-2006.pdf (accessed 27 March 2011).

Dodd, V. (2006) 'Universities urged to spy on Muslims', *The Guardian*, Monday, 16 October 2006. Available HTTP: www.guardian.co.uk/uk/2006/oct/16/highereducation.topstories3?INTCMP=SRCH (accessed 8 April 2011).

Dwyer, C. (2001) 'Negotiating diasporic identities: Young British South Asian Muslim women', *Women Studies International Forum* 23(4): 475–86.

Eade, J. and Garbin, D. (2005) *The Bangladeshi Diaspora: Community dynamics, transnational politics and Islamist activities* (London: Foreign and Commonwealth Office).

Engle, S.H. and Ochoa, A.S. (1988) *Education for Democratic Citizenship: Decision making in the social studies* (Columbia: Teachers College Press).

Fekete, L. (2004) 'Anti-Muslim racism and the European security state', *Race and Class* 46(1): 3–29.

Ferguson, N. (2004) 'The way we live now: Eurabia', *New York Times*, 4 April. Available HTTP: http://query.nytimes.com/gst/fullpage.html?res=9A05E1D61E30F937A35757C0A9629C8B63 (accessed 19 January 2008).

Gardner, F. (2006) 'Campus Radicals "growing problem"' BBC, 5 October 2006. Available HTTP: http://news.bbc.co.uk/1/hi/uk/5411172.stm (accessed 21 January 2008).

Garner, R. (2005) 'Imperial College bans students from wearing hoodies and veils', *The Independent*, 23 November 2005. Available HTTP: www.independent.co.uk/news/education/education-news/imperial-college-bans-students-from-wearing-hoodies-and-veils-516547.html (accessed 19 January 2008).

Gearty, C. (2005) '11 September 2001, counter-terrorism, and the Human Rights Act', *Journal of Law and Society* 32(1): 18–33.

Glynn, S. (2002) 'Bengali Muslims: the new East End radicals?', *Ethnic and Racial Studies* 25(6): 969–88.

The Guardian (2003) 'Minister's call to choose outrages British Muslims', 22 November 2003.

The Guardian (2006) 'Rammell backs University's Muslim veil ban', 11 October. Available HTTP: http://education.guardian.co.uk/higher/news/story/0,,1896776,00.html (accessed 19 January 2008).

Her Majesty's Government (2006) *Countering International Terrorism: The United Kingdom's strategy*, July 2006, Cm 6888, London: The Stationery Office.

Her Majesty's Government (2007) *The Governance of Britain*, Cm 7170, London: The Stationery Office.

Her Majesty's Government (2009) *Countering International Terrorism: The United Kingdom's Strategy*, Cm 7547, London: Stationery Office.

Home Affairs Committee (2005) *Terrorism and Community Relations: Sixth Report of Session 2204-05*, Vol. I, HC 165-I, London: The Stationery Office.

Home Office and Northern Ireland Office (1998) *Legislation against Terrorism: A consultation paper*, Cm 4178, London: The Stationery Office.

Hooper, J. (2002) 'Race card: Stoiber links terror to immigration: German challenger promises to deport 4,000 Islamists', *The Guardian*, 19 September.

House of Representatives (2005) 'Testimony of Claude Moniquet, Director General of European Strategic Intelligence and Security Center', *Hearing before the Subcommittee on Europe and Emerging Threats of the Committee on International Relations House of Representatives One Hundred Ninth Congress First Session April 27, 2005 Serial No. 109–34* (Washington: U.S. Government Printing Office). Available HTTP: http://democrats.foreignaffairs.house.gov/archives/109/20917.PDF (accessed 8 April 2011).

ICM and The Guardian (2005) *Muslims Poll*. Available HTTP: www.icmresearch.co.uk/pdfs/2005_july_guardian_muslim_poll.pdf (accessed 23 October 2007).

Iqbal, Sajid (2004) Interview with Sajid Iqbal, the editor of 'The Revival—Voice of the Muslim Youth' (Manchester/Southampton: K. Brown).

Islamic Human Rights Commission (ICHR) (2006) *Submission to the ICJ Eminent Jurists Panel on Terrorism, Counter-Terrorism and Human Rights* (London: Islamic Human Rights Commission).

Ismail, S. (2001) 'The paradox of Islamist politics', *Middle East Report*, No. 221. (Winter): 34–9.

Jackson, R. (2007) 'Constructing enemies: "Islamic terrorism" in political and academic discourse', *Government and Opposition* 42(3): 394–426.

Jopkke, C. (2004) 'The retreat of multiculturalism in the liberal state: Theory and policy', *British Journal of Sociology* 55(2): 237–57.

Kahn, W. (2006) 'Muslim students are not being influenced by extremists', *The Guardian (Leaders and Replies)* 21 April: 37. Available HTTP: www.guardian.co.uk/commentisfree/2006/apr/21/comment.highereducation (accessed 27 March 2011).

Kelly, R. (2007) 'Winning hearts and minds: Working together to defeat extremism', speech at the Muslim Cultural Heritage Centre, London, 5 April 2007. Available HTTP: www.communities.gov.uk (accessed 27 March 2011).

Klausen, J. (2008) *The Islamic Challenge: Politics and religion in Western Europe*, Oxford: Oxford University Press.

Le Figaro (2007) 'Londres Arriere-cour de l'extremisme islamique' (London's secret heart of Islamic extremism). Available HTTP: www.lefigaro.fr/international/20070205.FIG000000243_londres_arriere_cour_de_l_extremisme_islamique.html# (accessed 27 March 2011).

Lewis P. (1994) *Islamic Britain: Religion, politics and identity among British Muslims* (London: I.B. Tauris).

Lewis, P. (2006) 'Adding their voice to the debate', *The Guardian*, Tuesday 4 April. Available HTTP: www.guardian.co.uk/education/2006/apr/04/studentpolitics.highereducation (accessed 27 March 2011).

Lipsett, Anthea (2007) 'Universities vow to protect campus freedoms', *Education Guardian*, Wednesday, 14 November 2007. Available from: www.guardian.co.uk/

education/2007/nov/14/highereducation.uk1?INTCMP=SRCH (accessed 8 April 2011).

MacShane, D. (2006) 'Our failure to confront radical Islam is there for all to see', *Daily Telegraph*, 17 October.

McGhee, D. (2005) 'Patriots of the future? A critical examination of community cohesion strategies in contemporary Britain', *Sociological Research Online* 10(2). Available HTTP: www.socresonline.org.uk/10/3/mcghee.html (accessed 27 March 2011).

McGrory, D. (2006) 'Nervous informant who gave details of new terrorist device', *The Times*, 3 June.

Merali, A. (2004) 'Interview by author with Islamic Human Rights Commission representative Arzu Merali', London.

Modood, T. (2003) 'Muslims and the politics of difference', *Political Quarterly* 74(1): 100–15.

Muslim Council of Britain (2003) Muslim Council of Britain, Interview with the Chair of the Women and Family Committee of the Muslim Council of Britain, K. Brown, Southampton.

Muslim Council of Britain (MCB) (2004) *Government Discussion Paper – Counter-terrorism powers: Reconciling security and liberty in an open society: a response from the Muslim Council of Britain*, August.

Muslim Women's Helpline (2004) 'Telephone interview with coordinator of the Muslim women's helpline' (London: Southampton).

Muslimah Graduate Society (2004) 'Interview with representative of the Muslimah Graduate Society', London.

National Statistics Office (2001) Census: Religion. Available HTTP: www.statistics.gov.uk/StatBase/Expodata/Spreadsheets/D7681.xls or www.statistics.gov.uk/cci/nugget.asp?id=954 (accessed 8 December 2007).

National Statistics Office (2004) 'Ethnicity'. Available HTTP: www.statistics.gov.uk/cci/nugget.asp?id=957 (accessed 9 December 2007).

Newman, M. (2008) 'Research into Islamic terrorism led to police response', *Times Higher Education*, 22 May 2008. Available HTTP: www.timeshighereducation.co.uk/story.asp?storycode=402125 (accessed 27 March 2011).

Nielsen, J. (1999) *Towards a European Islam* (London: Macmillan Press).

Philips, M. (2006) *Londonistan: How Britain is creating a terror state within* (London: Gibson Square Books).

Quilliam Foundation (2010) *Quilliam Briefing Paper Radicalisation on British University Campuses: A case study*. Available HTTP: www.quilliamfoundation.org/images/stories/pdfs/radicalisation-on-british-university-campuses.pdf?dm_i=JI3,9VVO,2Q60WK,QMSG,1 (accessed 27 March 2011).

Qureshi, Mamooda (2004) *Interview with Mamooda Qureshi, former Sister in Charge of the Young Muslim Sisters* (Birmingham: K. Brown).

R (On the Application of Begum) v Headteacher and Governors of Denbigh High School [2006] UKHL 15 (Judgment of 22 March 2006).

Ramadan, T. (2004) *Western Muslims and the Future of Islam* (Oxford: Oxford University Press).

Ranger, T. (1996) 'Introduction', in T. Ranger, Y. Samad, and O. Stuart (eds.) *Culture, Identity and Politics: Ethnic minorities in Britain* (Aldershot: Avebury Press).

Raz, A. (2006) 'She who disputes – Muslim women shape the debate', November (London: Muslim Women's Network and the Women's National Commission). Available HTTP: www.thewnc.org.uk (accessed 27 March 2011).

Reisz, M. (2011) 'Contravene or intervene', *Times Higher Education*, 6 January 2011. Available HTTP: www.timeshighereducation.co.uk/story.asp?storycode=414746 (accessed 27 March 2011).

Ruby, C.L. (2002) 'Are terrorists mentally deranged?', *Analyses of Social Issues and Public Policy* 2 (December): 15–26.

Saggar, S. (2006) 'The one percent world: Managing the myth of Muslim religious extremism', *Political Quarterly* 77(3): 314–27.

Said, E. (1988) 'Identity, negation, violence', *New Left Review* 171 (September/October): 48–62.

Saleem, T. (2004) 'Interview with the Chair of the Islamic Society of Britain's Women's Participation Advisory Group', London.

Samad, Y. (2004) *Muslim Youth in Britain: Ethnic to religious identity*, Paper presented at the International Conference Muslim Youth in Europe: Typologies of religious belonging and socio-cultural dynamics, Edoardo Agnelli Centre for Comparative Religious Studies, Turin, 11 June.

The Scotsman (2006) 'Blair tells British Muslims to reject terrorists' ideals', 5 July.

The Security Service (MI5) (2006) *Countering International Terrorism: The UK strategy – preventing terrorism by countering the radicalisation of individuals* (London: Security Services). Available HTTP: www.mi5.gov.uk/ (accessed 27 March 2011).

Smith, G. and Stephenson, S. (2005) 'The theory and practice of group representation: Reflections on the governance of race equality in Birmingham', *Public Administration* 83(2): 323–43.

Smith, J. (2007) 'Home Secretary makes statement to Parliament, 2nd July'. Hansard, 2 July, Column 671–72.

Sparks, C. (2003) 'Liberalism, terrorism and the politics of fear', *Politics* 23(3): 200–6.

Stringer, D. (2008) 'UK police want to find campus extremists', Associated Press, 22 January. Available HTTP: http://news.lp.findlaw.com/ap_stories/i/1103/01-22-2008/20080122115039_78.html (accessed 10 February 2008).

Tarlo, E. (2007) 'Hidden features of the face veil controversy', *ISIM Review* 19: 24–5. Available HTTP: www.isim.nl/files/Review_19/Review_19-24.pdf (accessed 13 January 2008).

Taylor, M., Dodd, V. and Woodward, W. (2006) 'Anger over plans to spy on students', *The Guardian*, Tuesday, 17 October 2006. Available HTTP: www.guardian.co.uk/uk/2006/oct/17/highereducation.politics?INTCMP=SRCH (accessed 8 April 2011).

Taylor, M. and Smithers, R. (2005) 'Extremist groups active inside UK universities, report claims', *The Guardian*, Friday, 16 September 2005. Available HTTP: www.guardian.co.uk/uk/2005/sep/16/politics.students (accessed 8 April 2011).

Taylor, R. (2000) 'Straw tells police to get on with eradicating racism', *The Guardian*, 23 February 2000. Available HTTP: www.guardian.co.uk/uk/2000/feb/23/lawrence.ukcrime1 (accessed 27 March 2011).

The Times (2008) 'Appeal Court quashes convictions in blow for anti-terror strategy', 13 February 2008. Available HTTP: www.timesonline.co.uk/tol/news/uk/crime/article3363827.ece?token=null&offset=0 (accessed 14 February 2008).

Wæver, O. (1995) *On Security* (Bognor Regis: Columbia University Press).
Walker, C. (2002) *Blackstone's Guide to the Anti-terrorism Legislation* (London: Blackstone Press).
Werbner, P. (2007) 'Revisiting the UK Muslim diasporic public sphere at a time of terror: From local (benign) invisible spaces to seditious conspiratorial spaces and national media dialogue', *Keynote presented at symposium on 'Hyperdiversity Diaspora and Media' Centre for Cultural Research, University of Western Sydney*.
White, Vivian, Scott, Stephen, et al. (2004) *Covering up.* Panorama. UK, BBC.
Wiktorowicz, Q. (2005) 'A genealogy of radical Islam', *Studies in Conflict and Terrorism* 28: 75–98.
Wolfendale, J. (2006) 'Terrorism, security, and the threat of counterterrorism', *Studies in Conflict & Terrorism* 29(7): 753–77.
Young, I. (1990) *Justice and the Politics of Difference* (Oxford: Oxford University Press).

Index

Page numbers in *Italics* represent tables.
Page numbers followed by n represent endnotes.